COVENANT RENEWAL AT GILGAL

A Study of I Samuel 11:14—12:25

J. ROBERT VANNOY

MACK PUBLISHING COMPANY

Cherry Hill, New Jersey

For of him, and through him, and to him, are all things: to whom be glory for ever. Amen.
Romans 11:36

PROMOTOR:
PROF. DR. Nic. H. RIDDERBOS

To my mother

Margaret B. Vannoy

In memory of my father

Wesley G. Vannoy

February 28, 1900–September 3, 1976

TABLE OF CONTENTS

ACKNOWLEDGMENTS

It is with praise to God for his enablement and thanks to many individuals for their encouragement and assistance that this study is published.

The writer is particularly grateful to Prof. Dr. Nic. H. Ridderbos for his example of careful scholarship, and the readiness with which he gave generously of his time and expertise in the supervision of the writing of this dissertation. This writer has benefited in more ways than can be enumerated here from the tutelage of Prof. Ridderbos. I also express my appreciation to Dr. Allan A. MacRae, President and Prof. of Old Testament at Biblical School of Theology, Hatfield, Pa., for the inspiration and encouragement which he has been to me in biblical studies, initially as one of his students and in more recent years as a colleague and friend.

Thanks is also extended to the trustees of Biblical School of Theology whose grant of a sabbatical leave during the 1973-1974 school year enabled significant progress to be made in the research and writing of this work. Particular acknowledgment is due Prof. Thomas V. Taylor of Biblical School of Theology for his cheerful assumption of additional teaching responsibilities during my absence.

Many others have helped with this effort in a variety of ways contributing significantly to its completion. Thanks are extended to Mrs. William Taylor, typing; Dr. Perry Phillips, proof reading, checking citations; Mrs. James Pakala, proof reading; Mrs. Blair Ribeca, proof reading; my wife, Kathe, proof reading.

Finally, I express appreciation to my family for their encouragement, patience, and assistance during the time of the preparation of this study. It is not possible to convey in a few words the deep debt which I owe to my parents for their support through many years of educational pursuits and for their godly life and example. To my wife, Kathe, and our children, Anna, Robert, Mark, and Jonathan, I express my appreciation for their patience during the many hours that this study took from other activities in which they could also be actively involved.

I Chronicles 29:11-13

INTRODUCTION

There are few sections in the Old Testament which have been the object of more literary critical assessment than the narratives which describe the rise of the monarchy in Israel contained in I Samuel 8-12. During the first half of the 20th century these chapters were often pointed to by advocates of the documentary approach to the Old Testament as a showcase example for the combination of two contradictory sources (one considered to be early and pro-monarchial, and the other considered to be late and anti-monarchial) into a composite and historically dubious narrative sequence. The result of this approach was the obscuration of the historical setting for the rise of kingship which in turn contributed to the creation of many difficulties in evaluating the role of kingship in ancient Israel and especially its theological significance. It is inevitably the case that the question of origin has implications for understanding the nature of a given phenomenon as well as for assessing the course of its development. This is especially true with regard to kingship in Israel. When one considers the prominence which the notion of kingship assumes in connection with the Messianic theme in the Old Testament, it is certainly of great importance to understand the circumstances and conceptual considerations which were associated with the origin of the institution. Was kingship an aberration from the legitimate form of rule for the theocracy according to the Sinai covenant? Is kingship as conceived under David properly understood as a rejection of the covenant-kingship of Yahweh and in fundamental antithesis with it? Questions such as these with their many implications are inseparably related to the matter of how one understands I Samuel 8-12 which describes the events associated with the establishment of the monarchy. For this

1

reason the interpretation of these chapters is of great importance for understanding one of the central themes of the Old Testament.

It has generally been the case that I Samuel 11:14-12:25 has been granted little or no place in attempts by critical scholars to assess the historical situation in which Israelite kingship was established. This is largely due to the fact that I Samuel 11:14-12:25 has generally been regarded as a late and historically untrustworthy appendage to the preceding narratives of I Samuel 8-12. Even from the standpoint of conservative biblical scholarship, which has recognized the historical trustworthiness of I Samuel 12, it has generally been treated merely as Samuel's farewell address at the time of Saul's inauguration to be king and little further of significance has been attached to the events described in the chapter. It is our contention, however, that neither of these approaches do justice to the content and importance of this passage, and that instead of a relatively insignificant appendage to the preceding narratives, one here encounters the climax to the narrative sequence of I Samuel 8-12 in which the key to the interpretation of this section of I Samuel is found. It is also here that a perspective is found in which the pro and anti monarchial tension which has so often been pointed to in these chapters is to be understood. I Samuel 11:14-12:25 is thus to be regarded as a vitally important passage which is of great significance for understanding the concept of kingship in Israel at the time of its establishment and also for delineating the relationship which existed between human kingship and Yahweh's kingship.

In the discussion which follows it is our purpose to demonstrate by exegetical, literary critical, and form critical analysis that many features of I Samuel 11:14-12:25 strongly indicate that the assembly which is here described is properly understood as a covenant renewal ceremony, and that there is good reason to view this ceremony as an historically appropriate if not necessary event at this particular juncture in Israel's national existence. In our view the renewal of the covenant here described served a dual purpose. First, it served to restore the covenant relationship between Yahweh and his people after the people had abrogated the covenant by their sin in asking for a king "as the nations." And secondly, it provided a means for instituting the era of the monarchy in Israel in a manner which demonstrated that the suzerainty of Yahweh was in no way diminished by the establishment of kingship. It was Samuel's purpose, therefore, in calling for the assembly to provide for covenant continuity through a period of major restructuring of the theocracy.

In our study of I Samuel 11:14-12:25, Chapters I and II will be given to the translation and exegesis of I Samuel 12 and I Samuel 11:14-15 in that order. Chapter III will assess these same two units from a literary critical standpoint. Chapter IV will discuss the "covenant form" in the Old Testament and then investigate the implications which this form may have for the interpretation and unity of I Samuel 11:14-12:25. Chapter V will utilize the covenantal perspective found in I Samuel 11:14-12:25 for the assessment of the literary criticism of I Samuel 8-12, and particularly for suggesting a means for resolving the pro and anti monarchial tension which has so often been pointed to in this section of I Samuel.

A few additional words of comment concerning organization are in order at this point. First, as has already been indicated we have chosen to place the exegetical and literary critical discussion of I Samuel 12 before that of I Samuel 11:14-15. The reason for this is that I Samuel 12 in our view provides the basis for understanding I Samuel 11:14-15 as a brief synopsis of the Gilgal assembly prefaced to the narrative of I Samuel 12, which we take to be a more detailed description of the same assembly. Our exegesis of I Samuel 11:14-12:25 has no pretensions of providing a more or less complete exegesis. We have delved more deeply into only those

points which were considered of particular importance for
the purposes of this study.

Secondly, the survey of the history of the literary criticism of I Samuel 12 and I Samuel 11:14-15 precedes that of
the larger section of the book (I Samuel 8-12) for which they
form the concluding segment because our primary interest is
in these two units, and we have chosen to take them as the
starting point for our assessment of the larger section. This,
however, requires some overlap between Chapters III and V
because in certain instances it has been necessary to give a
general orientation to the criticism of the entire section
(I Samuel 8-12) in Chapter III in order to adequately describe the approach a given author has taken to the literary
criticism of I Samuel 12 and I Samuel 11:14-15. For this
reason the standpoint of certain authors is given three or four
times. This occurs from a different perspective in each case,
although of necessity some degree of repetition is involved.
This, of course, has its objections, but I hope that the
advantages will outweigh the disadvantages for the one who
reads or consults the book.

Thirdly, the greatest difficulty was caused by the structuring of Chapter IV. On the one hand, the issues which are
under discussion in this chapter are of very great significance
for our topic. On the other hand, such issues as the occurrence of the "covenant form" in the Old Testament, the origin
of the form, the significance of the form for the dating of
Deuteronomy, etc., are such broad matters that it is impossible to handle them satisfactorily in the scope of this dissertation. Let me make three remarks in this connection. 1) This
is not the first time that something has been written on these
issues. I have included a rather large number of references to
pertinent literature, particularly that which in my opinion
points in the right direction, although without ignoring literature in which other standpoints are defended. 2) Matters that
are of particular importance for my subject I have discussed
in more detail. 3) The discussion of the covenant form in the

Old Testament, Chapter IV, Section 1, does not, of course, stand by itself; it is an introduction to Chapter IV, Section 2 and to Chapter V. The discussion in Chapter IV, Section 1 depends to a great extent on the work of M. Kline (and others, such as K. A. Kitchen). I have tried to utilize the model which Kline has constructed in analyzing I Samuel 12, I Samuel 8-12. If some new light is thrown on these pericopes in this way, that in turn can argue that Kline has constructed his model correctly.

Fourthly, Chapter V is chiefly concerned with the implications which the covenantal character of I Samuel 11:14-12:25 may have for the literary critical assessment of I Samuel 8-12. It is not our purpose, in this chapter, to discuss literary critical matters which are not closely related to the covenantal perspective provided by I Samuel 11:14-12:15. It is our position that the tensions and irregularities between various segments of I Samuel 8-12 which have been pointed out and discussed by many, are not of a sort which requires one to conclude that contradictory sources have been linked together in this section of I Samuel. Where such matters have been raised in connection with specific statements in I Samuel 11:14-12:25 on which the covenant form has no particular bearing, they are discussed in our exegetical discussions of Chapters I and II.

PART I

TRANSLATION AND EXEGESIS OF I SAMUEL 11:14-12:25 WITH PARTICULAR EMPHASIS ON JURIDICAL AND COVENANT TERMINOLOGY AND CONCEPTS

I

TRANSLATION AND EXEGESIS OF I SAMUEL 12:1-25

I Sam. 12:1. And Samuel said to all Israel, "Behold I have listened to your voice[1] in all which you said to me, and I have placed a king over you.

The absence of a time or place designation at the beginning of I Samuel 12 is an indication that it is intended to be understood as related to the renewal of the kingdom at Gilgal which was briefly summarized in the last two verses of I Samuel 11. See further Chapter III, Sections 1 and 2 A.

Samuel's statement to the Gilgal assembly makes reference to what had transpired at two previous gatherings, one in Ramah (I Sam. 8:4, 5, 19-22) and the other in Mizpah (I Sam. 10:17-27). At Ramah the elders of Israel had come to Samuel and requested him to appoint them, "a king for us to judge, us like all the nations" (I Sam. 8:5).[2] Even though Samuel warned them that a king as the nations round about would be a burden rather than a blessing (I Sam. 8:10-18),[3]

---

1. For the use of שמע בקול in the sense of "yield to" or "obey" a request or entreaty see: *BDB* and *KBL*, s.v. שמע; cf. vv. 14, 15 below.

2. Bible quotations in most instances are from the *New American Standard Bible* (New York: 1963), with the modification that Yahweh has been used in place of LORD for the designation of the name of Israel's God (יהוה). Wherever it has been necessary to deviate from the *NASB*, I have given my own translation.

3. There is no need to assume that the description of the "manner of the king" contained in I Sam. 8:11-18 represents a late source expressing the bad experience that Israel and Judah had had with their kings, as has often been maintained. See, e.g.: H. P. Smith, *A Critical and Exegetical Commentary on the Books of Samuel* (ICC; Edinburgh: 1899) 55; G. Caird, "Introduction and Exegesis of I-II Samuel," *IB*, II (Nashville: 1953) 921-922; and M. Noth, *The History of Israel* (London: 1960²) 172, n. 2. For a rebuttal of this interpretation on the basis of texts from Alalakh and Ugarit which throw light on the practices of the city-state kings of Canaanite society from the 18th to 13th centuries B.C.,

the elders nevertheless insisted that they wanted a king
(I Sam. 8:19), and Yahweh instructed Samuel to acquiesce to
their request and, "appoint them a king" (I Sam. 8:22).
Subsequent to this, Yahweh made Saul known to Samuel as
he sought his father's stray asses, and after a private anointing, and the giving of signs to demonstrate to Saul that the
anointing was truly of Yahweh (I Sam. 9:1-10:16), Samuel
called all the people together to Mizpah (I Sam. 10:17-27)
for a public designation by Yahweh of the man who was to
be their king. After the lot had fallen on Saul, Samuel
addressed the Mizpah assembly and said, " 'Do you see him
whom Yahweh has chosen? Surely there is no one like him
among all the people.' So all the people shouted and said,
'Long live the king!' Then Samuel told the people the manner
of the kingdom and wrote it in a book and placed it before
Yahweh . . ." (I Sam. 10:24, 25).

Now at the gathering in Gilgal, which had been called by
Samuel to "renew the kingdom" after Yahweh had given Israel
victory in battle over the Ammonites under Saul's leadership,
Samuel had led the people in the formal inauguration of the
reign of Saul (I Sam. 11:15a, "they made Saul king before
Yahweh in Gilgal").[4] This having been accomplished, he now
presents the newly inaugurated king to the people, and says
that he has done what they had requested (I Samuel 8,
Ramah), and has placed a king over them (I Sam. 10:17-27,
Mizpah; I Sam. 11:15a, Gilgal).

---

see, I. Mendelsohn, "Samuel's Denunciation of Kingship in the Light of Akkadian
Documents from Ugarit," *BASOR* 143 (1956) 17-22. Mendelsohn (ibid., 22)
concludes, "In view of the evidence from the Akkadian texts from Ugarit it seems
obvious that the Samuel summary of 'the manner of the king' does not constitute
'a rewriting of history' by a late opponent of kingship, but represents an eloquent
appeal to the people by a contemporary of Saul not to impose upon themselves a
Canaanite institution alien to their own way of life." See further below, Chapter V, Section 2,A.

4. For discussion of when the inauguration of Saul took place, see below,
Chapter II.

I Sam. 12:2. And now,[5] behold, the king shall walk[6] before you; as for me, I have become old and grey headed, and behold, my sons are with you; and I have walked before you from my youth until this day.

With the twofold אֲנִי and the double use of Hithpael forms of the verb הלך for both himself and the newly inaugurated king,[7] Samuel draws attention to the transition in leadership which was being formally implemented at the Gilgal assembly. Just as Samuel had lived openly before the people for an entire lifetime, in the performance of a variety of public functions in the service of Yahweh, so now the king is to assume his public responsibilities under the guidelines which Samuel had previously explained to the king and the people at Mizpah (I Sam. 10:25).

In his introduction of the king Samuel makes allusion to his own advanced age, and to the presence of his sons among the people.[8] His age and his sons had both been cited by the

---

5. On the various uses of וְעַתָּה see H. A. Brongers, "Bemerkungen zum Gebrauch des Adverbialen *WeʿATTAH* im Alten Testament," *VT* 15 (1965) 289-299; and A. Laurentin, "*Weʿattah-Kai nun.* Formule caractéristique des textes juridiques et liturgiques," *Bib* 45 (1964) 168-195. וְעַתָּה is used to mark important transitions at three places in I Samuel 12: vv. 2, 7, 13 (16 [גַּם־עַתָּה]). It marks a secondary transition in v. 10, where it is used in Samuel's resumé of Yahweh's righteous acts. See further below, Chapter IV, Section 2,A,2.

6. *GK* §116 a.

7. In *BDB* (s.v.) this use of הִתְהַלֵּךְ is defined as, "fig. *walk about*=live; the king before (לִפְנֵי) his people I S 12:2, so of Samuel v. 2." S. R. Driver (*Notes on the Hebrew Text and the Topography of the Books of Samuel* [Oxford: 1913²] 38) comments: "To *walk before* any one is to live and move openly before him; esp. in such a way as a) to *deserve*, and consequently b) to *enjoy* his approval and favour." Smith (*Samuel*, ICC, 83) cites Num. 27:16 f. and comments: "the king is thought of as a shepherd walking before his flock." See further: G. Sauer, *THAT*, I, 491 f. on הלך .

8. Some commentators have questioned whether the expression, "I have become old and grey headed, and behold my sons are with you," is to be considered original. See for example: K. Budde, *Die Bücher Samuel* (KHC 8; Tübingen: 1902) 77; and H. Gressmann, *Die älteste Geschichtsschreibung und Prophetie Israels* (SAT II/1; Göttingen: 1921²) 45. There is, however, no textual evidence for eliminating this segment of the verse, and the allusion to Samuel's age and his sons does have relevance to the matters of concern at the Gilgal assembly. It is also not necessary to assume as does Caird (*IB*, II, 941) that, "the author must have forgotten their [the sons] misdemeanors, or he would not have committed the blunder of mentioning them at the very moment when Samuel is protesting his innocence from the crimes of which they had been accused."

elders as reasons for their initial request for a king at Ramah
(I Sam. 8:5). Samuel alludes to these matters here, however,
in neutral terms, indicating neither acceptance nor rejection
of their legitimacy as a basis for the establishment of kingship.[9] It was nevertheless, clear to all, that Samuel did not
have many more years to continue to give guidance and
counsel to the nation, and the people were well aware of the
unfitness of his sons to carry on in his place.

I Sam. 12:3. Here I am; testify against me[10] in the sight of Yahweh and
in the sight of his anointed. Whose ox have I taken? Or whose ass have I
taken? Or whom have I defrauded? Whom have I oppressed? Or from
whose hand have I taken a bribe[11] to pervert justice?[12] And I will repay
you."

---

9. It seems that for the people Samuel's age and the conduct of his sons
provided a convenient occasion for their request for a king. Their real desire,
however, particularly in the face of the Philistine and Ammonite threats to their
borders, was for a "king as the nations" round about to lead them in battle and
bring them deliverance (see especially I Sam. 8:20). The narratives of I Samuel
8-12 make it clear that the request for a king involved a rejection of the kingship
of Yahweh (I Sam. 8:7; 10:19; 12:12, 19). The people were seeking a national
hero, a symbol of national power and unity, and a guarantee of security which they
thought they could find in the person of a human king. See further the exegesis of
I Sam. 12:12 below, and A. A. Koolhaas, *Theocratie en Monarchie in Israël*
(Wageningen: 1957) 53-57.

10. For the use of עֲנֵה in the technical sense of responding as a witness or
testifying (with בְ of pers. usually meaning against) see *BDB,* s.v.I, 3. See also the
discussion of H. J. Boecker, *Redeformen des Rechtslebens im Alten Testament*
(WMANT 14; Neukirchen-Vluyn: 1964) 103.

11. כֹּפֶר is usually used in the sense of ransom for a forfeited life (Ex. 21:30;
Num. 35:31, 32). J. Herrmann, ("ἱλασμός," *TDNT,* III, 303) says of its use in
I Sam. 12:3 that the, "context leaves it uncertain whether he [Samuel] means an
expiatory ransom for a forfeited life, but there is nothing to rule out this view.
The same is true in Amos 5:12." In a similar vein Driver (*Notes,* 89) says, "In
Amos 5:12 the nobles of Samaria are denounced as לֹקְחֵי כֹפֶר . This being the
uniform usage of the word, it follows that what Samuel here repudiates is that he
has ever as judge taken a money payment on condition of acquitting a murderer
brought before him for justice." According to *KBL* (s.v. IV) כֹּפֶר has in I Sam.
12:3, Amos 5:12, and Prov. 6:35 (where it parallels שֹׁחַד, cf. also I Sam. 8:3 for
שֹׁחַד), however, a broader meaning: "hush-money" in general, so also, e.g., H. J.
Stoebe (*Das erste Buch Samuelis* [KAT VIII/I; Gütersloh: 1973] 232. This last
position appears preferable to me. There is insufficient basis for the restriction in
meaning indicated by Herrmann and Driver.

12. a) Literally, "so that I would have covered my eyes with it." On the use
of the imperfect here, see *GK* § 107r. Note also the statement in I Sam. 8:3 which
indicates that Samuel's sons were guilty of this very offense.

Samuel now proceeds to draw attention to his own past
leadership over the people. He does this by putting himself as

---

b) There is a variant reading for this phrase found in the LXX[AB], the
Old Latin Version, and confirmed in the paraphrase of Ben Sira (49:19). The
LXX version reads, καὶ ὑπόδημα; ἀποκρίθητε κατ᾽ ἐμοῦ, . . . which presupposes a
Hebrew text reading, . . .   ונעלים עני בי   (utilizing the Hebrew dual form of נעל
for a pair of shoes, cf., the Greek ὑποδημάτων of Ben Sira). The resulting
translation, ". . . (or from whose hand have I taken a bribe) and a pair of shoes?
Testify against me (and I will return it to you)," may appear to make little sense.
See, however, the discussion of this phrase by E. Speiser, "Of Shoes and Shekels,"
BASOR 77 (1940) 15-20. Speiser points out that the difference between the MT
and the reconstructed Hebrew text presupposed by the LXX is only the difference between an א and a נ (provided the comparison is on the basis of a purely
consonantal text). The question which naturally arises with the LXX rendering,
however, is why would a shoe be used in connection with a bribe? Smith (*Samuel,*
ICC, 85), supported by Driver (*Notes,* 89) understands the expression as representative of a bribe that would be something very insignificant, even something of
as little worth as a pair of shoes, but says that then one would expect the Hebrew
to read either נעלים כֵּ or וְאֵף נעלים . Both Smith and Driver feel that כפר and
נעלים do not agree well together, and that it is questionable whether a pair of
shoes is a likely bribe for a judge. They thus favor retention of the reading of the
MT.

Speiser, however, maintains on the basis of a similar mentioning of shoes as
legal symbols in two Nuzi texts that the shoes here are not to be understood
simply in the sense of something of little worth, but rather, as in the Nuzi texts,
in the sense of, "token payments to validate special transactions by lending them
the appearance of normal business practice." Speiser finds similar usages in the
OT in Ruth 4:7, Amos 2:6, and 8:6. His conclusion regarding Samuel's remark in
I Sam. 12:3 is that, "in his capacity as judge he had never accepted bribes or
gratuities from any litigant; what is more, he had had nothing to do with cases
where the law could be circumvented through some technicality." On the basis
that the more difficult reading deserves preference in matters of textual criticism,
Speiser, with this "outside support" favors the LXX version. While Speiser's
argument is interesting, and may well be the key to understanding the LXX
version, the argument of Smith and Driver that one would expect something other
than simple ו remains valid.

For another approach to this problem see: R. Gordis, "Na'alam and other
observations on the Ain Feshka Scrolls," *JNES* 9 (1950) 44-47. Gordis maintains
that in spite of Speiser's proposal, Driver's objections are still valid. He then
proposes another solution, namely that the word in question is a Hebrew noun
נֵעֶלֶם , (otherwise unknown) meaning literally "concealing substance" or bribe,
which is then a synonym for כפר. He translates the phrase, "From whose hand
have I taken ransom-money or a bribe; testify against me." His proposal is based
on the Hebrew Genizah text of Ben Sira which reads: כפר ונעלם ממי לקחגי .
Gordis says, "Unfortunately, scholars have emended it to read *kōpher v^ena
'alayīm*, 'ransom and shoes,' to conform with the Greek, ignoring the independent
testimony of the Syriac *šuhādā w^ekurbhānā*, 'bribe and offering.' This latter
rendering clearly presupposes a noun, probably נֵעֶלֶם (or נֵעֶלֶם) synonymous
with *kopher*."

it were on trial, and requesting legal testimony from anyone who could point to some irregularity or injustice in his own previous leadership of the nation.

This testimony is to be given before Yahweh and before the newly chosen king, who as king has now become the chief judicial officer in the land.[13] Samuel's referring to the king as Yahweh's anointed,[14] as well as granting to him the

---

In conclusion, it can be said that because of the indecisiveness of the available evidence, it is not possible to give *strong* preference to any one of these three alternatives for the best reading of the text.

With regard to the words עֵינַי בֹ , while they may have fallen out after יֹעַר בֹ because of their close similarity as is suggested by Driver (*Notes*, 89), it would seem better to follow the MT unless one chooses to adopt the entire LXX rendering, since the עֵינַי בֹ is not necessary for the sense of the verse. Note, however, that both the *RSV* and *NEB* incorporate the phrase "testify against me" (בֹ עֲנוּ) into their translation, but exclude "and a shoe" (וְנֶעְלָיִם).

13. Indications of the function of the king as judge are found in the time of David (II Sam. 15:1-6), and in the time of Solomon (I Kings 3:16, 28; and 7:7). From these and other references it appears that legal cases could either be appealed to the king from local jurisdiction, or in some cases be brought directly to the king. For discussion of the legislative and judicial powers of the king in Israel, see: R. de Vaux, *Ancient Israel, Its Life and Institutions* (New York: 1971) 152 166.

14. This is the first time in the OT (apart from the references of I Sam. 2:10, 35) that the king of Israel is referred to as Yahweh's anointed. E. Kutsch (*Salbung als Rechtsakt im Alten Testament und im Alten Orient* [BZAW 87; Berlin: 1963] 52-63) maintains that anointing of the king in Judah was done only by representatives of the people, and the idea of anointing by Yahweh through his representative represents a late "theologumenon," and thus the stories that utilize the expression "the anointed of Yahweh" in I Samuel in connection with Saul and David are late, and not historically reliable. For a variation of this view see R. Knierim, "The Messianic Concept in the First Book of Samuel," in *Jesus and the Historian*, ed. F. T. Trotter (Philadelphia: 1969) 20-51. Knierim agrees that anointment by the people was the original practice and suggests that the reference to the anointing of Saul through the people as contained in the LXX version of I Sam. 11:15 has been displaced in favor of a later "prophetic view" of Saul's anointing from Yahweh through Samuel his prophet. Knierim's view is adopted and elaborated on by B. C. Birch, "The Development of the Tradition on the Anointing of Saul in I Sam. 9:1-10:16," *JBL* 90 (1971) 55-68. This notion, however, has rightly been questioned by J. Scharbert in his review of Kutsch's work (*BZ* 9 [1965] 103, 104). Scharbert says, "Auch die Vorstellung von einer Salbung des Königs durch Jahwe bzw einen Gottesmann dürfte kein blosses Theologumenon sein, sondern in einem sakralen, tatsächlich geübten Ritus ihre Grundlage haben." He says, further; "Wenn Könige in Juda durch das Volk oder durch dessen Vertreter gesalbt wurden, schliesst das weder die Mitwirkung von Gottesmännern noch die Vorstellung aus, dass der König als von Jahwe gesalbt gilt." For further discussion of the phrase "the anointed of Yahweh" and its

function of the highest tribunal in the land reflects his positive disposition toward the king and kingship, now that Saul has been installed and is assuming his new responsibilities.

The brief formula by which Samuel elicits either his own indictment or exoneration touches on several major types of misdemeanors which frequently are characteristic of the abuse of power by public officials.

He first asks whose ox or whose ass he had taken. These two animals were probably the most important domestic animals for the Israelite.[15] Because of their importance it was not uncommon for them to be stolen, and accordingly this was specifically prohibited in the Pentateuch not only in the general terms of the apodictic laws, "You shall not steal" (Ex. 20:15), and "you shall not covet your neighbor's . . . ox, or his ass or anything that belongs to your neighbor" (Ex. 20:17, cf. Deut. 5:21), but also in the specific terms of the case laws of Exodus 21:37 (22:1); 22:3, 8 (22:4, 9).

It is striking that Moses defended the integrity of his leadership of the nation in a similar manner when he said to Yahweh at the time of the rebellion of Dathan and Abiram, "Do not regard their offering! I have not taken a single ass

---

significance see the essay by R. de Vaux "The King of Israel, Vassal of Yahweh," in *The Bible and the Ancient Near East* (New York: 1971) 152-166.

Apart from the above question it is certainly noteworthy, however, that Samuel in addressing the assembly speaks of Saul as the "anointed of Yahweh" as if this was something which was known to the people. How is this to be explained? Had he previously told them the story of chapters 9 and 10, or was Samuel publicly anointed prior to this statement in the Gilgal assembly itself (cf. LXX of I Sam. 11:14-15, and Chapter II, pp. 85-88 below)? However this may be answered, this is one of a number of indications that I Sam. 8-12 is a composite of originally separate sources (cf. below, Chapter V, Section 1,D and Section 2). In this connection it should be noted, however, that the account of the anointing of Saul by Samuel as the agent of Yahweh is found in I Sam. 10:1 which normally is assigned to the earlier more reliable "source," rather than to the "later source" often viewed as the prophetically influenced, less reliable, theological source.

15. For a discussion of their significance, see: E. Nielsen, "Ass and Ox in the Old Testament," in the Pedersen Festschrift, *Studia Orientalia* (Copenhagen: 1953) 163-174.

from them; nor have I done harm to any of them" (Num. 16:15). Now Samuel is bringing to the attention of the people that he has not used his position of leadership for his own personal advantage.[16]

In this connection, Samuel seems to be implying a contrast between his own past conduct in which he had not *taken* (לָקַח) anything from the people, and the warning which he had given to the people previously at Ramah (I Sam. 8:10-17) where he had said that a king as the nations round about would *take* their sons (v. 11), *take* their daughters (v. 13), *take* their fields (v. 14), *take* the tenth of their seed (v. 15), *take* their menservants, and maidservants (v. 16), and *take* the tenth of their sheep (v. 17).[17] It was often the case that kings in the ancient near East taxed and expropriated property and possessions from those over whom they ruled. Samuel had done nothing of this sort. He, like Moses before him, had performed his duties as a true servant of Yahweh and Yahweh's people.

Samuel then asks whom he has defrauded (עָשַׁק)[18] or oppressed (רצץ). The defrauding of a neighbor (Lev. 19:13),

---

16. G. von Rad, building on the work of K. Galling, has associated the series of questions in this verse with the *Gattung* of the "confessional list," although in doing so he questions the appropriateness of the label "confessional list" since innocence is being asserted rather than admission of shortcoming. See: K. Galling, "Der Beichtspiegel: eine gattungsgeschlichtliche Studie," *ZAW* 47 (1929) 125-130; and G. von Rad, "The Early History of the Form-Category of I Cor. 13:4-7," *The Problem of the Hexateuch and Other Essays* (New York: 1966) 301-317. To support his view of the origin of the literary type represented in the questions which Samuel asks, von Rad postulates an original list-form underlying the clauses (I have taken no man's ox, I have taken no man's ass, etc.). He then suggests that such professions were used outside the cultus in legal contexts or that perhaps it was the work of a late writer to place this procedure in a secular setting. The absence of firm evidence greatly weakens von Rad's thesis.

17. The מִשְׁפַּט הַמֶּלֶךְ (manner of the king) of I Sam. 8:9, 11 is not to be understood as descriptive of what the king of Israel ought to be, but rather descriptive of what a king such as "of all the nations" (I Sam. 8:5) would be like. See further: Koolhaas, *Theocratie en Monarchie*, 59-61.

18. Driver (*Notes*, 88) comments, "עָשַׁק is *to oppress*, in particular by defrauding a labourer or dependent of his due." See also *BDB*, s.v., where עָשַׁק is defined as, "oppress, wrong (oft. by extortion, ‖ גזל); c. acc. pers. I S 12:3, 4...."

or a hired servant that was poor and needy (Deut. 24:14) was also prohibited in the Pentateuch. Although רצץ does not occur in any specific legal prohibition in the Pentateuch, oppression was clearly contrary to the spirit of covenantal law particularly as it is summarized in the expression, "love your neighbor as yourself" (Lev. 19:18). This question then, just as the previous one, points to a particular category of political abuse. The practice of fraud (עשׁק), often in the form of extortion, as well as oppression (רצץ), by national leaders was frequent in ancient as well as modern times.[19]

Samuel next asks from whom he has taken a bribe to pervert justice (literally, to hide his eyes with it).[20] In Exodus 23:8[21] the taking of bribes was specifically forbidden because it, "blinds the clear-sighted and subverts the cause of the just." This prohibition is repeated in Deuteronomy in the context of regulations for local judges and officers throughout the land. "You shall not distort justice; you shall not be partial, and you shall not take a bribe, for a bribe blinds the eyes of the wise and perverts the words of the righteous" (Deut. 16:19).

Samuel's purpose is thus to establish publicly his adherence to the requirements of the covenantal law in the exercise of his leadership over the nation. Because he has been faithful to the covenant in the performance of his duties he has not used his position of leadership for his own enrichment, nor has he engaged in oppression, fraud or the obstruction or perversion of justice.

---

19. עשׁק and רצץ occur together in Amos's denunciation of the people of Samaria (Amos 4:1), and also in Hosea's denunciation of Ephraim (Hos. 5:11). They are also used together in Deut. 28:33 to describe the actualization of the covenant curse in the harsh treatment of Israel by a foreign nation through which Israel herself will experience what it means to be defrauded and oppressed.

20. See n. 11 and 12 above.

21. In Ex. 23:8 and also Deut. 16:19 שׁחד is used rather than כפר, see on שׁחד n. 11 above.

I Sam. 12:4. And they said, "You have not defrauded us nor oppressed us nor taken anything from the hand of any man."

Samuel receives complete exoneration by the people in response to his request.

I Sam. 12:5. And he said unto them, "Yahweh is witness overagainst[22] you and his anointed is witness this day that you have not found anything in my hand." And they said,[23] (They are)[24] "witness."

Samuel transposes the people's positive response into legal terminology to which the people respond again by asserting that Yahweh and the newly appointed king are witness to his innocence.

One might ask why Samuel was so interested in establishing his own covenant faithfulness at a public ceremony connected with the inauguration of Saul. It has often been suggested on the basis of his request for exoneration combined with his presentation of the king to the people, and the statement which he makes about his own age (v. 2), that he is here giving a "farewell address" before transferring his "office" to Saul and retiring from public life.[25]

A. Weiser has challenged this interpretation, and said that I Samuel 12:1-5 can hardly be understood as, "eine Art Indemnitätsverklärung, die er benötigt, um ordnungsgemäss von einem Amt (etwa wie meist angenommen als Richter)

---

22. As C. J. Goslinga (*Het Eerste Boek Samuël* [COT; Kampen: 1968] 245) notes, Yahweh and Saul are earwitnesses of the response of the people and therefore בכם is best taken as "overagainst" rather than "against."

23. The MT (with the exception of 18 MSS) reads, ויאמר. The LXX[BA], Syriac, Vulgate and Targum, however, all give a plural reading. Driver (*Notes*, 90, 91) discusses this variant reading at length because it is also suggested in the Masoretic note סביר. Driver (ibid., 91) points out that, "the סביר must be carefully distinguished from the קרי: in no case does it direct the suggested alternative to be *substituted* in reading for that which is written in the text." Perhaps the explanation of the MT is to be found in the idea that the people (cf. v. 6) responded as "one man."

24. For the suppression of the subject in an exclamatory statement see, *GK* §147c.

25. For a more complete discussion of this interpretation of I Samuel 12 see further the exegesis of v. 23, and also Chapter IV, Section 2,B, 1,a.

zurückzutreten."[26] He says further that the things for which
Samuel asks vindication are not simply typical of the moral-
ity of a judge, but those things which were incumbent on
every Israelite. Thus Samuel was simply seeking to establish,
"die Tatsache einer einwandfreien, bundesgemässen Lebens-
führung."[27] The confirmation of this by the king and the
people would mean that, "Samuel auch unter den neuen
Verhältnissen als Repräsentant des Jahwebundes aufzutreten
berechtigt und ermächtigt zu sein wünscht."[28] Weiser concludes that Samuel is not retiring or resigning, but that his
action is to be understood as, "ein kluger Schritt vorwärts,
der die Vertrauensbasis schafft für die durch die Einführung
des Königtums notwendig gewordene Neuordnung. . . ."[29]

Weiser is certainly correct in his opposition to the "farewell address" approach to this section of I Samuel 12, and in
his emphasis on the continuing function of Samuel; for
Samuel does not retire after the Gilgal ceremony, but continues to function as intercessor, as prophet, as priest, as the
one who brings the message of Yahweh's rejection of Saul,
and perhaps also even as judge (cf. I Sam. 7:15).

Yet at the same time there is an element of truth—
although not more than that—in the farewell hypothesis.
Samuel is transferring important elements of his former functions to the king, and precisely those functions in which
offenses such as those mentioned in verse three could be
committed. It is thus understandable that he desires an honorable discharge from these functions. In addition it is clear
from Samuel's advanced age (I Sam. 8:5; 12:2) that the time
is short in which he will continue as a leader in the nation,
and that here in the ceremony at Gilgal the matter of providing for an orderly transition in leadership is one of the major

---

26. A. Weiser, *Samuel. Seine geschichtliche Aufgabe und religiöse Bedeutung* (FRLANT, 81; Göttingen: 1962).
27. Ibid., 83.
28. Ibid., 83.
29. Ibid., 84.

concerns. It is clear then that there remains a significant distinction between Weiser's position on this point and my own, even though Weiser has provided a valuable corrective to the usual "farewell address" interpretation. Against Weiser's view it can also be noted that it seems clear that Samuel is doing more than merely seeking confirmation that he has lived as an ordinary Israelite in conformity to the covenant law. While it is true that all of the things which he mentions would be applicable to any citizen, in the context of the Gilgal assembly and his presentation of the newly inaugurated king to the people, they seem to have more specific reference to Samuel's role as a national leader.

Thus neither Weiser's suggestion nor the traditional view of the chapter as a "farewell address" does justice to the total picture. Samuel is not retiring, yet his advanced age is very real. He is not simply transferring his office to Saul, yet he is implementing a transition in national leadership and a reorganization of the theocracy. There must then, be some other over-arching explanation for this procedure of Samuel in the Gilgal assembly in which each of these aspects of his concern receives its due recognition. Further discussion of this matter must await examination of the remainder of the chapter, and our discussion of the "covenant form" and its implications for the interpretation of I Samuel 11:14-12:25.[30]

I Sam. 12:6. And Samuel said unto the people, "It is Yahweh[31] who

---

30. See below, Chapter IV, Section 2,B.
31. The LXX reading (λέγων Μάρτυς κύριος) is preferred by many because the sentence is not complete in the MT and because it is felt that עֵד could easily have dropped out by scribal error before or after יהוה. Among those favoring the LXX reading are: W. Nowack, *Richter, Ruth und Bücher Samuelis*, (HK I/4; Göttingen: 1902) 53; Driver, *Notes*, 92; K. A. Leimbach, *Die Bücher Samuel* (HSchAT III/I; Bonn: 1936) 56; and P. R. Ackroyd, *The First Book of Samuel* (CNEB; Cambridge: 1971) 98. This insertion of עֵד is in our opinion correctly opposed by, among others: A. Schulz, *Die Bücher Samuel* (EH 8/1; München in Westfalen: I, 1919) 168; H. W. Hertzberg, *I and II Samuel* (Philadelphia: 1964) 95, 98; Weiser, FRLANT, *Samuel*, 84; and Goslinga, *Het Eerste Boek Samuël*, COT, 245. For further discussion see exegesis below.

gave you[32] Moses and Aaron, and who brought your fathers up out of the land of Egypt.

This verse introduces a new section of the chapter in which Samuel turns from the matter of the character of his previous leadership over the people to the matter of the people's request for a king, which he views as a covenant-breaking act and a serious apostasy.

Samuel begins by turning the attention of the people back to their deliverance out of the land of Egypt by Yahweh himself. This was the foundation-event in the history of Israel as a nation. Israel owed her very existence as a nation to this gracious and mighty act of Yahweh performed in fulfillment of his promise to Abraham (Gen. 15:13-16) and Jacob (Gen. 46:3, 4). Yet in connection with this, Samuel emphasizes that Yahweh gave the people the necessary leaders, Moses and Aaron, to guide the nation through the critical period of her birth. In this way Samuel draws attention to Yahweh's past provision of leadership for the nation, which was one of the important issues to be considered at the Gilgal assembly.

Because of the somewhat awkward construction of the beginning of verse 6 in the MT where יהוה stands by itself followed by two relative clauses,[33] the LXX reading has often been preferred.[34] The acceptance of the LXX reading requires the insertion of עֵד before or after יהוה in the MT, with the resulting translation: "Yahweh is witness, who gave you Moses and Aaron, . . ." It should, however, be noted that there is no need for a repetition of the assertion that Yahweh is witness to the establishment of Samuel's innocence since this has already been explicitly stated by both Samuel and the people in verse 5. Furthermore, the acceptance of the LXX reading is, as might be expected, sometimes advocated

---

32. Literally: "who made (עָשָׂה) Moses and Aaron." See further in exegesis below.

33. Schulz (*Samuel,* EH, 168) suggests that הוא has dropped from the MT after יהוה and before אֲשֶׁר which is certainly a possibility, particularly since הוא begins with the last letter of יהוה and ends with the first letter of אֲשֶׁר.

34. See n. 31 above.

in connection with viewing verse 6 as the concluding verse to
the first section of the chapter.[35] In my opinion, however,
one in this way arrives at a wrong dividing point between two
important sections in the chapter. It should be noted that in
verse 6, as contrasted with verse 5, nearly the entire address
formula, "And Samuel said unto the people," is utilized as it
was in verse 1. There is thus good reason to view verse 6 as a
new beginning, and the introduction to what follows in
verses 7-15, for which view the insertion of עֵד is not at all
necessary.[36]

D. J. McCarthy also views the reading, "Yahweh is witness who . . ." as the most likely.[37] Nevertheless, he is of the
opinion that a new section begins with verse 6. His rationale
is that Samuel is here invoking Yahweh as witness to what
comes next in the narrative, and that the two relative clauses
following the statement that Yahweh is witness function,
"less as history than as a solemn designation of Yahweh. . . ."[38]

While this suggestion is much more attractive than the
approach to the insertion of עֵד which ties verse 6 to the
preceding section of chapter 12, it is in my opinion still not

---

35. See, e.g., S. Goldman (*Samuel* [SBB; London: 1962] 64) who says, "It
is better to follow Kimchi and treat this verse as the conclusion of Samuel's
self-justification. The sense is 'the Lord is witness, Who made Moses,' etc." See
also J. Muilenburg, "The Form and Structure of the Covenantal Formulations,"
VT 9 (1959) 362. Muilenburg does not advocate the insertion of עֵד, but does
view v. 6 as the "climactic" conclusion to the first section of the chapter.

36. There is not sufficient basis for the "garbled doxology" suggestion of K.
Baltzer in his book, *The Covenant Formulary* (Philadelphia: 1971) 66. Baltzer
finds v. 6 difficult to explain since it comes in between two clearly defined
sections in the chapter; vv. 1-5, the exoneration of Samuel, and vv. 7-13, containing the "antecedent history." Baltzer suggests that the verse may be the, "garbled
remnant of a doxology." He finds his primary support for this suggestion in 1QS
i. 18-19 where such a doxology occurs before the list of צדקות. In addition he
refers to the beginning of the doxology in Neh. 9:6; Ps. 115:15; 121:2; 134:3 and
passim. A glance at these texts, however, shows that they have little resemblance
to I Sam. 12:6 and in addition the Qumran text is clearly an invocation to praise
rather than a statement as is I Sam. 12:6.

37. D. J. McCarthy, *Treaty and Covenant* (AnBib 21; Rome: 1963) 141,
n. 1.

38. Ibid.

acceptable. In McCarthy's rendering, the stress is on Yah-weh-as-witness to the legal argument of Samuel which fol-lows. However, the emphasis in verse 7 is not on Yahweh as witness, but on Yahweh as judge, before whom a case is argued. It would thus seem best to retain the reading of the MT. Before Samuel gives a short summary of Israel's history (v. 8 ff.) he places as a sort of heading over this summary a statement of the fundamental redemptive fact, the deliver-ance out of Egypt. He then prefaces this with the statement that Yahweh had given leaders for this deliverance. As we already saw (p. 21) this is not strange: the provision of leaders was the important issue at the Gilgal assembly.[39]

It is in this connection that the unusual usage of עָשָׂה is perhaps best explained. It was Yahweh who had made Moses and Aaron what they were, and had enabled them to accom-plish what they did in connection with Israel's deliverance from Egypt.[40]

---

39. M. Noth views the mentioning of Moses and Aaron in both I Sam. 12:6 and 8 as later additions taken from the parallel expression of Josh. 24:5. See: M. Noth, *Überlieferungsgeschichtliche Studien* (Tübingen: 1967³) 59, n. 3. Notice, however, that this makes the, as it is, unusual use of עָשָׂה in v. 6 even stranger, since שָׁלַח is used in Josh. 24:5, and in the similar phrase of v. 8. Has the redactor replaced שָׁלַח by עָשָׂה in v. 6 for a particular purpose or just out of carelessness? In spite of this, Noth's suggestion is viewed as quite probable by H. J. Boecker, *Die Beurteilung der Anfänge des Königtums in den deuteronomistischen Ab-schnitten des I. Samuelbuches* (WMANT 31; Neukirchen-Vluyn: 1969) 71. Boecker remarks, "Alle text-kritischen Eingriffe in den Text, die an dieser Stelle erwogen worden sind, werden dann überflüssig. Der ursprüngliche Text lautet: 'Es ist Jahwe, der eure Väter aus dem Lande Ägypten herausgeführt hat.' " Stoebe (*Das erste Buch Samuelis*, KAT, 237) says that, "V 6 ist, wie das Fehlen einer Fortsetzung zeigt, Einschub, der einen Gedanken von V. 7 ff. vorausnimmt." All that Stoebe lets stand from verse 6 is: "And Samuel said to the people:".

All these proposed eliminations are quite arbitrary, lack textual support, and detract significantly from the force of the line of argumentation which Samuel is here beginning.

40. See: C. F. Keil, *The Books of Samuel* (Grand Rapids: 1956 [German original, Leipzig: 1864]) 116. Keil says that עָשָׂה is used here, "in a moral and historical sense, i.e. to make a person what he is to be. . . ." While this seems to be the best understanding of עָשָׂה in this context, it is also at least possible that it is used here as a word-play-tie to v. 7 where עָשָׂה occurs in connection with the righteous acts of Yahweh. Elsewhere in the OT עָשָׂה is used rather frequently in connection with the "great things" which Yahweh did (עָשָׂה) for his people (see, e.g.,: Deut. 11:7; Josh. 24:31; Judg. 2:7, 10). The emphasis in v. 6, then, is that

Samuel here echoes the Old Testament historical narratives of the exodus where Yahweh is consistently depicted as the deliverer of his people (see, e.g.: Ex. 14:13, 14, 25, 30, 31; 15:1b, 3, 6, 17). The statements of these verses indicate that from the very beginning of Israel's history as a nation, Yahweh was recognized as her deliverer and the provider for her well being. Included in his provision for the nation was the sending of the leaders which were appropriate and necessary to care for specific needs. But these leaders were clearly designated as instruments of the rule of Yahweh, who remained the nation's sovereign. The authority of these human leaders is not autonomous, but delegated, and their selection was the prerogative of Yahweh himself.

I Sam. 12:7. Now then, present yourselves[41] that I may enter into legal proceedings[42] with you before Yahweh[43] concerning all the righteous acts of Yahweh which He did with you and with your fathers.

The transition from Samuel's assertion of Yahweh's pri-

Moses and Aaron are not to be regarded merely as great national leaders, but rather as gifts of Yahweh to his people. Their capacity for leadership was to be viewed as attributable to Yahweh's doing.

41. For the use of התרצב in the sense of assembling before Yahweh for the purpose of witnessing what He is about to do either for or against his people, see: W. Harrelson, "Worship in Early Israel," *BR* 3 (1958) 1-14. See further n. 106.

42. a) For the pointing of the Niphal cohortative form of שפט see: *GK*, §51p.

b) For the Niphal use of שפט as meaning, "to go to law with someone," see: *GK* §51d. Cf. also Driver (*Notes*, 92, 93), who comments that the Niphal sometimes acquires, "a *reciprocal* force, as נשפט *to judge one another*, i.e., *to plead or dispute together in judgment*. ...." The sense here is thus of pleading a case as is done in a judicial procedure before a judge, who in this case is Yahweh himself.

c) For the use of *waw* with the cohortative, see: *GK* §108d.

43. The LXX has καὶ ἀπαγγελῶ ὑμῖν following יהוה. On this basis the insertion of ואגידה לכם in the MT has often been advocated. See, e.g.: Nowack, HK I/4, *Richter, Ruth und Bücher Samuelis*, 53; Driver, *Notes*, 93; and Ackroyd, *The First Book of Samuel*, CNEB, 94. It is, in our opinion, rightly opposed by: Smith, *Samuel*, ICC, 86; Schulz, *Samuel*, EH, 168; Goslinga, *Het Eerste Boek Samuël*, COT, 246; and Stoebe, *Das erste Buch Samuelis*, KAT, 233. The construction in the MT is admittedly somewhat awkward (שפט Niphal, and את כל-צדקות), but it is not impossible, cf. e.g., Ezek. 17:20. For further discussion see below in exegesis.

macy in the establishment of the nation to the initiation of
the second legal proceeding of the Gilgal assembly is made by
the use of וְעַתָּה.[44]

The legal character of what follows is indicated by the
combination of the Hithpael imperative form of יצב with
the subsequent Niphal form of שׁפט. H. J. Boecker has
pointed out that in legal cases it was customary for the judge
to sit, and for the parties to the case under consideration to
stand, and since there is no specific term in Hebrew meaning
to stand for trial, either עָמַד or יצב is normally utilized.[45]
While עָמַד and יצב are both used in a variety of different
ways, the sacral-legal sense of יצב in this verse is made clear
by the following phrase, וְאִשָּׁפְטָה אִתְּכֶם לִפְנֵי יהוה. The
scene is thus that of a legal proceeding, as in verses 2-5, but
now the relationship of the parties is reversed.[46] This time
Samuel is the accuser, the people are the defendants, and
Yahweh is the judge before whom the proceeding is held.

Contrary to what one might expect, Samuel does not
make the people's behavior the immediate and direct focus of
attention. Instead, he utilizes the judicial scrutiny of the
"righteous acts of Yahweh" as a foil for the people's conduct, and thereby an instrument for their indictment.

It has often been suggested (see already above) that the
sequence אֵת כָּל־צִדְקוֹת יהוה following וְאִשָּׁפְטָה requires the
insertion of וְאַגִּידָה לָכֶם , or the changing of וְאִשָּׁפְטָה אִתְּכֶם
to וְאֲסַפְּרָה לָכֶם.[47] Budde,[48] cites Ezekiel 17:20 as evidence
that one must insert וְאַגִּידָה לָכֶם or regard וְאִשָּׁפְטָה אִתְּכֶם as
a corruption or later insertion because the accusative in
Ezekiel 17:20 introduces the misdemeanour which is being

---

44. See above, n. 5.
45. Boecker, *Redeformen des Rechtslebens im Alten Testament,* 85; and
Die Beurteilung der Anfänge des Königtums, 72, n. 2. For the use of עָמַד in this
sense see: Ex. 18:13; Deut. 25:8; I Kings 3:16. For יצב see: Ex. 18:14.
46. A. F. Kirkpatrick, *The First Book of Samuel* (CambB; Cambridge:
1880) 119.
47. See above, n. 43, where we have appealed to Ezek. 17:20 for retaining
the MT.
48. Budde, *Die Bücher Samuel,* KHC, 79.

litigated. Boecker, however, has pointed out that, "In I Sam 12,7 wird ebenso wie in Ez 17:20b in akkusativischer Formulierung der Verhandlungsgegenstand der Rechtsauseinandersetzung genannt. Ein derartiger Verhandlungsgegenstand muss keineswegs immer ein Vergehen oder etwas Änliches sein. Das hängt ab vom Charakter der Rechtsauseinandersetzung. In unserem Fall liegt—in moderner Terminologie gesprochen—nicht so etwas wie ein Strafprozess vor; dazu würde eine Verhandlung über Vergehen oder Verbrechen passen; vielmehr wird hier ein Prozess anvisiert, den man als 'Feststellungsverfahren' bezeichnen könnte."[49] Samuel's purpose is to establish formally the covenant fidelity of Yahweh, which then itself indicts the people because they have turned away from Yahweh, in spite of his constant faithfulness, to seek deliverance from the internal and external difficulties which faced the nation by establishing an alien form of kingship.

In verses 8-11 Samuel summarizes the "righteous acts" of Yahweh in Israel's history, as manifest in Israel's deliverance from Egypt and possession of the land of Canaan (v. 8), and subsequently in the cycles of oppression and deliverance during the time of the judges (vv. 9-11). His purpose is to emphasize that Yahweh was at work in all of these historical experiences because it was Yahweh who sold Israel into the hand of Sisera, and into the hands of the Philistines and Moabites when Israel forgot Yahweh and served Baals and Astartes. It was also Yahweh who sent Jerubbaal, Bedan, Jephthah, and Samuel when the people cried out to him for deliverance and confessed their sin. These acts of Yahweh in Israel's history are here characterized as demonstrative of Yahweh's צדק and thus termed צדקות יהוה.

The expression צדקות יהוה occurs in the OT only in Judges 5:11; I Samuel 12:7; and Micah 6:5. In Psalm 103:6 one finds the expression עשה צדקות יהוה and in Daniel 9:16, אדני ככל־צדקתך .

---

49. Boecker, *Die Beurteilung der Anfänge des Königtums*, 73, 74.

There are few words in the OT which have been the object of more extensive investigation than that represented by the root צדק in its various forms.[50] In his recent very useful and comprehensive study of this root,[51] J. A. Ziesler concludes that righteousness is "behaviour proper to some relationship. . . . In the OT the relationship above all others within which behaviour occurs which may be called 'righteous' is the covenant."[52] He comments further: "Righteousness is neither a virtue nor the sum of the virtues, it is activity which befits the covenant. Similarly, on God's side it is not an attribute but divine covenant activity. If we must speak of

50. Cf., the nouns צֶדֶק and צְדָקָה, the adjective צַדִּיק, and the verb צָדֵק. For discussion of these terms see: G. Quell, "The Concept of Law in the OT," *TDNT*, II, 174-178; N. H. Snaith, *The Distinctive Ideas of the Old Testament* (London: 1944) 51-78; L. Köhler, *Theologie des Alten Testaments* (Tübingen: 1953³) 15; W. Eichrodt, *Theology of the Old Testament* (2 vols.; Philadelphia: 1961-1967) I, 239-249; G. von Rad, *Old Testament Theology* (2 vols.; New York: 1962-1965) I, 370-383; A. Jepsen, "צדק und צדקה im Alten Testament," in the Hertzberg Festschrift, *Gottes Wort und Gottes Land,* ed. H. G. Reventlow (Göttingen: 1965) 78-89; R. C. Dentan, *The Knowledge of God in Ancient Israel* (New York: 1968) 165-172; H. H. Schmid, *Gerechtigkeit als Weltordnung* (BZHT 40; Tübingen: 1968); E. Berkovits, *Man and God: Studies in Biblical Theology* (Detroit: 1969) 292-348. For a more complete literature listing, see H. H. Schmid, ibid., 1, n. 1, and the additional citations below.

51. J. A. Ziesler, *The Meaning of Righteousness in Paul* (Cambridge: 1972). Although Ziesler's study is directed to elucidation of the meaning of the concept of righteousness in the writings of Paul, he considers it important to examine all the usages of the word which are likely to have some bearing on Pauline usage. This inevitably involves a study of the root צדק in the OT and elsewhere. Ziesler (ibid., 14) notes that: "As far as possible the analysis has been exhaustive, all cases being examined, but in one or two instances this has proved impracticable; in the Rabbinic writings because of the sheer volume of the material; and in Josephus, partly because of the relatively minor importance of the material." In general one can say that Ziesler's view is the view which has been dominant in recent decades with respect to צדק. In my opinion his view at least in its major emphases is correct (see, however, my critical remark in n. 53). There are, however, also other viewpoints, see especially that of H. H. Schmid (cf. above, n. 50) which are also influential.

52. Ibid., 38. Cf. the definition of K. Dronkert, "Liefde en gerechtigheid in het Oude Testament," in *Schrift en Uitleg* (jubileum-bundel W. H. Gispen; Kampen: 1970) 51. Dronkert says, "De kernbetekenis van het woord is 'handelen naar de *mišpāṭ*.' Moeilijk is het om precies te zeggen wat onder die *mišpāṭ* verstaan wordt, omdat zij immers (zie boven) zo'n typisch karakter heeft. Het is een rechtswaarde in de meest uitgebreide zin van het woord. Die rechtswaarde nu moet in de praktijk worden gebracht door de *ṣᵉdāqā(h)*. Doet men dat en handelt men naar de *mišpāṭ* dan is men *ṣaddīq* en staat men in de kring van *ṣᵉdāqā(h)*."

norms, then the norm is the covenant and whatever is appropriate to it. . . . We must recognize that on this view God's righteousness may take many forms. Sometimes it may take the form of gracious, merciful, saving action, but it is too simple to say that it is always this and that severity is never meant by the term. . . . So God's righteousness means mercy in one situation, triumph in another, judgment in another, the establishment of good government and good justice in another."[53] As can be inferred from these comments, the specific meanings which the various forms of the root צדק assume may vary considerably according to the context, yet these meanings can all be subsumed under Zeisler's above definition.[54]

A prayer of Daniel (Dan. 9:3-19) is particularly instructive in this regard. The prayer begins with confession of the nation's rebellion against the commandments of Yahweh (vv. 5, 11) and then links the disastrous situation in Israel to the actualization of the covenant curse poured out upon the people because of their sin (v. 11). For Daniel this judgment is demonstrative of Yahweh's צדקה (v. 7). He says further (v. 14): "Therefore Yahweh has kept the calamity in store and brought it upon us: for Yahweh our God is righteous (צדיק) with respect to all His deeds which He has done: but we have not obeyed his voice." The calamity which has come

---

53. Ziesler, *The Meaning of Righteousness in Paul*, 40, 41. While this last statement of Ziesler is certainly born out by an examination of the use of the various forms of צדק, it is at the same time clear that the emphasis is again and again on salvation, although not to the exclusion of punishment because of unfaithfulness. Dronkert ("Liefde en gerechtigheid in het OT," in *Schrift en Uitleg,* 53) comments: "De mens kan op Hem aan. God handelt altijd recht op Zijn doel af en concreet naar Zijn *mišpāṭ.* Dat is Zijn *ṣedāqā(h),* Zijn gerechtigheid, die in al Zijn werken tot uitdrukking komt. Hij is rechtvaardig en Hij handelt rechtvaardig. . . . Opmerkelijk is, dat de gerechtigheid Gods in het O.T. in hoofdzaak betrokken wordt op de gunst van God jegens de mens en dat Zijn recht en gerechtigheid in hoofdzaak een reddend karakter dragen."

54. In Ziesler's vocabulary analysis of the forms of the root צדק used in relation to God's activity (cf. ibid., 28-32) he includes the following categories: a) Legal activity; b) Gracious, saving activity; c) Vindication, giving victory or prosperity; d) Acting reliably, trustworthily, faithfully; e) Right speaking; f) God's forensic or relational righteousness.

upon Israel is acknowledged as the "just" result of Israel's failure to take their covenant obligations seriously, as well as their persistence in turning a deaf ear to warnings of judgment.[55] In verse 15 the prayer turns from confession to supplication, and Daniel addresses Yahweh as the one who has delivered his people from Egypt. He then requests that Yahweh's fury be turned away from Jerusalem "in accordance with all your righteousness."[56] This is a striking statement when it is placed in connection with the use of צדיק in verse 14. There, Daniel says Yahweh is righteous in bringing judgment. Here, he appeals to Yahweh's righteousness as the basis for deliverance. He is explicit in stating that the appeal is not made on the basis of the people's צדקות, but on the basis of Yahweh's רחמים (Dan. 9:18),[57] and in accordance with his צדקות (Dan. 9:16). As John Calvin pointed out so well in commenting on Daniel 9:16: "Those who take this word 'righteousness' to mean 'judgment' are in error and inexperienced in interpreting the Scriptures; for they suppose God's justice to be opposed to his pity. But we are familiar with God's righteousness as made manifest, especially in the benefits he confers on us. It is just as if Daniel had said that the single hope of the people consisted in God's having regard to himself alone, and by no means to their conduct. Hence he takes the righteousness of God for his liberality, gratuitous

---

55. As G. Kennedy (*IB*, VI, 489) comments: "God is not to be mocked. Since men were perverse he executed his judgment, and in doing so he acted rightly." G. Ch. Aalders (*Daniël* [COT; Kampen: 1962] 206) says, "Daniël erkent ten volle de rechtvaardigheid van het oordeel dat God over Israël heeft gebracht, nooit kan Hem enige onrechtvaardigheid worden ten laste gelegd; en hij accentueert dat nog eens door de herhaling: 'wij hebben geen gehoor gegeven aan zijn stem' (vgl. vs. 10.11)." See also Neh. 9:33 where after a lengthy recapitulation of Israel's history with particular stress on the judgments brought on the nation because of her apostasy, it is stated that Yahweh has been, "just (צדיק) in all that has come upon us, for Thou hast dealt faithfully (כי־אמת עשית) but we have acted wickedly."

56. Cf. *GK* § 124e (pl. intensivus).

57. רחמים has reference to Yahweh's compassion exhibited in his covenant fidelity. It is used in parallelism with חסד in Jer. 16:5; Hos. 2:21; Ps. 40:12 and 103:4. Note also the use of a verbal form of the root רחם in Deut. 30:3 with reference to Yahweh's promise to turn Israel's captivity.

favour, consistent fidelity, and protection, which he promised his servants. . . ."[58] It is this latter use of צדקות which is
of particular significance in connection with I Samuel 12:7.

In Judges 5:11 the expression צדקות יהוה occurs in the
Song of Deborah which celebrates the victory which Yahweh
had given the Israelites over the forces of Jabin of Hazor. B.
Holwerda has commented that this song is, "de profetische
vertolking van het gebeurde in cap. IV, en is vooral hierom
van belang, dat het aanwijst waar het eigenlijk om ging: het
toont dat het niet zuiver menselijke en militaire gebeurtenissen waren, maar dat het hierin om de VERLOSSING DES
HEREN ging."[59] The reference to singing of the צדקות יהוה
is here to be understood as the singing of Yahweh's covenant
fidelity as demonstrated in Israel's historical experience. Holwerda comments that צדקות in verse 11, "is het zich houden
aan verbondsafspraken, hier dus practisch 'trouwbe-
wijzen.' "[60]

The use of the expression צדקות יהוה in Micah 6:5 is
nearly identical to its use in I Samuel 12:7. The setting in
Micah as in I Samuel is that of a legal proceeding in which a
recapitulation of Yahweh's righteous acts is utilized to indict
an apostate nation.

Samuel's use of the term צדקות יהוה thus emphasizes
the constancy of Yahweh's covenant faithfulness toward his
people as demonstrated in their past history. As we noted
above, the question in I Samuel 12:7 is not that of judging or
vindicating God's righteous acts, but that of calling Israel to
the bar in view of all God's righteous acts on her behalf. The
emphasis here is on Yahweh's acts of deliverance although

58. J. Calvin, *Commentaries on the Book of the Prophet Daniel,* II (Grand
Rapids: 1948 [ET of the 1561 Latin original] 177. Aalders (*Daniël*, COT, 206)
says in speaking of צדקות "Hieronder moeten gerekend worden al de daden ter
verlossing van zijn volk, in de eerste plaats het in het vorige vers genoemde voeren
van Israël uit Egypte, maar verder ook alle andere heilsdaden waarin God zich
tegenover zijn volk als de trouwe Verbondsgod geopenbaard heeft."
59. B. Holwerda, *Seminarie-Dictaat, Richteren I* (Kampen: n.d.) 21.
60. Ibid., 24.

the expression need not be taken as referring exclusively and only to salvific actions.[61]

I Sam. 12:8. When Jacob went into Egypt[62] and your fathers cried unto Yahweh, then Yahweh sent Moses and Aaron, and they brought your fathers out of Egypt, and made them[63] to dwell in this place.

Samuel begins his recapitulation of the צדקות יהוה with a statement of the exodus (cf. already verse 6) and the conquest. Yahweh had heard the cry of the children of Israel in Egypt when they suffered there in bondage (Ex. 2:23; 3:7; Deut. 26:7), and, "God remembered His covenant with Abra-

---

61. The *RSV* translates צדקות יהוה in I Sam. 12:7 as "the saving deeds of the LORD." This translation is supported by, among others, Caird (*IB*, II, 942, 943) who says, "the righteous acts of the Lord (lit. 'righteousnesses') are those acts in which he has appeared as the deliverer of his people, and so has manifested that righteousness which consists in the vindication of the helpless (cf. 2:8). The word is therefore well translated *saving deeds* (*RSV*)." This translation, however, places too much of a one-sided emphasis on the term. Goslinga (*Het Eerste Boek Samuël*, COT, 247) comments: "Ook deze pijnlijke kastijdingen van Gods hand kunnen gerekend worden bij zijn צדקות (vs. 7), daar zij ten doel hadden Israël weer in de rechte verhouding tot Hem te brengen."

62. The LXX adds καὶ ἐταπείνωσεν αὐτοὺς Αἴγυπτος after Egypt. On this basis Driver (*Notes*, 93) adds ויענום מצרים to the MT saying, "The words are needed on account of the following ויזעקו : a copyist's eye passed from the first מצרים to the second." While this explanation is certainly possible, it seems preferable to leave the verse as it stands in the MT because adopting the LXX reading raises the additional problem of the singular "Jacob," and the plural suffix of the verb "oppressed them." This in turn necessitates another addition to the verse, which in fact is also included in the LXX (καὶ οἱ υἱοὶ αὐτοῦ = ובניו), so that the verse reads, "When Jacob and his sons went to Egypt...." This, however, has the problem of a plural subject and a singular verb (בא), and the absence of ובניו is not so easily explained as could be the absence of the previous phrase.

63. The MT gives a plural reading (וישבום), while the LXX^BL (κατῴκισεν αὐτούς), Targum^B, Syriac, and Vulgate presuppose a singular form (וישיבם). Driver (*Notes*, 93) comments, " וישיבום | expresses just what Moses and Aaron did not do." He then advocates reading the singular form with Yahweh as the subject and says, "The unpointed וישבם has been filled in wrongly in the MT." It would seem more likely, however, from the flow of the sentence that the plural form is original and that Samuel is speaking in broad general terms. Goslinga (*Het Eerste Boek Samuël,* COT, 246) says, "De oude vertalingen hebben hier een oneffenheid willen gladstrijken. Over het tijdperk der richteren is Samuël breder, dat is betrekkelijk nog recent, vss. 9-11." In this connection it should be noted, that several versions (LXX^A, Targum, Vulgate) also have a singular form (with Yahweh as subject) for ויציאו . Cf. Stoebe, *Das erste Buch Samuelis*, KAT, 233.

ham, Isaac, and Jacob" (Ex. 2:24; cf., Gen. 46:1-4). It was in response to this cry, and in keeping with his promises to Abraham, Isaac, and Jacob that Yahweh appeared to Moses and commissioned him to lead his people out of Egypt. Moses was to say to the people, "I AM has sent (שׁלח) me to you" (Ex. 3:14). And he was to tell the people that Yahweh had said, "I will bring you up out of the affliction of Egypt to the land of the Canaanite, . . . to a land flowing with milk and honey" (Ex. 3:17). The exodus and conquest remained throughout Israel's history the outstanding examples of Yahweh's gracious and righteous acts on her behalf, and are frequently cited in the OT literature as that which obligates Israel to be loyal to Yahweh (cf., e.g.: Deut. 26:5-9; Josh. 24:4-8; Judg. 2:1-2; 6:8-10; 10:11-13; Amos 2:10; Ps. 105; Neh. 9:9-25).

I Sam. 12:9-11. But they forgot Yahweh their God and he sold them into the hand of Sisera, chieftain of the army of[64] Hazor, and into the hand of the Philistines, and into the hand of the king of Moab, and they fought against them.

And they cried unto Yahweh, and they said,[65] "We have sinned, because we have forsaken Yahweh, and served the Baals and the Astartes; but now deliver us from the hand of our enemies, and we will serve you."

And Yahweh sent Jerubbaal and Bedan,[66] and Jephthah, and

---

64. The LXX[L] (Ιαβω βασιλέως) presupposes a Hebrew text reading שׂר צבא (יבין מלך) הצור.   Driver (*Notes,* 93) says that this is more in accord with Hebrew usage. Schulz, (*Samuel,* EH, 169), however, points out that the addition is not necessary and that, "die Ausdrucksweise 'Heerführer von Hasor' ist gestützt durch I Kn 2,32 ('Heerführer von Israel' und 'H. von Juda'). . . ." It seems likely that the LXX is expanded with data from Judg. 4:2.

65. The K^etîb is singular. It is not impossible that this is correct: elsewhere in the Old Testament one finds sudden alternations of singular and plural.

66. Bedan is an otherwise unknown judge (the name Bedan occurs elsewhere in the OT only in I Chron. 7:17 where it designates another person). For this reason most commentators give preference to the reading of the LXX (βαρακ) and Syriac. Keil (*The Books of Samuel,* 118) after considering and rejecting several possibilities such as rendering Bedan as an appellative, i.e., the Danite (ben-Dan), and thus connecting the name to Samson, concludes, "there is no other course left, therefore, than to regard *Bedan* as an old copyist's error for Barak (Judg. iv.), as the LXX, Syriac, and Arabic have done,—a conclusion which is favored by the circumstance that Barak was one of the most celebrated of the judges, and is

Samuel,[67] and he delivered you from the hand of your enemies on every side, and you dwelt securely.

In these verses Samuel gives a brief summary of the period of the judges in which he clearly portrays the cycle of:

a) apostasy;

b) oppression;

c) repentance and confession accompanied by a request for deliverance;

d) deliverance through the instrumentality of leaders sent by Yahweh.

The ideas which Samuel incorporates in this survey of the history of the period of the judges are found elsewhere also. The terminology by which he frames the cyclical character of the course of events is similar to that found in the book of Judges, and some of it is rooted originally in Deuteronomy. Similar expressions are subsequently to be found in the Psalms and prophetical books as well. The cycle is formulated with the phrases:

---

placed by the side of Gideon and Jephthah in Heb. xi. 32." Similar views are advocated by: Smith, *Samuel,* ICC, 86; Schultz, *Samuel,* EH, 170; and Leimbach, *Samuel,* HSchAT, 57. Goslinga, (*Het Eerste Boek Samuël,* COT, 247), with hesitation, also adopts this view saying, "de lezing Barak staat toch wel het sterkst . . . te meer omdat door hem het leger van Sisera (vs. 9) verslagen is." This represents a change in position from Goslinga's earlier commentary (C. J. Goslinga, *I Samuël* [KV; Kampen: 1948] 151) where he said, " 't is moeilijk denkbaar dat een afschrijver Bedan zou schrijven, indien er geen richter van die naam was opgetreden. Maar ook is moeilijk aan te nemen, dat Samuël wel de verdrukking van Sisera zou noemen (vs. 9) en niet de held, die Sisera overwon. Daarom lijkt de beste oplossing, dat Bedan een andere naam (bijnaam?) voor Barak is en dat deze aan Samuëls hoorders evengoed bekend was als wij b.v. Gideons bijnaam Jerubbaäl kennen." This suggestion of Goslinga seems to be more plausible than to assume a scribal error since the name of Barak was so well known as to make that highly unlikely. It also seems preferable to seeing here the name of a judge not mentioned in the book of Judges at all as do a number of commentators, including: J. de Groot, *I Samuël* (TeU; Groningen: 1934) 123; Goldman, *Samuel,* SBB, 65; and Stoebe, *Das erste Buch Samuelis,* KAT, 233. Nevertheless, Stoebe is, in my opinion, perhaps correct when he suggests that the occurrence of this name here is indicative of an independent tradition.

67. The LXX[L] and the Syriac read Samson instead of Samuel. This is most likely a correction due to the feeling that Samuel is speaking and he would not place his own name on the list of judges he mentions. See further the discussion below in the exegesis.

apostasy:

"forgot Yahweh" (וישכח את יהוה , verse 9);[68]

oppression:

"he sold them into the hand of" (וימכר אתם ביד , verse 9);[69]

repentance and confession, accompanied by request for deliverance:

"they cried unto Yahweh" (ויזעקו אל־יהוה , verse 10);[70]

"we have sinned" (חטאנו, verse 10);[71]

"we have forsaken Yahweh" (עזבנו את יהוה, verse 10);[72]

"we have served the Baals and Astartes" (ונעבד את־הבעלים ואת העשתרות, verse 10);[73]

"deliver us from the hand of our enemies" (הצילנו מיד איבינו, verse 10);[74]

deliverance through the instrumentality of leaders sent by Yahweh:

"Yahweh sent . . ." (וישלח יהוה , verse 11);[75]

"and Yahweh delivered you from the hand of your enemies" (ויצל אתכם מיד איביכם , verse 11).[76]

The cumulative effect of the phraseology is to focus on Yahweh's works of judgment and deliverance. It was Yahweh who gave Israel into the hand of her enemies when she sinned

---

68. Deut. 6:12; 8:11, 14, 19; Judg. 3:7; Isa. 17:10; 51:13; Hos. 2:15 (13); 13:6; Jer. 2:32; 3:21; 13:25; 18:15; 23:27; Ezek. 22:12; 23:35.

69. Deut. 32:30 (אם־לא כי־צורם מכרם); Judg. 2:14; 3:8; 4:2; 10:7.

70. Judg. 3:9, 15; 6:6-7; 10:10; I Sam. 7:8-9; 8:18; Hos. 7:14; 8:2; Joel 1:14; Mic. 3:4; Ps. 22:6 (5); 107:13, 19; Neh. 9:28.

71. Num. 14:40; 21:7; Deut. 1:41; Judg. 10:10, 15; I Sam. 7:6; I Kings 8:47; Jer. 3:25; 8:14; 14:7, 20; Ps. 106:6; Lam. 5:16; Dan. 9:5, 8, 11, 15; Neh. 1:6; I Chron. 6:37.

72. Deut. 28:20; Josh. 24:16; 24:20; Judg. 2:12; 2:13; 10:6; 10:10; 10:13; I Sam. 8:8; I Kings 9:9; 11:33; II Kings 22:17; Isa. 1:4; 1:28; Jer. 1:16; 2:13; 5:19; 16:11; 19:4; Hos. 4:10; II Chron. 7:22.

73. Judg. 2:11 (only Baals); 2:13; 3:7; 10:6; 10:10 (only Baals).

74. Judg. 10:15 (the exact wording of this phrase is not paralleled in the OT).

75. Ex. 3:15; 7:16; Num. 16:28-29; Josh. 24:5; Judg. 6:8; I Sam. 12:8; Isa. 19:20; Jer. 23:21; Mic. 6:4; Ps. 105:26.

76. Ex. 18:9-10; Josh. 24:10; Judg. 6:9; 8:34; I Sam. 7:3; 10:18.

and forsook him. But it was also Yahweh who sent deliverers when Israel repented. The victories of these deliverers were in reality Yahweh's victories, and it was therefore accurate for Samuel to conclude that Yahweh had delivered them out of the hand of their enemies, so that they could live securely. It was this repeated provision for Israel's deliverance from her enemies which was of particular importance for Samuel's demonstration of the people's apostasy in desiring a king (cf. verse 12). Although it is true that the judges themselves were sometimes referred to as Israel's deliverers,[77] it is clear that this is to be understood only in a secondary sense, as instruments of Yahweh's deliverance (Judg. 2:18). It was Yahweh who sent them (Judg. 6:14; I Sam. 2:11) to be the agents of his deliverance.[78]

This is made particularly clear, for example, in the case of Gideon. When the Israelites forsook Yahweh in the time of Gideon they were delivered into the hands of the Midianites who oppressed them for seven years (Judg. 6:1-5). When they cried (ויזעקו , verses 6-7) unto Yahweh, a prophet was sent, who (much like Samuel at the Gilgal assembly) utilized a brief recapitulation of Israel's previous history to explain the reason for her present distress (Judg. 6:8-10). The emphasis in this historical recapitulation is that Yahweh had delivered Israel out of Egypt, and Yahweh had given Israel the land of Canaan, but Israel had turned away from Yahweh to idolatry. Yahweh, however, had now heard the cry of the Israelites for deliverance, and Gideon is to become Yahweh's instrument to achieve this end.

Gideon asked for a sign, and said that by the sign he

---

77. Judg. 3:9, 15, 31; 6:14; 10:1; 13:5.

78. When the root ישע is used with reference to the activity of a human leader, some indication that he was sent by Yahweh is normally made explicitly clear in the context. See, e.g.: Judg. 2:16; 3:9, 15; 6:14; 13:5; I Sam. 9:16; II Kings 13:5; Neh. 9:27. The only exceptions I have noticed are Judg. 3:31; 10:1.

In Judg. 8:22 one finds an expression of the apostate idea that Gideon was the deliverer. A similar idea (although expressed negatively) with reference to Saul is found in I Sam. 10:27 and perhaps 11:3.

would, "know that Thou [Yahweh] wilt deliver (תושיע)
Israel through me, as Thou hast spoken" (Judg. 6:37). After
receiving the sign and proceeding to organize his military
force, Gideon was told to reduce the number of men in the
force so that Israel would not "become boastful" and say,
"My own power has delivered (ידי הושיעה) me" (Judg. 7:2).
Yahweh told Gideon that, "I will deliver (אושיע) you with
the three hundred men who lapped and will give (ונתתי) the
Midianites into your hands . . ." (Judg. 7:7). After surveying
the host of the Midianites, and after hearing the dream of one
of the Midianites which depicted a victory for the Israelites
over the Midianites, Gideon called his force to advance on the
camp and said, "Arise for *Yahweh* has given (נתן) the camp
of Midian into your hand" (Judg. 7:15).

After the victory the men of Israel came to Gideon and
asked him to establish dynastic rule over Israel saying, "Rule
over us, both you and your son, also your son's son, for *you
have delivered us* (הושעתנו) from the hand of Midian" (Judg.
8:22). Gideon rejected their request,[79] however, because it
betrayed the apostate idea that the human leader was the real
deliverer rather than the instrument of Yahweh's deliverance,
and it sought to exchange the rule of Yahweh for the rule of
a man (Judg. 8:23).

Because Samuel's purpose was to demonstrate Yahweh's
constant fidelity to the covenant throughout the period of
the judges (cf. צדקות יהוה , verse 7), and contrastingly the
people's repeated apostasy, he stresses the cycle of oppressions and deliverances rather than historical details of the
period. Accordingly, he mentions only three oppressors and

---

79. The interpretation of this passage has provoked a great deal of discussion. J. Bright (*A History of Israel* [London: 1972²] 173) rightly comments on
the offer of kingship to Gideon that, "he is said flatly to have refused—and in
language thoroughly expressive of the spirit of early Israel." He adds in a footnote
(ibid., 173, n. 84): "It is frequently asserted (e.g., G. Henton Davies, *VT,* XIII
[1963], pp. 151-157) that Gideon actually accepted the kingship. But the language of ch. 9: 1 ff. certainly does not require this conclusion; cf. J. L. McKenzie,
The World of the Judges (Prentice-Hall, Inc., 1966), pp. 137-144." See also below,
p. 77, n. 51.

four deliverers, and neither the oppressors nor the deliverers are cited in the order in which they appear in the book of Judges.[80]

It is, however, significant that Samuel places his own name last in the list of deliverers, and thereby brings the historical recapitulation right up to the time in which the matter of kingship had become an issue. There is no need to regard the appearance of Samuel's name as a scribal error for Samson,[81] nor to view it as either a later insertion[82] or an indication of the authorship of Samuel's speech by a 'deuteronomic editor.'[83] In fact, it was quite necessary for Samuel to make very clear that Yahweh had continued to provide for the national defense and leadership even during his own lifetime (cf., I Samuel 7; esp. vv. 3, 8, 10, 12), in order to make his case relevant to the current situation, and the request for a king. In addition as Goldman has pointed out, "if it be remembered that the figure of a trial is being employed, the third person is not strange. Samuel the accuser, dissociates himself from Samuel, the saviour, who is cited as evidence against his people."[84]

---

80. The oppressors to which Samuel refers are: Sisera, the Philistines, and the king of Moab, in that order. It would appear that he has reference to episodes recorded in the books of Judges and I Samuel in which the order is: Eglon, king of Moab (Judg. 2:12-30); the Philistines (Judg. 3:31); Sisera (Judg. 4, 5); and perhaps subsequent Philistine threats (Judg. 10:7; 13:1 ff.; I Sam. 4-7). The deliverers which Samuel mentions are Jerubbaal, Bedan, Jephthah, and Samuel, in that order. The activities of these deliverers are described in Judges and I Samuel in the following order: Bedan (if this is another name for Barak, cf. above, n. 66, Judges 4, 5); Jerubbaal (Judg. 6-8); Jephthah (Judg. 11:1-12:7); Samuel (I Samuel 7). Here also (see the end of n. 66) one must consider the possibility that Samuel had access to traditions not contained in the book of Judges; see also, Judg. 10:11 f.

81. Gressmann, SAT II/1, *Die älteste Geschichtschreibung,* 45; cf., for instance, above, n. 67.

82. Goslinga, *Het Eerste Boek Samuël,* COT, 247.

83. Caird, *IB,* II, 943. Caird views the introduction of the name of Samuel in this summary of the period of the judges as a "frank admission" that this is a "Thucydidean speech" and the product of a deuteronomic editor. A similar view is expressed by Ackroyd, *The First Book of Samuel,* CNEB, 99. See further Chapter IV, Section 2,A,1 and Section 2,B,2,b; Chapter V, Section 2,C.

84. Goldmann, *Samuel,* SBB, 65.

I Sam. 12:12. But when you saw that Nahash the king of the Ammonites came against you, you said to me, No! but a king shall reign over us, whereas[85] Yahweh your God was your king.

Samuel now comes to the climax of his historical recapitulation in which the people's desire for a king to safeguard themselves from the threat of Nahash, is represented as a rejection of the kingship of Yahweh, and thus as the last of the long series of apostasies.

The mentioning of Nahash in connection with the request for a king is often viewed as contradictory to chapters 8 and 11, since in chapter 8 internal problems are mentioned as the motivation for the request, and in chapter 11, according to the opinion of many, the desire for a king arose after rather than before the threat from Nahash. For this reason it has often been suggested that I Samuel 12:12a is best explained as a later insertion.[86] Others have suggested that this verse as well as the rest of I Samuel 12 is to be viewed as the free formulation of the deuteronomistic history writer.[87] Still others see here evidence of an independent tradition which is in conflict with chapters 8 and 11, and lays stress on the importance of the Ammonite threat for the rise of the desire of the people for a king.[88]

While it certainly is to be admitted that from a reading of

85. See *GK* (§141e, §156a) for a discussion of the syntax of a noun-clause connected by a *waw* to a verbal clause.

86. See, e.g.: Budde, *Die Bücher Samuel*, KHC, 80; and Schulz, *Samuel*, EH, 170.

87. Noth, *Überlieferungsgeschichtliche Studien*, 60. More recently, Boecker (*Die Beurteilung der Anfänge des Königtums*, 75, 76) says, "In I Sam 12 werden die Berichte über die Entstehung des Königtums zusammengefasst und das Ereignis abschliessend gewertet. V. 12 ist als das Ergebnis solch abschliessender Zusammenfassung verschiedener Berichte anzusehen, wobei sich einmal mehr zeigt, wie wenig die Deuteronomisten Geschichtsschreiber in modernem Sinne waren. Sie verbinden in diesem Vers den von ihnen in ihr Werk übernommenen Bericht von der Nachaschgeschichte mit der von ihnen selbst konzipierten Erzählung von dem an Samuel herangetragenen Königswunsch des Volkes, wobei die dadurch entstehende sachliche Spannung sie offenbar weniger belastet als den modernen Leser."

88. Weiser, *Samuel*, FRLANT, 72-74, 86; Stoebe, *Das erste Buch Samuelis*, KAT, 237.

chapters 8, 10:17 ff., and 11 one could not conclude that the desire for a king was specifically tied to the Ammonite threat; it must also be admitted that there is nothing in chapters 8, 10:17 ff., and 11 which contradicts this idea. Goslinga comments that here is "een van de oneffenheden die in ons boek meer aangetroffen worden, zonder dat een bepaalde tegenspraak valt te constateren."[89] Even though Nahash is not mentioned in chapter 8, there is reference to the desire for a king to lead Israel in battle (I Sam. 8:20), and it is not at all impossible that the threat of attack from Nahash was already a matter of concern at that time.[90] It should also be noticed, that when Samuel spoke to the people gathered at Mizpah for the public selection of Saul to be king, he placed the matter of desiring a king in the context of seeking a savior (צל), and said that in desiring a king Israel had rejected their God who had saved them out of the hand of the Egyptians, and all the other kingdoms which had oppressed them (I Sam. 10:18, cf. also v. 19, ישע). In addition, after Saul's selection, there were those who objected to him by asking, "how is this man going to save (ישע) us?" (I Sam. 10:27), betraying their fear that he was not adequate to the task of delivering Israel from her enemies. The manner of expression "No! but . . ." indicates the people's response to a preceding rejection of the kingship by Samuel. Samuel and the elders must have repeatedly negotiated this matter (cf. I Sam. 8:19; 10:19).

Samuel's statement in I Samuel 12:12 is thus compatible with chapters 8, 10, and 11, but more important is that it reveals his own analysis of the motivation behind the initial request of the elders for a king. In the face of the combined pressures of the Philistines in the west (I Sam. 9:16) and the

89. Goslinga, *Het Eerste Boek Samuël,* COT, 248.
90. See: J. Schelhaas, "De instelling van het koningschap en de troonbestijging van Israëls eerste koning," *GTT* 44 (1944) 270, n. 62; B. J. Oosterhoff, "De boeken 1 en 2 Samuël," *Bijbel Met Kanttekeningen,* eds. J. H. Bavinck and A. H. Edelkoort (Baarn: n.d.) II, 237; Goslinga, *Het Eerste Boek Samuël,* COT, 248.

Ammonites from the east, the Israelites desired a human king, a national hero, and a symbol of national power and unity in whom they thought they could find a guarantee of security and rest. They were seeking their deliverance in the person of a human king.[91] This, however, constituted a rejection of the kingship of Yahweh, and betrayed a loss of confidence in his care for the welfare of the nation. For Yahweh was the deliverer of Israel (Ex. 3:8, נצל ; Deut. 20:4, ישע). He had promised to fight for them against their enemies and to deliver them. He had remained faithful to this promise throughout the periods of the exodus, the conquest and the judges.[92]

I Sam. 12:13. And now behold the king whom you have given preference to,[93] whom you have requested,[94] and behold, Yahweh has given a king over you.

---

91. Koolhaas, *Theocratie en Monarchie*, 53-57. Koolhaas (ibid., 57) sums up his discussion of Israel's request for a king by saying, "Zo wordt in het Oude Testament als achtergrond van de vraag naar een koning gezien: wantrouwen jegens de koningsheerschappij van Jahwe, vrees voor de vijanden en een eigenmachtig streven naar veiligheid en eenheid."

92. See, e.g.: (ישע) Ex. 14:30; Num. 10:9; Judg. 2:18; 10:13; 12:3; I Sam. 7:8; 10:19; (נצל) Ex. 3:8; 6:6; 18:8, 9, 10; Josh. 24:10; Judg. 6:9; 8:34; I Sam. 7:3; 10:18; 12:11. Yahweh continued to be Israel's deliverer in the kingdom period. Cf. (ישע) I Sam. 14:6, 23, 39; 17:47; II Sam. 3:18; I Kings 14:27; II Kings 19:34; I Chron. 11:14; II Chron. 10:9; 32:30; (נצל) I Sam. 17:37; II Kings 17:39; 20:6.

93. The suggestion of Stoebe (*Das erste Buch Samuelis*, KAT, 234) following, among others, M. Buber ("Die Erzählung von Sauls Königswahl," *VT* 6 [1956] 160) to retain אשר שאלתם (see n. 94b below) but to delete אשר בחרתם has no textual evidence in its support. According to Keil (*The Books of Samuel*, 19) the use of בחר is best understood as referring to the choice of Saul by lot in I Sam. 10:17-25. There, however, the emphasis is not on the people's choice but rather on the fact that Saul is the one whom *Yahweh* has chosen (cf. v. 24). In view of this it seems that בחר both here and in I Sam. 8:18 may be best translated in the sense of "give preference to" (i.e., over Yahweh). See *KBL* s.v.

94. a) see *GK* 44d and 64f for the pointing of שאלתם. b) The LXX[B] omits אשר שאלתם, and the phrase is therefore regarded by many commentators as a gloss. See, e.g.: O. Thenius, *Die Bücher Samuels* (KeH IV; Leipzig: 1898³) 53; Smith, *Samuel*, ICC, 88; and Driver, *Notes*, 94. The textual evidence for deletion, however, is not strong and Goslinga (*Het Eerste Boek Samuël*, COT, 249) is right in saying that the phrase in question is, "zonder twijfel oorspronkelijk, en juist in Samuëls mond zeer begrijpelijk, omdat hij in dit vragen en zelfs eisen van een koning een zondige daad zag, zie vs. 17."

Samuel now draws the attention of the people to the king, and stresses that it is Yahweh who has given them this king. In spite of the sinfulness of the people's request, Yahweh has chosen to incorporate kingship into the structure of the theocratic government of his people.[95] Kingship has been given by Yahweh to his people, and from this time forward is to function as an instrument of his rule over them.

I Sam. 12:14. If you will fear Yahweh, and serve him, and listen to his voice, and not rebel against the commandment of Yahweh; then both you and the king who reigns over you shall follow Yahweh your God.

It has long been the general consensus of interpreters that this verse contains only a protasis and ends with an aposiopesis.[96] The translation normally adopted is similar to that of the *RSV*: "If you will fear the LORD and serve him and hearken to his voice and not rebel against the commandment of the LORD, and if both you and the king who reigns over you will follow the LORD your God, *it will be well*" (italics mine). The last phrase does not occur in the MT and must be added to complete the sentence. As Smith, however, has pointed out, "to begin the apodosis with וְהָיִתֶם is grammatically the correct thing to do...."[97] Yet Smith feels that to do so produces a redundancy because, "it makes an identical proposition: *if* you fear Yahweh ... then you will follow Yahweh.[98]

A comparison of verse 14 with verse 15, however, con-

---

95. I Sam. 12:13 with its juxtaposition of the people's request and Yahweh's response points to the resolution of the kingship issue which has been the focal point of the narratives of I Sam. 8-12 (see further the exegesis of I Sam. 12:14). This verse cannot be reconciled with the assignment of I Sam. 12 to an "anti-monarchial" source as often has been done. See further below: Chapter IV, Section 2,A,2 and Chapter V, Section 1 and 2,A.

96. See, e.g.: Smith, *Samuel*, ICC, 88 (see further below in the exegesis); Nowack, HK I/4, *Richter, Ruth und Bücher Samuelis*, 54; Schultz, *Samuel*, EH, 171; Driver, *Notes*, 94; Goslinga, *Het Eerste Boek Samuël*, COT, 249; J. Mauchline, *I and II Samuel* (NCB; London: 1971) 109; and Stoebe, *Das erste Buch Samuelis*, KAT, 234.

97. Smith, *Samuel*, ICC, 88.

98. Ibid.

firms Smith's observation that as a matter of fact the apodosis does begin with והיתם.

protasis a (verse 14)	ושמעתם בקולו	אם־תיראו את יהוה . . .
protasis a (verse 15)	תשמעו בקול יהוה . . .	ואם־לא
protasis b (verse 14)		ולא תמרו את־פי יהוה
protasis b (verse 15)		ומריתם את־פי יהוה
apodosis (verse 14)		והיתם
apodosis (verse 15)		והיתה

The two verses display a remarkably close parallelism in
wording and structure, and because the apodosis is introduced in verse 15 with והיתה, the parallelism strongly supports beginning the apodosis of verse 14 with והיתם.[99]
The objection which Smith makes to beginning the
apodosis of verse 14 with והיתם, while understandable, is not
conclusive, since it turns on his understanding of the phrase
והיתם . . . אחר (יהוה). This phrase (היה אחר or היה אחרי)
is found in several other places in the OT (II Sam. 2:10;
15:13; I Kings 12:20; 16:21), in all of which it is used to
indicate that the people of Israel, or a certain segment of the
people, have chosen to follow a particular king in a situation
where there was another possible alternative.
II Samuel 2:10 relates the decision of Judah to follow
David while Isbosheth reigned over the remainder of the

---

99. It is noteworthy that in both verses "Athnah" stands under [את־פי]
יהוה, indicating that in the opinion of the Masoretes the principal division
within the verse is to be made at that point. Cf. *GK* § 15b,c.

nation. I Kings 12:20 relates that Judah followed the house of David at the time of the division of the kingdom. I Kings 16:21 relates the people's divided loyalties between Tibni and Omri after the death of Zimri. Particularly instructive, however, is II Samuel 15:13. At the height of the rebellion of Absalom, David is told that, "the hearts of the men of Israel are after Absalom" (היה לבאיש ישראל אחרי אבשלום). The clear meaning of the phrase here is that the men of Israel had chosen to give their allegiance to Absalom and to recognize him as king rather than David. Boecker, in his discussion of these passages comments as follows: "Es handelt sich an all diesen Stellen um eine inhaltlich geprägte und in bestimmter Richtung qualifizierte Ausdrucksweise. Die Aufnahme dieses Ausdrucks dürfte in I Samuel 12, 14 im Sinn der genannten Parallelstellen erfolgt sein. Ist dort die Anerkennung eines menschlichen Königs das Thema, so hier die Bestätigung der Königswürde Jahwes. Paraphrasiert lautet V. 14b—wiederum ausserhalb des syntaktischen Zusammenhanges—'sowohl ihr als auch der König, der über euch regiert, werdet Jahwe, euren Gott, als König anerkennen.' "[100] When . . . והיתם אחר יהוה in I Samuel 12:14 is understood in this way then there is no need to postulate an aposiopesis, because there is a meaningful apodosis to the sentence.[101]

---

100. Boecker, *Die Beurteilung der Anfänge des Königtums,* 80.

101. This also makes unnecessary the various suggestions for emendation which have frequently been made in an effort to avoid what is felt to be either an identical proposition or incompleteness in the verse. LXX^L has added καὶ ἐξελεῖται ὑμᾶς in an attempt to complete the verse. J. Wellhausen (*Der Text der Bücher Samuelis* [Göttingen: 1871] 79) gives והיתם as the reading of some Hebrew MSS in place of והיתה , but points out that this does not fit with אחר יהוה . Smith (*Samuel,* ICC, 88), while noting Wellhausen's objection, and also noting that De Rossi "denies the manuscript authority" nevertheless concludes: "As a conjecture the reading recommends itself, even without any external authority. I have therefore adopted it, omitting the clause אחר יהוה אלהיכם , which was probably added after the corruption to והיתם had taken place." Others have read the verse in a way that does not require an apodosis either stated or unstated. Budde (*Die Bücher Samuel,* KHC, 80) advocates reading אך יראו in the place of אם תיראו by analogy with v. 24 and Josh. 24:14. He explains that the corruption is due to v. 15. There is, however, no textual basis for his suggestion. Keil (*The Books of Samuel,* 119) and others come to a similar

At the assembly in Gilgal Israel is confronted with the commencement of a new era in which the old covenant conditional (cf. Ex. 19:5, 6; Deut. 8:19; 11:13-15, 22-25, 26-28; 28:1 ff., 15 ff.; 30:17, 18; Josh. 24:20; I Sam. 7:3) takes on a new dimension. With the institution of kingship the potential for divided loyalties of the people and conflict of interest between Yahweh and the human king is created. In this new situation Samuel challenges the people to renew their determination to obey Yahweh, and not to rebel against his commandments, and thereby to demonstrate that they continue to recognize Yahweh as their sovereign. This challenge is extended not only to the people, but also to the newly inaugurated king, who is to recognize that his kingship is a vice-regency, and that he, just as all the other people, is obligated to follow Yahweh. It is Yahweh who has given Israel a king, but Israel must not replace her loyalty to Yahweh by loyalty to her human ruler. Israel is to recognize that these loyalties lie on two different levels and total loyalty to Yahweh must remain inviolate.

It is then not necessary to conclude as does Smith that the expression, "if you fear Yahweh . . . then you will follow Yahweh" is an identical proposition. Rather this is the expression of the basic covenant conditional in terms of the new era which Israel was entering. If Israel fears Yahweh, and serves him, and obeys his voice, and does not rebel against his commandments, then she will show that even though human kingship has been introduced into the structure of the theocracy, she continues to recognize Yahweh as her sovereign.[102] The implication of this in terms of the covenant

---

result as Budde without modification of the text; they read אם in the sense of a wish, "Oh that ye would only. . . ." None of these proposals give sufficient weight to the clear structural parallel between vv. 14 and 15.

102. The terms "fear" and "serve" Yahweh in I Sam. 12:14, 20 (ירא ; עָבד is used differently here than it is in vv. 14 and 24), 24 are used to characterize Israel's fundamental obligation of loyalty to Yahweh to be expressed in obedience to the covenant stipulations. "To fear" Yahweh and "to serve" Yahweh is to be obedient to the commandments, statutes and judgments of the covenantal law. The antecedents for the terminology utilized here by Samuel are to be found in

conditional is that Israel and her king can then continue to expect Yahweh's help in war and enjoy the benefits of Yahweh's rule as described in the blessings of the covenant (Deut. 28:1 ff.) which are received as the concomitant of

---

such places as Deut. 6:1-2; 10:12-13; 11:13; 17:19; 28:58; Josh. 22:5; 24:14. For ירא in v. 20, see ad locum.

For a discussion of the meaning of ירא את־יהוה in Deuteronomy, see: B. J. Oosterhoff, *De Vreze des Heren in het Oude Testament* (Utrecht: 1949) 34-39. He concludes (ibid., 39), "In Deuteronomium is Jahwe vrezen het gehoorzamen aan Zijn geboden met een hart vol diep ontzag voor Jahwe enerzijds, maar ook vol dankbare wederliefde voor de liefde, die Hij bewees aan Zijn volk anderzijds." See also S. Plath, *Furcht Gottes. Der Begriff* ירא *im Alten Testament* (Arbeiten zur Theologie II/2; Stuttgart: 1962).

For a discussion of the meaning of עבד את־יהוה in the sense of total commitment to obedience to Yahweh's commandments, see the extremely useful study of C. Lindhagen, *The Servant Motif in the Old Testament* (Uppsala: 1950). Lindhagen (ibid., p. 155) comments: "As Yahweh's servant, Israel owes her lord unconditional obedience. Her service implies that she hearkens שמע to the voice and commandments of Yahweh.... For Israel, serving Yahweh means keeping שמר his commands and statutes and doing עשה the commandment and the law.... As lawgiver for Israel Yahweh appears in his royal function: Israel here stands before Yahweh as a subject (i.e., עבד) before his king. The demands of the Torah apply to both cult and morals; the whole of Israel's ethos is to be moulded by the will of Yahweh. To rebel against the commandment of Yahweh מרה את־פי יהוה   [I Sam. 12:14] is incompatible with Israel's position as a servant."

Both of these expressions ("to fear" and "to serve" Yahweh) are sometimes used in the OT in a narrower sense to indicate cultic worship of Yahweh. Oosterhoff (ibid., 45) finds this usage of ירא particularly in the historical books and comments: "Nu betekent in Deuteronomium Jahwe vrezen zijn geboden onderhouden en daar deze geboden voor een groot deel betrekking hebben op de cultische verering van Jahwe, kan Jahwe vrezen de betekenis krijgen van 'Jahwe cultisch vereren,' op de wijze, die Hij aan Zijn volk in Zijn wet heeft voorgeschreven." See further, Oosterhoff (ibid., 40-47). To serve Yahweh is also used in this way, although as Lindhagen (ibid., 90-91) points out one must be careful in drawing too rigid a distinction. As he notes: "To serve Yahweh means allowing the whole of one's conduct to be ruled by obedience to the will of Yahweh. As the cult is part of what Yahweh commanded, every right act of worship is an act of obedience." Yet, on the other hand, as becomes clear on the basis of numerous passages "this does not prevent the word being used in the OT not only in a general sense but also in contexts where the ethical or cultic aspect more or less wholly predominates." Some of the passages in which the cultic aspect is primary are: Ex. 3:12; 4:23; 7:16, 26 (8:1); 8:16(20); 9:1, 13; 10:3, 7, 8, 11, 24; 12:31. On this usage see also, G. Schmitt, *Der Landtag von Sichem* (Arbeiten zur Theologie I/15; Stuttgart: 1964) 40, 41.

The use of the terms in I Sam. 12:14, 20 (עבד), 24 in connection with Samuel's challenge to Israel to renew her allegiance to Yahweh as her sovereign favors understanding the terms here in the broader more inclusive sense of obedience to all of Yahweh's commands.

covenant loyalty to Yahweh. Kingship is here being incorporated into the structure of the theocracy in a manner designed to safeguard the continued recognition of the rule of Yahweh over his people.

I Sam. 12:15. And if you will not listen to the voice of Yahweh, and rebel[103] against the commandment of Yahweh; then shall the hand of Yahweh be against you as it was against your fathers.[104]

The alternative to recognizing Yahweh as the supreme authority over the nation and thereby to receive the benefits of the covenant blessings, is to refuse to submit to Yahweh's authority and in so doing to evoke Yahweh's wrath as expressed in the covenant curses and experienced by the ancestors of the people to whom Samuel spoke. Here, then, Israel is faced with the same alternatives which long before had been presented by Moses to the people in the plains of Moab (Deut. 28:1-62; 30:15-20). The introduction of kingship into Israel's socio-political structure, bringing with it a new potential for either good or evil, has not changed the fundamental nature of Israel's relationship to Yahweh.

The alternatives which are here opened to the Israelites can be traced in their realization in Israel's subsequent his-

---

103. Note the Qal form of מרה here, but the Hiphil form in v. 14. No difference in meaning is involved; it would appear to be merely variety in expression.

104. The LXX$^{L(BA)}$ reads καὶ ἐπὶ τὸν βασιλέα ὑμῶν in place of the ובאבתיכם of the MT. Driver (*Notes,* 95) adopts this reading of LXX$^{L(BA)}$ and points out that the mentioning together of "you" and "your king" agrees with vv. 14 and 25b. The LXX^L adds at the end of the verse ἐξολοθρεῦσαι ὑμᾶς = להשבידכם , which reading is favored by Budde (*Die Bücher Samuel,* KHC, 80) and Smith (*Samuel,* ICC, 88). Hertzberg (*I and II Samuel,* 96) combines the LXX and MT and translates the phrase: "... the hand of the LORD will be against you and against your king to destroy you like your fathers." The Targum and Syriac translate the phrase, "as it was against your fathers." This translation is defended by Keil (*The Books of Samuel,* 119) and Goslinga (*I Samuel,* KV, 153) based on the use of ו in a comparative sense. More recently Goslinga (*Het Eerste Boek Samuël,* COT, 249) suggests: "Verreweg het eenvoudigst is aan te nemen, dat een oorspr. כ bij het afschrijven is vervangen door ו, zo dat het vs. besluit met een vergelijking: *tegen u evenals tegen uw vaderen.*" This is certainly a reasonable conclusion.

tory. The history of the northern and southern kingdoms with few exceptions is a history of apostasy and turning away from the commandments of Yahweh. This led to repeated actualizations of the covenant curses in plagues, droughts, and foreign oppressions, eventually resulting in captivity, first to the northern and later to the southern kingdom.[105]

I Sam. 12:16. Now therefore, present yourselves and see this great thing which Yahweh will do before your eyes.

With this verse a new section of the report of the Gilgal assembly is introduced. Samuel has presented his case demonstrating Yahweh's faithfulness to the covenant, and by contrast the people's apostasy in requesting a king. He has pointed out that Yahweh has chosen to give them a king but it is their responsibility to continue to recognize Yahweh as their sovereign in the new era of the monarchy. He now calls for the attention of the people to observe something which Yahweh himself will do in order to authenticate that which he has been saying, and in order to remind the people that Yahweh's power to actualize the covenant curses is very real. Yahweh will do this by the performance of a "great thing" which will be a tangible demonstration of his existence and power, as well as his involvement with his people in the issues being faced at the Gilgal assembly.

This was to be an event of such highly unusual significance that Samuel introduces it in terminology resembling that of Moses when he announced Yahweh's deliverance of his people at the Red Sea.[106]

---

105. That this is the case is no reason to conclude that these verses must have been written after 587 BC. See, e.g., Hertzberg's statement (*I and II Samuel,* 100) that vv. 14 and 15 give a "survey of the period of the kings which is now beginning. . . . The standpoint of the preacher and his audience accordingly lies in the time after 587."

106. W. Harrelson (*BR* 3[1958] 4, 5) has drawn attention to the specialized meaning of התיצב in a number of its OT occurrences. Although in certain places the word means simply to stand (Ex. 2:4; II Sam. 18:13, 30; Ps. 36:5(4); Prov. 22:29) or to stand against, as in battle (Deut. 7:24; 9:2; 11:25), Harrelson points out that the use of the term in Ex. 14:13; 19:17; Judg. 20:2; I Sam. 10:19; 12:7,

I Sam. 12:16a: . . . . ‫ . . . . ‫התיצבו וראו‬

Ex. 14:13a: . . . . ‫ . . . התיצבו וראו‬

I Sam. 12:16b: ‫וראו את־הדבר הגדול הזה אשר יהוה עשה לעיניכם‬

Ex. 14:31a: ‫וירא ישראל את־היד הגדולה אשר יהוה עשה‬

I Sam. 12:17. Is it not wheat harvest today? I will call unto Yahweh that he may send thunderings and rain; then you shall know[107] and see that your evil is great which you have done in the eyes of Yahweh, in asking[108] for yourselves a king.

In a season during which rain rarely fell (cf. Prov. 26:1), Samuel says that he will call on Yahweh to send thunderings (‫קולות‬) and rain as a sign that Israel has sinned in asking for a king.[109] In this way the people can assuredly know (expressed by the imperative ‫ודעו‬) that the words of Samuel are true.

---

16 "suffice to indicate that to take one's stand, or to present oneself, is an act of fundamental meaning for Israelite worship. When the congregation is summoned to assemble before Yahweh, the first thing to be done is for Israel to take her stand in expectancy and holy fear. The outcome of such gatherings cannot be predicted in advance. The people are present for the purpose of witnessing what Yahweh is about to do. They are not mere bystanders by any means, but they are gathered first of all to hear from Yahweh, before they are to make confession, do acts of sacrifice or otherwise to demonstrate their loyalty or devotion." In v. 7 the people present themselves (‫התיצב‬) before Yahweh for indictment in a sacral-legal proceeding, now they present themselves (‫התיצב‬) to await a sign (‫הדבר הגדל‬) from Yahweh authenticating all that Samuel had been saying. For other references to "great things" which Yahweh had done for his people see: Deut. 20:21; 11:7; Josh. 24:17; Judg. 2:7; Ps. 106:21.

107. *GK* §110i.

108. *GK* §114o.

109. Mauchline (*I and II Samuel*, NCB, 109) misconstrues the intent of this verse when he says, "the editor of this chapter cannot be reconciled to royal rule (17) and has a final condemnation of it put on record. . . . This chapter is commonly associated with chs. 7 and 8 but at this point it seems to go beyond them in exalting Samuel and in denigrating royal rule." See further below, Chapter V.

It has often been asserted that the reference to the time of wheat harvest in this verse demonstrates that there was no original connection between the events described in I Samuel 11 and those of the Gilgal assembly.[110] On the basis of the statement in I Samuel 11:5 that Saul was coming from the field behind the oxen it is concluded that the events of chapter 11 took place at ploughing time which was in the rainy season of November to January and not at the time of wheat harvest in the dry season of May and June.

De Groot, however, has rightly pointed out that the remark in I Samuel 11:5 is better interpreted as a reference to threshing, not only because of the agreement which this establishes between chapters 11 and 12, but also because warfare was not normally carried on in the rainy season, and according to I Samuel 11:1, Nahash had already brought his military force against Jabesh-Gilead.[111] Goslinga adds to this that the crossing of the Jordan by a military force (I Sam. 11:11) also fits much better with the dry season than it does with the rainy season, when this would be extremely difficult.[112] It should also be noted that I Samuel 11:11 appears to contain a reference to the cessation of fighting due to the severity of the mid-day heat (cf. v. 9, and Judg. 8:13; Neh. 7:3) which would be characteristic of harvest time, not of the season for ploughing.[113]

---

110. See, e.g.: Budde, *Die Bücher Samuel,* KHC, 81; and Schulz, *Samuel,* EH, 172.

111. De Groot, *I Samuël,* TeU, 121, 122.

112. Goslinga, *Het Eerste Boek Samuël,* COT, 250. Stoebe's comment (*Das erste Buch Samuelis,* KAT, 239) that the thunder storm's occurrence at the time of wheat harvest is emphatically against the assignment of the proceedings of this assembly to a "hypothetical covenant renewal celebration" is apparently based on the assumption that a covenant renewal ceremony must take place on a fixed date, most likely at the time of the Feast of Tabernacles in the fall (cf. Deut. 31:10, 11). There is no firm evidence however for concluding that covenant renewal ceremonies were always held at fixed times. Cf. Baltzer, *The Covenant Formulary,* 61; Dentan, *The Knowledge of God in Ancient Israel,* 248, n. 11. For further discussion see Chapter IV, Section 2,B,1,a.

113. For a discussion of climatic conditions referred to in the Old Testament including those alluded to in I Samuel 11 and 12 see: R. B. Y. Scott,

I Sam. 12:18. And Samuel called on Yahweh and Yahweh sent thunderings and rain on that day, and all the people greatly feared Yahweh and Samuel.

Yahweh responded to Samuel's prayer and sent thunderings and rain with the result that the people feared for their very lives (v. 19), being convinced that Samuel's indictment was correct, and that they had incurred upon themselves the wrath of Yahweh. This is not the only place in the Old Testament where it is noted that the Israelites feared for their lives when Yahweh revealed himself in the thunderstorm (cf. Ex. 19:16; 20:18-20; Deut. 18:16). Neither is this the only place in the Old Testament where an expression similar to the unusual combination at the end of the verse (Yahweh and Samuel) is found. On another historic occasion it is said that the Israelites "feared Yahweh and believed Yahweh and his servant Moses" (Ex. 14:31), in response to the manifestation of Yahweh's power at the Red Sea.[114]

It is sometimes questioned whether this event is to be regarded as a theophany or merely as an authenticating sign that what Samuel had said was correct.[115] However one may answer this,[116] it is clear that the people understood the

---

"Meteorological Phenomena and Terminology in the Old Testament," *ZAW* 64 (1962) 11-25.

114. Notice also the statement in Josh. 4:14 after the Israelites had seen the waters of the Jordan cut off to permit them to cross: "On that day Yahweh exalted Joshua in the sight of all Israel; so that they feared him, just as they feared Moses all the days of his life." See further below, n. 122b.

115. Stoebe (*Das erste Buch Samuelis*, KAT, 238) contrasts the thunder and rain in I Sam. 12:18 with Ex. 19:18 where he sees the thunderstorm at the concluding of the covenant as a sign of the power of Yahweh, and bearing the character of a theophany. In I Sam. 12:18 he says there is no thought of this and he views the storm as an unexpected event authenticating a mandate. Stoebe argues that here rain is mentioned, "und Regen gehört nun sicherlich nicht zu einer theophanieschilderung" (239); (cf., however, Judg. 5:4). Baltzer (*The Covenant Formulary*, 67, n. 20) suggests that the sign in vv. 16-18 has replaced an original theophany.

116. The question is more complicated than would appear from Stoebe's comments. Various authors (see, e.g.: Th. C. Vriezen, *An Outline of Old Testament Theology* [Oxford: 1970²] 190 f.; Nic. H. Ridderbos, "Die Theophanie in Ps. L 1-6," *OTS*, XV [1969] 213-226, esp., 216 f., and the literature there cited) make a distinction between an epiphany and a theophany. Ridderbos (216, n. 1)

thunder and rain as an attestation to Samuel's words, but at the same time as a revelation of the power of Yahweh. Perhaps the closest parallel to be found in the OT is the sending of fire from heaven in response to the prayer of Elijah on Mt. Carmel (I Kings 18:36-39), which let the Israelites know that Yahweh was God, and that Elijah had performed his ministry at the mandate of Yahweh. In both instances authentication is primary. Thus while a theophany cannot be spoken of in the normal technical sense of that term on either of these occasions, there is nevertheless in both instances a manifestation of the power of Yahweh which revealed something of the awesomeness of his person and which to that extent can be said to have theophanic aspects.[117]

It is noteworthy that here when the people of Israel are challenged to renew their loyalty to Yahweh and to resolve to keep their covenantal obligations, a sign is given which might well remind them of the establishment of the covenant at Sinai where there were, "thunder and lightning flashes and a thick cloud upon the mountain" (Ex. 19:16).[118]

comments, "Wenn Gott erscheint, um seinem Volk (durch einen Mittler) etwas zu sagen, spricht man von einer Theophanie; erscheint Gott zur Rettung seines Volkes im Kampf mit den Feinden, so handelt es sich um eine Epiphanie (die Definitionen des Unterschieds weisen bei den einzelnen Verfassern gewisse Abweichungen auf). Eine solche Unterscheidung kann gewiss klärend wirken. . . ." Vriezen (*An Outline of Old Testament Theology,* 190), however, rightly remarks that "in the stories concerning Mount Sinai the descriptions are closely allied to those of the epiphanies, though these stories are meant to describe theophanies." Ridderbos (217, n. 1) with reason adds to this that the same can be said of Ps. 50. We make mention of this here merely to indicate the complexity of the question involved. We are using the term theophany, however, in the customary manner, i.e., the designation of an appearance of God which is accompanied by extraordinary natural phenomena.

117. For discussion of the revelatory significance of signs and wonders in the Old Testament, see: G. F. Oehler, *Theology of the Old Testament* (Grand Rapids: n.d. [German original, Stuttgart: 1891] 139, 140); C. A. Keller, *Das Wort OTH als "Offenbarungszeichen Gottes"* (Basel: 1946); G. Quell, "Das Phänomen des Wunders im Alten Testament," in: *Verbannung und Heimkehr,* Festschrift W. Rudolph (Tübingen: 1961) 253-300; F. J. Helfmeyer, "אות," *TDOT,* I, 167-188. On theophany in general see: J. Jeremias, *Theophanie. Die Geschichte einer Alttestamentlichen Gattung* (WMANT, 10; Neukirchen-Vluyn: 1965).

118. Cf. especially the plural קוֹלוֹת in I Sam. 12:17-18 and in Ex. 19:16;

I Sam. 12:19. And all the people said[119] unto Samuel, "Pray[120] for your servants unto Yahweh your god that we die not,[121] because we have to all our sins added evil in asking for us a king."

The people's fear motivated them to confess their sin and request Samuel to intercede for them unto Yahweh. As they look to Samuel to mediate between themselves and Yahweh, they are strongly conscious that from their side they had broken the covenant relationship with Yahweh. This being so they do not even dare to refer to him as "our God," but ask Samuel to pray to Yahweh "your God" (in contrast cf. I Sam. 7:8). The evil (רעה) to which the people refer is (as in v. 17) the request for a king with its accompanying implications. The people recognize that this evil did not stand alone, as they have become aware that Samuel was right when he spoke at length of the pervasiveness of their sinful condition throughout the centuries.

It is not explicitly stated that Samuel acceded to their request. Yet we may conclude from verse 23 that he did. This prayer of Samuel must have been a prayer of confession, and a request for mercy, much like that of Moses after the apostasy of the golden calf worship (Ex. 32:31-32; 33:12-17), and the unbelief at Kadesh Barnea (Num. 14:13-19). This and other intercessions (cf., e.g., I Sam. 7:8, 9; 12:23)

20:18 (according to Mandelkern the plural occurs only twelve times in the entire OT). It is, of course, true that there are considerable differences between Ex. 19 and 20, and I Sam. 12 (note, e.g., the absence of rain in Ex. 19 and 20; see n. 115 above). But, on the other hand, in view of the connection which Nic. H. Ridderbos (*OTS*, XV, 213-226) has suggested between Ps. 50 and a covenant renewal, it is apparent that to an Israelite the concluding and renewing of the covenant with Yahweh is apt to be accompanied by thunder (see Ps. 50:1 ff.). See further below, Chapter IV, Section 2,A,4.

119. Subject sing., predicate pl., cf. *kᵉtîb* in v. 10.

120. Driver (*Notes*, 35) defines התפלל as "to interpose as mediator, especially by means of entreaty. . . ." Although in general usage the term is about as neutral as the verb "to pray" in English, it is often used in the sense of "asking for someone else." J. Herrmann ("εὔχομαι," *TDNT*, II, 785) notes that 25 out of 60 occurrences of the word are intercessory. Cf. the similar requests for prayer addressed to Moses in the wilderness: Num. 11:2; 21:7. See further: P. A. H. de Boer, "De voorbede in het OT," *OTS*, III (1943) 124-132; D. R. Ap-Thomas, "Notes on some terms relating to prayer," *VT* 6 (1956) 225-241.

121. *GK* §107p.

later cause Samuel to be regarded as an intercessor comparable to Moses, and otherwise unequalled in the course of Israel's history (Jer. 15:1; Ps. 99:6). The effectiveness of Samuel's prayers appears in I Samuel 7:10 and 12:18.

I Sam. 12:20. And Samuel said to the people, "Fear not![122] You indeed have[123] committed all this evil, only do not any longer turn away from following Yahweh, but serve Yahweh with all your heart."

In words of comfort and admonition, also in some ways reminiscent of those which Moses spoke to the children of Israel at Sinai (cf. Ex. 20:20), Samuel tells the people not to fear in spite of the evil which they had done[124] and the awesome sign which Yahweh had given. Samuel subsequently (v. 22) explains the grounds on which he can tell the people not to fear, but he first reminds them of their responsibility toward Yahweh. Their duty remains to serve Yahweh with all their heart. In this expression Samuel states concisely the fundamental obligation of the covenant relationship (cf. Deut. 10:12; 11:13; Josh. 22:5).[125]

Here Samuel again brings to focus the central issue in the controversy surrounding the establishment of kingship in Israel. The evil was not kingship in itself, but turning away from following Yahweh. In this admonition Samuel again uses the terminology (מאחרי יהוה) which he had used earlier to formulate the covenant conditional in verse 14 (אחר

---

122. a) *GK* §109c. b) Samuel's exhortation in this verse not to fear utilizes ירא in a different sense than in vv. 14, 24. See n. 102 above and n. 144 below. We can say that the meaning of ירא in v. 18 is in between that in v. 14 and 24 and that in v. 20.

123. *GK* §135a; Driver, *Notes*, 95.

124. There is no well founded basis for seeing here in Samuel's encouraging words a badly harmonized tension with the previous verse as does Stoebe (*Das erste Buch Samuelis,* KAT, 239) who suggests that when the people have come to the realization of their arrogance (v. 19) this is weakened with the "yes-but" idea of v. 20. Rather than tension, here is an expression of the idea that when Israel in repentance resumes her proper relationship to Yahweh (i.e., that of serving him) He will not forsake them for his great name's sake (v. 22). Stoebe, however, views vv. 21 and 22 as a late insertion. On this question, see further below.

125. See above, n. 102.

יהוה).[126] The supreme obligation of the children of Israel has not changed with the establishment of the monarchy. Their duty now, just as previously, is to follow Yahweh, which is to serve Yahweh with all their heart.

I Sam. 12:21. And turn not[127] away[128] after vain things which do not profit or deliver because they are vain things.

The alternatives for Israel are again made clear. They can follow Yahweh and find prosperity and security or follow vain things (התהו) which cannot profit or deliver because they are vain (תהו). Samuel here broadens the frame of reference from the focus on the evil (רעה, vv. 17, 19) of requesting a king, and now warns the people to turn from every attempt to find security outside of obedience and loyalty to Yahweh.

From the construction of the sentence it is clear that התהו is to be understood in a collective sense.[129] The term תהו is usually interpreted as a reference to turning aside after heathen gods or idols.[130] Because idolatry is not the issue in

---

126. See above, 41-46.

127. Here the stronger form of prohibition is used, לא and the imperfect, rather than אל and the jussive, which was used in v. 20, cf. *GK* §107o, §109b.

128. The כי which appears here in the MT is regarded by many as a copyist's error and thus to be eliminated. See, e.g.: Thenius, *Die Bücher Samuels,* KeH, 53; Wellhausen, *Der Text der Bücher Samuelis,* 79; Driver, *Notes,* 95; and Smith, *Samuel,* ICC, 89. Keil (*The Books of Samuel,* 121) suggests that following the כי after תסורו the same verb should be supplied from the context thus yielding the translation: "Do not turn aside (from the LORD) for (ye turn aside) after that which is vain." A. B. Ehrlich (*Randglossen zur Hebräischen Bibel* [7 vols.; Leipzig: 1908-1914] III, 209) suggests that since the removal of כי leaves an incorrect sentence because סור אחרו is not used in Hebrew, but rather סור מאחרי , it may be better to view כי as a mutilation of an original לבת with סור as in Deut. 11:28; 28:14. More recently Stoebe, (*Das erste Buch Samuelis,* KAT, 234) following P. A. H. de Boer (*Research into the Text of I Samuel I-XVI* [Amsterdam: 1938] 52) advocates retaining כי as an emphatic particle.

In my opinion the resolution of de Boer is preferable. But whichever of these alternatives is adopted, the meaning of the verse remains unchanged. The presence of *paseq* points up the problem, but may not be used to give precedence to any particular solution (cf. *GK* §15 f., n. 2).

129. Note the plural verb forms which follow התהו and the pronoun המה at the end of the sentence.

130. See, e.g.: Keil, *The Books of Samuel,* 121 ("false gods"); Kirkpatrick,

the context, and because the use of תהו is considered by many to be an indication that this verse cannot be dated prior to the time of the author of "deutero-Isaiah" (c. 540 B.C.), it is frequently suggested that this entire verse should be regarded as a later insertion.[131] Such a position, however, rests on too narrow an understanding of the meaning of תהו , and on the unprovable assumption that the word could not have been used in the time of Samuel. Certain occurrences of the word in Isaiah (where eleven of its twenty occurrences are found), show that it is sometimes used to express the weakness or nothingness not only of molten images (Isa. 41:29), but also of nations (Isa. 40:17), and their rulers (Isa. 40:23), when these are compared to the power of Yahweh. The term is thus not to be confined in its meaning in I Samuel 12:21 to the "nothingness" of heathen idols, but rather has reference to the "nothingness" of anything that would exalt itself against Yahweh. Samuel thus uses the term here to exhort the people to turn aside from everything, whether that be a person, a king, a nation, a god or idol, which entails a reduction or replacement of service to Yahweh. For to follow anything or anyone to the deprecation of following Yahweh is to follow a "nothing" (תהו) and a "nothing" cannot deliver (נצל , Hiphil).

I Sam. 12:22. For Yahweh will not forsake his people, on account of his great name's sake, for Yahweh has resolved to make you a people for himself.

The double use of כי serves to indicate the basis on

Samuel, CambB, 122 ("false gods"); Nowack, *Richter, Ruth und Bücher Samuelis,* HK I/4, 55 ("fremden Götter"); A. R. S. Kennedy, *I and II Samuel* (CentB; Edinburgh: 1904) 95 ("idols of the heathen"); and Goslinga, *Het Eerste Boek Samuël,* COT, 251 ("heidense afgoden").

131. See, e.g.: Budde, *Die Bücher Samuel,* KHC, 81; Kennedy, *Samuel,* CentB, 95; Caird, *IB,* II, 945; and Stoebe, *Das erste Buch Samuelis,* KAT, 239. Schulz (*Samuel,* EH, 173) also questioning the use of תהו by Samuel proposes a reconstruction of the verse in which on the basis of the Targum he suggests replacing התהו with התועבה. His proposal, however, is quite involved and requires other changes in wording as well, for which there is no textual evidence.

which Samuel's previous words of comfort and admonition
rest. First of all, Samuel asserts categorically that Yahweh
will not forsake (נטש) his people for his great name's sake
(בעבר שמו הגדול). While נטש is used rather infrequently in
the OT in an expression of this type (normally a verb such as
עזב is used) Samuel's statement is directly paralleled in Psalm
94:14a. Here נטש is used in synonymous parallelism with
עזב . Samuel is thus restating the well known promise of
Deuteronomy 31:6, 8 and Joshua 1:5.

The guarantee to the people for the validity of the
promise of Yahweh's faithfulness to them rests in the integrity of Yahweh himself (שמו הגדול).[132] The idea that
Yahweh will do certain things for the sake of his own name is
equivalent to saying that Yahweh will be faithful to his own
self revelation. Yahweh cannot deny himself.[133] It was on
this same basis that both Moses and Joshua had interceded
for the Israelites after previous incidents of serious apostasy
(Ex. 32:12-14; Num. 14:15-20; Josh. 7:9); and in Deuteronomy it is emphasized that the basis for Israel's selection to
be Yahweh's people does not lie in any quality or merit of
the people themselves, but in the oath which Yahweh had
given to Abraham, Isaac, and Jacob (Deut. 7:7, 8; 9:4, 5).
This idea persisted throughout Israel's history as a nation, so
that during the exile Ezekiel is found assuring the people in
captivity that Yahweh was not finished with them, and in
spite of their present condition, Yahweh would again act on
their behalf for his holy name's sake. "Thus says Yahweh
God, It is not for your sake, O house of Israel, that I am
about to act, but for My holy name, which you have profaned among the nations where you went. And I will vindi-
cate the holiness of My great name which has been profaned
among the nations . . ." (Ezek. 36:22, 23, see further Ezek.
36:22-38).

---

132. For similar expressions see: Isa. 48:9; Jer. 14:7; Ps. 106:8.
133. For discussion of the theological significance of the use of the term
"name" of Yahweh in this way, see: G. A. F. Knight, *A Christian Theology of the
Old Testament* (Richmond: 1959) 60-64, esp. 61.

Samuel then undergirds this assertion with a statement
introduced by the second בְּ which explains that the ultimate
basis for Israel's special relationship to Yahweh is the unconditional free choice of Yahweh's elective grace to make Israel
his own people. The use of יָאַל (Hiphil) to express the idea
of divine determination or "good pleasure" is found elsewhere only in II Sam. 7:29; Job 6:9; I Chron. 17:27. Nevertheless, it clearly expresses an idea which finds repeated stress
in Deuteronomy (Deut. 4:37; 7:6; 10:15; 14:2; 26:18, 19),
and which constitutes one of the most important and central
ideas of the OT.[134]

For the simple reason that Yahweh had chosen Israel to
be his people, the people can be assured that he will not
forsake them. Yet this position is not simply one of privilege
without obligation. Yahweh's choice of Israel demanded response and created a particular responsibility. The form
which the response was to take found its definition in the
stipulations of the Sinaitic covenant. These stipulations were
to be observed as an expression of the people's thanksgiving
and loyalty to Yahweh, who had revealed himself to them,
delivered them out of Egypt, and remained constantly faithful to his covenant with them and their fathers.[135]

---

134. For discussion of the OT idea of election see: K. Galling, *Die Erwähl-
ungstraditionen Israels* (BZAW 48; Giessen: 1928); H. H. Rowley, *The Biblical
Doctrine of Election* (London: 1950); G. E. Wright, *God Who Acts* (SBT 8;
London: 1952) 50-54; Th. C. Vriezen, *De Verkiezing van Israel* (Exegetica,
Nieuwe reeks, II; Amsterdam: 1974).

135. D. J. McCarthy (*Treaty and Covenant*, 175, 176) makes the following
comment on the relation between election and covenant while discussing the
giving of the decalogue to Israel at Sinai: "To retain its special relationship with
Yahwe Israel must obey the commands. Thus in the oracle Yahwe Himself has
made known the conditions for continued covenant; or better, obedience to these
provisions is the living expression of Israel's special relation to Yahwe. It does not
produce this relationship. We may remark that this becomes even more clear when
the covenant comes to be expressed in the treaty form. It is not the stipulations
which produce the relationship; they are the obligations which are revealed by
God as resulting from that relationship rather than bringing it about." C. Lindhagen (*The Servant Motif in the Old Testament*, 153, 154) points out: "The
election was an election to a service of Yahweh. As Yahweh's servant, Israel is no
longer entitled to go her own way. Her τέλος from then onwards is to perform the
will of another, to effectuate the purpose that Yahweh laid down in the elec-

I Sam. 12:23. As for myself,[136] far will it be from me that I should sin against Yahweh, that I should cease to pray for you; but I shall instruct you[137] in the good and the right way.[138]

Samuel assures the people not only of Yahweh's continued commitment to them (v. 22), but also of his own continued interest in their well being. Samuel's great concern is that Israel should walk in the way of the covenant, and he intends to do all that he can to see that this is done. It is clear from this statement that he is not planning to withdraw from a role of leadership in the nation.[139] First, he will continue (cf. v. 19) to intercede for the people, but in addition he will instruct them in their covenantal obligations.[140] These are essentially the same functions which he was performing in convening and directing the Gilgal assembly.

This continued activity of Samuel was to be of great

tion. . . . As Yahweh's obedient servant, Israel will receive blessing and life. But if she tries to free herself from Yahweh's sovereignty, the unfaithful servant will be led into a curse and death." This does not mean, however, that Yahweh's covenant with his people is dissolved. When the people turn away from their covenant obligations they will experience the covenant curses (Deut. 28.15 ff., cf. 29:11[12]) or what is termed in Lev. 26:25 the "vengeance of the covenant." Yet the curses and the vengeance are not antipathetic to the covenant, nor do they void the covenant, but rather belong to it. As Lindhagen (ibid., 154) notes: "Even if Israel immediately started on the path of apostasy (the golden calf), Yahweh never let go his servant: in the new covenant, everyone was both to know and to do the will of Yahweh." For further discussion of the relation between election and covenant see: M. G. Kline, *By Oath Consigned* (Grand Rapids: 1968) 26-38; J. Jocz, *The Covenant: A Theology of Human Destiny* (Grand Rapids: 1968) 40-43; D. J. McCarthy, *Old Testament Covenant* (Richmond: 1972) 53-56, and the additional literature cited below in Chapter IV, n. 10.

    136. *KBL*[3] s.v. ‏כב‎, 4, cf. Gen. 32:19(18) etc.
    137. *GK* §112x.
    138. *GK* §126x. See further Chapter IV, n. 113.
    139. This chapter is not properly understood when it is viewed as Samuel's farewell speech. See above, 18-20 and below, Chapter IV, Section 2,B,1,a. For this reason statements such as that of Kennedy (*Samuel,* CentB, 95): "Samuel divests himself of his authority as Yahweh's representative in the theocracy, reserving only the privilege of being his people's intercessor" do not do justice to the continuing role of Samuel in the national life.
    140. That the good and the right way (‏בדרך הטובה והישרה‎) is the way of covenantal obedience is clear from comparison of this expression with Deut. 6:18 and 12:28 (see also I Kings 8:36). Samuel is here carrying on with one of the most important functions which Yahweh had previously entrusted to Moses (see Ex. 24:12). See further Chapter IV, Section 2,B,1,b,3.

significance to Saul. While from this time on Saul would assume a position of leadership in the nation, particularly in political and military matters, his actions would remain subject to review by Samuel, who would not hesitate to rebuke him should his actions be in violation of the revealed will of Yahweh, the description of the responsibilities of the king drawn up at Mizpah previously (I Sam. 10:25), or of covenantal law generally.

More importantly, however, Samuel's continuing activity establishes the pattern for all the future occupants of the throne in Israel, in that their actions would always be subject to assessment by a prophet of Yahweh.[141] Samuel is here laying the structural foundation for the functioning of the theocracy in the new era of the monarchy which was now beginning; and in so doing he is seeking to insure covenantal continuity through a time of transition and into the new epoch.

I Sam. 12:24. Only fear[142] Yahweh, and serve him faithfully with all your heart, for consider what great things he has done[143] for you.

Speaking to the people, Samuel now describes how they may walk, "in the good and the right way" (v. 23b). Much as Joshua had done previously at the covenant renewal ceremony at Shechem (Josh. 24:2-14a), Samuel frames the essence of the people's covenant obligation in words demanding complete loyalty to Yahweh out of gratitude for the great things which he has done for them.[144] The great things to

141. E. F. Campbell ("Sovereign God," *McCormick Quarterly* 20 [1967] 182) comments that the role of the prophet in Israel, "is dramatic evidence that no man is king in Israel in an absolute sense, and that a vital office exists side by side with the office of kingship which will never let the king forget who is really sovereign in Israel."

142. *GK* §75oo.

143. The Hebrew expression here is difficult. Perhaps this is an elliptic formulation: אֵת מַעֲשָׂיו אֲשֶׁר הִגְדִּיל cf. Eccl. 2:4.

144. To fear Yahweh, and serve him faithfully with all your heart is to live in obedience to the covenantal obligations (see n. 102 above). Oosterhoff's comment (*De Vreze des Heren in het Oude Testament*, 43) that "to fear" Yahweh in I Sam. 12:24 has particular reference to, "de cultische dienst van Jahwe in

which he refers are all the manifestations throughout the centuries of Yahweh's care for his people which Samuel has summarized previously (vv. 8 ff.), but they also include the more recent manifestations of Yahweh's care for his people such as the victory over the Ammonites (I Sam. 11:13), the giving of a king to the people in spite of the sinfulness of their request (I Sam. 12:13), and the sending of the thunder storm as a sign of Yahweh's concern for the condition of his people (I Sam. 12:16, אֶת־הַדָּבָר הַגָּדוֹל). Yahweh has been faithful to his people; their obligation is total loyalty to him in gratitude for his great and gracious acts on their behalf.

I Sam. 12:25. (But) if you on the contrary do evil, both you and your king will be swept away.[145]

Samuel concludes by warning the people that persistent rejection of Yahweh will ultimately lead to the destruction of the nation. Previously (vv. 17, 19, 20) Samuel focused on the evil (רָעָה) of seeking a king, which betrayed Israel's rejection of the kingship of Yahweh (v. 12). Now a king has been given to the nation with Yahweh's sanction (v. 13); but his role is to be that of an instrument of the rule of Yahweh (v. 14, see also 10:25). Should the nation or the king now persist in covenant breaking conduct, then they will bring upon themselves their own destruction.[146]

---

tegenstelling met de verering der afgoden" is too restrictive in this context. Lindhagen (*The Servant Motif in the Old Testament,* 158) notes that "the fear-serve combination is associated with ideas like hearkening to the voice of Yahweh [Dt 13:5(4), I S 12:14; cf. Ecclus 2:15], not being rebellious [I S 12:14], cleaving to Yahweh [Dt 10:20, 13:5(4)], being followers of Yahweh [Dt 13:5(4), I S 12:14], walking in his ways [Dt 10:12; cf. Dt 8:6, Is 63:17, Ps 128:1, Pr 14:2], keeping his commandments and statutes [Dt 10:12f; cf. Dt 5:29(26), 6:2,24, 8:6, 17:19, 28:58 (שָׁמֹר לַעֲשׂוֹת), 31:12 (*do.*), Ps 19:10, 112:1, Ecclus 23:27 and the explanation וִירֵאתָ מֵאֱלֹהֶיךָ in 'the law of Holiness' Lev 19:14,32, 25:17,36,43. Cf also 2 K 17:34], swearing by his name [Dt 6:13, 10:20]."

145. סָפָה, Niphal (which is also used in I Sam. 26:10; 27:1) appears in the Pentateuch only in Gen. 19:15, 17; Num. 16:16. In Deuteronomy only the Hiphil is used (Deut. 32:23, in the sense of "heap up"). Similar expressions occur frequently in Deuteronomy but using forms of אבד or שמד.

146. The alternation of promise and warning as found here is characteristic of the exhortations of Deuteronomy (see, e.g., Deut. 28 and 29).

TRANSLATION AND EXEGESIS OF I SAMUEL 11:14-15

I Sam. 11:14. And Samuel said unto the people, "Come, let us go to Gilgal and renew the kingdom there."

After the great victory over the Ammonites (I Sam. 11: 1-13) which demonstrated to the people not only that Saul was competent to lead them in battle, but more importantly that Yahweh was willing to bring victory to the Israelites through Saul's leadership,[1] Samuel called for the people to assemble in Gilgal to renew the kingdom.

By far the most significant phrase in I Samuel 11:14 is the expression "renew the kingdom." The question of how this expression is to be understood is inseparably tied to the question of how one interprets the relationship between the event here referred to and those which precede and immediately follow in the sequence of events associated with Saul's being made king in Israel.[2]

Currently the most common approach to the phrase is to

---

1. In I Sam. 11:13 Saul says that "Yahweh has worked salvation (עָשָׂה־יְהוָה תְשׁוּעָה) in Israel." This appears to be a response to the questions of those who opposed Saul's selection to be king at Mizpah, and who then asked, "How is this man going to save us?" (מַה־יִּשִׁעֵנוּ זֶה, I Sam. 10:27; cf. also I Sam. 11:12). The important point being made is that it is not merely *this man* who delivered Israel, but that the promise of Deut. 20:4 ("For Yahweh your God goes with you to fight for you against your enemies to save you" [לְהוֹשִׁיעַ].) is still operative. Even though Israel is now to have a king to lead them in battle, this does not mean that Yahweh is being replaced, but that he will continue to lead Israel in battle, sometimes through the instrumentality of the human king, and sometimes through the extraordinary utilization of psychological and natural forces. The victory of the Israelites over the Ammonites is thus to be seen as an additional confirmation that Yahweh had chosen Saul to be king.

2. For the literary critical background to this problem see below, Chapter III, Section 1, and Chapter V, Section 1.

view it as a "harmonizing redactional insertion."[3] This view transcends many of the differences in approach to the literary analysis of I Samuel 8-12,[4] and its advocates regard the expression "renew the kingdom" as an ineffectual editorial attempt to arrange I Samuel 10:17 ff. and I Samuel 11:15 (which are viewed as two separate and conflicting traditions of the establishment of the monarchy) as sequential rather than juxtaposed parallel accounts.

Those who do not view the phrase "renew the kingdom" as a harmonizing redactional insertion generally interpret חדשׁ (renew) as inaugurate,[5] confirm,[6] or celebrate.[7] The Gilgal

---

3. B. C. Birch, (*The Rise of the Israelite Monarchy: The Growth and Development of I Sam. 7-15* [unpublished Ph.D. dissertation, Yale University, 1970] 101), says, "Most scholars have regarded this verse as the clearest evidence of redactional activity in this chapter and there would seem to be little reason for challenging this conclusion." Note, for example, the following expressions of this viewpoint: Ackroyd, (*The First Book of Samuel*, CNEB, 92), writes, "The text represents an attempt at harmonizing the various divergent statements about the origins of the monarchy." N. K. Gottwald, "The Book of Samuel," *Encyclopedia Judaica* (Jerusalem: 1971) XIV, 793, 794: "The disruption of the story line is only imperfectly dealt with by the harmonizing reference 'Let us go to Gilgal and there renew the kingdom' (11:14)." Hertzberg, *I and II Samuel*, 94: "The final compiler sees this account as a continuation of the earlier ones. This may explain the word 'renew'; originally it will have been no 'renewal,' but an institution of the kingship. We are also able to see in the sequel that here an editorial hand has tried to represent things as a succession rather than a juxtaposition of accounts." See also the similar viewpoints of: Weiser, *Samuel*, FRLANT, 78; Stoebe, *Das erste Buch Samuelis*, KAT, 229; Smith, *Samuel*, ICC, 80. Many more commentaries as well as introductions could be cited which represent this viewpoint.
   4. See below, Chapter III, Section 1,B, and Chapter V, Section 1.
   5. J. Schelhaas, "De instelling van het koningschap en de troonbestijging van Israëls eerste koning," *GTT* 44 (1944) 268.
   6. Goslinga, *Het Eerste Boek Samuël*, COT, 242; Th. C. Vriezen, "De Compositie van de Samuël-Boeken," in *Orientalia Neerlandica* (Leiden: 1948) 181; Leimbach, *Samuel*, HSchAT, 55; O. Eissfeldt, *Die Komposition der Samuelisbücher* (Leipzig: 1931) 10.
   7. A. H. Edelkoort, *De Profeet Samuel* (Baarn: 1953) 149. Others with this same general viewpoint propose the emendation of חדשׁ to קדשׁ (consecrate). See, e.g.: Ehrlich, *Randglossen*, III, 205, 206; and K-H. Bernhardt, *Das Problem der Altorientalischen Königsideologie im Alten Testament* (VTS, VIII; Leiden 1961) 142, n. 1. While this approach avoids the questionable interpretations of חדשׁ as inaugurate, confirm, or celebrate (see below), it suffers from a complete lack of textual evidence. A. Schulz (*Die Bücher Samuel*, EH, 163) correctly rejects the emendation approach saying, "Das ist aber nicht angängig, weil der Text sicher ist."

assembly of I Samuel 11:14, 15 is then viewed as an additional step in the process of establishing Saul's kingship, rather than a conflicting parallel account to I Samuel 10:17-27. In this category of approach some[8] would view I Samuel 11:14, 15 as a *military* recognition of the previous *civilian* acclamation of Saul as king at Mizpah.[9] In this case, the "renewal of the kingdom" would be interpreted as the formal acceptance of Saul as military chief by the army. Unfortunately, however, there is no firm basis in the language of the text for viewing the action at Gilgal as confined to the military.[10]

---

8. A. R. Hulst (I en II Samuël, *Commentaar op de Heilige Schrift*, ed. J. A. van der Hake [Amsterdam: 1956] 270) says, "Saul is immers reeds gezalfd; door zijn eerste krijgsdaad heeft hij getoond ook in feite koning te kunnen zijn; vandaar, dat het leger (de heirban) hem ook voor de toekomst als koning, bevelhebber, aanvaardt." De Groot (*I Samuël*, TeU, 122, 123) says, "Als wij de uitdrukking 'het geheele volk' mogen opvatten als beteekenende 'alle soldaten'— en dit is o.i. zeer wel geoorloofd–, dan hebben we hier geen plomp duplicaat van het verhaal in 10:17vv. (zelfs den meest onnoozelen redactor zouden we daartoe niet in staat mogen achten), doch moeten we hierin zien een voortzetting en wel speciaal de militaire erkenning van de kroningsplechtigheid te Hammispa (hoofdstuk 10)." De Groot's point regarding the redactor is well made, but his interpretation of "renew" as a military recognition is questionable. Koolhaas (*Theocratie en Monarchie*, 66) expresses a similar view and says, "Na het verslaan der Ammonieten wordt in Gilgal het koningschap vernieuwd. Deze samenkomst kan gezien worden als een voortzetting van de plechtigheid te Mizpa, waar het volk Saul, na zijn verkiezing tot koning, erkende en huldigde. In Gilgal riep de heerban hem tot koning uit en bekrachtigde zo de koningskeuze."
9. Here the position of M. Buber (*VT* 6 [1956] 155, 156) can also be mentioned. Buber takes the position that the opposition to Saul's selection as king as expressed in I Sam. 10:27 was not merely that of a few detractors, but to the contrary represented the great majority of the people, while those who acclaimed Saul were only a small group whose "hearts God had touched" (v. 26). He thus feels it is appropriate to speak of "renewing" Saul's kingdom in I Sam. 11:14. This interpretation, however, does not give adequate recognition to I Sam. 10:24.
10. In I Sam. 11:14 and 15a *"the people"* (הָעָם) are called to Gilgal to "renew the kingdom" and "make Saul king before Yahweh." In verse 15b *"all the men of Israel"* (וְכָל־אַנְשֵׁי יִשְׂרָאֵל) rejoiced greatly. In I Sam. 12:1 Samuel speaks to *"all Israel"* (כֹּל יִשְׂרָאֵל).
These terms in themselves are indecisive in regard to whether or not they are intended to have military significance, since all three are used elsewhere with either civilian or military connotation depending on their context.
Three things, however, should be noted. First, there is no terminology that is clearly military in vv. 14 and 15 such as, e.g., the terms "men of war" (אַנְשֵׁי הַמִּלְחָמָה) or "warriors" (חֵיל צָבָא). Second, the term *"the people"* is also used in I Sam. 10:24, 25 without military connotation. When Saul had been chosen by

Furthermore, one can raise serious questions as to whether the translations "inaugurate," "confirm," and "celebrate" do justice to the meaning of חדש.[11]

In the places where חדש occurs in the OT it consistently presupposes as an object something that already exists which is to be renewed or made anew.[12] The verb occurs nine times in the Piel. In four of these occurrences it expresses the idea of repairing a material object which is in a state of deterioration (Isa. 61:4; II Chron. 15:8; 24:4, 12). Among the five other occurrences there is a poetical usage in Psalm 104:30 where God's creative power is referred to as *renewing* the face of the earth (apparently with reference to springtime); and then four instances where the object to be renewed is something non-material (I Sam. 11:14; Ps. 51:12[10]; Job 10:17; Lam. 5:21). Thus in all of its occurrences חדש speaks of the restoration or repair of something that already exists, be that a material or immaterial entity,[13] but which in some sense is in a condition of deterioration.[14]

---

lot, *"the people"* shouted and said, "Long live the king!" (v. 24). Samuel then told *"the people"* the manner of the kingdom and sent *"the people"* to their houses (v. 25). In I Sam. 12:6, 19, 20, 22 *"the people"* (הָעָם) are again referred to without any indication of military connotation. In I Sam. 11 the term "the people" (הָעָם) is used with two different senses. In vv. 4, 5, 7, 12 it would appear to refer to the general populace, while in v. 11 it appears to have military significance. The important thing, however, for the question under consideration is that the expression *"the people"* is used in I Sam. 10 when Saul was chosen by lot to be king, and also in I Sam. 11:14, 15 when the kingdom was to be renewed, with no clear indication in the context that a distinction between a civilian and a military recognition is intended as the distinguishing difference between the two ceremonies. Thirdly, the phrase, *"the men of Israel"* occurs in I Sam. 8:22 where it has no military connotation and where it is used interchangeably with *"the people"* (vv. 7, 10) and *"the elders of Israel"* (v. 4). Its use in I Sam. 11:15b is, therefore, not a clear reference to the military.

11. Stoebe (*Das erste Buch Samuelis*, KAT, 223) comments, " נחדש darf weder geändert (Ehrlich נקדש,...) noch durch erleichternde Übersetzung beseitigt werden (Dhorme, 'inaugurer'; Klostermann, 'ein Volksfest feiern')."

12. *KBL*, s.v.; *BDB*, s.v.

13. M. Buber (*VT* 6 [1956] 155) in his discussion of the word under consideration says that renew means, "die Stärke, Konsistenz und Gültigkeit von etwas wiederherstellen." He rejects the translations of Wiesmann and Dhorme (inaugurieren) as well as that of Leimbach (bestätigen).

14. It appears, however, that חדש is used in a more relative sense in Job 10:17. As J. H. Kroeze (*Het Boek Job* [COT; Kampen: 1961] 142 comments:

If then the kingdom is to be renewed at Gilgal this means that something which was already established, but which subsequently had deteriorated, needed to be restored to the position of strength and validity which was proper to it. One might ask why Saul's kingdom would need restoration so soon after his selection at Mizpah. What had occurred in the intervening time to necessitate a renewal at Gilgal? Goslinga is of the opinion that it didn't need to be "renewed" and says that there is, "geen grond in de tekst en evenmin in de historische situatie" for such a conception.[15] He then cites with favor the views of Leimbach (bestätigen), Wiesmann and Dhorme (inaugurieren), and concludes that what was done at Gilgal was that Saul was "confirmed" (bevestigd) as king.[16]

As was noted above, however, such a translation of חדשׁ has little support from its usage elsewhere.[17] The translation

---

"Wat Job vreest en verwacht dat God zal doen, wordt in dit vs. vermeld: U zult uw getuigen tegen mij vernieuwen, d.w.z. nieuwe getuigen laten verschijnen. Die getuigen zijn z'n lijden en rampen als bewijzen van zijn schuld, 16:8."

15. Goslinga, *Het Eerste Boek Samuël*, COT, 242.

16. In his conclusion on this matter Goslinga (ibid.) also cites with favor both Koolhaas (*Theocratie en Monarchie*) and J. H. Kroeze (*Koning Saul* [Potchefstroom: 1962]). Goslinga comments, "Hetgeen men te Gilgal gedaan heeft was niet een plompe herhaling maar wel een bekrachtiging (vgl. Koolhaas, blz. 66) van de koningskeuze te Mispa." He then quotes Kroeze and says, "Nu Saul getoond had wat hij waard was, had de huldiging te Gilgal ook meer waarde en dieper zin dan die te Mispa, 10:24." For the view of Koolhaas, however, see above, n. 8.

The position of Kroeze is more general. He sees no need to view 10:17 and 11:14, 15 as a doublet, and he says (ibid., 49, 50) that the word "renew," "toon duidelik aan dat die 'Gilgal-verhaal' die 'Mispa-verhaal' veronderstel." Thus Saul was chosen king at Mizpah: "Tog het daar te Mispa, vergeleke by Gilgal, iets ontbreek. Dit was meer iets van psigologiese aard. Daar was geen merkbare verandering van situasie nie. Elkeen het na sy huis gegaan, Saul inkluis. Was Israel nou regtig 'n koninkryk?" But this is changed after the events of chapter 11. The king had acted in his role, "Daarom gaan die volk nou na Gilgal om Saul daar voor die aangesig van die HERE koning te maak; nie weer deur verkiesing of enige andere formele handeling nie, maar deur *hulde-betoon*, deur erkenning van sy dade. Die nuwe instelling, die koningskap, het, om so te sê, in twee etappes tot stand gekom."

As will appear below I am in general agreement with much of what Goslinga, Koolhaas, and Kroeze write, but in my opinion as long as they continue to apply חדשׁ to the kingdom of Saul, they cannot do justice to the meaning of the word.

17. Bernhardt (*Königsideologie*, 142, n. 1) comments that with this inter-

of the *NEB*, "renew our allegiance to the kingdom" suggests a better alternative. Strictly speaking it was not the kingdom which had deteriorated and needed renewal, but rather the recognition of the kingdom by the people. Yet even with the introduction of this distinction, both Goslinga's suggestion and that of the translation of the *NEB* are still confronted with the difficulty of explaining the relationship between this renewal of allegiance to the kingdom and the statement in verse 15 that at Gilgal all the people "made Saul king before Yahweh." How could Saul's kingdom be renewed (i.e., allegiance to it be renewed), if he had not yet been officially inaugurated (to be distinguished from his having been selected to be king at Mizpah) and therefore had not yet assumed his royal functions and begun his reign?[18] It would appear that the renewal of the kingdom referred to in I Samuel 11:14 must be regarded as distinct from the inauguration of Saul (I Sam. 11:15), even though his inauguration was enacted as an important subsidiary action of the Gilgal assembly.[19]

pretation, "man allerdings in V. 14 statt נחדש mit Kittel נקדש lesen müsste." Yet as was also noted above, this emendation has no textual support.

18. Note the comment of G. Wallis (*Geschichte und Überlieferung* [Arbeiten zur Theologie II/13; Stuttgart: 1968] 74-75) that, "Erneuern aber kann man nur, was in der Substanz vorhanden, vielleicht überholt oder hinfällig geworden ist. Betrachten wir aber das gesamte Kap. 11, so sehen wir in Saul einen Bauernsohn, von Jahwes Geist ergriffen, handeln, aber keinen, der schon zuvor König war. . . . Ein Aufruf zur Erneuerung setzt aber die Bekanntschaft des Volkes mit dem Königtum voraus. Aber davon lässt der Erzähler wiederum gar nichts erkennen." The conclusion which Wallis draws from this is quite different than ours (see below, Chapter III, Section 1,B,1,a,5), yet the point which he makes here certainly has merit.

19. See, H. Wildberger, "Samuel und die Entstehung des israelitischen Königtums," *ThZ* 13 (1957) 442-469. Wildberger (449) says, "Wenn V. 14 vom Erneuern (chaddeš) des Königtums spricht, so steht das mit V. 15, wo ja nicht von seiner Erneuerung, sondern der Neuerrichtung gesprochen wird, im Widerspruch." Wilderberger's conclusion is that vv. 12-14 are a redactional insertion to link chapter 11 with chapter 10 (see below, Chapter III, Section 1,B,1,a,4). Note also Birch's comment (*The Rise of the Israelite Monarchy*, 93): "It has long been recognized that the exhortation of Samuel 'to renew the kingdom' נחדש שם המלוכה at Gilgal stands in contradiction to vs. 15 which indicates that it was on this occasion at Gilgal that Saul was actually 'made king' וימלכו שם את־שאול by the people. This discrepancy must be taken into account in any attempt to treat the development of I Sam. 7-12."

The central issue here revolves around the question of what the term "kingdom" refers to in I Samuel 11:14. Does it refer to the kingdom of Saul, or does it perhaps have reference to something more fundamental, namely the *kingdom of Yahweh*? Considering the ramifications of the total historical situation depicted in I Samuel 8-12, it is certainly clear that renewed recognition of the kingdom of Yahweh was in order. Had not the people already expressed their disdain for the kingship of Yahweh by their request for a king to rule over them "as the nations" round about? Was there not the implicit danger that with the establishment of the kingship of Saul, the recognition of the continuing rule of Yahweh over his people would become eclipsed in the new order of Israel's civil government?

The pivotal question which runs through the narratives in I Samuel 8-12 is that of how the monarchy was to be integrated with the already existing rule of Yahweh over Israel, without nullifying the latter.[20] When the elders asked Samuel to give them a king "like all the nations" (I Sam. 8:5), Samuel discerned that the type of kingship which they were requesting was such that it would exclude the continued recognition of the kingship of Yahweh over his people (cf. I Sam. 8:7; 10:19; 12:12, 17). To this, Samuel expressed his opposition.[21] Yet in the sequence of events described in I Samuel 8-12 it becomes clear that a human kingship integrated with the kingship of Yahweh in a manner that would not detract from Yahweh's rule over his people but rather be an instrument of that rule was Yahweh's intention for his people, and that which Samuel led in establishing (cf. I Sam. 8:22; 9:16, 17; 10:1, 24, 25; 12:13-15, 20).

It may be objected that to interpret הַמְּלוּכָה in I Samuel

---

20. Cf. D. J. McCarthy, "The Inauguration of Monarchy in Israel," *Int* 27 (1973) 401-412.

21. Samuel's attitude toward kingship is not properly characterized as anti-monarchial. His opposition was to the kind of kingship desired and the reasons for which it was requested.

11:14 as a reference to the kingdom of Yahweh does violence to the immediate context, since מֶלֶךְ is used with reference to Saul in I Samuel 11:12, 15 and I Samuel 12:1, 2. Yet it should be noticed that the preceding statement of Saul in verse 13 makes the explicit assertion that the deliverance from the Ammonite threat was the work of Yahweh,[22] and while it is true that the מֶלֶךְ terminology in the immediate context refers to Saul, it must also be recognized that מֶלֶךְ terminology is applied to Yahweh several times in the larger context (I Sam. 8:7; 12:12; cf. also 10:19), and the continued recognition of the kingship of Yahweh is the primary issue in the narratives of I Samuel 8-12. In this regard it is certainly also of significance that it is not the kingship of Saul which is the central focus of the proceedings of the Gilgal assembly as that assembly is described in I Samuel 12, but rather renewed allegiance to the kingship of Yahweh, at the time of the establishment of the kingship of Saul.[23] Saul's name is not once mentioned in chapter 12, and he appears to be strangely and inexplicably in the background if the basic purpose of the Gilgal gathering was to renew the recognition of his kingship. In addition, it is extremely difficult to satisfactorily explain the phrase in the very next verse (I Sam. 11:15), "they made Saul king" if the renewal of the kingdom in verse 14 refers to renewed recognition of Saul's already established kingdom.[24] There are then, strong contextual arguments for interpreting הַמְּלוּכָה in verse 14 as Yahweh's kingdom, in spite of the references to the kingship of Saul immediately preceding and following.

---

22. This demonstrated Yahweh's sanction of the choice of Saul to be king, but at the same time it also demonstrated Saul's realization that he was merely an instrument in the accomplishment of Israel's deliverance, which, rightly understood, was to be regarded as a work of Yahweh.

23. Notice particularly the formulation of the covenant conditional in I Sam. 12:14-15, where at the climax of Samuel's discourse before the Gilgal assembly, the challenge to the people is presented in the terminology of renewed allegiance to Yahweh as king. See above, Chapter I, 41-47. For the relationship between I Sam. 11:14-15 and I Sam. 12 see below, Chapter III, Section 2,A.

24. See below.

This interpretation, however, also raises the vexing question of whether or not Yahweh's relationship to his people, conceived as that of a king to his kingdom, was an early or late conception in ancient Israel.[25] Many have maintained

25. On this issue see particularly M. Buber, *Kingship of God* (New York: 1967[3]) in which he has argued that Israel understood her relationship to Yahweh as that of the relationship of a people to her king from the very inception of her existence as a nation when a "kingly covenant" was concluded at Sinai after Yahweh had delivered his people out of the land of Egypt. Buber's book provoked an extensive debate after its original publication in 1932. In the prefaces to the 2nd and 3rd editions of his book Buber interacts with many criticisms of his position in a manner which is helpful in bringing into focus the issues involved.

For a contrasting position see: A. Alt, "Gedanken über das Königtum Jahwes," *Kleine Schriften zur Geschichte des Volkes Israel,* I (München: 1953) 345-357. Alt (345) maintains that the paucity of references to the kingdom of God in the earlier writings of the OT is very much against the idea "dass man die Vorstellung vom Königtum Jahwes für eine Urgegebenheit der israelitischen Religion halten dürfte, die ihr von jeher zu ihrem Selbstverständnis unentbehrlich gewesen wäre." Nevertheless, Alt does conclude that the kingship of Yahweh over a circle of subordinate divine beings (cf. his discussion of I Kings 22:19 ff.; Gen. 3:22; 11:7) was an idea present in pre-monarchic Israel, probably bearing some relationship to the idea of a monarchistic order in the world of the gods which was extant among neighboring peoples.

For the viewpoint of G. Fohrer see: *History of Israelite Religion* (New York: 1972) 166. Fohrer comments: "Although the earliest explicit literary evidence (Isa. 6:5; cf. Num. 23:21 [E]) dates only from the eighth century, the use of the title 'king' for Yahweh is undoubtedly earlier and represents a Canaanite heritage." In this way Fohrer adopts a nuanced standpoint with its attendant advantages and disadvantages.

G. von Rad (" מֶלֶךְ and מַלְכוּת in the OT," *TDNT,* I, 565-571) while noting that the application of the term מֶלֶךְ to the Godhead is common to all the ancient Orient, says (568) that: "In Israel the emergence of this view may be fixed with some precision. As is only natural, references are first found only after the rise of the empirical monarchy; Nu. 23:21; Dt. 33:5; 1K. 22:19 and Is. 6:5 are among the earliest." He notes further (570): ". . . Yahweh is never called *melek* prior to the monarchy. There is certainly no exegetical basis in the text for regarding the Sinaitic covenant as a royal covenant."

Koolhaas, (*Theocratie en Monarchie,* 23-37) gives careful consideration to this question, including various facets of the "Buber debate" and concludes (ibid., 133), "The idea of the royal power of Yahweh did not arise after the empirical kingship had come into existence, but we may assume with sufficient certainty that the nucleus of it existed among the Israelites after Yahweh's revelation at mount Sinai." See also John Bright, *The Kingdom of God* (New York: 1953) 19, where he comments, "in the heritage of Moses himself, we shall find the beginnings of her [Israel's] hope of the Kingdom of God. For this was no idea picked up along the way by cultural borrowing, nor was it the creation of the monarchy and its institutions, nor yet the outgrowth of the frustration of national ambition, however much all of these factors may have colored it. On the contrary it is

that it was a late conception derived from the already existing human institution of kingship. Even if this were correct,
it is difficult to deny that I Samuel 8-12, as they lie before
us, present the idea that the maintenance of the kingship of
Yahweh was the central issue at the establishment of the
human kingship. Even if the statements of I Samuel 8:7;
12:12 do not derive from the time of Samuel, they can still
be of importance for the exegesis of I Samuel 11:14 (see also
below).

This, however, is not to deny that the question of
whether the idea of Yahweh as king over Israel is early or late
is of great significance for the exegesis of I Samuel 11:14,
and for the subject of our study in general. It should be
noted that while it is true that the Hebrew root מֶלֶךְ is not
frequently utilized either as a title for Yahweh or for the
characterization of his rule over his people in OT passages
dealing with the period from the exodus to the establishment
of the monarchy, nevertheless, it does occur, and not only in
passages which are often regarded as "late."[26]

Because of the importance of this issue in this connection

linked with Israel's whole notion of herself as the chosen people of God, and this
in turn was woven into the texture of her faith from the beginning." He says
(ibid., 28) further, "The Exodus was the act of a God who chose for himself a
people that they might choose him. The covenant concluded at Sinai could, then,
be understood in Hebrew theology only as a response to grace. . . . *The notion of
a people of God called to live under the rule of God, begins just here, and with it
the notion of the Kingdom of God.*" See further: A. von Gall, "Über die Herkunft
der Bezeichnung Jahwehs als König," in Wellhausen Festschrift (BZAW 27;
Berlin: 1914) 145-160; O. Eissfeldt, "Jahweh als König," *ZAW* 46 (1928) 81-105;
J. Gray, "The Hebrew Conception of the Kingship of God: Its Origin and
Development," *VT* 6 (1956) 268-285; L. Rost, "Königsherrschaft Jahwes in
vorköniglicher Zeit?" *TLZ* 85 (1960) 722-723; W. Schmidt, *Königtum Gottes in
Ugarit und Israel. Zur Herkunft der Königsprädikation Jahwes* (BZAW 80; Berlin:
1966²) 80-97; J. A. Soggin, "מֶלֶךְ," *THAT,* I (München: 1971) 908-920, esp.
914 f.

26. Buber (*Kingship of God,* 36) says, "For the assertion that it is certain
that JHWH, before the period of the kings, is not designated as *melekh,* no proof
has up to now been offered either by von Rad or by any one else." See also Th. C.
Vriezen, *The Religion of Ancient Israel* (Philadelphia: 1967) 154-178. Vriezen
says (160): "One can fully accept, therefore, from a historical standpoint, that
such a mentality should stipulate Yahweh's sole right to the kingly title and could
reject the earthly status of a king (Judg. 8:22 f. and 9:8 ff.)."

we will look briefly at the passages involved, noting particularly the evidence for an early date for this material.

The noun מֶלֶךְ occurs in the Hebrew Bible prior to I Samuel 11:14 as a designation of Yahweh in Numbers 23:21 and Deuteronomy 33:5.[27]

The first of these occurrences is contained in the second discourse of Balaam the Mesopotamian diviner who was hired by the Moabite king Balak to curse Israel. Balaam, however, could only speak that which Yahweh put in his mouth (Num. 23:26), and instead of cursing Israel he prophesied of great and good things which Yahweh would give to them. In Numbers 23:21 he says that, "The shout for a king is among them." The context makes it clear that the reference is not to a human king but to Yahweh himself. The preceding phrase says that "Yahweh his God is with them," and the following phrase states that, "God brings them out of Egypt." It was Yahweh their king who led Israel from Egypt. It was Yahweh who gave Israel victory over the Amorites (Num. 22:2) and He is the one who has promised to give them the land of Canaan. There is thus every reason for the shout for king-Yahweh to be in the camp of Israel.

The unity and authenticity of the Balaam narrative has been defended by numerous scholars in the tradition of conservative biblical scholarship.[28] The advocates of the documentary theory of the origin of the Pentateuch have customarily divided the Balaam narrative (in a variety of different ways) into J, E, JE, and P components thus assigning the

---

27. The noun occurs elsewhere as a designation of Yahweh in: I Sam. 12:12; Isa. 6:5; 33:22; 41:21; 43:15; 44:6; Jer. 8:19; 10:7, 10; 46:18; 48:15; 51:57; Mic. 2:13; Zeph. 3:15; Zech. 14:9, 16, 17; Mal. 1:14; Ps. 5:3(2); 10:16; 24:7, 8, 9, 10; 29:10; 44:5(4); 47:3(2), 7(6), 8(7); 48:3(2); 68:25(24); 74:12; 84:4(3); 95:3; 98:6; 99:4; 145:1; 149:2; Dan. 4:34(37); cf., Eissfeldt, *ZAW* 46 (1928) 89.

28. See, e.g.: G. Ch. Aalders, *Oud-Testamentische Kanoniek* (Kampen: 1952) 147; E. J. Young, *An Introduction to the Old Testament* (Grand Rapids: 1964²) 84-93; W. H. Gispen, *Het Boek Numeri* II (COT: Kampen: 1964) 66-72, 110-112; R. K. Harrison, *Introduction to the Old Testament* (Grand Rapids: 1969) 614-634.

material to various times long after the Mosaic era.[29] There is, however, a tendency in recent years even among certain advocates of the documentary theory to recognize the antiquity of much of the material in the Balaam narratives,[30] and particularly to make a distinction between the oracles, which are regarded as old, and the narrative framework which is often considered to be of later origin. W. F. Albright in his study of the Balaam oracles concluded that Balaam was a genuine historical personality and that, "we may also infer that the Oracles preserved in Numbers 23-24 were attributed to him from a date as early as the twelfth century, and that there is no reason why they may not be authentic, or may not at least reflect the atmosphere of his age."[31]

In the introduction (Deut. 33:1-5) to the blessings which Moses pronounced on the tribes of Israel just before his death, he speaks of Yahweh's kingship over his people which was exhibited in the giving of the covenantal law by Yahweh at Sinai ("And he was king [מֶלֶךְ][32] in

---

29. See the survey of positions given by Gispen, *Het Boek Numeri*, COT, II, 66-69.

30. M. Noth, e.g., (*Das vierte Buch Mose. Numeri* [ATD VII; Göttingen: 1966] 13, 163 considers the Balaam narrative to be composed of J and E strands, but finds it quite difficult to divide the material between the two sources. He comments (13), however, that, "die 'alten Quellen,' soweit sie im 4. Mosebuch zu Worte kommen, auf sehr frühe Traditionen zurückgehen, die anfangs mündlich weitergegeben worden waren, ehe sie in die Erzahlungswerke J und E Eingang fanden, ist nich zu bezweifeln. Das gelt für . . . die Bileamgeschichte in Kap. 22-24. . . ."

31. W. F. Albright, "The Oracles of Balaam," *JBL* 63 (1944) 233. See Gispen (*Het Boek Numeri*, COT, II, 112) for an analysis of Albright's translation of Num. 23:21.

32. That מֶלֶךְ is here used as a designation of Yahweh is made clear in the context and is interpreted in that way by most commentators. See, e.g., the comments of S. R. Driver (*A Critical and Exegetical Commentary on Deuteronomy* [ICC; Edinburgh: 1901³] 394); J. Ridderbos (*Het Boek Deuteronomium*, II [KV; Kampen: 1964²] 124); and M. H. Segal (*The Pentateuch. Its Composition and Its Authorship and Other Biblical Studies* [Jerusalem: 1967] 100, 101). G. von Rad (*Deuteronomy. A Commentary* [London: 1966] 205), however, writes: "Probably the sentence is to be applied to the rise of the earthly kingdom in Israel." In my opinion this idea is contrived and von Rad's arguments are not convincing. Thus his statement: "Elsewhere the conception of Yahweh as king is understood to be confined to a kingdom over the gods and the nations . . ." is, as

Jeshurun,[33] When the heads of the people were gathered, The tribes of Israel together" [Deut. 33:5]). Here Yahweh's kingship over his people is closely tied to the establishment of the covenant at Sinai.[34]

The Mosaic origin of this chapter has had many defenders.[35] We do not know if Moses put the material in written form himself (cf. Deut. 33:1) but the chapter is represented as containing his own words. Those who deny a Mosaic origin for Deuteronomy 33 are divided over its date,[36] but as with the Balaam oracles there is increasing recognition of its antiquity among critical scholars.[37]

Verbal forms of מלך as a predicate of Yahweh in the Hebrew Bible prior to I Samuel 11:14 occur in Exodus 15:18

---

a generalization, certainly incorrect. A view similar to von Rad's is advocated by O. Eissfeldt (*ZAW* 46 [1928] 98-99).

33. A title for Israel (apparently meaning "the upright") which is used also in Deut. 32:15; 33:26 and Isa. 44:2.

34. M. Kline (*Treaty of the Great King. The Covenant Structure of Deuteronomy: Studies and Commentary* [Grand Rapids: 1963] 145) comments, "As Yahweh's earthly representative, Moses gave his covenant with its kingdom promises to Israel (v. 4) and by the covenant ceremony Yahweh's theocratic kingship over Israel was ratified (v. 5)."

35. See, e.g.: J. Ridderbos (*Het Boek Deuteronomium*, I [KV; Kampen: 1963²] 29); idem, *Deuteronomium*, II, 120-122) and Young, *Introduction*, 104. Segal (*The Pentateuch*, 99-102) comments that, "its [The Blessing of Moses] ascription in the heading to Moses immediately before his death is much more plausible than the imaginary and contradictory dates assigned to it by its modern critical interpreters" (102). Harrison (*Introduction*, 660) concludes that, "there is no warrant whatever for assigning the blessing to some date within the period of the divided monarchy, as Riehm, Stade, and other earlier critics did."

36. Driver (*Deuteronomy*, ICC, 387) dates the chapter shortly after the rupture of the kingdom under Jereboam I or in the middle of the reign of Jereboam II (c. 780 B.C.). Both O. Eissfeldt (*The Old Testament. An Introduction* [New York: 1965] 228-229) and A. Weiser (*The Old Testament: Its Formation and Development* [New York: 1961] 117-118) maintain that no certainty can be had for the date of the chapter but they regard certain unspecified parts of it to be "old" without indicating more precisely how old that might be.

37. See the discussion of M. Cross and D. N. Freedman, "The Blessing of Moses," *JBL* 67 (1948) 191-210; cf. also the comments of Albright, "The Old Testament and the Archaeology of the Ancient East," in *OTMS*, ed. H. H. Rowley (Oxford: 1951) 33, 34; and P. C. Craigie, "The Conquest and Early Hebrew Poetry," *TB* 20 (1969) 76-94.

and I Samuel 8:7.[38] In Exodus 15:18   יְהוָה יִמְלֹךְ is found in
the climactic phrase of the song sung by Moses and the
people of Israel to celebrate their deliverance from the Egyptians at the Sea of Reeds. This is the first occurrence of the
root מָלַךְ in connection with Yahweh in the Old Testament.
This text is only of secondary importance for us, because
here Yahweh's kingship *over Israel* is not specifically mentioned. Nevertheless, this text also deserves our attention. It
is in this connection certainly not without significance that
already in ancient times Yahweh's kingship in general was
spoken of. And perhaps it is significant that this expression is
associated with Israel's deliverance from Egypt which led to
the establishment of her nationhood under the rule of Yahweh at Sinai.[39]

Although this song has been given a late date by many
scholars,[40] some of the more recent studies of its vocabulary,

---

38. Verbal forms of מָלַךְ as a predicate of Yahweh also occur in Isa. 24:23;
52:7; Ezek. 20:33; Mic. 4:7; Ps. 47:9; 93:1; 96:10; 97:1; 99:1; 146:10; I Chron.
16:31; (=Ps. 96:10); cf. Eissfeldt, *ZAW* 46 (1928) 90.

39. See the illuminating discussion of M. Kline (*The Structure of Biblical
Authority* [Grand Rapids: 1972] 76-88) in which he draws attention to the
theme of divine triumph and house-building in the book of Exodus. The exodus
victory of Yahweh issued in Yahweh's house building which was of two kinds:
first, the structuring of the people Israel into the formally organized "house of
Israel," a living habitation of Yahweh, and second, the constructing of the more
literal house of Yahweh, the tabernacle. Kline points out (81) that this idea of,
"victorious kingship followed by palace-building is discovered as a thematic
pattern within the briefer unity of the Song of Triumph at the sea (Exod.
15:1-18)...."

40. See, e.g.: R. H. Pfeiffer (*Introduction to the Old Testament* [New York:
1941] 281) who dates the poem to the 2nd half of the 5th century B.C., and
terms it a "homiletic and devout paraphrase of Miriam's Song by a 'pseudo-
poet.'" A. Weiser (*The Old Testament: Its Formation and Development,* 106) is
uncertain of the date of the song, but considers it as certain that it was composed
after the time of David and Solomon. G. Fohrer (*Überlieferung und Geschichte
des Exodus: eine Analyse von Ex 1-15* [BZAW 91; Berlin: 1964] 112, 115) gives
it a late pre-exilic date while J. P. Hyatt (*Commentary on Exodus* [NCB; London:
1971] 163) suggests the 7th century. Although it is now generally agreed that Ex.
15:1-18 is not to be considered as belonging to any of the JED or P strands of the
Pentateuch, no alternative consensus on the date or manner of its origin has been
achieved. The view that the song was used as a liturgy in a Jerusalem enthronement festival as advocated by A. Bentzen (*Introduction to the Old Testament*
[Copenhagen: 1952] I, 143) and others has influenced their opinion of its date.

poetic form and general content have yielded firm evidence for its unity and antiquity,[41] including the statement in verse 18 that, "Yahweh shall reign for ever and ever" (It should be noted, however, in this connection that some authors do not hereby have in mind specifically a reigning over Israel).[42]

The date of the use of מֶלֶךְ to designate Yahweh in I Samuel 8:7 is normally regarded as closely connected with the date of similar statements in I Samuel 10:19 and 12:12. The three passages in which these statements are found are

---

See, however, the comments of W. H. Gispen (*Het Boek Exodus*, I [KV; Kampen: 1964³] 160) in opposition to this view.

41. See particularly F. M. Cross, and D. N. Freedman, "The Song of Miriam," *JNES* 14 (1955) 237-250. Cross and Freedman emphasize that the poem does not find its origin in the late cultus and they assert that its metrical style and strophic structure precisely fit the pattern of old Canaanite and early Hebrew poetry. They say further (237, 238) that, "the repetitive parallelism, mixed meter, and the complex makeup of the strophes suggest an early date of composition. At the same time, the unity of the pattern and the symmetry of the strophic structure indicate that the poem is substantially a single, unified composition." While not fixing a precise date for the poem they conclude (240) that the poem, "is scarcely later than the twelfth century in its original form." W. F. Albright (*Yahweh and the Gods of Canaan* [New York: 1969] 12) says that, "The oldest Israelite poetry of any length, judging from stylistic indication, confirmed by content, is the song of Miriam, which I should date in the thirteenth century B.C., preferably in the first quarter." See also M. H. Segal, (*The Pentateuch*, 38, 39) for a similar position.

42. Cross and Freedman (*JNES* 14 [1955] 250) comment, "The kingship of the gods is a common theme in early Mesopotamian and Canaanite epics. The common scholarly position that the concept of Yahweh as reigning or king is a relatively late development in Israelite thought seems untenable in the light of this, and is directly contradicted by the evidence of the early Israelite poems; cf. Num 23:21; Deut 33:5; Ps 68:25; Ps 24:9." F. C. Fensham (*Exodus* [POT; Nijkerk: 1970] 86) who also dates the song between the 13th and 11th centuries B.C. says of verse 18, "Het is beslist onnodig deze woorden te beschouwen als een exilische of postexilische toevoeging, omdat de idee van het eeuwige koningschap van YHWH eerst in de dagen van de tweede Jesaja volop uitgesproken zou zijn. Reeds in oudhebreeuwse gedichten als Deuteronomium 32 (vs. 5) Psalm 68 (vs. 25) en Numeri 23 (vs. 21) treffen wij deze gedachte aan. Overigens wordt al heel vroeg in de kanaänitische wereld het koningschap van een bepaalde vorst als eeuwig gekwalificeerd...." A similar position is adopted by J. Muilenburg ("A Liturgy on the Triumphs of Yahweh," in *Studia Biblica et Semitica* [jubileumbundel Th. C. Vriezen; Wageningen: 1966] 233-251, especially, 249, 250) who says that the closing celebration of the kingship of Yahweh is not necessarily late; "it may well have been the central affirmation in the credo of the early tribal federations (Num 23:31; Judg 8:23; 1 Sam 8:7; 12:12)."

frequently considered to compose the "late anti-monarchial source" which is detected by many critical scholars in I Samuel 8–12. It is our contention, however, that the מלך terminology of I Samuel 8:7 and 12:12 is closely related to Samuel's invitation in I Samuel 11:14 for all the people to come to Gilgal to "renew the kingdom" (המלוכה). Moreover, the late date of all this material as well as its anti-monarchial character are being increasingly called in question in many of the more recent studies of its interpretation and literary origins.[43]

The abstract nouns ממלכה, מלוכה/ מלכה, מלכות are used in reference to Yahweh prior to I Samuel 11:14 only in Exodus 19:6 (ממלכה).[44] In this passage commentators are sharply divided over both the meaning of the phrase ממלכת כהנים[45] as well as its date.[46] As can be seen from the discussion by B. S. Childs,[47] the critical theories which have been advanced to explain the composition of Exodus 19 are notoriously complex, and no consensus has been reached. It is our position, however, that this passage also is to be understood as evidence for the existence of the idea of Yahweh's kingship over

---

43. See further below, Chapter V.

44. Other places in which מלכות is used with reference to Yahweh are: Ps. 103:19; 145:11, 12, 13; Dan. 3:33 (4:3); 4:22, 29, 31 (4:25, 32, 34); 5:21; 6:27; I Chron. 17:14; 28:5; II Chron. 13:8. מלוכה is used in: Ps. 22:29; Obad. 21. ממלכה is used in I Chron. 29:11; cf. Eissfeldt, *ZAW* 46 (1928) 91.

45. For discussion of various interpretations of the phrase see esp.: R. B. Y. Scott, "A Kingdom of Priests (Exodus xix 6)," *OTS*, VIII (1950) 213-219; W. L. Moran, "A Kingdom of Priests," in *The Bible in Current Catholic Thought*, ed. J. L. McKenzie (New York: 1962) 7-20; G. Fohrer, " 'Priesterliches Königtum,' Ex. 19,6," *ThZ* 19 (1963) 359-362.

46. For a good summary of various positions on the date of Ex. 19:3b-8 see: B. S. Childs, *The Book of Exodus. A Critical Theological Commentary* (Philadelphia: 1974) 344-351, 360-361. Positions ranging from the Mosaic era to exilic times have been advocated.

47. Ibid. It would take us beyond the scope of our thesis to discuss here the details of the various critical theories. Childs comments (344): "The extreme difficulty of analyzing the Sinai pericope has long been felt. In spite of almost a century of close, critical work many of the major problems have resisted a satisfactory solution." Child's own conclusion concerning Ex. 19:3b-8 is (361): "In sum, although the passage contains old covenant traditions, probably reflected through the E source, its present form bears the stamp of the Deuteronomic redactor."

his people in pre-monarchial times, and for the close linkage of the ideas of covenant and kingship.[48] The Israelites as subjects of the kingdom of Yahweh are to fulfill a priestly task among the nations.[49]

Also indicative of the early existence of the idea of the kingship of Yahweh are certain Hebrew personal names including Elimelech,[50] Abimelech,[51] and Melchishua (see above, the remarks on Yahweh's kingship in general in the discussion of Exodus 15:18). The most important of these for the purposes of our discussion is Melchishua (I Sam. 14:49; 31:2; I Chron. 8:33; 9:34; 10:2) who was one of the sons of Saul. In most cases Hebrew personal names utilizing the root מלך are considered theoforic, that is, names which include a title

---

48. For a more detailed development of this position see: W. Beyerlin, *Origins and History of the Oldest Sinaitic Traditions* (Oxford: 1965) 67-77. Although Beyerlin regards Ex. 19:3b-8 as an Elohistic tradition, he nevertheless places its roots in pre-monarchic times and comments (74): "Exod xix. 3b-8, the kernel of which goes back to Israel's early history, as stated, thus provides very early evidence of Yahweh's kingship. . . ." Such a position, in our view, is to be preferred over that of M. Noth (*Exodus. A Commentary* [Philadelphia: 1962] 157) who says: "There is no particular emphasis on the word 'kingdom' in this expression; it may be understood to mean 'state' in just the same way as the nations on the earth are usually organized into states.

49. Note the comment of W. H. Gispen (*Het Boek Exodus* [KV; Kampen: 1951²] II, 54): "En Hij legt den nadruk op Israëls heerlijke bestemming en dure verplichting: konninkrijk van priesters (de dienst, dien het voor den HERE moest verrichten als onderdanen van zijn rijk, is dus van priesterlijken aard) en een heilig, afgezonderd, rein, aan God gewijd, Gode toebehorend, volk moeten zij zijn (vs 6a)."

50. Cf. Ruth 1:2. The name means, God is King. Cf. M. Noth, *Die israelitischen Personennamen im Rahmen der gemeinsemitischen Namengebung* (BWANT III/10; Stuttgart: 1928) 70, 90-99, 141-142; B. J. Oosterhoff, *Israelietische Persoonsnamen* (Exegetica 1/4; Delft: 1953) 9, 28, 36, 55.

51. Cf. Judg 8:31. The name means, Father is King, but as Oosterhoff (*Het Koningschap Gods in de Psalmen* [Alphen: 1956] 26, n. 7) comments, "Evenals in de andere eigennamen in de Bijbel, die samengesteld zijn met *ab*, is ook in de naam Abimelech *ab* een aanduiding voor God. . . . De opmerking van Kittel, dat uit de naam Abimelech blijkt, dat Gideon wel het koningschap heeft aanvaard en dat de mededeling van de Bijbel, dat Gideon het koningschap niet heeft aanvaard het gevolg is van een latere wijziging, is er dan ook geheel naast, R. Kittel, *Geschichte des Volkes Israel*, II, 1925, bl. 31, aant. 2."

For the use of אב and אח as theoforic elements in Hebrew personal names see: Noth, *Die israelitischen Personennamen*, 66-82; Oosterhoff, *Israelietische Persoonsnamen*, 28-31; Bright, *History of Israel*, 98.

or name of God in their construction.[52] The meaning of Melchishua is thus "the king-Yahweh has delivered."[53] By giving his son this name, Saul is testifying in a forceful way to his belief that King-Yahweh is the deliverer of his people.[54] Here then is an important indication that precisely at the time of the establishment of the earthly kingship in Israel, the recognition of the kingship of Yahweh was extant, and confessed by Saul who became Israel's first earthly monarch.[55]

---

52. For the use of מלך as a theoforic element in Hebrew personal names see: Noth, *Die israelitischen Personennamen,* 118-119; Oosterhoff, *Israelietische Persoonsnamen,* 26-28.

53. Noth (*Die israelitischen Personennamen,* 147) says: "Eine grosse Reihe von Namen bringt eine Beziehung zur Gottheit oder eine Seite des göttlichen Wesens zum Ausdruck, die geeignet ist, das Vertrauen des Menschen zur Gottheit zu erwecken oder zu stärken. Wir werden sie daher am besten Vertrauensnamen nennen." Noth includes Melchishua among this category of names. With regard to the etymology of שוע Noth (ibid., 154, n. 2) comments, "Man pflegt dieses Element mit dem hebräischen שוע=edel, freigebig zusammenzubringen (vgl. Gray S. 146 f.; König, Wörterbuch), doch liegt es näher, an eine Nebenform vom Stamme שוע zu denken (so richtig Hommel, Altisr. Überl. S. 52 u. ö.; Zimmern KAT³ S. 481 Anm 4), denn auch die Wurzel שוע =freigebig sein tritt im Arabischen als *wsʿ* auf, und שוע =helfen haben wir im Hebräischen מ... ה... ל... in שוע, (vgl. אושיע תשוע בשוע u.a.) und in Pi.=Hilfe schreien." See also Oosterhoff, *Israelietische Persoonsnamen,* 35, 40. Oosterhoff comments, "Vele zijn de namen, die ons melden, dat God een helper is. Helpen behoort tot het wezen van God (Ps 33:10; 70:6; 115:9; 146:5). Abiëzer: 'Vader is een hulp'; Ahiëzer: 'Broeder is een hulp'; ... Ongeveer dezelfde betekenis hebben de namen Abisua: 'Vader heeft verlost'; Elisua: 'God heeft verlost'; Malkisua: 'De Koning heeft verlost'; Jozua: 'De HERE heeft verlost.' De afgekorte naam is Sua."

54. It is striking that Saul's statement after the victory over the Ammonites (I Sam. 11:13) expresses the very idea which is incorporated in the name given to his son Melchishua. On that occasion Saul said that none of those who had opposed his selection to be king should be put to death, "for today Yahweh has accomplished deliverance in Israel" (היום עשה יהוה תשועה בישראל).

55. Cf. further: A. H. Edelkoort, *De Christus-verwachting in het Oude Testament* (Wageningen: 1941) 49-107, esp. 51-55; Koolhaas, *Theocratie en Monarchie,* 24-31; Oosterhoff, *Het Koningschap Gods in de Psalmen,* 4-5; D. H. Odendaal, *The Eschatological Expectation of Isaiah 40-66 With Special Reference to Israel and the Nations* (Philadelphia: 1970) 38-41.

G. Fohrer (*History of Israelite Religion,* 166-167), who considers the application of the title "king" to Yahweh to be closely related to the bringing of the ark to Jerusalem in the time of David, and the construction of the temple in the time of Solomon, and therefore a development subsequent to the establishment of the Israelite monarchy, makes the rather unconvincing statement with respect to the name Melchishua that: "such official use [of the title "king" for Yahweh] does not exclude the possibility that the title was used earlier and elsewhere as a more or less private form (I Sam. 14:49)." Eissfeldt (*ZAW* 46

It should also be said that the hesitation to utilize מֶלֶךְ
terminology for Yahweh in the narratives of the history of
early Israel is at least partially explicable as a deliberate
attempt to avoid the potential for confusing Israel's relationship to Yahweh with the mythological divine-kingship ideolo-
gies of various ancient near eastern peoples.[56] In any case the

---

[1928] 89, 104), who considers Isa. 6:5 as the oldest biblical text which speaks
of the kingship of Yahweh concludes that names such as Elimelech, Abimelech,
and Melchishua, although theoforic names, must not have originally had reference
to Yahweh. He says: "Die noch in anderem Zusammenhang zu wertende
Tatsache, dass der deutlich auf Jahwe das Prädikat מֶלֶךְ anwendende Personenname
מַלְכִּיָּהוּ (Jer 38:6) erst seit der Zeit Jeremias nachweisbar ist, rechtfertigt den
Verdacht, dass in den genannten Namen unter מֶלֶךְ ursprünglich nicht Jahwe,
sondern ein anderer Gott zu verstehen ist." This argument is also hardly convincing particularly with regard to Melchishua (cf. I Sam. 11:13).

56. Koolhaas (*Theocratie en Monarchie*, 24) says, "Maar daar Jahwes koningsheerschappij zo geheel anders was dan die van de andere goden en daar de titel
mlk bij goden en koningen gevuld was met een geheel andere inhoud en door
heidense mythologieën belast, had Oud-Israël in bepaalde tijden een afkeer om
deze naam voor Jahwe te gebruiken en bezigde men andere uitdrukkingen om
Jahwes heerschappij aan te geven.... Het ontbreken van deze titel houdt echter
niet in dat de gedachte, die later door deze titel tot uitdrukking werd gebracht,
niet aanwezig was.... Het getuigt juist van een uiterst fijn aanvoelen van deze
heerschappij van Jahwe dat men besefte dat, daar deze titel bij andere volken zo
anders gevuld was, het gevaar bestond dat Israël, door het gebruik van deze titel,
de heerschappij van Jahwe ook zou vullen met een inhoud die in strijd was met de
openbaring van Jahwe."

Buber (*Kingship of God*, 37-38) also noting that this terminology is not
widely used, points out that it is found, "only in passages where it appears to be
representatively important, even indispensable. The four passages of the Pentateuch ... which I treat in the seventh chapter, emphatically have such a focal
significance. After the successful liberation the people proclaim its king (Exodus
15:18); the King establishes His constituency with the marking out of His 'kingly
domain' (Exodus 19:6); the mantic representative of universal man bows before
the divine kingship in Israel (Numbers 23:21); Moses remembers before dying,
before he blesses the people at parting, with the last words before the beginning
of the blessing, the hour at Sinai when over the united tribes 'a king there was in
Jeshurun' (Deuteronomy 33:5). One might investigate whether the designation
melekh in any of the four passages was dispensable, but also whether it was
indispensable in any other passages beside these four. Those responsible for the
textual selection preserved what had to be preserved, no less, but also no more. In
the book of Judges which swarms with *melekh*s (cf. the second chapter), in the
decisive passage 8:22 ff., the application of the word, noun or verb, to JHWH is
carefully avoided. Here it can be avoided because it is not yet a matter of the
historical fact of the Israelitish kingship with which the divine kingship is to be
confronted in the same linguistic expression, but only the first unrealized striving
after it. It can no longer be avoided in the confrontation with the historically
realized kingship: I Samuel 8:7; 12:12, 14. ... Because here the vocable *melekh* is

absence of a particular terminological label does not necessarily mean that the reality of the function legitimately associated with that label might not be operative.[57] Thus in spite of the paucity of references to Yahweh as king in the parts of the OT dealing with early Israel it is clear that these same parts nevertheless portray Israel as the kingdom of Yahweh, and particularly in the realms of law and warfare represent Yahweh as king over his people.[58]

In fact, it is precisely the early Israelite conception of the kingdom of Yahweh[59] which most adequately explains the rather amazing fact of the relatively late origin of the monarchy in the history of the Israelite socio-political structure.[60]

Out of what we have argued above it is also clear that in ancient Israel a close relationship existed between the kingdom of Yahweh and the covenant, see especially Exodus 19:6; Deuteronomy 33:5. It was in the Sinaitic covenant that Yahweh's rule over his people was formally structured, and it was in the covenant ratification that Yahweh's kingdom was

---

given for the human ruler, it must, in the confrontation, be applied to the divine ruler also."

57. Note the similar debate occasioned by the infrequent use of the word covenant by the prophets before Jeremiah. See further Chapter IV, n. 41.

58. For the development of this basic thesis see A. E. Glock, "Early Israel as the Kingdom of Yahweh," *CTM* 41 (1970) 558-605, and G. E. Mendenhall, *The Tenth Generation. The Origins of the Biblical Tradition* (Baltimore: 1973). In Mendenhall's work see particularly Chapter I, "Early Israel as the Kingdom of Yahweh: Thesis and Methods."

59. The idea of Israel as the kingdom of Yahweh has often been characterized by the term "theocracy." For discussion of this term see: Buber, *Kingship of God,* 23, 24, 56-58, 93, 139-162; Koolhaas, *Theocratie en Monarchie,* 28; and Oehler, *Theology of the Old Testament,* 199, 200.

60. Koolhaas (*Theocratie en Monarchie,* 53, 54) discusses various explanations which have been advanced for the late rise of the monarchy in Israel such as geographical factors or bondage to customs of the nomadic times, and concludes: "Al kunnen deze bovengenoemde feiten, historisch gezien, zeker als argumenten gelden voor het late opkomen van het koningschap in Israël, toch is dit niet de zienswijze van het Oude Testament, dat het late opkomen niet als een historische, maar als een principiële kwestie ziet. Israël was door Jahwe uitverkoren om zijn eigendom te zijn, waarover Hij zelf koning was en in welks midden Hij woonde, waarvan de ark als zijn troon het teken was. Het feit dat Israël zo lange tijd zonder menselijke koning leefde, komt vooral voort uit het koningschap van Jahwe."

formally constituted.[61] It is accordingly the allegiance to this kingdom, and hence this covenant, which now at the time of the institution of the monarchy was in urgent need of renewal.

Here then (I Sam. 11:14), is one of those moments in which, to borrow Buber's expression, the מָלַךְ terminology is "indispensable."[62] Precisely because the kingdom of Saul was being formally established, the kingdom of Yahweh must not be forgotten. The introduction of the monarchy in Israel required that it be understood within the framework of the provisions of the Sinaitic covenant so that the continued rule of Yahweh in the new political order would be recognized. In addition, because of the people's sin in seeking a human king to replace Yahweh, there was also the necessity that formal confession of their apostasy be made, and that they renew their allegiance to Yahweh in the context of the introduction of the new civil order.

All of these considerations indicate that we should understand Samuel's summons to the people to meet at Gilgal "to renew the kingdom" as a summons for them to renew their allegiance to the rule of Yahweh. The Gilgal assembly was thus not simply a duplication of that which had occurred previously at Mizpah, nor the recognition by the military of

---

61. There is the possibility here of distinguishing between two OT conceptions of the "kingdom of God." G. Vos (*Biblical Theology, Old and New Testaments* [Grand Rapids: 1959] 398) comments, "In the O.T. the thing later called the Kingdom of God relates as to substance to two distinct conceptions. It designates the rule of God established through creation and extending through providence over the universe. This is not a specifically redemptive Kingdom idea, cf. Psa. 103:19. Besides this, however, there is a specifically-redemptive Kingdom, usually called 'the theocracy.' The first explicit reference to the redemptive Kingdom appears at the time of the exodus, Ex 19:6, where Jehovah promises the people, that if obeying His law, they shall be made to Him 'a Kingdom of priests.' " It is in this latter sense that we speak of Yahweh's kingdom being constituted at Sinai. See also Oehler, *Theology of the Old Testament*, 199, 200. It is not necessary here to discuss further the questions which are raised by this distinction.

62. Buber does not include I Sam. 11:14 in the list of passages where he finds מָלַךְ terminology utilized for the rule of Yahweh (see n. 51 above). His argument, however, can be appropriately applied to this verse.

Saul's authority, nor even merely the inauguration or celebration of Saul's kingship (although this was a subsidiary and contributing cause for the calling of the assembly, cf. v. 15). It was rather a solemn covenant renewal ceremony, in which at a time of important transition in leadership, and covenant abrogation because of apostasy, Saul was made king, in connection with the people's confession of sin, and renewed recognition of the continuing suzerainty of Yahweh the Great King.

It is not surprising that Samuel selected Gilgal[63] near the Jordan river as the appropriate place for the gathering to be held. For it was at Gilgal that the Israelites first encamped in the promised land (Josh. 4:19-24); it was there that all those who were not circumcised during the period of the wilderness wandering were circumcised (Josh. 5:2-9);[64] and it was there

---

63. The precise geographical location of the Gilgal mentioned in I Sam. 11:14 is a matter of dispute. There are those who argue for a location near Shechem including: E. Sellin, *Gilgal. Ein Beitrag zur Geschichte der Einwanderung Israels in Palästina* (Leipzig: 1917) 17-18; Keil, *The Books of Samuel*, 114; Kroese, *Koning Saul*, 19; Edelkoort, *De Profeet Samuel*, 149; and J. H. Kroese, *Het Boek Jozua* (COT; Kampen: 1968) 63.

Others, including the following, favor a location near the Jordan: J. Mauchline, "Gilead and Gilgal: Some Reflections on the Israelite Occupation of Palestine," *VT* 6 (1956) 29-30; H.-J. Kraus, *Worship in Israel* (Richmond: 1966) 152-154; A. Alt, "The Formation of the Israelite State in Palestine," in *Essays on Old Testament History and Religion* (New York: 1968) 251; Goslinga, *Het Eerste Boek Samuel*, COT, 189, 241-242.

It is this latter location which is to be preferred (see particularly the reasons adduced by Goslinga, 241-242) yet there is an additional question over the precise identification of the ancient site. Some favor *chirbet el-mefjir* located to the north of *tell es sultan*. See, e.g., J. Muilenburg, "The Site of Ancient Gilgal," *BASOR* 140 (1955) 11-27. Others favor either *chirbet en-netheleh* or a site in its near vicinity. See, e.g.: J. Simons, *The Geographical and Topographical Texts in the Old Testament* (Leiden: 1959) 269. This latter location seems to be preferable in view of the reference in Josh. 4:19 which places Gilgal east of the territory of Jericho, but as J. Stoebe says (*Das erste Buch Samuelis*, KAT, 222-223) its precise location remains a matter of uncertainty.

64. C. J. Goslinga (*Het Boek Jozua* [KV; Kampen: 1927] 60) interprets the abstention from circumcision during the wilderness period as attributable to the brokenness of the covenant relationship. He bases this interpretation on the statement in Num. 14:33 reading, "your children shall wander in the wilderness forty years, *and bear your harlotries* ..." (italics mine). Goslinga maintains that by the term "harlotries" the sin of apostasy or covenant breaking is pointed to. He says, "Doordat het volk niet naar Kanaän wilde, stelde het zich feitelijk buiten het

that the first observance of the passover was held in the land of Canaan (Josh. 5:10, 11).[65]

Gilgal was tied historically not only to these covenant renewal traditions, but also to events related to the conquest of Canaan which demonstrated Yahweh's power to deliver the land into the hand of the Israelites, and his faithfulness to his promise to lead Israel in the conquest of Canaan. For it was at Gilgal that twelve stones were set up to remind the Israelites that Yahweh had, "dried up the waters of the Jordan . . . that you may fear Yahweh your God forever" (Josh. 4:23, 24). It was at Gilgal that the "captain of the host of Yahweh" appeared to Joshua (Josh. 5:13-15). It was at Gilgal that Joshua was told of the remarkable manner in which Yahweh would give the city of Jericho into the hand of the Israelites (Josh. 6). It was also from Gilgal (Josh. 10:8, 9) that Israel went to the aid of Gibeon, and the biblical

verbond met Jehovah, die het juist daartoe uit het diensthuis had uitgeleid. De Heere heft nu wel zijn verbond met het volk als zoodanig niet op, maar spreekt toch den ban uit over het uit Egypte getogen geslacht en over deszelfs kinderen, welke ban eerst zal worden opgeheven als het oudere geslacht geheel is vergaan. Het 'dragen van de hoererijen' der vaderen, hield zonder twijfel ook in, dat de kinderen niet mochten besneden worden. . . . Ten bewijze dat de verbondsverhouding thans weder volkomen normaal is, laat de Heere nu diegenen die het verbondsteeken nog missen, besnijden. Hij neemt hen daarbij tot Zijn volk aan in de plaats hunner ongehoorzame vaderen (vs 7)."

Goslinga's interpretation is challenged by Kroeze (*Jozua*, COT, 65-69) who maintains that the abstention from circumcision was not due to a prohibition but was merely negligence.

While it must be admitted that there is no specific prohibition given in Numbers against continuation of circumcision, it seems strange that, as Josh. 5:5 says, "*all* the people who were born in the wilderness . . . had not been circumcised" (italics mine), if this was simply a matter of negligence. It would seem likely that at least *some* of the people would have continued the practice if it had been permissible.

Goslinga's position can be strengthened, I believe, by notice of the expression in Num. 14:34(33) which says that, "forty years you shall spend—a year for each day—paying the penalty of your iniquities. *You shall know what it means to have me against you*" (וִידַעְתֶּם אֶת תְּנוּאָתִי : *NEB*, italics mine).

65. Goslinga (*Jozua*, KV, 62) also places the observance of the passover (which he views as the first passover observance since the second year after the exodus) in the context of covenant renewal upon entering the promised land. He says (ibid.), "Van God zelf gaat dan ook het bevel tot besnijdenis uit. Hij vernieuwt aldus Zijn verbond met Israel en verzekert het volk daarna door het Pascha, dat Hij zijn Bondgenoot is ook in den komenden strijd."

narrative relates that, "Yahweh fought for Israel" and an extraordinary victory was gained (Josh. 10:14, 15). The picture of the conquest contained in Joshua is that it is Yahweh who gives Israel victory over the inhabitants of the land, and the remembrance of this is rooted more firmly in Gilgal than in any other single site in Canaan.[66]

Gilgal's unique historical credentials, therefore, made it a fitting place for the convening of a covenant renewal ceremony in which the issue of Yahweh's continued leadership over his people was the focal issue.[67]

I Sam. 11:15. And all the people went to Gilgal, and there they made Saul king before Yahweh in Gilgal, and there they sacrificed peace offerings before Yahweh, and there Saul and all the men of Israel rejoiced greatly.

I Samuel 11:15 is a condensed description of what took place at the Gilgal assembly. The verse functions as a sort of "lead sentence" to the more detailed description of certain parts of the same ceremony which is contained in I Samuel 12:1-25.[68] The primary purpose of the assembly was renewal

---

66. G. von Rad located what he termed the "settlement tradition" at the sanctuary in Gilgal. See: G. von Rad, *Das Formgeschichtlich Problem des Hexateuch* (BWANT 4, Heft 26; Stuttgart: 1938). In von Rad's theory of the origin of the Hexateuch the Yahwist used this "settlement tradition" as the basic core material to which he fused the Exodus and Sinai traditions, all of which von Rad views as originally distinct and independent tradition units. Building on von Rad's approach, but advocating a different means for the fusion of the Sinai and Exodus-Conquest traditions is H.-J. Kraus, "Gilgal-ein Beitrag zur Kultusgeschichte Israels," *VT* 1 (1951) 181-199, and also *Worship in Israel,* 152-165. His idea is that the union of the traditions occurred when the Shechem cult was displaced to Gilgal.

For a critical analysis of these theories see, e.g., H. B. Huffmon, "The exodus, Sinai and the Credo," *CBQ* 27 (1965) 101-113. For a more general analysis of von Rad's approach to the historical narratives of the OT, see: B. J. Oosterhoff, *Feit of Interpretatie* (Kampen: 1967).

67. The idea that Gilgal was chosen for this occasion because at this time Gilgal was the "central sanctuary" of the "amphictyonic tribal confederation" is a matter of speculation for which there is no firm biblical evidence. On the question of whether or not it is proper to speak of the pre-monarchial period of Israel's tribal organization as an amphictyony, see the literature cited below, Chapter IV, n. 37.

68. See below, Chapter III, Section 2,A and Chapter IV, Section 2,B.

of allegiance to Yahweh (v. 14). The two subsidiary actions mentioned in verse 15, (first the people made Saul king before Yahweh, and second, they sacrificed peace offerings) correspond to the two historical realities which called for renewal of allegiance to Yahweh. First, it was of great importance that the kingship of Saul be inaugurated in the context of a challenge to renewed allegiance to Yahweh. And secondly, covenant fellowship needed to be restored after Israel's apostasy in desiring a king "like all the nations" to replace Yahweh as the source of her national security.

The question of what is to be understood by the phrase the people "made Saul king before Yahweh" is related to one's interpretation of what is to be understood by the phrase "renew the kingdom" in the preceding verse. The two expressions are usually regarded as nearly synonymous, with both referring to the kingship of Saul. The relationship of חדש to verse 15 has already been discussed above from the standpoint of the meaning of חדש.[69] Here we must give further attention to the same question but with particular emphasis on the meaning of the term ימלכו. If one regards both נחדש and ימלכו as referring to the kingship of Saul, one creates the problem of how Saul's kingdom could be "renewed" if he had not yet been "made king."[70]

In attempting to alleviate this problem some interpreters are of the opinion that the phrase (וימלכו . . .) is a reference to a public anointing (cf. I Sam. 10:1, a private anointing) of Saul by Samuel at the Gilgal renewal of Saul's kingdom.[71] This interpretation assumes that Saul had actually already been "made king" previously in the ceremony at Mizpah (I Sam. 10:17 ff.), and thus his kingdom could be renewed at Gilgal in a ceremony of confirmation and celebration which then also included a public anointing. Goslinga, for example,

---

69. See above, pp. 62-66.
70. See above, p. 68.
71. See: Caird, *IB*, II, 940; and Goslinga, *Het Eerste Boek Samuël*, COT, 242.

says: "Op de vraag wat wij precies denken moeten bij de woorden וימליכו enz. is wrsch. te antwoorden, dat Saul door Samuël gezalfd is. De LXX zegt και ἐχρισεν Σαμουηλ ἐκει τον Σαουλ en het uitvallen van het Hebr. equivalent is door een homoioteleuton (שאול) zeer goed denkbaar. Voor deze lezing (in elk geval voor haar zakelijke inhoud) pleit zeer sterk dat Saul vlak daarna, 12:3, 5, maar ook later met grote nadruk de gezalfde van Jahwe (24:7, 26:9; II 1:16) genoemd wordt en dat David blijkens II 2:4, 5:3 ook publiek gezalfd is."[72] While it is true that the LXX reads, "and Samuel anointed Saul there to be king before Yahweh in Gilgal," it seems much more likely that this is the LXX's interpretation of וימלכו rather than an indication that the MT has dropped a phrase due to homoeoteleuton.[73] In fact, the assumption that a phrase is dropped due to homoeoteleuton is pure hypothesis.[74] Goslinga's point that David's anointing was repeated is of interest in this connection, and calls attention to the possibility that an anointing could be repeated under certain circumstances, but it certainly does not prove that this was necessarily the case in the instance of Saul.[75]

In addition it should be noted that the expression "to make a king" (Hiphil forms of the verb מלך) is consistently utilized to designate the official inauguration of someone's rule as king.[76] This may or may not be associated with

---

72. Ibid.

73. Budde (*Die Bücher Samuel*, KHC, 76) sees this LXX interpretation as an additional attempt to relate this tradition of Saul's rise to the monarchy to that of I Sam. 10:17 ff. He says, "Die Anpassung an 10:17 ff ist auch hier in LXX weiter vorgeschritten indem sie statt וימלכו bietet καὶ ἔχρισεν Σαμουήλ . . . εἰς βασιλέα." Others who state a preference for the MT are: Smith, *Samuel*, ICC, 81; and Leimbach, *Samuel*, HSchAT, 55.

74. Notice that there is no evidence in either the MT or LXX for supposing the presence of an additional mentioning of the name Saul in the original text.

75. Keil, *The Books of Samuel*, 113.

76. There are forty-nine occurrences of Hiphil forms of מלך in the OT. Among these I Chron. 23:1; 29:22 are the only places where the term is not clearly a reference to the inauguration of someone's rule as king. I Chron. 23:1 says: "when David reached old age, he made his son Solomon king (וימלך) over Israel." In I Chron. 29:22 we read: "they made Solomon the son of David king (וימליכו) a second time." What is the relationship between these two statements?

anointing as a simultaneous act. The important thing is that "to make someone king" is to formally invest him with the prerogatives and responsibilities of his office.

Saul's anointing had taken place previously (I Sam. 10:1); subsequent to this he was publicly designated as the one whom Yahweh had chosen to be king at the gathering in Mizpah (I Sam. 10:17-27). At this time Samuel was careful to explain to Saul and to the people exactly what the responsibilities and obligations of Saul as king would be (I Sam. 10:25). All the people, with a few exceptions, rejoiced in his selection and said, "Long live the king!" (I Sam. 10:24), but nowhere is it said in the report of the Mizpah assembly that Saul was "made king," nor is there any indication that he assumed the responsibilities and prerogatives of a newly installed king at that time.[77]

W. Rudolph (*Chronikbücher* [HAT I/21; Tübingen: 1955] 194) says that the phrase "a second time" in I Chron. 29:22 is an "Einschub wegen 23I, dessen Überschriftcharakter verkannt wurde," and is to be deleted. If this is the case then I Chron. 23:1 is a heading for the entire following section and it has reference to the same event as does I Chron. 29:22, and therefore also refers to the inauguration of rule. In support of Rudolph's statement it can be noted that שׁנית does not appear in LXX[BA] and one might suggest it has been inserted in the MT in an attempt to harmonize I Chron. 29:22 with I Chron. 23:1. A similar position is also advocated by R. Kittel (*Die Bücher der Chronik* [HK I/6; Göttingen: 1902] 85, 104); J. Goettsberger (*Die Bücher der Chronik Oder Paralipomenon* [HSchAT IV/1; Bonn: 1939] 165, 199; and A. van den Born (*Kronieken* [BOT; Roermond: 1960] 125. Generally speaking we have objections to the views of Rudolph on the relationship of I Chron. 23 ff. and 28-29, but it is possible that his statement cited above is correct.

77. It is also noteworthy in this connection that the regular formula used to begin the report of a reign ("... was ... years old when he began to reign, and he reigned. ...") occurs with reference to the reign of Saul right after the report of the Gilgal assembly in I Sam. 13:1, rather than after the Mizpah gathering in Chapter 10. This favors the view that Saul's reign was initiated at Gilgal rather than previously at Mizpah. Although the regular formula for initiation of a reign clearly occurs here, the present state of the Hebrew text only enables one to estimate the length of Saul's reign and his age when he began to reign. The MT reads, "Saul was ... years old when he began to reign, and he reigned *two* years over Israel" (italics mine). It is clear that a numeral has dropped out of the text in both clauses. Various conjectures have been made in attempting to reconstruct the original reading, but evidence is lacking for certainty. See, Driver, *Notes*, 96-97, and Stoebe, *Das erste Buch Samuelis*, KAT, 242-243 where extensive literature is cited. K. A. Kitchen (*Ancient Orient and Old Testament* [London: 1966] 75) notes a similar omission of the year-date in Babylonian Chronicles.

Saul's subsequent activity in the events surrounding the threat of the Ammonites against the inhabitants of Jabesh-gilead (I Sam. 11:1-13) does not rest on public recognition of his kingship and royal authority, but rather leads to this recognition and the inauguration of his reign. For it was only after Yahweh confirmed Saul's selection to be king, by bringing victory to the Israelites over the Ammonites under his leadership, that Saul was formally invested with his kingly office in the Gilgal ceremony.[78] This investiture was done "before Yahweh" indicating the sacral-cultic character of the ceremony in which Saul was inaugurated in the context of a challenge to a renewed recognition of the kingship of Yahweh over his people.

It is significant that the sacrifices which are mentioned in connection with the Gilgal ceremony are the ‏זבחים שלמים‎. The common characteristic of this category[79] of sacrifice was that one portion was offered to God upon the altar while the remainder was eaten by the one or ones offering it in a meal which signified the fellowship and communion of God with his people.

The name "peace offering" follows the translation normally given by the LXX ($\vartheta v\sigma i a\ \epsilon i\rho\eta\nu\iota\kappa\acute{\eta}$) and the Vulgate (*victima pacifica*); see further, W. H. Gispen (*Leviticus*, COT, 62) for an enumeration of the translations of the LXX and the Vulgate. These translations reflect the view that ‏שלמים‎ is connected with the Kal, ‏שלם‎, to be complete or be sound. In more recent times other suggestions have been made for the designation of this sacrifice including: "communion sacrifice,"[80] and "covenant offering."[81] The Hebrew word, with

78. See n. 72.
79. Lev. 7:12-17 and 22:21-23, 29-30 distinguish three different types of this sacrifice. For discussions of its different uses and significance, see: R. de Vaux, *Studies in Old Testament Sacrifice* (Cardiff: 1964) 27-51, especially 33; and Oehler, *Theology of the Old Testament*, 287, 288.
80. De Vaux, *Studies in Old Testament Sacrifice*, 27-51.
81. J. Pedersen, *Israel. Its Life and Culture* III/IV (London: 1940) 335; R. Schmid, *Das Bundesopfer in Israel* (StANT 9; München: 1964).

the exception of Amos 5:22, is always in the plural form; this is explained in different ways.[82]

Rudolph Schmid, who has recently made an extensive study of the nature, origin, and significance of the שְׁלָמִים, maintains that the communal meal, which is the distinguishing feature of this offering, emphasizes the relation of the sacrifice to the covenant. Schmid concludes his study by saying, "Deutlicher sprach das alttestamentliche selamim-Opfer den Bundesgedanken aus, das die Bundesgemeinschaft schloss, wiederherstellte und starkte."[83] While Schmid's study successfully demonstrates the close relationship of this sacrifice to covenant making, restoration, and strengthening in various contexts, his designation of the sacrifice in translation as covenant offering may be questioned. H. H. Rowley comments that this term, "would seem well to define the character of the offerings made at the sacred mount at the time of the conclusion of the covenant, but less certainly to cover all the cases of these sacrifices."[84] This caution of Rowley's is certainly justified,[85] but at the same time it

---

82. De Vaux (*Studies in Old Testament Sacrifice*, 50, 51) suggests that the name was borrowed from the Canaanites noting that the Ras Shamra texts refer to the communion sacrifice as *šlmm*. He says that the "pseudo-plural form *šelāmîm* is explicable on these grounds, and it can be compared to other loan-words in the religious vocabulary: *ʾūrîm, tummîm, tᵉrāpîm,* which in their primitive form, are singulars with mimation." See further in relation to this question David Gill, "Thysia and sᵉlamim: Questions to R. Schmid's Das Bundesopfer in Israel," *Biblica* 47 (1966) 255-261. W. H. Gispen (*Het Boek Leviticus* [COT; Kampen: 1950] 61-69) suggests the plural is "pluralis van het abstractum" (62).

83. Schmid, *Das Bundesopfer,* 125.

84. H. H. Rowley, *Worship in Ancient Israel. Its Forms and Meaning* (London: 1967) 122, 123. Accordingly, Rowley gives the translation, "peace offering." In a similar vein D. J. McCarthy in his review (*CBQ* 26 [1964] 503) of Schmid's *Das Bundesopfer* says: "If it is certain that *zebah šelāmîm* was often associated with covenant, it is not clear that this was always and necessarily the case as will be seen from the very instance cited (p. 83), Ex 10, 25, as well as from the sacrifice of Jethro in Ex 18, which leaves open the possibility that the rite was simply a means to honor God whether there was a covenant or not."

85. A. Rainey ("Peace offering," *Encyclopedia Judaica* XIV, 603, 604) points out that among the events which called forth the peace offering were: "cessation of famine or pestilence (II Sam. 24:25), acclamation of a candidate for kingship (I Kings 1:9, 19), or a time of national spiritual renewal (II Chron.

remains apparent that the זבחי שלמים did have a particularly close relationship not only to the establishment, but also
to the maintenance and strengthening of the covenant, and
Rowley himself summarizes their purpose by saying that,
"these sacrifices were for the maintenance or restoration of
good relations with God."[86]

The זבחי שלמים were an important element in the original ceremony of covenant ratification at Sinai (Ex. 24:5,
11).[87] On that occasion after sprinkling half of the blood of
the sacrifice on the altar, Moses read the book of the covenant to the people, and then when the people had affirmed
their willingness to keep the covenant obligations Moses
sprinkled the people with the other half of the blood saying,
"Behold the blood of the covenant, which Yahweh has made
with you in accordance with all these words" (Ex. 24:8). At
the conclusion of this ceremony the elders of Israel, as
representatives of the people, ate the covenantal meal demonstrating the communion of Yahweh with his people.[88]

This particular sacrifice was thus part of the ceremony
establishing the covenant relationship at Sinai, and it represented symbolically the communion or peace that was to
exist between Yahweh and his people when they lived in
conformity to their covenant obligations. It is, therefore,
certainly appropriate, and even to be expected, that at the
"renewal of the kingdom" at Gilgal the same sacrifices were
offered which had comprised an important element in the
original ceremony of covenant ratification at Sinai.

Finally, it is said that Saul, and all the men of Israel
rejoiced greatly. Rejoicing (שמח) is associated with peace

29:31-36). At the local level they were sacrificed for the annual family reunion
(I Sam 20:6) or other festive events such as the harvesting of the firstfruits (I Sam
9:11-13, 22-24; 16:4-5)."

86. Rowley, *Worship in Ancient Israel*, 123. Cf. further Gispen, *Leviticus*,
COT, 61-69; J. C. de Moor, "The peace-offering in Ugarit and Israel," in *Schrift
en Uitleg* 112-117.

87. See the discussion of Eichrodt in: *Theology of the Old Testament*, I,
156-157.

88. See: Oehler, *Theology of the Old Testament*, 264.

offerings in Deuteronomy 27:7, II Chronicles 29:36 (cf. 29:35), 30:25 (cf. 30:22), and with "eating before Yahweh" in Deuteronomy 14:26 and 27:7. שמח appears as an activity associated with covenant renewal in the time of Joash (II Kings 11:20; cf. II Chron. 23:21), in the time of Asa (II Chron. 15:15), and in the time of Hezekiah (II Chron. 29:36; cf. 29:10). Here in I Samuel 11:15 the rejoicing is to be understood as the expression of a people who has renewed its commitment to Yahweh, has confessed its sin (cf. I Sam. 12:19) and has been given a king.

PART II

LITERARY-CRITICAL AND GENRE-HISTORICAL
ANALYSIS OF I SAMUEL 11:14–12:25

III

I SAMUEL 11:14-12:25 AS A COMPOSITE UNIT

The position which we are seeking to develop and defend on the basis of exegetical, literary-critical, and genre-historical analysis is that I Samuel 11:14-12:25 is best understood as a composite unit,[1] descriptive of a covenant renewal ceremony held in Gilgal in connection with the inauguration of kingship in Israel. In this chapter we will concern ourselves with the literary critical analysis of I Samuel 11:14-12:25 before looking in Chapter IV at the form-critical assessment of I Samuel 12 and the implications which this might have for its literary character and interpretation.

Section 1
A Survey of the Literary Criticism
of I Samuel 11:14-12:25

In the survey of the literary criticism of I Samuel 11:14-12:25 which follows, no attempt will be made to be exhaustive, but the main varieties of approach which have been followed in the literary-critical assessment of this material will be indicated, and resumés of the positions of important representatives of the major categories of viewpoint will be given.[2] We will treat I Samuel 11:14-15 and I Samuel 12:1-25 separately, beginning with I Samuel 12:1-25.

---

1. The question can be raised if the material of this section of I Samuel was originally an oral unity. It would lead us too far astray here to go into the complicated question of the relation of oral and written traditions. Given our view of I Sam. 11:14-12:25 it appears improbable to us that this would have ever existed as an oral tradition. See Section 2,A, below.

2. As much as possible the authors discussed in Section A have also been discussed in Section B. There is not complete correspondence, however, since

A. I Samuel 12:1-25

The literary analysis of I Samuel 8-12 can be divided into four broad categories of approach.[3] There is the documentary-source theory, which distinguishes two or three literary strands within I Samuel 8-12, basing itself largely on the general orientation of the various sections which are characterized either as "pro" or as "anti" monarchial. Secondly, there is what can be termed the "fragmentary approach" which finds in I Samuel 8-12 the linkage of a number of originally independent tradition units. More recently a third approach has developed which combines elements of the "documentary" and "fragmentary" viewpoints by finding the present narrative to be the end result of a process of growth in which originally independent traditions became linked into clusters, and the clusters in turn became fused into the present narrative so that various stages of tradition growth are represented in the final product. And fourthly, there are those who regard I Samuel 8-12 as the work of a historian who utilized the materials at his disposal to construct a reliable historical record of the rise of the Israelite monarchy and its attendant circumstances.[4]

I Samuel 12:1-25 has presented particular difficulty for the advocates of all the above mentioned approaches to the material in I Samuel 8-12. The result is that scholars who otherwise are in general agreement in their basic approach to

some authors have not discussed both sections in detail, and in some instances have said little or nothing about one of the sections. Notice, e.g., that Buber is discussed in Section A and not in Section B, and Wildberger is discussed in Section B but not in Section A.

3. See further below, Chapter V, Section 1.

4. This classification has its deficiencies. At least the later advocates of the documentary-source theory and the fragmentary approach have also engaged in traditions-history research, sometimes rather extensively. It is therefore, sometimes also difficult to determine in which category a specific author should be discussed (see Chapter V, n. 2). Particularly the line between the third and the fourth category is not to be drawn too rigidly. The distinction between these categories is that those in the fourth category lay more emphasis on the work of the final historian (what those of the third category might designate as the final redactor), they regard his sources as closer in time to the events which they describe, and in connection with this are more inclined to view chapters 8-12 as a

the literary criticism of I Samuel 8-12 have often differed in
their analysis of I Samuel 12, while contrarily, scholars who
hold quite divergent views about the literary character of
I Samuel 8-12 as a whole are in many instances in close
agreement in their assessment of I Samuel 12. For this reason
we will organize our survey of the literary criticism of I Samuel 12 differently than our discussion of the literary criticism
of I Samuel 8-12 as a whole (see Chapter V, Section 1).[5] For
the present our interest focuses primarily on the degree and
kind of literary unity or disunity which is ascribed to I Samuel 12, separating this as much as is possible from other
considerations. We will reserve for Chapter IV, Section 2,B
and Chapter V the discussion of questions related to the
process or means by which I Samuel 12 has been given its
present form, and its relationship to other pericopes in I Samuel 8-12.[6] In this way it is possible to classify the approaches
to the composition of I Samuel 12 in three general categories: 1) the chapter represents an original unity; 2) the
chapter represents an original unity modified by varying
degrees of redactional reworking and supplementation; 3) the
chapter represents a composite-construction of originally disparate materials.

---

fairly continuous unity, which has, among other things, implications for their
historical reliability.

5. This has strange results. For example, it means that in Section 1,A
Gressmann is handled before Budde, and it means that Wellhausen and Noth come
into discussion in close succession. This arrangement has its disadvantages, but it
also has the benefit that lines of approach become clear that often remain
obscured.

6. At this point it is not our *primary* concern to deal with questions such as
whether or not the chapter is a free composition of a deuteronomistic historian of
exilic (post-exilic) time; whether or not the chapter is part of the "E source" of
pentateuchal criticism extended into the historical books; whether or not the
chapter is a separate independent tradition unit or part of a larger narrative
strand; whether or not the chapter contains a historically trustworthy report of
the Gilgal assembly; and whether or not the chapter contains discernible evidences
of deuteronomistic redaction; but rather with the question of the chapter's unity
or disunity. Nevertheless, it is not possible to separate totally the question of the
chapter's unity from many of the above mentioned questions (this is particularly
the case with the question of evidences of deuteronomistic redaction). These
questions will thus be referred to here, but only in so far as they have a relation to
the extent and nature of the chapter's unity or disunity.

1. *I Samuel 12 as an original unity.*

Those who view I Samuel 12 as an original unity may be divided into three categories. There are, first of all, those who view I Samuel 12 as all-of-a-piece, and a historically reliable record of the proceedings of the Gilgal assembly. According to this view I Samuel 12 is included in the carefully constructed books of I and II Samuel along with the accounts of many other events surrounding the lives of Samuel, Saul, and David, and particularly those concerned with the foundations of Israelite kingship. Secondly, there are those who view I Samuel 12 as the composition of a "deuteronomistic historian" who (even though the record of I Samuel 12 is a fiction) presents a picture of the Gilgal assembly which is internally consistent, since it is governed in its content by the deuteronomist's theologically determined view of Israel's history. Thirdly, there are those who view I Samuel 12 as an independent tradition unit which has its own unique history of development, but which is nevertheless an organic unit.[7]

a. *I Samuel 12 as a reliable historical record.*

1) *Representatives of "conservative biblical scholarship."*—There is a long history of what is often termed "conservative biblical scholarship" which has maintained the historical reliability and unity of I Samuel 12 as the report of the Gilgal assembly which marked the close of the period of the judges and the beginning of the period of the monarchy.[8]

---

7. These categories cannot be rigidly applied and are utilized here primarily as a means of organizing the material to be considered. There is, for example, possibility of overlap between the first and third categories as can be seen in the approach of Robertson (see further below 99 ff. and 103 ff.). Generally speaking, however, those we have placed in the first category have neither emphasized nor attempted to reconstruct the tradition-history of the component parts of the books of Samuel.

8. Representatives of this approach do not deny that the author of I and II Samuel utilized various sources in his composition of the book, but they view the work as non-contradictory in its various parts. The advocates of this approach have given little or no attention to the bearing which a form critical analysis might have on the chapter's unity and interpretation. See further below, Chapter IV.

A recent extensive treatment of this chapter from this perspective is that of C. J. Goslinga, *Het Eerste Boek Samuël*, COT, 17-60, 191, 243-252.[9]

2) *E. Robertson.*—Although Edward Robertson's general approach to the literature of the Old Testament must be distinguished from that of the above mentioned scholars, he nevertheless considers I Samuel 12 to be a unity and a historically reliable account of the Gilgal assembly. In his assessment of the composition of I Samuel 1-15 he concludes that the attempts to divide the material into two or three documentary sources have not been convincing, and he adopts the view that the book is the work of a compiler who has utilized numerous literary fragments, which along with his own *supplementa*, have been ordered into the present carefully constructed book.[10] He maintains, however, that the principle of organization is more thematic than strictly chronological so that in some cases stress must not be placed on the present sequence of events.[11]

Robertson divides I Samuel 1-15 into six sections, each of which is either concluded or introduced by *supplementa* from the compiler's own hand. His fourth section contains the narratives of the establishment of Saul's kingship and is divided into two sub-sections, I Samuel 8:1-10:27 (*supplementa* 10:25-27), and I Samuel 11:1-15 (*supplementa* 11: 14-15), and then a conclusion to the whole of I Samuel 8-12 which he finds in I Samuel 12:1-25.[12]

---

9. For other representatives of this basic approach see: W. Möller, *Einleitung in das Alte Testament* (Zwickau: 1934) 75-83; idem, *Grundriss für alttestamentliche Einleitung* (Berlin: 1958) 156, 157; Schelhaas, *GTT* 44 (1944) 240-272; Aalders, *Kanoniek*, 181-191; Young, *Introduction*, 177-187; Harrison, *Introduction*, 695-718.

10. E. Robertson, *Samuel and Saul* (reprint from *BJRL* 28 [1944] 175-206; Manchester: 1944) 1-17.

11. Robertson feels, for example, that the election of Saul by lot (I Sam. 10:17-27) may have chronologically followed the battle recorded in I Sam. 11:1-11; and I Sam. 8:1-6 he feels is placed before the following pericopes because it raises the question of kingship and thus introduces a theme, although some of the events related after this he regards as having occurred before the events of I Sam. 8:1-6.

12. Ibid., 20-22.

Robertson regards the materials used by the compiler as dating from the early days of the monarchy, and he maintains that they have been arranged so that they can tell their own story without the infusion of the compiler's own viewpoint into the early history.[13] He sees the age-long struggle for supremacy between civil and religious power reflected in the tensions between Samuel and Saul.[14]

b. I Samuel 12 as the composition of a "deuteronomistic historian."

The view that I Samuel 12 is to be considered the work of a deuteronomistic historian of the 6th or 5th century B.C. has had many adherents.

1) *J. Wellhausen.*—J. Wellhausen associated I Samuel 12 with a late deuteronomistic, anti-monarchial strand of the book of Samuel which he felt was also discernible in I Samuel 7:2-17; 8:1-22; and 10:17-27. He viewed this strand as historically unreliable, asserting that there, "cannot be a word of truth in the whole narrative,"[15] and considered it as a product of exilic or post-exilic Judaism which had lost all knowledge of the real conditions behind the rise of kingship in Israel and had simply transported an idealized picture back into the earlier times.[16] Yet as a part of this narrative strand Wellhausen considered I Samuel 12 to be all-of-a-piece and an authentic representation of the deuteronomist's theologically determined anti-monarchial reconstruction of the events associated with the establishment of the monarchy.

2) *H. P. Smith.*—Similar to the view of Wellhausen as it pertains to I Samuel 12 is that of H. P. Smith. Smith detects two strands in the narratives of I Samuel 1-15 which he labels as a "life of Samuel" (*Sm.*) and a "life of Saul" (*Sl.*).

---

13. Ibid., 5, 32.

14. Ibid., 29, 31.

15. J. Wellhausen, *Prolegomena to the History of Ancient Israel* (German original: 1905[6]; New York: 1957) 249.

16. J. Wellhausen, ibid., 245-256; and *Die Composition des Hexateuchs und der historischen Bücher des Alten Testaments* (Berlin: 1899[3]) 240-243.

He assigns chapter 12 to the "Sm." source which he says idealizes persons and events and is dominated by a theological idea which is in line with, "the latest redactor of the Book of Judges, who embodied the Deuteronomistic theory of history in the framework of that book."[17] Smith rejects the identification of this narrative strand with E of the Pentateuchal sources saying that there are too many resemblances to D or the deuteronomic school, and that there is not sufficient evidence for identifying these resemblances as secondary deuteronomistic expansions as had been advocated by K. Budde.[18] With regard to stylistic features of I Samuel 12, Smith notes affinities of language with J, E, JE, D, and R^D and concludes that this chapter, along with the other passages which he assigns to the "Sm." source, shows indications of being composed at a late date, perhaps during or after the exile.

3) *M. Noth (H. J. Boecker).*—M. Noth asserts that Wellhausen was entirely right when he declared that on the basis of their language and content I Samuel 7:2-8:22; 10:17-27 and 12:1-25 belong together, are deuteronomic in character, and presuppose the older tradition in I Samuel 9-11.[19] He then assigns all of these passages to the anonymous deuteronomistic historian whom he views as the author-editor of all the material contained in Deuteronomy to II Kings.

In Noth's opinion I Samuel 12 is particularly significant because it is one of the key passages of the deuteronomist's own composition by which he structured his history work and attempted to tie together the various epochs of Israel's history. It is Noth's view that at important junctures in the historical narrative of Joshua–II Kings the deuteronomistic historian inserted passages containing a retrospective evaluation of what had gone before and a preview of what was to come. According to Noth these interpretive reflections on

17. Smith, *Samuel,* ICC, xx. See further, xvi-xxii and 81-89.
18. For Budde's viewpoint see below, 104 f.
19. Noth, *Überlieferungsgeschichtliche Studien,* 54-55.

Israel's history were, whenever possible, placed in the mouth of a leading figure in the narrative in the form of a speech.[20] Noth regards Samuel's speech in I Samuel 12 as one of these passages, here serving to mark the end of the period of the judges and the beginning of the monarchy, and expressing the deuteronomist's own anti-monarchial assessment of the establishment of kingship in Israel.[21] Accordingly, he considers the chapter a unity. He sees little evidence of redactional reworking and rejects, for example, the view that I Samuel 12:12a is an insertion,[22] viewing it instead as evidence for the dependence of the narrative strand represented in I Samuel 7:2-8:22; 10:17-27a; 12:1-25 on the traditions contained in 9:1-10:16; 10:27b-11:15.[23]

4) *R. H. Pfeiffer.*—Also adhering to this general view of I Samuel 12 is R. H. Pfeiffer, who, while differing from Wellhausen, Smith, and Noth in discerning two pre-deuteronomic narrative strands in I Samuel, isolates I Samuel 12 from both of them, maintaining that the deuteronomists who edited the books from Genesis to Kings added this final address of Samuel as their own free composition.[24] He says of I Samuel 12 (along with I Kings 2:1-12) that, "no other

---

20. Ibid., 5. According to Noth such speeches are found in Josh. 1:11-15; Josh. 23; I Sam. 12, and I Kings 8:14-61. Where a speech could not easily be utilized, the deuteronomist's reflections were inserted directly in the text as for instance in II Kings 17:7-23.

21. Ibid., 60. Noth says that the deuteronomist had difficulty in combining his negative view of kingship with the traditions possessing a more positive attitude toward the monarchy which he incorporated in his history work. He nevertheless regards this negative assessment of kingship as one of the "wesentlichen Zügen seiner Gesamtgeschichtsauffassung," and he says that the deuteronomist gives an account of the rise of kingship which makes it very clear that "dieses eine zeitlich sekundäre und seinem Wesen nach sogar unsachgemässe und daher grundsätzlich abzulehnende Einrichtung war ..." (ibid., 110, 95, resp.).

Boecker in his recent work (*Die Beurteilung der Anfänge des Königtums*) adopts Noth's position with regard to the unity of I Sam. 12. Boecker, however, rejects Noth's view that I Sam. 8; 10:17-27; 12:1-25 are basically anti-monarchial. See further below, Chapter V, Section 1,B,2.

22. See above, Chapter I, n. 86.

23. Ibid., 60. In a note Noth comments: "Auch die Bezeichnung des neuen Königs als des 'Gesalbten Jahwes' dürfte eine Anspielung auf 10, 1 sein."

24. Pfeiffer, *Introduction,* 338-373 (esp. 359-368).

passages in our book can be attributed with equal assurance to the Deuteronomic school."[25]

c. I Samuel 12 as an independent tradition unit.

1) *H. Gressmann.*—Hugo Gressmann pioneered in the application of the methodology developed by Herman Gunkel to I and II Samuel. Following Gunkel's lead he directed his attention to the independent narrative units of the book, rather than to the documentary sources or strands of the then prevalent literary critical approach. In the pericopes of I Samuel 8-12 he found examples of sagas and legends, but viewed I Samuel 11 as the only "Geschichtserzählung," and thus the only historically reliable record of the rise of Israelite kingship. I Samuel 12 he considered as one of the later legends in the entire section. In Gressmann's view the representation in this chapter of Samuel as a judge and administrator, as well as the notion that kingship was a violation against God are false ideas of a later time. He regarded the chapter as an independent tradition unit, and maintained that the book of I Samuel was constructed by a late editor from many such independent tradition units of varying lengths.[26]

2) *A. Weiser.*—A. Weiser also maintains that the division of I Samuel 8-12 into either two or three literary strands has proven to be an unsatisfactory solution to the problem of its literary origin, and adopts the view that the material is composed of a collection of originally independent traditions which arose in different places and which later were placed side by side and welded into the literary composition which we now have.[27] Weiser accordingly views I Samuel 12 as a unity but he objects to the assignment of the chapter either to an E strand or to the deuteronomistic historian because in

---

25. Ibid., 368.
26. Gressmann, *Die älteste Geschichtsschreibung,* SAT II/1, 24-47.
27. A. Weiser, *The Old Testament. Its Formation and Development,* 158-170; idem, *Samuel,* FRLANT, 79-94.

his opinion neither approach has been able to solve the difficulties encountered in the literary analysis of the chapter.

Weiser seeks the origins of I Samuel 12 in the cult tradition of the Gilgal sanctuary which he maintains was developed in prophetic circles which regarded Samuel as their ancestor. In Weiser's opinion this is the reason that the material of I Samuel 12 shows a relationship to the E source which he feels arose later in these same circles. With regard to the "deuteronomistic" phraseology in the chapter which has often led to theories of either deuteronomistic authorship or deuteronomistic redaction Weiser says, "Auf die Frage nach dem sog. deuteronomistischen Stil in 1. Sam 12, die meist in der Form einer äusserlichen Wortstatistik verhandelt wird, näher einzugehen, versage ich mir: so lange über das Wesen, die Herkunft und Geschichte dieses 'Stils' keine Klarheit gewonnen ist, kann er nicht als Beweismittel für das literarkritische Problem dienen."[28]

2. I Samuel 12 as an original unity modified by redactional reworking.

The second general category of critical approaches to I Samuel 12 is that of those who view the chapter as an original unity but think its present form evidences varying degrees of later redactional reworking and additions.

a. K. Budde

K. Budde divided the pre-deuteronomic content of I Samuel into two sources which he identified with the J and E strands of the Pentateuch.[29] He assigned I Samuel 12 to the E strand and said it originally connected directly with I Samuel

---

28. Weiser, *Samuel,* FRLANT, 85, n. 80. See also R. C. G. Thornton, "Studies in Samuel," *CQR* 168 (1967) 413-423, for a view of I Sam. 12 very similar to that of Weiser's.

29. K. Budde, "Sauls Königswahl und Verwerfung," *ZAW* 8 (1888) 223-248; idem, *Die Bücher Samuel,* KHC, xii-xx, 76, 77.

10:24. He saw a parallel between I Samuel 12 and the farewell address of Joshua in Joshua 24, and said that as long as Joshua 24 in its original form is ascribed to E, I Samuel 12 in its original form must also be viewed as belonging to E. He maintained, however, that just as the deuteronomistic school reworked Joshua 24, so also a deuteronomistic redactor repeatedly intervened in I Samuel 7; 8; 10:17 ff. and 12 even though his reworking and additions are not always easily and precisely distinguishable from the elohistic original. Nevertheless Budde felt that the deuteronomist's hand could be clearly seen in the following expressions of I Samuel 12: "he sold them into the hand of" (v. 9); "your enemies all around" (v. 11); "and not rebel against the command of Yahweh" (v. 14); "and rebel against the command of Yahweh" (v. 15); "which you have done in the sight of Yahweh by asking for yourselves a king" (v. 17).[30] In addition "angesichts des klaren Aufbaus, den Rje in Cap. 8ff. hergestellt hat," he considered the association of the Ammonite threat with the request for a king which is contained in verse 12 as, "so grosse Gedankenlosigkeit, dass nicht dieser, [Rje] sondern nur ein Überarbeiter dafür verantwortlich gemacht werden kann."[31] He accordingly maintained that the first half of the verse stemmed from Rd at the earliest. Verse 21 he viewed as belonging to neither E nor Rd, and labeled it as a very late gloss.[32]

b. S. R. Driver

S. R. Driver viewed the pre-deuteronomic content of I Samuel 8-12 as a combination of two originally independent narratives. The later of the two narrative strands, to which he assigned I Samuel 12, he regarded as akin to the E strand of the Pentateuch, but not actually written by the same hand. The combined narrative he regarded as having

---

30. Budde, *Die Bücher Samuel,* KHC, 77-81.
31. Ibid., 80.
32. Ibid., 81.

been expanded by a later writer whose style and viewpoint were similar to Deuteronomy and the compiler of the book of Judges.[33] This expansion is said by Driver to be particularly noticeable in I Samuel 12:9 ff. However, he specifically designates only the reference of Samuel to himself in verse 11, and the association of the Ammonite threat with the request for a king in verse 12, as attributable to later expansion.[34]

c. O. Eissfeldt

O. Eissfeldt views I Samuel 12 as part of the E strand of the Hexateuch and the book of Judges which later underwent a deuteronomistic redaction. He maintains, however, that the deuteronomistic redaction interfered with the material only very slightly and he gives no indication of specific evidences of this in I Samuel 12.[35]

d. G. B. Caird

G. B. Caird finds an early and a late source in I Samuel which in his opinion show affinity with the J and E sources of the Pentateuch, although he considers it unlikely that they are direct continuations of J and E. He assigns I Samuel 12 to his late source. He maintains that the two sources were united prior to a deuteronomistic revision, but he says that the language of the late source is not sufficiently different from that of the deuteronomist for one to be confident at any point in distinguishing between them.[36]

e. M. Buber

M. Buber views the original core of I Samuel 12 as a unity, but in his detailed literary analysis of the chapter he

---

33. S. R. Driver, *Introduction to the Literature of the Old Testament* (New York: 1913⁹ [reprinted, 1956]) 175-178.

34. Expansions manifesting characteristically deuteronomistic style and viewpoint are not specified by Driver.

35. Eissfeldt, *Komposition*, 6-11; idem, *Introduction*, 262, 263, 268-280.

36. Caird, *IB*, II, 855-862.

limits this original material to verses 1-5 and 13-15, 24, 25. The remainder of the chapter he regards as produced in late prophetic circles through a complex process of insertions. He says, for example, that the "Mirakelgeschichte" (vv. 16-19) had nothing to do with the original account, and he views verse 21 as an insertion within an insertion, and the only verse representing a post-exilic voice in the chapter.[37]

Buber sees verses 1-5 as the record of Samuel's discharge after completion of the task which is described in I Samuel 9:16. He suggests that the last ten words of verse 12 originally appeared between verse 1a and 1b, and were to be understood parenthetically ("Behold I have listened to your voice in all that you said to me,—you said, 'No but a king shall reign over us,' and Yahweh your God is your king!—and I have made a king over you").[38] He also suggests that verse 2ab ("but I am old and gray, and behold my sons are with you") is not likely to be original.[39]

Buber considers verses 13-15, 24 and 25 to be the message which Samuel as the prophetic representative of Yahweh gave to the king and the people at the beginning of Saul's rule. Even within these verses Buber eliminates a number of phrases which appear to him to be later insertions[40] and proposes a compact original text reading as follows:

"Und nun, da ist der König, den ihr erwünscht habt, da, gegeben hat *JHWH* über euch einen König. Werdet ihr *JHWH* fürchten und auf seine Stimme hören, dann sollt ihr leben, so ihr, so der König, der nach *JHWH* eurem Gott über euch König wurde. Werdet ihr aber nicht auf *JHWHs* Stimme hören, dann wird *JHWHs* Hand wider euch und wider euren

37. Buber, *VT* 6 (1956) 156-162. See above, Chapter I, 54 f.
38. Ibid., 156, 157.
39. See above, Chapter I, n. 8.
40. In v. 13 he eliminates אשר בחדתם (see above, Chapter I, n. 93). In v. 14 he eliminates the phrases, "and serve him," and "and not rebel against the commandment of Yahweh," and he adopts והיתם in place of והיה (see above, Chapter I, n. 101). In v. 24 he eliminates, "and serve him in truth with all your heart," because יראו and כי ראו belong close together as a word-play.

König sein. Fürchtet nur *JHWH!* Denn scht, welch Grosses er
an euch erzeigt hat! Treibt böse, böse ihr's aber, dann werdet
ihr, so ihr, so euer König, hinweggerafft."[41]

f. G. Wallis

G. Wallis sees in I Samuel 8-12 three separate accounts of
Saul's selection to be king, recorded respectively in: a) I
Samuel 11; b) I Samuel 9:1-10:16; and c) the narrative
strand contained in I Samuel 8; 10:17-21ba, 24-26. To explain the differences in the accounts he chooses a different
course than the above named authors. It is his opinion that
these accounts originated in different times and places and
represent the gradual development and extension of Saul's
dominions in the consolidation of his kingship over expand-
ing areas.[42]

Wallis notes that I Samuel 12 links appropriately with
I Samuel 10:24 and can be regarded as an extension of this
tradition, but he rejects the view that it reflects a late
negative assessment of kingship. He views it rather as a record
of Samuel's retirement as a judge, in which a cool and
reserved attitude toward the new order under the monarchy
is expressed. He comments that kingship was a legally determined entity in the view of the judge Samuel, and its continued existence was to be dependent on whether or not the
people would reject the rule of Yahweh with the accession of
their human king.[43] Wallis thus feels that the basic core of
I Samuel 12 can be traced back to Samuel himself or at least
to the feelings of his contemporaries. Yet he regards the
miracle account of verses 16-23 as a secondary element which
adds nothing to the text and is actually disturbing; he thinks
the survey of the conquest and period of the judges (vv. 6b-

---

41. Ibid., 161.
42. G. Wallis, "Die Anfänge des Königtums in Israel," *WZ* 12 (1963)
239-247, incorporated in G. Wallis, *Geschichte und Überlieferung* (Arbeiten zur
Theologie, II/3; Stuttgart: 1968) 45-66.
43. Wallis, "Die Hoheit des Königs im Alten Testament," *Geschichte und
Überlieferung,* 88-108, esp. 93-95.

11) fits poorly in the mouth of Samuel; and he considers the connection of the request for a king with the Ammonite war (v. 12) to be inconsistent with I Samuel 8.[44] He therefore regards these passages as insertions of a deuteronomistic revision, leaving I Samuel 12:1-6a, 13-15, 24, 25 as original.[45]

g. B. C. Birch

A recent extensive treatment of the narratives of I Samuel 8–12 is found in the dissertation of B. C. Birch, *The Rise of the Israelite Monarchy: The Growth and Development of I Samuel 7–15* (1970). Birch views this part of Samuel as the end product of a long process of tradition development, the various stages of which he attempts to reconstruct. He concludes that initially a large variety of traditions concerning the rise of kingship in Israel circulated independently. A pre-deuteronomic editor belonging to northern prophetic circles of the late 8th century B.C. brought the traditions together into a single edition which also included material of his own composition. Subsequently the deuteronomistic historian (whom Birch dates at approximately the time of Josiah) incorporated the prophetic edition into his own history work adding only a few sections including I Samuel 7:3-4, 13-14; 8:8, 10-22; 12:6-24; 13:1. Birch claims that although the deuteronomist had a less positive view of kingship than did the prophetic editor, his view was sufficiently close to that of the previous edition that he allowed the earlier material to remain relatively unchanged.[46]

As can be seen from the above summary Birch divides I Samuel 12 into two sections (vv. 1-5 and 6-24) which he assigns to different stages of the tradition growth. He views verses 1-5 as showing likeness to the material of preceding chapters which he assigned to the "prophetic edition." He

---

44. See above, Chapter I, p. 38 ff.
45. Wallis, *Geschichte und Überlieferung*, 94-96. Wallis eliminates some additional phrases even in these verses.
46. Birch, *The Rise of the Israelite Monarchy*, 176-211.

cites for example the use of the title משיח for the king in I Samuel 12:3, 5 which previously appears only in I Samuel 9:16 and I Samuel 10:1. According to Birch this implies a much more positive attitude toward the king than is to be found in the remainder of I Samuel 12 (vv. 6-24) where the term משיח is not utilized. In addition he sees I Samuel 12:1-5 as the logical continuation of the concern expressed in I Samuel 11:12, 13 which he views as indicative of the transfer of certain sacral-legal responsibilities from Samuel to the king.[47] Since I Samuel 12:1-5 shows the king now functioning in the sacral-legal realm (vv. 3, 5), and Samuel retiring from office, Birch feels that these verses are best regarded as a report added to the notice of the Gilgal assembly recorded in I Samuel 11:12-14.[48]

Birch then assigns I Samuel 12:6-24 to the deuteronomistic historian and regards this section of the chapter as having been added in a supplementary fashion after the previous material in I Samuel 7-11 had been brought together in the earlier prophetic edition. In verses 6-15 Birch sees evidence of the influence of the covenant form to which a theophanic sign is attached for additional force and authority. Verses 20-25 he finds to be similar to the paranetic sections of Deuteronomy, but with Samuel instead of Moses in the role of preacher and teacher. Whether verse 25 is to be regarded as part of the deuteronomist's final exhortation or as a post-exilic addition is not clear according to Birch.[49]

h. N. Gottwald

N. Gottwald views I Samuel as the product of a deuteronomistic author-editor who worked with clusters of tradition units (rather than extant parallel documentary sources). He associates I Samuel 12 with what he labels the "Mizpah-

47. Ibid., 102-105. Birch derives his view on this matter from R. Knierim ("The Messianic Concept," in *Jesus and the Historian*, F. T. Trotter, ed.).
48. Ibid., 108-113.
49. Ibid., 113-121.

Ramah story of the rise of the monarchy" (I Sam. 7:3-12; 8:1-22; 10:17 ff.; 12; 15) and concludes that the original tradition unit has been reworked and expanded by the deuteronomistic compiler, although he attributes the essential structure of the chapter to the original source. He maintains that I Samuel 12 and II Samuel 7 display the most extensive rewriting or expansion by the deuteronomistic author-editor, although he admits that the extent of the deuteronomist's work may be debated. He gives no further indication of the specific verses or phrases within I Samuel 12 which he would assign to the deuteronomist.[50]

i. H. J. Stoebe

The view of H. J. Stoebe is rather complex. He considers I Samuel 12 to represent in its original core an independent tradition unit rather than simply the continuation of the documentary source of I Samuel 8 and 10:17-27. He nevertheless considers it unlikely that the chapter is a free composition of the deuteronomistic school because of the tensions in details between this chapter and those preceding it. He also notes, however, that when measured on likenesses, the chapter is not to be totally separated from I Samuel 8 and 10:17-27, and that it therefore does belong with these traditions to a complex entity whose central ideas are brought to expression by the working together of various traditions.

Stoebe does not regard I Samuel 12 to be anti-monarchial and says that the impression that it is, arises from the

---

50. Gottwald, *Encyclopedia Judaica*, XXIV, 787-797. Gottwald's view has affinity with the positions of Fohrer (E. Sellin—G. Fohrer, *Introduction to the Old Testament* [New York: 1968] 218-225) and Mauchline (*I and II Samuel*, NCB, 18-20, 31, 107-110). Fohrer, however, ascribes a lesser role to the deuteronomist than does Gottwald. Mauchline sees the origin of I Sam. 12 in a "prophetic interpretation of history"; the strongly deuteronomic character of the chapter causes him to date its present form at the earliest in the late seventh century and perhaps in the sixth century BC. He does not attempt to specify the extent of the deuteronomic editing, but instead refers only to marks of the deuteronomic style which may or may not be due to a secondary reworking.

deuteronomistic revisions which obscure its original positive attitude toward kingship. The particular difficulty which Stoebe finds in I Samuel 12 is that here, as contrasted with chapter 8, it is not possible to clearly separate the original tradition from its revisions because the original account was characterized by prophetical thought.[51]

3. *I Samuel 12 as a composite of disparate material.*

a. *I. Hylander*

I. Hylander attempts to reconstruct the history of tradition development which lies behind the present literary deposit in I Samuel 1-15.[52] In doing this he begins, much like Gressmann, by concentrating on the character of the individual tradition units, but he differs from Gressmann in that he attempts to disentangle what he regards as the interlaced threads of the various tradition units in the final literary composite. This accomplished, he attempts to reconstruct each tradition unit into what he regards as its original form.[53]

Hylander finds four stages of tradition development reflected in the present narrative, with his fourth stage representing the coalescence of traditions into the present text. He divides the bulk of the material of I Samuel 12 between two of these layers, assigning I Samuel 12:1-5 to the second layer,[54] and I Samuel 12:7-25 to the third layer.[55] He views verse 6 as belonging to the first stratum; this verse, Hylander suggests, perhaps originally preceded I Samuel 10:25.[56] The

51. Stoebe, *Das erste Buch Samuelis,* KAT, 234-240.

52. I. Hylander, *Der literarische Samuel-Saul Komplex (I Sam. 1-15) traditionsgeschichtlich untersucht* (Uppsala: 1932).

53. Hylander's argumentation is extremely complicated and at points highly arbitrary in its conclusions. H. W. Hertzberg in his review of Hylander's work (*TLZ* 59 [1934] 226) says "Der Rezensent muss bekennen, noch nie ein Buch zur Besprechung durchgearbeitet zu haben, das ihn auch nur annähernd so viel Geduldsaufwand gekostet hat wie dieses."

54. He views this layer as having originated in the priestly circles at Anathoth to which Abiathar fled after being expelled by Solomon (ibid., 301).

55. Hylander views this layer as emanating from an elohistic circle in the time of Jeremiah (ibid., 237, 238).

56. Ibid., 130, 131.

inevitable conclusion of this approach for I Samuel 12 is that it comes to be regarded as a composite of at least two originally separate traditions which have been fused together by the compiler of the book.

b. H. Seebass

H. Seebass views I Samuel 12 as a construction of the deuteronomistic historian designed to portray kingship as an unnecessary and superfluous institution, the establishment of which was motivated by the desire of Israel to be like the other nations.[57]

Seebass suggests that the deuteronomist utilized an older tradition in I Samuel 12:1-15, but in doing so he significantly altered its original sense, especially by removing a statement of the "law of the king" and replacing it with a resumé of the righteous acts of Yahweh which is now contained in verses 6-12. In Seebass's opinion the original form of I Samuel 12:1-15 was found by the deuteronomist in a different setting (i.e., between vv. 24 and 25 of I Samuel 10), and was part of a narrative strand which was primarily interested in showing how the request for a king led to the formulation of the "law of the king" in connection with the inauguration of Saul.[58]

Seebass suggests that verses 16-25 were modeled after I Samuel 7:5-12 and attached to verses 1-15 by the deuteronomist in order to emphasize that even though Yahweh consented to the establishment of kingship, the request for a king was a sin against Yahweh, and earthly kingship was a heathen institution which did not properly belong to Israel's essence as a nation.[59]

---

57. H. Seebass, "Traditionsgeschichte von 1 Sam 8, 10:17 ff. und 12," *ZAW* 77 (1965) 286-296 (esp. 288-292). See also by the same author: "I Sam 15 als Schlüssel für das Verständnis der sogenannten königsfreundlichen Reihe I Sam 9:1–10:16; 11:1-15; und 13:2–14:52," *ZAW* 78 (1966) 148-179; and, "Die Vorgeschichte der Königserhebung Sauls," *ZAW* 79 (1967) 155-171.

58. Seebass, *ZAW* 77 (1965) 288-292; *ZAW* 79 (1967) 170, 171.

59. Seebass, *ZAW* 77 (1965) 289, 292-295.

4. Provisional conclusion.

As can be seen from the above summary of positions, the unity of I Samuel 12 has had many advocates, including representatives of widely differing approaches to the literary criticism of I Samuel 8–12 as a whole. Those who regard the chapter as containing expansions of a deuteronomistic editor admittedly find it difficult to distinguish the deuteronomistic additions from the earlier material, and the more recent advocates of this position have given up the attempt to identify precisely the alleged deuteronomistic additions. Those who suggest that large segments of the chapter are secondary, or that the chapter is composed of originally separate traditions engage in highly speculative reconstructions of the text which give insufficient weight to the chapter's inner unity in its present form. We will discuss these questions further in Chapter IV, Section 2,B when we consider the implications which a form critical analysis of the chapter has for its literary unity.

B. I Samuel 11:14-15

Aside from the position which considers I Samuel 11:14-15 to be an original and integral part of I Samuel 11 f., and the beginning of the authentic record of the assembly of all Israel at Gilgal[60] which was called together by Samuel to "renew the kingdom" (regardless of how this phrase may be interpreted),[61] there is nearly a consensus among scholars that verse 14 represents a redactor's effort to harmonize the contents of verse 15 with the account of Saul's selection to be king by sacred lot at Mizpah contained in I Samuel 10:17 ff. Verse 15 is then generally considered to contain the most credible of the two (or three) versions of how Saul became king which are alleged to be contained in the narratives of I Samuel 8–12.

---

60. See, e.g., Goslinga, *Het Eerste Boek Samuël*, COT, 17-60, 240-242, and the other authors mentioned in n. 9 above.

61. See above, Chapter II, 61 ff.

The extent of the redactional insertion is, however, a matter of dispute. Some investigators regard the entirety of verses 12-14 as redactional, while others confine the redactor's work to the phrase "renew the kingdom" in verse 14.

An alternate position is to view I Samuel 11:12-14(15) or I Samuel 11:14-15 as a whole to be an originally separate tradition which has been linked to Saul's Ammonite victory.[62]

1. I Samuel 11:14 as a redactional introduction to I Samuel 11:15.

a. Entirety of I Samuel 11:12-14 as redactional.[63]

1) *J. Wellhausen.*—J. Wellhausen who was the most influential advocate of the documentary approach to I Samuel 8-12 maintained that, "the renewal of the kingdom (xi. 14), after a month's interval, is a transparent artifice of the author of viii. 10, 17 seq. to incorporate in his own narrative the piece which he had borrowed from some other quarter [i.e., 11:1-11]: the verses xi. 12-14 are due to him."[64]

2) *H. P. Smith.*—In a similar way H. P. Smith, who isolated a "Sm. source" and a "Sl. source" in I Samuel 8-12, claims that while not many redactional alterations were made in the fusing of these two documents, "the most marked is 11:12-14 where the proposition to *renew* the kingdom is a concession to the other document."[65] He says further, "the

---

62. There is not necessarily a contradiction between this position and that of those mentioned in n. 60 above, although none of the above mentioned scholars have advocated it.

63. One must remember that our concern is with the vv. 14 and 15 and thus we will not enter into discussion of problems related to vv. 12 and 13. Various authors, as will appear, consider vv. 12-14 as redactional, constituting a bridge between I Sam. 10:17-27 and I Sam. 11:15. Sometimes it is not clear whether these authors consider these verses as pure fiction simply to form the bridge or whether some historical reality lies behind them. In addition it should be noted that the line between our categories a and b is in certain cases not to be drawn too rigidly (cf. Driver's view below).

64. Wellhausen, *Prolegomena*, 250, 251. See also, idem, *Composition*, 241. Here he comments, "die Erneuerung des Königtums v. 14 ist eine höchst durchsichtige Naivität des Verfassers von Kap. 8, 10, 17-27. Kap. 12, der auf diese Weise das ältere Stück Kap. 11. seiner Version einverleibte."

65. Smith, *Samuel*, ICC, xxii. It seems clear that Smith considers vv. 12 and

word *renew* the kingdom is a palpable allusion to the preceding account and therefore redactional."[66]

Similar positions are also advocated by Budde,[67] Schulz,[68] Caird,[69] and Birch.[70]

3) *H. Gressmann.*—As we noted above, Hugo Gressmann rejects a documentary approach to the narratives of I Samuel 8-12, and advocates a "fragmentary approach."[71] Nevertheless, his assessment of the literary character of I Samuel 11:12-14 is in basic agreement with the above mentioned advocates of the documentary approach. In Gressmann's view I Samuel 11:1-11, 15 is an independent tradition unit representing the only "Geschichtserzählung" about the rise of the Israelite kingship contained in I Samuel 8-12. In its present form he regards it as a continuation of the story in I Samuel 9:1-10:16, but he maintains that the two stories originally had nothing to do with each other.[72]

In Gressmann's view after the Ammonites were punished for their presumption, the thankful people crowned their conquering leader in Gilgal. He notes that the Hebrew text of verse 15 does not mention the participation of Samuel in the establishment of Saul as king, and maintains that in the original narrative nothing separated verses 11 and 15, so that verses 12-14 are to be regarded as a secondary insertion. Gressmann says nothing further, however, concerning the origin of this secondary material. Concerning verse 15, and its relation to I Samuel 9:1-10:16 he comments: "Wäre ein innerer Zusammenhang vorhanden, so hätte ein Hinweis auf die heimliche Salbung nicht fehlen dürfen; mindestens hätte

13 also to be the redactor's attempt to tie the two sources together (cf. 10:17). It seems probable that, for example, Gressmann, Bentzen, et. al. have a similar view of vv. 12 and 13.

  66. Ibid., 80.
  67. Budde, *Die Bücher Samuel*, KHC, 73, 76; and *ZAW* 8 (1888) 227.
  68. Schulz, *Samuel*, EH, 176, 177.
  69. Caird, *IB*, II, 940.
  70. Birch, *The Rise of the Israelite Monarchy*, 99-105.
  71. See above, Section 1,A,1,c,1).
  72. Gressmann, *Die älteste Geschichtsschreibung*, SAT, II/1, 43.

Samuel den Saul krönen müssen, wie die griechische Übersetzung (v. 15) mit Recht empfunden, aber mit Unrecht gelesen
hat."[73]

4) *H. Wildberger.*—In H. Wildberger's analysis[74] of the
narratives of Saul's rise to kingship, I Samuel 11 is regarded
as a separate and reliable tradition unit, but misplaced in the
present narrative sequence. Wildberger maintains that I Samuel 11 should precede the narratives of I Samuel 8–10, and
asserts that the victory over the Ammonites could have
occurred years if not decennia prior to Saul's elevation to
kingship.[75] According to Wildberger I Samuel 11:1-11 pic-
tures Saul in the likeness of the charismatic leaders of the
period of the judges, and after his victory over the Ammonites he became an obscure farmer again. Then, when the
Philistine crisis arose, the elders in consultation with Samuel
turned to Saul and entrusted him with a greater task, that of
the kingship. In order to advance this theory, Wildberger
must propose some explanation for the material in I Samuel
11:12-15 which stands in contradiction with this picture of
the course of events. He does this by characterizing I Samuel
11:12-14 as a redactional insertion intended to link I Samuel
11 (in its at present misplaced position) with I Samuel 10:
17 ff. especially verse 27.[76] Verse 15 he regards as the continuation of the old tradition, but he theorizes that something
has been eliminated from the original account between
verses 11 and 15 which explained the long process by which
Saul had risen from the position of an obscure farmer to that
of the kingship.

Wildberger's reconstruction results in the conclusion that
although it now appears in the text of I Samuel 11 that Saul
was made king in Gilgal directly after the victory at Jabesh,
in actuality there was a long interval involving other impor-

---

73. Ibid., cf. above, Chapter II, 85 ff.
74. Wildberger, *ThZ* 13 (1957) 442-469.
75. Ibid., 466, 467.
76. Ibid., 449, cf., Chapter II, n. 19.

tant historical developments (including the rise of the Philistine threat) between this victory and Saul's being made king.[77]

5) *G. Wallis.*—As we noted above G. Wallis, as many others, discerns three separate traditions of Saul's selection as king contained in the narratives of I Samuel 8-12. Yet, unlike many others, Wallis rejects the supposition that these three traditions represent three divergent but parallel accounts. He instead advances the idea that Saul did not become king over *all* Israel *simultaneously,* and that the narratives of I Samuel 8-12 indicate that individual tribes at different times: a) anointed him to be *nagid* (Ephraim, I Sam. 9:1-10:16); b) acclaimed him as king after victory in battle (armies of Jabesh and Gilead, I Samuel 11); and c) elevated him to be king by sacred lot (Benjamin, I Sam. 10:17-21). Each of these three actions Wallis claims were later represented as involving all Israel, and because the compiler did not want to eliminate any of them, they were connected and harmonized.[78]

With regard to I Samuel 11, Wallis maintains that the acclamation of Saul to be king after the victory at Jabesh originally took place in Jabesh itself, and that it was only at a later time associated with Gilgal (I Sam. 11:15) where other traditions of Saul's life were preserved.[79] He accordingly regards I Samuel 11:12-14 as a redactional insertion and says that the expression "renew the kingdom" as well as the indication of Samuel's involvement in the crowning of Saul are disturbing in the context of the spontaneous acclamation of the people, by which Saul was made their king after his striking military victory at Jabesh.[80]

---

77. Ibid., 468.
78. Wallis, *WZ* 12 (1963) 239-247.
79. Ibid., 243.
80. Wallis, *Geschichte und Überlieferung,* 74, 75.

b. The phrase "renew the kingdom" (verse 14) as redactional.

1) *S. R. Driver.* —S. R. Driver who views I Samuel 8-12 as a composite of two independent documentary sources regards the expression "renew the kingdom" of I Samuel 11:14 as a redactional adjustment made for the purpose of harmonizing I Samuel 11:15 with I Samuel 10:17 ff. He is not certain whether I Samuel 11:12, 13 should also be regarded as redactional, saying, "perhaps 11:12 f. are inserted likewise; but the precise relation of these verses to 10:25-27a is uncertain."[81]

2) *R. Press.* —R. Press considers the material in I Samuel 1-15 to be derived from three different independent tradition complexes whose origins he ascribes to priestly, royal, and prophetic circles respectively. He regards I Samuel 11 as a unity and while he sees a certain disharmony in verses 12 and 13, he finds explicit altering only in the phrase "renew the kingdom" (v. 14) which he attributes to a redactor's attempt to link I Samuel 10:17 ff. and I Samuel 11 in a temporal sequence.[82]

3) *K. Möhlenbrink.* —K. Möhlenbrink maintains that Saul's victory over the Ammonites recorded in I Samuel 11 was originally the victory of only three tribes (Gad, Reuben, and Benjamin) rather than that of all Israel. He argues that Gilgal had once been the cultic center of these three tribes, before it was replaced by the prominence of Shechem and Shiloh. With the disintegration of the twelve tribe league, the campaign of Saul against the Ammonites represents for Möhlenbrink the restitution of the old amphictyony of Gilgal in a time of crisis. In connection with this he views the "core" of I Samuel 11:14 to be historical. That is, he consid-

---

81. Driver, *Introduction,* 176. A very similar view is expressed by Pfeiffer (*Introduction*, 364).

82. R. Press, "Der Prophet Samuel. Eine traditionsgeschichtliche Untersuchung," *ZAW* 56 (1938) 177-225 (esp. 204-205).

ers it likely that Samuel did issue an invitation to assemble at Gilgal after the victory of the three tribes over the Ammonites. But he regards the expression "renew the kingdom" and also the indication that this gathering involved all Israel as secondary accretions. His view is that the summons to assemble was issued to only the part of Israel in which Samuel enjoyed esteem, namely Ephraim and Manasseh, and that the significance of this is to be seen in assuming that this was an attempt by Samuel to erase the old opposition between the Gilgal confederation and the Shiloh confederation, when the latter no longer functioned, by reestablishing a tribal league centered in Gilgal.[83]

4) *M. Noth.*—M. Noth regards the phrase "renew the kingdom" as the attempt of the deuteronomistic historian to harmonize I Samuel 11:15 and I Samuel 10:17-27.[84] He views I Samuel 11:15 as the authentic record of Saul's establishment as king and I Samuel 10:17-27 as a later construction of the deuteronomistic historian. He comments: the original sense of I Samuel 11:14, 15 "musste Dtr mit Rücksicht auf 10, 17ff. verwischen durch die unmotivierte und unbeholfene Bemerkung, dass es sich jetzt nur noch um eine 'Erneuerung des Königtums' gehandelt habe."[85]

5) *A. Weiser.*—A. Weiser, as we have seen above, views I Samuel 8-12 as the combination of dissimilar literary traditions which originated in different localities, but which have been placed side by side without extensive adjustment of their differences. He accordingly considers the accounts of Saul's rise to kingship in I Samuel 10:17-26 and I Samuel 10:27-11:15 to be parallel accounts, the former deriving from Mizpah and the latter from Gilgal. The collector linked the two traditions by designating Saul's inauguration in Gilgal

83. K. Möhlenbrink, "Sauls Ammoniterfeldzug und Samuels Beitrag zum Königtum des Sauls," *ZAW* 58 (1940) 57-70.

84. Noth, *Überlieferungsgeschichtliche Studien,* 54-59; and, *The History of Israel,* 167-173.

85. Noth, *Überlieferungsgeschichtliche Studien,* 59, n. 2.

as a "renewing of the kingdom."[86] In spite of this editorial subordination of the Gilgal tradition to the Mizpah tradition, Weiser regards I Samuel 10:27-11:15 as preserving the oldest material concerning Saul's rise to kingship, so that it presents, in his opinion, a closer approximation of the actual historical events than the traditions of chapters 8 and 10.[87]

6) *H. W. Hertzberg.*—H. W. Hertzberg, much like Weiser, regards I Samuel 8-12 as the combination of a variety of traditions preserved in different localities. He says that occasionally the hand of the compiler is evident in ordering and connecting his material, and the description of the enthronement in Gilgal as a "renewal of the kingdom" is one such instance.[88] According to Hertzberg this was originally not a renewal but rather the institution of kingship.[89]

2. *I Samuel 11:12-14(15) as part of an originally separate tradition.*

a. Th. C. Vriezen

Th. C. Vriezen feels that the great mistake made in literary critical research on the Samuel books is that pentateuchal criticism has often been the starting point, and this has brought with it the search for the J and E sources. In Vriezen's view I and II Samuel are a great political-historical work that describe and defend the right of David's descendants to the throne of Israel as successors of Saul. He feels that the literary analysis of the books must begin with the "succession narrative" contained in II Samuel 11-I Kings 2. This succession history is, however, tied to a history of David, which is tied to a history of David's relationship to Saul, which in turn is tied to the stories of Saul's rise to the kingship.

---

86. Weiser, *Samuel,* FRLANT, 69, 78.
87. Ibid., 78. See also Weiser's earlier discussion of the composition of I Samuel in *The Old Testament. Its Formation and Development,* 163, 165-170.
88. Hertzberg, *I and II Samuel,* 133.
89. Ibid., 94.

Vriezen finds great difficulties in the Saul narratives and concludes that the origin of Saul's kingship is told in three separate versions (I Sam. 9:1–10:16; 10:17 ff., and 11). In Vriezen's opinion I Samuel 11:1-11, 15 was part of the original Saul-David-Solomon narrative. The other two accounts of the rise of kingship were worked into the present narrative at different times in the process of the gradual enlargement and modification of the original Saul-David-Solomon history. I Samuel 11:12-14 was in Vriezen's opinion originally tied to the complex of traditions now found in I Samuel 7; 8; 10:17 ff.; 11:12-14; 15. This Samuel-Saul history was worked into the beginning of the Saul-David complex by placing I Samuel 7 and 10:17 ff. before I Samuel 11:1-11 while I Samuel 11:12-14 which tells of the confirmation at the Gilgal sanctuary of the previous selection of Saul to be king (at Mizpah), was given a place before the old Gilgal tradition of the original story (I Sam. 11:15). In this way the noticeable splitting of the verses I Samuel 10:27 and I Samuel 11:12-14 are explained in a natural manner, and the expression "renew the kingdom" (I Sam. 11:14) is explained by its connection with the Mizpah tradition of I Samuel 10:17-27.[90]

b. H. Seebass

H. Seebass subjects the narratives of I Samuel 1–15 to a drastic rearrangement in the course of which he separates I Samuel 11:1-11 from I Samuel 11:12-15 and places them in widely divergent historical contexts. He views Saul's victory over the Ammonites (I Sam. 11:1-11 as the first sign in a long time that Yahweh was again ready to help his people. Subse-

---

90. Vriezen, "Compositie," in *Orientalia Neerlandica,* 167-189 (esp. 172, 173, 177, 181). Note that Vriezen's position requires the interpretation of the phrase "renew the kingdom" (I Sam. 11:14) as a "confirmation" ("bevestiging," 181) of the Mizpah ceremony (see, however, above, Chapter II, 62 ff.). Cf. also Th. C. Vriezen, A. S. van der Woude, *Literatuur van Oud-Israël* (Wassenaar: 1973⁴) 207-213, where Vriezen in broad lines maintains the position developed in 1948.

quent to this victory a Philistine threat arose and Samuel who
was a judge in the Bethel, Gilgal, and Mizpah circuit, anointed Saul as *nagid* with the instruction that he was to defeat
the Philistines (I Sam. 9:1-10:16). To the Israelites' surprise
Saul defeated the Philistines in a first encounter at Geba
(I Sam. 13:4). Later he was victorious over the Philistines at
Michmash in a manner which could only be described as a
miracle of Yahweh (I Sam. 13:5-14:23). It was only then, in
Seebass's opinion, that the elders of Israel sought to give the
nagid-calling of Saul a political form by establishing a kingdom (I Sam. 8). Since the land was freed from the threat of
the Philistines, Samuel could call an assembly in Mizpah in
order to obligate the people to the "law of the king" (I Sam.
10:17-25). After this the people elevated Saul to be king in
Gilgal (I Sam. 11:12-15). Seebass thus avoids designating
I Samuel 11:12-15 as redactional, but he does place the
events recorded in these verses in an entirely different historical context than they presently occupy in I Samuel 11.[91]

c. N. Gottwald

N. Gottwald[92] views I Samuel 11 as an erratic bloc of
material that does not fit smoothly into either what he terms
the "Gilgal" or "the Mizpah-Ramah" story clusters which tell
of the rise of the Israelite kingship. Therefore he regards
I Samuel 11:12-15 as a third version of the enthronement of
Saul which the deuteronomistic compiler had at his disposal
in addition to the Gilgal story (I Sam. 9:1-10:16; 13:1-
14:46)[93] and the Mizpah-Ramah story (I Sam. 7:3-12; 8:1-
22; 10:17 ff.; 12; 15). He concedes that I Samuel 11:1-11
may have belonged to the Gilgal source, aiming to demon-

---

91. Seebass, *ZAW* 79 (1967) 164-169, cf. above, p. 113. Seebass' position
bears certain similarities to those of Wildberger (see p. 117 f. above) and Wallis
(see p. 118 above).

92. Gottwald, *Encyclopedia Judaica*, XXIV, 793-796.

93. Gottwald links this material to Gilgal because of the reference to Gilgal
in 10:8 and the offering of sacrifices by Saul at Gilgal to initiate the war against
the Philistines (13:4, 8 ff.).

strate Saul's inspired military prowess against the Ammonites preparatory to his attacks on the more powerful Philistines. Yet he says that I Samuel 11:12-15 can only be understood as another version of how Saul was made king. The disruption of the story line, he feels is only partially reduced by the harmonizing reference of the redactor, "Let us go to Gilgal and there renew the kingdom."

d. H. J. Stoebe

H. J. Stoebe does not consider I Samuel 11:12-15 originally to have been part of the account of Saul's victory over the Ammonites contained in I Samuel 11:1-11. He considers it also unlikely that I Samuel 11:12, 13 were originally connected with I Samuel 10:27 because of differences in the choice of words and nuance of meaning. And he considers verses 12 and 13 to be subordinate and supplementary to verse 14 and perhaps to verses 14 and 15. Stoebe finds it very difficult, however, to establish the origin of the tradition contained in the latter two verses. He comments that this tradition can not have arisen too late. He considers the "contorted" and in itself impossible use of חדש to be an indication that an old tradition or at least the memory of an old tradition is represented here. He then comments that this points to a parallelism between these verses and I Samuel 10:17 ff. which is difficult to explain. He rejects the explanation that the one tradition concerns the selection of Saul to be king (I Sam. 10:17 ff.), while the other relates the confirmation or celebration of his kingship (I Sam. 11:14-15). He concludes that I Samuel 11:14-15 show the strength of the memory that the root of the kingship of Saul lay in his charismatic leadership, and in addition that Samuel played an important role as a prophetic figure in Saul's rise to kingship; this memory stood in Stoebe's opinion in close connection with the Benjaminite sanctuary in Gilgal. Stoebe concludes that because originally parallel accounts have been coordinated to a sequence, a type of temporal succession has been developed in the present narrative behind which one cannot go in order to reconstruct the actual course of historical events.[94]

e. E. Robertson

As was noted above[95] Edward Robertson considers I Samuel 1-15 to be the work of a compiler who has linked a number of literary fragments and his own *supplementa* into a unified literary document. He points out that each of the six sections into which he divides I Samuel 1-15 is either concluded or introduced by what he terms the *supplementa.* These *supplementa* contain brief summary notes or additional bits of information. In the MT they are invariably separated from the preceding and following section by ‫ ס‬or ‫ פ‬.[96] Robertson comments, "So far as the *supplementa* are concerned, the paragraphs so distinguished, appear to be independent pieces of information with no intimate connection with the preceding text and would seem to be drawn from other sources."[97] Robertson considers I Samuel 11 to be a subdivision of the fourth of the six major sections into which he divides I Samuel 1-15. The beginning of this subdivision he places at I Samuel 11:1, and he designates verses 14 and 15 as a *supplementum.* He notes that these two verses are isolated before and behind respectively by ‫ פ‬and ‫ ס‬, and he regards them as the conclusion to the subsection, with I Samuel 12 as the conclusion to the whole of his fourth section of the book (I Samuel 8-12).[98]

94. Stoebe, *Das erste Buch Samuelis,* KAT, 228, 229, see further comments on pages 177, 178.
95. See above 99 f.
96. See, E. Würthwein, *The Text of the Old Testament* (Oxford: 1957) 16. How much significance is to be attached to these markings is difficult to determine.
97. Robertson, *Samuel and Saul,* 17.
98. Ibid., 20.

3. Provisional conclusion.

I Samuel 11:14, especially the expression "renew the kingdom," has rather generally been regarded by critical scholars as a redactor's attempt to harmonize I Samuel 11:15 with I Samuel 10:17 ff. As was noted above (cf. Chapter II, 61-68, 85-88) the expression "renew the kingdom" is admittedly puzzling if it is to apply to the kingdom of Saul. How is it to be satisfactorily related to the subsequent phrase in verse 15 that "they made Saul king in Gilgal?" What is the explanation for the appropriateness or necessity of a "renewal" of Saul's kingdom at this particular time?

It is our contention, however, that the phrase in question does not have reference to the kingdom of Saul, but rather to the kingdom of Yahweh, and there is accordingly no necessity to regard it as a redactional attempt to harmonize I Samuel 11:15 with I Samuel 10:17 ff., nor is there sufficient warrant for considering I Samuel 11:14, 15 to be one of several separate accounts in I Samuel 8-12 which reflect a gradual extension of Saul's dominions.[99] I Samuel 10:17 ff. is an account of Saul's selection to be king, while I Samuel 11:15 has reference to Saul's inauguration which took place in Gilgal as part of a ceremony in which the people not only made Saul their king (v. 15), but also renewed their allegiance to Yahweh as the supreme authority over the nation.[100]

The other alternative which has been suggested by a few scholars is to regard I Samuel 11:12-14(15) as a separate tradition unit in which "renew" is understood as meaning "celebrate" or "confirm." This suggestion (Vriezen, Seebass), however, does not do justice to the meaning of חדשׁ,[101] and when verse 15 is also included as part of the separate tradi-

---

99. Cf. the views of Wildberger, p. 117 above and Seebass, p. 122 f. above.

100. See above Chapter II.

101. See above Chapter II, 61-68.

tion unit (Seebass), the tension remains between חדש and the subsequent phrase, "they made Saul king in Gilgal."[102]

Section 2
The Structure of I Samuel 11:14-12:25

A. The relationship of I Samuel 11:14-15 to I Samuel 12:1-25.

As we have noted above there is nearly universal agreement among scholars that I and II Samuel show evidence of having been written by someone who utilized a greater or lesser variety of sources for the composition of his historical narrative. In certain places it appears that these source materials were incorporated into the narrative by the author with little or no modification of their original form. The resulting unevenness in the narrative flow has occasioned certain problems of interpretation and contributed to many elaborate theories on the literary origins of the book. While it is indisputable that the author utilized different sources in his composition and that in places this causes certain difficulties in interpretation, it is quite a different matter to conclude, as some have, that the final form of the book includes contradictory parallel accounts of the same event which the author has attempted to link together in a sequential fashion. It is our contention that a proper analysis of the content of the book does not lead one to such a conclusion, and in particular that the narratives of I Samuel 8-12 do not lend support to such a theory.

Nevertheless the fact remains that when one examines the pericopes of the books of Samuel with a view to establishing their mutual relationships, one must consider the possibility that the author has utilized more than one source in his description of a given historical event.

I Samuel 11:14-12:25 provides a good illustration of this

---

102. See above, Chapter II, 85-88.

point. It seems quite apparent that the author intended the
reader to conclude that Samuel's words to "all Israel" contained in I Samuel 12:1 ff. were spoken on the occasion of
the assembly called to "renew the kingdom" at Gilgal which
is introduced in I Samuel 11:14.[103] I Samuel 12 begins with
no additional time or place designation, but simply relates
what Samuel said to a national gathering. Had·it been the
author's intent to separate the assembly described in I Samuel 12 from the Gilgal assembly referred to in I Samuel
11:14-15, it is only reasonable to assume that he would have
inserted some indication that I Samuel 12 was descriptive of
a separate occasion.[104]

Furthermore, when one studies the content of I Samuel
12 it becomes apparent that it is complementary to that of
I Samuel 11:14-15. In I Samuel 12 there are two subordinate
matters which receive special attention. First, there is the
establishment of Samuel's covenant faithfulness in his past
leadership of the nation (I Sam. 12:1-5), as well as an indication of his continuing role in the future (I Sam. 12:23) as the
human kingship assumes its legitimate place in the structure
of the theocracy (I Sam. 12:13). Secondly, there is the people's confession of their sin particularly as this related to
their wrongly motivated desire for a king. These two foci of
attention, namely transition in leadership and confession of
sin, are both set in the context of Samuel's forceful challenge
to the people to renew their allegiance to Yahweh, which is

103. On the basis of literary critical considerations the events of I Sam. 12
have often been assigned to Mizpah in spite of the indications in the context to
the contrary. See, e.g.: Nowack, *Richter, Ruth und Bücher Samuelis,* HK I/4, 52;
Hertzberg, *I and II Samuel,* 97.

104. See further the comments of Goslinga (*Het Eerste Boek Samuël,* COT,
243) who notes that the time factor is also a significant consideration. After the
victory over the Ammonites the Israelites could expect a counter action by the
Philistines. "Israël moest zich gereedmaken voor de strijd tegen de erfvijand en
onderdrukker en zo mogelijk de eerste slag toebrengen. Aan te nemen is dan ook
dat de gebeurtenissen van cap. 11v, zeer spoedig door die van cap. 13 gevolgd
zijn."

the dominating and major emphasis of the chapter (I Sam. 12:14, 15, 20, 24, 25).

The foci of attention in I Sam. 11:14-15 parallel those of I Samuel 12. I Samuel 11:14-15 speaks of an assembly at which transition in leadership was formalized with the inauguration of Saul (I Sam. 11:15a), and fellowship with Yahweh was restored with the sacrificing of peace offerings (I Samuel 11:15b).[105] All of this was done in an assembly called for the primary purpose of renewing allegiance to Yahweh (I Sam. 11:14).

I Samuel 12 differs from I Samuel 11:14-15 in that while both pericopes are concerned with transition in national leadership, this transition is seen in I Samuel 12 in a discussion of the past and future role of Samuel in the life of the nation, as well as in the indication that the human kingship was now to occupy a legitimate place in the new order of the theocracy, while it is seen in I Samuel 11:14-15 in the reference to the act of the formal investiture of Saul (v. 15a). In addition, while both pericopes are concerned with the matter of restoration of fellowship with Yahweh, this is indicated in I Samuel 11:15 by the reference to sacrificing of peace offerings, while it is indicated in I Samuel 12 by recounting the people's confession of their sin in requesting a king and their appeal to Samuel to intercede for them and by relating Samuel's reassuring (v. 20a, 22) and admonishing (v. 20b, 24, 25) words. It is then certainly reasonable to assume that in connection with their confession and Samuel's intercession, peace offerings were offered signifying and sealing the restoration of fellowship between Yahweh and his people.

Thus both I Samuel 11:14-15 and I Samuel 12 speak of an assembly which was convened to provide an occasion for the people of Israel to renew their allegiance to Yahweh at a

---

105. Cf. Ex. 24:5 f. and note the comment of Nic. H. Ridderbos (*De Psalmen,* II [KV; Kampen: 1973] 155) on Ps. 50:5 with regard to the peace offering: "... elk brengen van een (vrede) offer kan een vernieuwing van het verbond genoemd worden. ..." See above, Chapter II, 88-91.

time in which the need for restoration of fellowship with Yahweh was apparent, and kingship was being formally inaugurated.

It is accordingly our position that instead of regarding I Samuel 11:14 as a redactional attempt to connect I Samuel 11:15 with I Samuel 10:17 ff., it is much more appropriate to regard the brief resumé of the Gilgal ceremony contained in I Samuel 11:14-15 as a sort of "lead sentence" or "summarizing introduction" prefacing the more detailed account of the same Gilgal ceremony contained in I Samuel 12. While these two accounts are complementary and not contradictory, and while in their major emphases they agree, they nevertheless reflect differences in detail and formulation to an extent that suggests they must have had separate origins. The author of the book has utilized both however, in order to give a fuller although still not complete picture of what transpired at the Gilgal assembly.

It is for these reasons that we maintain that I Samuel 11:14-12:25 is best regarded as a composite unit descriptive of the important Gilgal ceremony where Israel renewed their allegiance to Yahweh. Whether or not I Samuel 11:14-15 was originally separate from I Samuel 11:1-13 is a question that cannot be answered with certainty. It is clear that the last phrase of I Samuel 11:13 brings the narrative of the Ammonite conflict to its conclusion, with the statement that "today Yahweh has accomplished deliverance in Israel." This statement also provides the basis for Samuel to call for an assembly at which the people can renew their allegiance to Yahweh and install Saul as their king. The Gilgal assembly is the sequel to the victory which Yahweh gave over the Ammonites under Saul's leadership, and is the final episode in the series of events which led to the establishment of kingship in Israel. Thus whether or not I Samuel 11:14-15 was originally a part of the narrative of I Samuel 11:1-13 is not of great importance, but it is important to recognize that it now serves as the introduction to I Samuel 12.

B. Structural Elements of I Samuel 12:1-25

Although clearer insight into the structural elements of I Samuel 12 and the inter-relationship of its parts may be gained by a form critical analysis of the chapter, it is nevertheless possible to divide the chapter into the following sections based on the exegetical observations given above.

The chapter as a whole presents Samuel's challenge to Israel to renew her allegiance to Yahweh on the occasion of the introduction of kingship into the socio-political structure of the nation.

I Samuel 12:1-5. Samuel secures a vindication of his own covenant faithfulness during the previous conduct of his office as he presents the one who is to assume the responsibilities of kingship.

I Samuel 12:6-12. Samuel utilizes a recapitulation of the righteous acts of Yahweh in the events of the exodus and the period of the judges in order to judicially establish Israel's apostasy in requesting a king.

I Samuel 12:13. Samuel indicates that in spite of this apostasy, Yahweh has chosen to utilize kingship as an instrument of his rule over his people.

I Samuel 12:14-15. By a restatement of the "covenant conditional" Samuel confronts Israel with her continuing obligation of total loyalty to Yahweh with the integration of human kingship into the structure of the theocracy.

I Samuel 12:16-22. A sign is given from heaven at Samuel's request serving to underscore the seriousness of Israel's apostasy in asking for a king to replace Yahweh (vv. 16-18a). This leads to a confession of sin (vv. 18b-19), a challenge to renewed covenant faithfulness (vv. 20, 21), and a reminder of the constancy of Yahweh's faithfulness to his people (v. 22).

I Samuel 12:23-25. Samuel describes his own continuing function in the new order (v. 23) and concludes his remarks with a repetition of Israel's central covenantal obligation (v. 24) reinforced by the threat of the covenant curse if Israel again apostasizes (v. 25).

IV

THE COVENANT FORM IN THE OLD TESTAMENT
AND I SAMUEL 11:14-12:25

Section 1
The Covenant Form in the Old Testament
A. The Covenant-Treaty Analogy

Ever since G. Mendenhall's ground breaking work, *Law and Covenant in Israel and the Ancient Near East*,[1] a great deal of attention has been devoted to the covenant form in the Old Testament.[2] Mendenhall's work demonstrated the correspondence between the structural elements of the second millennium B.C. Hittite suzerainty treaties[3] and certain cove-

---

1. G. E. Mendenhall, *Law and Covenant in Israel and the Ancient Near East* (Pittsburgh: 1955), reprinted from *BA* 17 (1954) 26-46, 49-76. Now also in, *The Biblical Archaeologist Reader* 3 (New York: 1970) 3-53.

2. The number of studies stimulated by Mendenhall's work is far too great to list here. See the comprehensive review by D. J. McCarthy (*Old Testament Covenant. A Survey of Current Opinions* [Richmond: 1972]), including the extensive bibliography on pages 90-108. See further the many literature citations in the remainder of this chapter. G. E. Wright (*The Old Testament and Theology* [New York: 1969] 106) comments: "During the years since the publication of Mendenhall's work, so many fresh studies of various aspects of Israel's covenant life have been stimulated that one must say that his thesis has been the single most suggestive and provocative hypothesis of this generation in Old Testament studies."

3. There have been a number of international treaties uncovered in the excavations at Boghazköi amid the ruins of the capitol of Hattusas and the royal archives of the Hittite empire. The treaties all derive from the new Hittite empire during the reigns of the "Great Kings," Suppiluliumas I, 1380-1346; Mursilis II, 1345-1315; Muwatallis, 1315-1296; Hattusilis III, 1289-1265; and Thudhaliyas IV, 1265-1235 (chronology taken from O. R. Gurney, *The Hittites* [Harmondsworth: 1969⁷] 216). The transcriptions and translations of these treaties may be found in various places, but unfortunately they have not been collected and made available in a single volume. See the following: D. D. Luckenbill, "Hittite Treaties and Letters," *AJSL* 37 (1921) 161-211; E. F. Weidner, *Politische Dokumente aus*

nantal passages in the Old Testament. In agreement with V. Korošec's[4] earlier juristic analysis of the Hittite treaty form, Mendenhall noted six basic elements in the composition of the treaty texts including: 1) preamble; 2) historical prologue; 3) stipulations; 4) provision for deposit in the temple and periodic public reading; 5) lists of gods as witnesses; 6) curses and blessings formula.[5] In addition to the written form, Mendenhall also noted other standard elements associated with the ratification of the treaty document including: 7) an oath by which the vassal pledged his obedience; 8) a solemn ceremony accompanying the oath; 9) a form for initiating procedure against a rebellious vassal.[6] The significance of Mendenhall's essay, however, lay primarily in its calling attention to the presence of many of these same

---

Kleinasien. Die Staatsverträge in akkadischer Sprache aus dem Archiv von Boghazköi (Boghazköi Studien, VIII and IX; Leipzig: 1923); J. Friedrich, "Staatsverträge des Hatti-Reiches in hethitischer Sprache," *MVÄG* 31/I (1926) and 34/I (1930); A. Goetze, trans., "Hittite Treaties," *ANET*, ed. J. B. Pritchard (Princeton: 1955²) 201-206.

Here it can also be noted that besides these Hittite treaties, there are also other treaties under discussion. Attention is given below to the treaties of Esarhaddon, which concern his succession, and the Aramaic treaties of Sefire. There are also other treaties (see, e.g., the enumeration of S. R. Külling, *Zur Datierung der "Genesis-P-Stücke"* [Kampen: 1964] 229-237, and R. Frankena "The Vassal Treaties of Esarhaddon and the Dating of Deuteronomy," *OTS*, XIV [1965] 122 f.) which did not appear necessary to discuss further.

4. V. Korošec, *Hethitische Staatsverträge. Ein Beitrag zu ihrer juristischen Wertung* (Leipziger Rechtswissenschaftliche Studien 60; Leipzig: 1931).

5. Mendenhall, *Law and Covenant*, 31-34. K. Baltzer (*The Covenant Formulary*, 9-18) gives a slightly different schema for the component parts of the treaty form in which he eliminates element four (provision for deposit and public reading) of Korošec and Mendenhall and inserts between element two (historical prologue) and element three (stipulations) what he terms a "statement of substance [*Grundsatzerklärung*] concerning the future relationship of the partners to the treaty." Baltzer's schema thus includes: 1) preamble; 2) antecedent history; 3) statement of substance; 4) specific stipulations; 5) invocation of gods as witnesses; 6) blessings and curses. In the opinion of this writer Baltzer's classification is an improvement over that of Korošec and Mendenhall because references to deposit and public reading are not constant enough in the extant Hittite treaties to warrant inclusion as a regular characteristic of the treaty form and because the "*Grundsatzerklärung*" expressing general imperatives for loyalty on the part of the treaty signatory is of such importance that it deserves a place in any schematization of the treaty form.

6. Mendenhall, *Law and Covenant*, 34-35.

elements in the Old Testament covenantal pericopes of Exodus 20 and Joshua 24.[7] Others following Mendenhall's lead have pointed out similar treaty-covenant parallels in numerous additional covenantal passages in the Old Testament, including, as most notable, the structure of the book of Deuteronomy.[8] The potential literary, exegetical, and theological implications of Mendenhall's thesis are many and it is to be expected that they will continue to receive a great deal of attention in the future.

It is beyond the scope of our investigation to enter into a lengthy discussion of the Old Testament concept of covenant, yet it is necessary to give some indication of the sense in which we use the word "covenant" when we speak of the "covenant form" in the Old Testament. In general it can be said that the term "covenant" (ברית) is used in the Old Testament to designate an arrangement between two parties which is established under sanctions,[9] and which involves

---

7. Ibid., 35-44.

8. See particularly: H. B. Huffmon, "The Covenant Lawsuit in the Prophets," *JBL* 78 (1959) 285-295; J. Muilenburg, "The Form and Structure of the Covenantal Formulations," *VT* 9 (1959) 347-365; Baltzer, *The Covenant Formulary;* F. C. Fensham, "Malediction and Benediction in Ancient Near Eastern Vassal-Treaties and the Old Testament," *ZAW* 74 (1962) 1-9; W. L. Moran, "The Ancient Near Eastern Background of the Love of God in Deuteronomy," *CBQ* 25 (1963) 77-87; F. C. Fensham "Clauses of Protection in Hittite Vassal-Treaties and the Old Testament," *VT* 13 (1963) 133-143; Kline, *Treaty of the Great King;* McCarthy, *Treaty and Covenant;* D. R. Hillers, *Treaty Curses and the Old Testament Prophets* (BibOr 16; Rome: 1964); J. A. Thompson, *The Ancient Near Eastern Treaties and the Old Testament* (London: 1964); idem, "The Near Eastern Suzerain-Vassal Concept in the Religion of Israel," *JRH* 3 (1964) 1-19; Külling, *Zur Datierung der "Genesis-P-Stücke";* J. Wijngaards, *Vazal van Jahweh* (Baarn: 1965); Kitchen, *Ancient Orient and Old Testament,* 90-102; Kline, *By Oath Consigned;* D. R. Hillers, *Covenant: The History of a Biblical Idea* (Baltimore: 1969); J. B. Payne, "The B'rith of Yahweh," in *New Perspectives on the Old Testament,* J. B. Payne, ed. (Waco: 1970) 240-264; C. L. Rogers, "The Covenant with Moses and its Historical Setting, *JETS* 14 (1971) 141-155; Kline, *The Structure of Biblical Authority.*

9. G. Vos (*Biblical Theology,* 277) points out that the only idea always present in the Old Testament use of the word b^erith is that of, "a solemn religious sanction" (see further, ibid., 33, 137-138). It is in this connection that the ratificatory oath assumes great importance in the biblical covenants. Indicative of this importance is the use of covenant (ברית) in parallelism with oath (אלה), and the expression "to make a covenant" (כרת ברית) in parallelism with "to swear"

certain specified obligations. Covenants are represented as being concluded between individuals (e.g., Gen. 21:22-34; 31:44-55; I Sam. 18:3; 23:18), between states or their representatives (e.g., Josh. 9; I Kings 15:19; 20:34), and most importantly between God and man (e.g., Gen. 15; 17; Ex. 19-24; II Sam. 7:4-17). From the wide variety of relationships for which בְּרִית is used in the Old Testament it is clear that while the above definition is valid as a generalization, further differentiation between various types of covenants is necessary.[10] This is apparent not only because בְּרִית is used of agreements between man and man on the one hand, and man and God on the other, but also because not every covenant in either of these categories is of an identical type. There is a noticeable difference, for example, between the covenants which Yahweh made with Abraham (Gen. 15; 17) and David (II Sam. 7:4-17) on the one hand, and the covenant he made with his people Israel at Sinai on the other (Ex. 19-24, Deut.). M. Kline, noting the distinction between these covenants, has designated the former as "promise covenants" and the latter as a "law covenant."[11] It is particularly, al-

---

(שׁבַע). See, e.g.: Gen. 26:28a, 31; Gen. 21:31, 32; Deut. 29:11(12), 13(14); Josh. 9:15; II Kings 11:4; Ezek. 17:13, 16, 18, 19. See further, G. M. Tucker, "Covenant Forms and Contract Forms," *VT* 15 (1965) 487-503, and particularly Kline, *By Oath Consigned,* 14-25, and Payne, "The B'rith of Yahweh," in *New Perspectives on the Old Testament,* 243, 244.

10. For extended discussions of the Old Testament concept of covenant see the following recent articles: M. Weinfeld, "בְּרִית," *TWAT,* I (1972) 781-808; idem, "Covenant," *Encyclopedia Judaica,* V, 1012-1022; E. Kutsch, "בְּרִית//berīt Verpflichtung," *THAT,* I (1971) 339-352; W. Eichrodt, "Covenant and Law: Thoughts on Recent Discussion," *Int* 20 (1966) 302-321; D. N. Freedman, "Divine Commitment and Human Obligation. The Covenant Theme," *Int* 18 (1964) 419-431; G. E. Mendenhall, "Covenant," *IDB,* I, 714-723; A. Jepsen, "Berith. Ein Beitrag zur Theologie der Exilszeit," in *Verbannung und Heimkehr* (Rudolph Festschrift, A. Kuschke, ed.; Tübingen: 1961) 161-179; G. Quell, "The OT Term בְּרִית," *TDNT,* II, 106-124. See further, E. Kutsch, *Verheissung und Gesetz. Untersuchungen zum sogenannten 'Bund' im Alten Testament* (BZAW 131; Berlin: 1973) and the extensive bibliography given by H. H. Rowley, in *Worship in Israel,* 31, n. 2.

11. M. Kline (*By Oath Consigned,* 13-19) points out that both of these types of covenants are sanction-sealed commitments to maintain a particular relationship, and that this commitment is expressed by an oath sworn in the covenant ratification ceremony. According to Kline it is in the swearing of the

though not exclusively,[12] the "law covenant" pericopes in the Old Testament to which parallels have been noted with extra-biblical vassal treaties. For the purpose of our discussion we include only covenantal pericopes of this type in our references to the covenant form in the Old Testament.

It is also not within our purpose to enter extensively into the intricacies of the treaty-covenant analogy discussions.[13] Some have questioned the validity of the analogy itself,[14] and

ratificatory oath that a means is provided for distinguishing a law covenant from a promise covenant. He maintains (16) that, "if God swears the oath of the ratification ceremony, that particular covenantal transaction is one of promise, whereas if man is summoned to swear the oath, the particular covenant thus ratified is one of law." In the opinion of this writer, Kline has pointed out an important distinction between these two types of covenants in the Old Testament although it is sometimes maintained that an oath was not foundational to the Sinaitic covenant (see, e.g., Mendenhall, *Law and Covenant,* 40). For Kline's treatment of this question as well as whether or not the Deuteronomic covenant was based on a bilateral oath, see, *By Oath Consigned,* 17-21. For Kline's discussion on the compatibility of the Sinaitic "law covenant" with the Abrahamic "promise covenant" see, ibid., 22-38. M. Weinfeld ("Covenant," *Encyclopedia Judaica,* V, 1018) makes a similar distinction between the Mosaic covenant and the Abrahamic-Davidic covenants, terming the former the "obligatory type" and the latter the "promissory type." In his article, "The Covenant of Grant in the Old Testament and in the Ancient Near East" (*JAOS* 90 [1970] 184-203) Weinfeld notes that while the covenant between Yahweh and Israel was based on the ancient Near East treaty pattern and is of the obligatory type, the covenants with Abraham and David are modeled on the "royal grant" the classical form of which is found in the Babylonian *kudurru* documents (boundary stones) but which occurs also among the Hittites and others, and is of the promissory type (cf. esp. 184-186).

    12. See, e.g., Külling, *Zur Datierung der "Genesis-P-Stücke,"* 228-249; and the more recent resumé of this dissertation by the same author, "The Dating of the So-Called 'P-Sections' in Genesis," *JETS* 15 (1972) 67-76.

    13. In the enormous volume of literature which has grown up around the treaty-covenant analogy in the past two decades, different directions have been taken in the assessment of its significance and the implications which may be drawn from it, even among those accepting the validity of the analogy. We will discuss these matters only in so far as they have a bearing on the covenantal character of I Sam. 11:14–12:25.

    14. See, e.g., the scepticism of A. Jepsen ("Berith," in *Verbannung und Heimkehr,* Rudolph Festschrift, 161, 175) based largely on his view that *berith* in the Old Testament designates an assurance or promise of God rather than a legal relationship. Cf., however, Eichrodt's (*Int* 20 [1966] 303-306) critical analysis of Jepsen's position. See further the negative attitude of C. F. Whitley ("Covenant and Commandment in Israel," *JNES* 22 [1963] 37-48) who says (37), "we may doubt if the Hittite treaties offer a close parallel to the Hebrew covenant." F. Nötscher ("Bundesformular und 'Amtsschimmel,' " *BZ* 9 [1965] 181-214) also raises serious ques-

others, while granting its presence elsewhere,[15] have denied the presence of the treaty pattern in the Old Testament passages which record the establishment of Yahweh's covenant with his people at Sinai (Ex. 19–24). Nevertheless, it is the opinion of this writer that compelling evidence exists that the treaty form is reflected in varying degrees in Old Testament passages concerned with *both* the establishment and perpetuation of the Sinaitic covenant between Yahweh and his people.[16]

tions concerning the treaty-covenant analogy, but cf., D. J. McCarthy's (*Der Gottesbund im Alten Testament* [Stuttgarter Bibelstudien 13; Stuttgart: 1967²] 37-40) critique of Nötscher's article. Note further the rejection of the parallel between treaty and covenant by L. Perlitt (*Bundestheologie im Alten Testament* [WMANT 36; Neukirchen-Vluyn: 1969]), but again see the extensive critical review of Perlitt's book by McCarthy ("bᵉrît in Old Testament History and Theology," *Bib* 53 [1972] 110-121).

15. See particularly D. J. McCarthy (*Treaty and Covenant*, 154) who finds only a remote resemblance to the treaty form in Exodus 19-24, although generally he is one of the leading defenders of the treaty-covenant analogy. McCarthy comments: "if our present text in Ex. 19 ff. does reflect the covenant form, it reflects it only remotely. . . . Moreover, we must ask ourselves how much of the resemblance to the covenant form is due to the present composite and rearranged text." Cf., however, the critique of McCarthy's position on this issue by Kline (*By Oath Consigned*, 38, n. 10) and Kitchen (*Ancient Orient and Old Testament*, 101, n. 53). G. Fohrer (*History of Israelite Religion* [New York: 1972] 80, 81) is also sceptical of the treaty-covenant analogy particularly with respect to the Sinai traditions. He says, "Quite apart from the fact that the word bᵉrît does not mean 'treaty, covenant,' there is really no parallelism: the Sinai tradition is not modeled after a treaty form."

16. For advocacy of the presence of the treaty form in Ex. 19-24 in addition to Mendenhall (*Law and Covenant*, 35-44) see: W. Moran ("Moses und der Bundesschluss am Sinai," *VD* 40 [1962] 3-17), and W. Beyerlin (*Origins and History of the Oldest Sinaitic Traditions*, 50-77). Beyerlin considers the treaty form to have had a formative influence on the various tradition units included in what he regards as the composite account of the establishment of the covenant at Sinai in Ex. 19-24. He says (54, 55), e.g., of the decalogue that, "the parallels between the above Hittite covenant-treaties and the Israelite Decalogue are so numerous and so striking that one can hardly avoid the view that the Ten Commandments are—formally—modeled on the covenant-form that is revealed in the vassal-treaties of the Hittites and was probably in general use in the Near East of the second millennium B.C." See further in a similar vein: Huffmon, *CBQ* 27 (1965) 101-113; Baltzer, *The Covenant Formulary*, 27-31; Hillers, *Covenant: The History of a Biblical Idea*, 46-71; J. A. Thompson, "The Cultic Credo and the Sinai Tradition," *RThR* 27 (1968) 53-64, esp. 55-56; Rogers, *JETS* 14 (1971) 141-155.

Apart from the discussion over the presence of the treaty form in Ex. 19-24

We will not here enter into detailed analyses of individual covenantal pericopes in order to demonstrate either the structural and terminological treaty-covenant parallels or the repetition of characteristic features of the Old Testament "covenant form" in various covenantal pericopes in the Old Testament. This has been detailed elsewhere and need not be repeated here.[17] A general indication of the results of these investigations is, however, necessary.

B. Characteristic Features of the Old Testament Covenant Form

In a number of instances investigators have simply utilized the literary pattern of the Hittite treaties as a structural model for elucidating the corresponding structural elements in various Old Testament covenantal pericopes.[18] Although this has sometimes been done with a rigidity which tends to

---

there is widespread agreement with regard to its presence in other passages which are concerned with the perpetuation of the Sinaitic covenant. The point of issue then becomes not the presence or absence of the treaty form in the Old Testament but rather the time of its origin and reason for its utilization in the covenantal traditions of the Old Testament. For further discussion of these questions, see below. For the present, however, note the comment of G. von Rad (*Old Testament Theology*, I, 132): "Comparison of ancient Near Eastern treaties, especially those made by the Hittites in the fourteenth and thirteenth centuries B.C., with passages in the Old Testament has revealed so many things in common between the two, particularly in the matter of the form, that there must be some connexion between these suzerainty treaties and the exposition of the details of Jahweh's covenant with Israel given in certain passages in the Old Testament. As a result, with particular passages and groups of passages, we may speak of a 'covenantal formulation,' in which the various formal elements found in the treaties recur feature for feature, though sometimes freely adapted to suit the conditions obtaining in Israel...." Cf. his similar comments in: *Deuteronomy, A Commentary* (London: 1966) 21-22. D. J. McCarthy comments (*Old Testament Covenant,* 14), "Despite many difficulties in detail, the evidence that Israel uses the treaty-form in some, at least, of its religious literature, and uses it to describe its special relationship with Yahweh is irrefragable. There is not another literary form from among those of the ancient Near East which is more certainly evident in the Old Testament. The question is, just where and at what stage of the tradition it is to be found."

17. See especially the literature cited in n. 8 above.

18. This has been done with minor variations by a number of scholars particularly with Ex. 19-24, the entire book of Deuteronomy, and Josh. 24. See, e.g.: Mendenhall, *Law and Covenant,* 35-44; Baltzer, *The Covenant Formulary,*

obscure the variations of the Biblical material from the treaty documents in a way that does not do justice to the unique-ness of the covenantal traditions of the Old Testament, it nevertheless has served to draw attention to the treaty-covenant parallel and to delineate a number of the character-istic features of the covenant form in the Old Testament. The following resumé of J. A. Thompson's and K. A. Kitchen's presentations of the correspondence between structural ele-ments of the treaty formulary and similar features in the composition of Exodus 19-24, Deuteronomy 1-32 and Joshua 24 illustrates this approach.[19]

1. Preamble: (Kitchen) Ex. 20:1; Deut. 1:1-5; Josh. 24:2. (Thompson) Ex. 19:3; 20:2a; Josh. 24:2a.
2. Historical prologue: (Kitchen) Ex. 20:2; Deut. 1:6-3:29; Josh. 24:2-13. (Thompson) Ex. 19:4; 20:2b; Deut. 1-4; Josh. 24:2b-13.
3. Statement of substance: (Kitchen) Ex. 20:3-17, 22-26; Deut. 4-11. (Thompson) Ex. 19:5a; 20:3; Deut. 5-11; Josh. 24:14.
4. Stipulations: (Kitchen) Ex. 21-23; Deut. 12-26; Josh. 24:14-15. (Thompson) Ex. 20:4-17; Deut. 12-26; Josh. 24:25.
5. Witnesses: (Kitchen) Ex. 24:4; Deut. 31:16-30; 31:26; 32:1-47; Josh. 24:22. (Thompson) ... Josh. 24:22, 27.

19-36; Kline, *Treaty of the Great King*, 13-49; McCarthy, *Treaty and Covenant*, 109-151 (excluding Ex. 19-24, see n. 15 above); Thompson, *The Ancient Near Eastern Treaties and the Old Testament*, 20-23; Hillers, *Covenant: The History of a Biblical Idea*, 46-71; Kitchen, *Ancient Orient and Old Testament*, 92-102.

It is also noteworthy that G. von Rad pointed out similarities in the struc-tural elements of Ex. 19 ff., Deuteronomy and Josh. 24 (*Das formgeschichtliche Problem des Hexateuchs* [BWANT 4/26; Stuttgart: 1938]) long before discus-sions of the treaty-covenant analogy were popular. Von Rad considered these similarities to be reflections of a cultic setting for the Sinai tradition which he localized in an ancient covenantal festival at Shechem. As was noted above (cf. n. 16) von Rad has more recently pointed out the relationship between the Old Testament covenantal formulations (including those of Ex. 19 ff., Deuteronomy, and Josh. 24) and the suzerainty treaty form.

19. Our resumé (with modified terminology) is taken from the works of Thompson and Kitchen as mentioned in n. 18 above and is representative merely of the basic skeleton of their presentations. They both give added details and discuss various problematic aspects of the parallels.

6. Curses and blessings: (Kitchen) Deut. 28:1-14, 15-68;
    Josh. 24:19-20. (Thompson) Ex. 19:5b, 6a; 20:5b, 6, 7b,
    12b; Deut. 27–30.

While there is value in such analyses for drawing attention
to the treaty-covenant analogy, the noting of recurring structural features in the Old Testament covenantal passages themselves is of far more importance, for this points to the
existence of a covenant form intrinsic to the Old Testament.
It is in this area that J. Muilenburg's work is of particular
value.[20] Muilenburg's analysis of Exodus 19:3-6 led him to
the conclusion that this passage, "is a special covenantal
Gattung, and it is scarcely too much to say that it is *in nuce*
the *fons et origo* of the many covenantal pericopes which
appear throughout the Old Testament."[21] Although Muilenburg notes that it is likely that the pattern distinguished in
Exodus 19:3-6 and other covenantal pericopes is an ancient
literary form and that its terminology and structure may be
derived from royal compacts or treaties, he is not interested
so much in the extra-biblical parallels as he is in tracing the
consistency of the covenant form in the Old Testament. He
does this with Exodus 19:3-6, Joshua 24, and I Samuel 12.
He concludes that although there is diversity in these passages
because covenant speech comes to include more varied and
richer terminology, and because the formulations are influenced by their particular settings, nevertheless the essential
features originally derived from Exodus 19:3-6 are often
reiterated.[22]

The features which Muilenburg presents as persistent in

---

20. Muilenburg, *VT* 9 (1959) 347-365.

21. Ibid., 352.

22. Muilenburg (ibid., 350-351, 360) ascribes priority to the Ex. 19:3-6
pericope over both Deuteronomy and Josh. 24. He says (350): "The Book of
Deuteronomy is the covenant book κατ᾽ ἐξοχὴν. But it comes to us as a 'second
law' and is based in its prevailing terminology upon the formulation of the
covenant in Ex. xix-xxiv. G. von Rad has shown convincingly that the general
structure of the two correspond." He says further (360) with regard to Josh. 24
that a "comparison of the relationship between the two passages favors the
priority of Ex. xxiv (*sic,* xix) 3b-6."

many covenant contexts include the following elements: 1) the presence of the covenant mediator; 2) the motif of the witness ("you have seen for yourselves"); 3) the pronounced I-Thou style; 4) the recital of the mighty acts; 5) the emphatic call to obedience; 6) the inclusion of apodictic requirements; 7) the conditional sentence; 8) the transitional *and now* (וְעַתָּה). He notes also that the deliverance from Egypt continues to be the decisive redemptive event (Josh. 24; Lev. 26:45; Deut. 8:11-20; 11:3-4; I Sam. 12, etc., etc.).[23]

It is the repeated occurrence of many of these features in Old Testament passages concerning either the establishment or the perpetuation of the Sinaitic covenant which legitimatizes the use of the term "covenant form" in the Old Testament.[24]

---

23. Ibid., 355-356. As can readily be seen there is an overlap between the features which Muilenburg finds to be characteristic of the covenantal formulations in the Old Testament and the features of the treaty form outlined above (note particularly Muilenburg's features 4, 5, 6 and 7).

24. We are using the term "form" here in the broad sense of a literary category characterized by certain structural and terminological features: or in certain instances of elements of such a category combined in different ways. We have refrained from using the more technical term *Gattung* because of the variety and freedom which is apparent in the adaptation of what we have labeled as "covenant form" to different uses in the Old Testament. Various distinctions can be made between the divergent uses of the covenant form according to the particular purpose and setting of a given passage (e.g., covenant lawsuit, covenant renewal account, etc., see further below). Baltzer (*The Covenant Formulary*, 38) believes that on the basis of his analysis of Josh. 24, Ex. 19-24, and Deuteronomy, "it is possible to say that the covenant formulary, as a literary type, was familiar in Israel." In the remainder of his book he attempts to show, "the ways in which this formulary was employed and transformed." Von Rad (*Theology of the Old Testament*, I, 132) concludes, as we noted above, that as a result of the correspondence between treaty and covenant forms it is possible with particular Old Testament passages and groups of passages to "speak of a 'covenantal formulation,' in which the various formal elements found in the treaties recur feature for feature though sometimes freely adapted to suit the conditions obtaining in Israel." Nötscher (*BZ* 9 [1965] 205) concludes: "Ein Bundesformular mag es in Israel gegeben haben, wie auch Baltzer (S.47) auf Grund der von ihm untersuchten Texte (Jos 24; Ex 19-24; Dt 1, 1-4, 40; 5-11; 28-31) annimmt, aber darin eine festgefügte literarische Gattung zu sehen, heisst doch wohl dem Formdenken zu grosse Bedeutung beimessen und die freie geistige Beweglichkeit zu gering einschätzen."

C. Extent and Variety of Utilization of the
Old Testament Covenant Form

In addition to Exodus 19-24, the book of Deuteronomy, and Joshua 24, the covenant form has been found to be reflected in numerous other places in the Old Testament. K. Baltzer traces the pattern, noting the variations and adaptations for different settings, in the following passages: Exodus 34; Nehemiah 9-10; Ezra 9-10; Daniel 9:4b-19; Joshua 23; I Samuel 12; I Chronicles 22-29; II Kings 11.[25] Others have noted the reflection of the covenant form in the "covenant law-suits" etc. of especially the prophetic books where Yahweh is depicted as entering into judgment with his people for breaking the covenant (note particularly: Deut. 32; Isa. 1:2-3, 18-20; 3:13-15; Jer. 2:4-13; Hos. 2:4-17; 4:1-3, 4-6; 12:3-15; Mic. 6:1-8; Mal. 3:5).[26] In addition, the reflec-

---

25. Baltzer, *The Covenant Formulary.*

26. The covenantal nature of the prophetic function and the influence of the covenant form in the writings of the latter prophets has been noted in recent years in a number of studies. W. F. Albright (*From the Stone Age to Christianity,* 17) has stated that his earlier analysis of the origin and development of the prophetic movement in Israel was not sufficiently penetrating, "largely because I failed to grasp the full significance of the Covenant principle... The dominant pattern of prophecy, as found in the earliest rhapsodist ('writing') Prophets of the eighth century, is firm belief in the validity of the ancient Covenant between God and His people according to whose terms Israel would be severely punished for its sins, both moral and cultic, but would ultimately be 'restored' because of the mercy or grace of God (*ḥésed*) which exceeded the formal terms of the Covenant and thus made it more binding than it would otherwise have been." R. E. Clements (*Prophecy and Covenant* [SBT 43; London: 1965] 127) says that the distinctiveness of the canonical prophets "lay in their particular relationship to, and concern with, the covenant between Yahweh and Israel." J. Muilenburg concludes his article "The 'Office' of the Prophet in Ancient Israel," (in *The Bible in Modern Scholarship* J. P. Hyatt, ed. [Nashville: 1965] 97) with the statement that the prophets were "Yahweh's messengers, his covenant mediators, intercessors for the people, speakers for God. They are sent from the divine King, the suzerain of the treaties, to reprove and to pronounce judgment upon Israel for breach of covenant." M. Kline (*The Structure of Biblical Authority,* 58) describes the prophets as "representatives of Yahweh in the administration of his covenant over Israel to declare his claims and enforce his will through effective proclamation." P. A. Verhoef (*Maleachi* [COT; Kampen: 1972] 59) comments: "De verbondsgedachte is niet alleen maar de grote veronderstelling achter Maleachi's prediking maar wordt ook met zoveel woorden uitgesproken terwijl we ook verscheidene typische elementen van het verbond in zijn prediking terugvinden."

tion of the covenant form in varying degrees in certain Psalms
has been noted by various investigators and may suggest that
the covenant form exerted its influence to some degree on
the liturgy of the temple worship.[27] Others have discussed

He mentions among these the preamble, the historical prologue, stipulations,
sanctions and blessings and curses.

On the covenant lawsuit itself and the question of its derivation see: E.
Würthwein, "Der Ursprung der prophetischen Gerichtsrede," *ZThK* 49 (1952)
1-16; J. Harvey, "Le 'RÎB-Pattern,' réquisitoire prophétique sur la rupture de
l'alliance," *Bib* 43 (1962) 172-196; idem, *Le Plaidoyer prophétique contre Israël
après la rupture de l'alliance,* (Studia 22; Paris: 1967) 9-30; Boecker, *Redeformen
des Rechtslebens im Alten Testament,* 91 f. Each of the above discusses the
question of where the form of the רִיב originated; whether in the sphere of the
court at the gate (Boecker), the cult (Würthwein), or international relationships
(Harvey). In an excellent survey of the issues involved, J. Limburg ("The Root
רִיב and the Prophetic Lawsuit Speeches," *JBL* 88 [1969] 304) concludes that it
"appears that the prophet, speaking as Yahweh's messenger, is employing forms
of speech which originated in the sphere of international relationships. The figure
of the royal messenger, bringing a complaint against a people, provides a kind of
model for understanding the figure of the prophet, announcing that Yahweh has a
complaint against *his* people."

For additional discussions of the covenant form in the prophetic books, see:
Huffmon, *JBL* 78 (1959) 285-295; G. E. Wright, "The Lawsuit of God: A
Form-Critical Study of Deuteronomy 32," in *Israel's Prophetic Heritage* (Muilen-
burg Festschrift, B. W. Anderson, W. Harrelson, eds.; New York: 1962) 26-67; F.
C. Fensham, "Common Trends in Curses of the Near Eastern Treaties and
Kudurru-inscriptions Compared with the Maledictions of Amos and Isaiah," *ZAW*
75 (1963) 155-175; idem, "The Covenant-idea in the book of Hosea," in *Studies
on the books of Hosea and Amos* (OTWSA; Potchefstroom: 1964/65) 35-49;
Hillers, *Treaty Curses and the Old Testament Prophets;* W. Brueggemann, "Amos
IV 4-13 and Israel's Covenant Worship," *VT* 15 (1965) 1-15; A. S. van der Woude,
"Micha II 7a und der Bund Jahwes Mit Israel," *VT* 18 (1968) 388-391; J. S.
Holladay, Jr., "Assyrian Statecraft and the Prophets of Israel," *HTR* 63 (1970)
29-51; R. North, "Angel-Prophet or Satan-Prophet?" *ZAW* 82 (1970) 31-67; M.
O'Rourke Boyle, "The Covenant Lawsuit of the Prophet Amos: III 1–IV 13," *VT*
21 (1971) 338-362; T. M. Raitt, "The Prophetic Summons to Repentance," *ZAW*
83 (1971) 30-49.

27. J. Muilenburg (*VT* 9 [1959] 356) comments: "A cursory inspection of
such psalms as 1, lxxxi, lxxxix, and cxxxii will reveal the degree to which the
covenant terminology and form was adapted for use in worship." A. Weiser (*The
Psalms* [London: 1962] 23-52) considers the cult, and specifically his reconstructed "covenant festival" to be the source of the majority of the Old Testament psalms. Weiser's theory has been applied in a modified way by M. Manatti
and E. de Solms (*Les Psaumes,* 4 vols. [Cahiers de la Pierre-qui-Vire, 26-29;
Bruges: 1966 ff.]). We cannot discuss the merits of Weiser's "covenant festival"
theory here, but as Kline (*Structure of Biblical Authority,* 63) points out, "the
covenantal function of the Psalter does not depend on a theory (like Weiser's)
that would assign much in the Psalter a role in some one annual covenant renewal
festival, speculatively reconstructed. Rather, the Psalter served broadly as a cultic

the relationship of the covenant form to the wisdom literature of the Old Testament.[28] M. Kline has argued that the
various component parts of the Old Testament itself, including history, law, wisdom, and prophecy are functional exten-
sions of the main elements of the treaty-covenant form, and
the Old Testament is therefore best characterized as a "covenantal corpus."[29] It is not possible for us here to do more
than indicate something of the prevalence of the covenant
form in the Old Testament. For detailed discussions of the
various ways in which the form is utilized one must consult
the literature cited above. There is, however, substantial
evidence that the covenant form was persistently utilized
throughout Israel's history in a wide variety of adaptations
and applications.

D. *Sitz im Leben* of the Old Testament Covenant Form;
Historical Implications of Its Presence

As has been noted, there is widespread agreement that
the "covenant form" is a discernible and important literary
feature of the Old Testament. There is, however, no corresponding agreement on the origin of this phenomena and
consequently on the historical implications which may or
may not be drawn from its admitted presence. In fact, there
is an expressed resistance to the attempts which some have
made to draw historical conclusions from the presence of the
literary form.[30] Caution is certainly in order at this point,

instrument in the maintenance of a proper covenantal relationship with Yahweh."
See further: R. Millard, "For He is Good," *TB* 17 (1966) 115-117; N. H.
Ridderbos, *OTS,* XV, 213-226; J. H. Tigay, "Psalm 7:5 and Ancient Near Eastern
Treaties," *JBL* 89 (1970) 178-186. For a survey of Psalm research since 1955 see:
D. J. A. Clines, "Psalm Research Since 1955: I. The Psalms and the Cult," *TB,* 18
(1967) 103-126; idem, "Psalm Research Since 1955: II. The Literary Genres," *TB*
20 (1969) 105-125.
    28. D. A. Hubbard, "The Wisdom Movement and Israel's Covenant Faith,"
TB 17 (1966) 3-33; Kline, *The Structure of Biblical Authority,* 64-67.
    29. Ibid., 47.
    30. Baltzer (*The Covenant Formulary,* 7, n. 49) commenting on Menden-
hall's article "Law and Covenant in Israel and the Ancient Near East," (*BA* 17
[1954] 26-76) says: "He is more interested in historical questions, while the

particularly because one of the most serious weaknesses of the form critical method as it has often been practiced is its tendency to encourage speculative and hypothetical reconstructions of a *Sitz im Leben* for particular forms, sometimes with little or no corroborating evidence. While recognizing the danger in this procedure and the excesses to which it has led, there nevertheless remains a definite validity to the notion that the presence of a particular form presupposes a historical setting which has given rise to the form in question and which accordingly provides insight into the reasons for and significance of its utilization. It is therefore apparent that judicious attempts to delineate the historical setting for particular forms can be a useful interpretive tool, and in the case of the "covenant form" the questions of when and how it was adopted in Israel are certainly matters of fundamental significance whose avoidance impoverishes the study of the forms and may contribute to misinterpretation of their significance.

---

present work limits itself to the form-critical approach. No doubt further conclusions, not least in the historical sphere, can be drawn on the basis of this beginning; but I consider it methodologically dangerous to bring both sets of questions together prematurely." J. J. Stamm ("Dreissig Jahre Dekalogforschung," *ThR* 27 [1961] 214) says that W. Zimmerli while admitting the treaty-covenant parallel, warns rightly against too hastily drawn historical conclusions, commenting: "Die geschichtlichen Wege, auf denen sich die Nähe der hethitischen Vasallenvertragstexte zu den alttestamentlichen Bundesformulierungen erklären lässt, sind noch ganz undurchsichtig. . . ." (*TLZ* 85 Sp. 481-498). P. J. Calderone (*CBQ* 25 [1963] 138) notes in his review of Baltzer's, *The Covenant Formulary:* "B. insists throughout on a sharp separation between his form critical investigation and the historicity of the episodes narrated. This reserve toward matters historical, which still lies far short of skepticism, owes its vigor to the influence of Alt, Noth, and von Rad. In this way B. has successfully avoided hasty and premature conclusions. An author has the right to delimit his scope and material, but it is disappointing that B. eschews historical conclusions." McCarthy (*Biblica* 53 [1972] 120) in his review of Perlitt (*Bundestheologie im Alten Testament*) says concerning the treaty-covenant analogy: "No doubt too much has been claimed for the analogy, and, especially, illegitimate historical conclusions have been drawn from it. Still, this does not invalidate such evidence as there is for the analogy. . . ."

1. The nature of the covenant form and its origin—cultic or historical?

Some have sought the explanation for the widespread occurrence of the "covenant form" in Old Testament literature by positing its derivation from the cult. We cannot here enter into the complexities of this thesis whose most prominent advocate has been G. von Rad,[31] but in this writer's opinion, there is good reason to conclude that a cultic-origin hypothesis does not provide an adequate or complete explanation for the nature of the form in question. This is not to deny the possibility of a recurring covenant festival in ancient Israel, the existence of which many have suggested,[32] either in connection with the feast of tabernacles every seven years (cf. Deut. 31:9-13), or, perhaps, even more frequently. Nor is this to deny that cultic observances may have contributed to the perpetuation and shaping of various utilizations of the "covenant form" as represented in the literature of the Old Testament. Nevertheless, such cultic observances in themselves do not provide an answer to the more fundamental questions of the reason for and the time of the initial adoption of this particular form in ancient Israel.

J. A. Thompson,[33] in discussing von Rad's view, writes: "There seems little reason to doubt that the historical prologue in the secular treaties was a basic aspect of any treaty. Nor need we doubt that it represented, albeit, perhaps, in some enhanced form, a correct outline of the preceding

---

31. von Rad, *The Problem of the Hexateuch,* 1-78; see also, Schmidt, *Der Landtag von Sichem,* 87-88. The dilemma "cultic or historical origin" is deficient, but the sense in which I use it should be clear. In his later writings von Rad himself seems also to indicate that a purely cultic explanation cannot provide the final answer. He comments (*Deuteronomy,* 22): "However, the question is still quite open how and when Israel came to understand its relationship to God in the form of these early Near Eastern treaties with vassals."

32. S. Mowinckel, *The Psalms in Israel's Worship* (Nashville: 1963); A. Alt, *Die Ursprünge des israelitischen Rechts* (Leipzig: 1934), ET: *Essays on Old Testament History and Religion* (New York: 1968) 103-171; von Rad, *The Problem of the Hexateuch,* 1-78; Weiser, *The Psalms,* 23-35.

33. Thompson, *RThR* 27 (1968) 53-64.

historical events which were paraded as a strong argument for the acceptance of the treaty by the vassal. . . . Von Rad does, of course, take note of the historical recital of the Sinai events when he discusses Deuteronomy and Exodus 19-24. But for him this historical narration is merely a cultic legend of very doubtful historicity.[34] But the question should be asked whether a cultic legend could serve the purpose demanded by the historical prologue to a covenant demand. . . . It ought not be assumed that a cultic liturgy should be divorced from underlying historical events."[35]

It is possible to find fault with Thompson's article. For example, von Rad's view of the historicity of Old Testament history writing is more complex than would appear from Thompson's discussion. Nevertheless the remarks of Thompson cited above merit serious consideration.

In any case, as we have seen above, a purely cultic derivation for the covenant form is unsatisfactory. The relationship between Yahweh and his people, of which the establishment or renewal is narrated in connection with the appearance of the covenant form in the Old Testament, is explicitly and conceptually connected with the antecedent historical relationship of the covenant partners. Such a relationship, while it may be renewed or celebrated in the cult, presupposes a specific historical occasion on which it was originally and formally established (which, of course, could also have taken place in a cultic ceremony, see n. 31). The question is: what was this occasion?

M. Noth has suggested that the real historical event behind the traditions which are joined together in what has now been identified as the "covenant form" is the assembly held at Shechem described in Joshua 24, where an amphictyonic twelve-tribe league was established under the leadership of

---

34. Thompson's contention has particular relevance to von Rad's suggestion that the "exodus tradition" and the "Sinai tradition" were originally separate. See further below, p. 161 ff., n. 68.

35. Ibid., 57, 58.

Joshua in which covenantal allegiance to Yahweh was the unifying force.[36] There are serious objections, however, which can be advanced against the amphictyonic hypothesis,[37] and even if one accepts Noth's general theory[38] there are good reasons for seeking the origins of Israelite unity and covenant allegiance to Yahweh prior to the assembly at Shechem.[39] G. W. Anderson, after pointing out various weaknesses in Noth's reconstruction, comments: "It seems natural, therefore, to look for the establishment of this unity, not in the emergence of an amphictyony in Canaanite soil in the wake of the invasion, but rather, where so much ancient Israelite tradition would lead us to expect to find it, in the period before the settlement, and, more specifically, in the establishment of the Sinai covenant between Yahweh and the Israelite tribes."[40]

It is the Sinai event described in Exodus 19–24 which provides the most likely setting for the entrance of the "covenant form" into the experience of ancient Israel. The

36. M. Noth, *Das System der zwölf Stämme Israels* (Stuttgart: 1930); idem, *The History of Israel*, 85-138.

37. See: H. Orlinsky, "The Tribal System of Israel and Related Groups in the Period of the Judges," *OrAn* I (1962) 11-20; G. Buccellati, *Cities and Nations of Ancient Syria* (StSe 26; Rome: 1967); G. W. Anderson, "Israel: Amphictyony; 'AM; ḴĀHĀL; 'ĒDÂH," in *Translating and Understanding the Old Testament*, Essays in honor of H. G. May; H. T. Frank and W. L. Reed, eds. (Nashville: 1970) 135-151; A. D. H. Mayes, *Israel in the Period of the Judges* (SBT, 2nd series, 29; Naperville: 1974). See also the discussion and literature cited by Fohrer (*History of Israelite Religion*, 89-94).

38. See, e.g., Bright, *A History of Israel*, 158, n. 45.

39. F. C. Fensham ("Covenant, Promise and Expectation in the Bible," *ThZ* 23 [1967] 313, 314) comments: "Some scholars are of the opinion that in Jos. 24 the real historical background of the covenant of Sinai occurs. The conquering tribes from the desert and those tribes which were already in possession of the country for a long time decided to make a covenant accepting Yahweh as God and each other as brothers of the covenant.... Taking into consideration its final form, however, and its relation to covenantal descriptions in the Pentateuch, it seems as if this chapter gives a description of a renewal of covenant. It is quite probable that groups which had associated themselves with the conquering tribes, were taken into the covenant at Shechem, but not as a covenant for the first time instituted."

40. Anderson, "Israel: Amphictyony . . . ," in *Translating and Understanding the Old Testament*, 149.

significance of this event for Israel's subsequent history, including the nature of her faith, the forms of her worship and literature should not be obscured or de-historicized as many have done in the past. The increasing recognition in recent years of the formative importance of the Mosaic era, is at least partially due to the growing admission that the historical basis for the extensive utilization of the covenant form in the life and literature of ancient Israel is to be found in the event of the establishment of the covenant at Sinai under the leadership of Moses.[41]

41. W. Eichrodt (*Int* 20 [1966] 308, 309) after noting the Hittite treaty structure and manner of treaty making says that "the oldest traditions of the Sinai Covenant are filled with the same conceptions of the content and way of making a covenant." He notes that Beyerlin has shown how this conception was preserved and renewed in cultic celebrations, but he also states, "it is quite clear that the origin of this liturgical tradition is not to be sought in the cult but in history. The tradition originated in the decisive hour in which the tribes, led out of Egypt into freedom engaged themselves—through the medium of Moses—to an exclusive service of the God known for his mercy at the Exodus and while they wandered in the wilderness, the God who then received them into a covenant relationship. . . . The tenacity with which the Hittite type of treaty maintained itself throughout the centuries in Israel vouches for the antiquity of this form of covenant-making, given the constancy of fixed liturgical form. A covenant formulation with great authority, going back into remote antiquity must have so impressed itself on Israel's celebrations that a covenant without this form would have been inconceivable. The literary application of the form in the Old Testament texts confirms such an influence in spite of the various styles. This renders hopeless any attempt to explain the adoption of the form as a fortuitous and arbitrary event of a later time and the means of theological reflection and interpretation." J. Bright, (*A History of Israel*, 148, 149) speaking of the treaty-covenant parallel and of the "extreme antiquity and centrality of the covenant in Israel," says: ". . . we may believe that this form was determinative for Israel's self-understanding and corporate life since the beginning of her history as a people—indeed brought her into existence as a people." See further: E. F. Campbell, "Moses and the Foundations of Israel," *Int* 29 (1975) 141-154. Although this view is finding increasing support it is by no means universally accepted. Note, e.g., the comment of M. Smith ("The Present State of Old Testament Studies," *JBL* 88 [1969] 30): "The historicity of the Sinai covenant was argued from its similarity to Hittite treaties, but the same essential structure appears in the treaties of Esarhaddon of Assyria where the parallels are so close to Deuteronomy as to argue its literary dependence . . . so one has to ask, When did the Israelites become familiar with this enduring Mesopotamian diplomatic convention? And the answer is surely not while they were slaves in Egypt or nomads along the desert, but after they became a kingdom, and perhaps, indeed, only after the revival of Assyria. Thus the 'ancient near eastern archeological evidence'

2. The evolution of the treaty form and its implications for the date of the book of Deuteronomy.

Recognizing the "covenant form" in the description of the Sinai event recorded in Exodus 19–24 and ascribing the adoption of this form to the Mosaic era is further substantiated by the structural, terminological and conceptual parallels to the Hittite treaties which are to be found in the book of Deuteronomy.

M. Kline has argued that the book of Deuteronomy "is a covenant renewal document which in its total structure exhibits the classic legal form of the suzerainty treaties of the Mosaic age."[42] Kline's case for the origin of Deuteronomy in the Mosaic era is made in part by noting what he describes as a "discernible evolution" of the documentary form of the suzerainty treaties, and by pointing out that Deuteronomy agrees with the classic stage in the evolution of the treaty form. It is his contention that the suzerainty treaties of later times diverge from the pattern followed by the Hittites, and it is the classic pattern of the Hittite treaties which is reflected in the book of Deuteronomy.[43] Whether or not the Hittite treaties of the 14th–13th centuries B.C. exhibit a "classical form" which does not survive in the treaties of later times, as, for example, in the 8th century Aramaic treaties from Sefîre

---

is actually evidence for a rather late date." (However, see our discussion of this view below.)

It should also be noted in this connection that the infrequent use of the word "covenant" by the prophets before Jeremiah is not necessarily evidence for the late origin of the concept. As Eichrodt (*Theology of the Old Testament*, I, 17, 18) has pointed out: "The crucial point is not as an all too naïve criticism sometimes seems to think—the occurrence or absence of the Hebrew word $b^e r \hat{\imath} t$, but the fact that all the crucial statements of faith in the OT rest on the assumption, explicit or not, that a free act of God in history raised Israel to the unique dignity of the People of God in whom his nature and purpose were to be made manifest. The actual term 'covenant' is, therefore, so to speak, only the code-word for a much more far-reaching certainty, which formed the very deepest layer of the foundations of Israel's faith, without which indeed Israel would not have been Israel at all."

42. Kline, *Treaty of the Great King*, 28; see also 42 ff.

43. Ibid., 43.

in northern Syria,[44] or the 7th century vassal treaties of Esarhaddon of Assyria,[45] is therefore a matter of importance for Kline's argument, as well as our own position, and thus merits further consideration.

   a. The vassal treaties of Esarhaddon compared with the Hittite suzerainty treaties.

An examination of the vassal treaties of Esarhaddon reveals that certain elements of these treaties are much the same as those of the earlier Hittite treaties. Yet in spite of these basic similarities, one cannot but notice that there are important differences as well. Perhaps the most noticeable difference is that of the schema or arrangement of the Assyrian treaties.

   1) *Absence of a historical prologue.*—As we noted above[46] the Hittite treaties adhere to a rather consistent form with little deviation. The most striking contrast between the Assyrian and Hittite treaties is that the second section of the schema in the Hittite treaties, the historical prologue, is not found in the Assyrian treaties. This is an important difference because the historical prologue sets the tone for the Hittite treaties. It is on the basis of his prior beneficent acts that the Great King justifies his demand for observance of the stipulations which follow. This historical prologue follows immediately after the preamble in every presently available Hittite

---

44. Cf., André Dupont-Sommer and Jean Starcky, "Les inscriptions araméennes de Sfiré (Stèles I et II)," *Mémoires présentés par divers savants à l'Académie des Inscriptions et Belles-Lettres* 15 (1958) 197-351, plus 29 plates. Also by the same authors: "Une inscription araméenne inédite de Sfiré," *Bulletin du Musée de Beyrouth* 13 (1956) 23-41, (Stèle III). See also: F. Rosenthal, "Notes on the Third Aramaic Inscription from Sefire-Sujin," *BASOR* 158 (1960) 28-31; J. A. Fitzmyer, "The Aramaic Inscriptions of Sefire I and II," *JAOS* 81 (1961) 178-222; J. A. Fitzmyer, *The Aramaic Inscriptions of Sefire* (BibOr, 19; Rome: 1967).

45. Cf., D. J. Wiseman, "The Vassal-Treaties of Esarhaddon," *Iraq* 20 (1958) 1-91. These treaties are essentially duplicates, differing only in the names of the various rulers with whom they were made and concern the subject of the royal succession of Ashurbanipal to the Assyrian throne.

46. See p. 132 ff.

treaty of the 14th-13th centuries B.C.[47] The historical prologue immediately introduces the pronunciation of the loyalty obligation of the vassal to the Great King.[48]

The absence of a historical prologue contributes to the
very cold and harsh tone of Esarhaddon's treaties. The wording of these treaties typifies the ruthless Assyrian imposition
of its power over surrounding nations, and the lack of a
historical prologue is consistent with this spirit. There is no
hint of any merciful Assyrian actions on behalf of the vassals
which would merit their loyalty and thankfulness, but rather
only the blunt declaration of their obligation, secured by
threats of horrible curses if they are not followed. The lack
of the historical prologue therefore is not only an important
difference in the literary form, but it also indicates from the
outset the vast difference in spirit between the Hittite and
Assyrian treaties. Consequently, a difference in the quality of
the relationship established between the suzerain and his
vassal exists.

2) *Absence of a Grundsatzerklärung.* A second structural difference is the lack of an Assyrian equivalent for the
"Grundsatzerklärung" of the Hittite treaties. The declaration
of allegiance to the head partner by the vassal flows from the
historical prologue in the Hittite treaties. This is an extremely
important element in the Hittite treaties because this, more
than anything else expresses the spirit of the relationship
between the treaty partners. Because of the gracious acts
performed in the past by the Great King, the vassal expresses

47. Korošec (*Hethitische Staatsverträge*, 13) says of the historical prologue
that, "Das ständige Wiederkehren von solchen Ausführungen zeigt, dass man sie in
Ḫattušaš als einen wesentlichen Bestandteil jedes Vasallenvertrags ansah. . . ." D.
J. McCarthy (*Treaty and Covenant,* 26, 30-31, 98-99) contests this assertion and
argues that several of the Hittite treaties do not have a historical prologue and
consequently that "the history was not an essential element of the treaty form."
For a detailed analysis of McCarthy's position on this question see H. Huffmon,
CBQ 27 (1965) 109-110, whose analysis supports the statement of Korošec
above.

48. This is Baltzer's "statement of substance (*Grundsatzerklärung*) concerning the future relationship of the partners to the treaty," cf. n. 5 above, and, *The
Covenant Formulary,* 12, 13.

his thanks by declaring his allegiance and loyalty. Naturally, such a declaration following the historical prologue does not appear in the Assyrian treaties because in these treaties the historical prologue is non-existent. Instead of this the Assyrian treaties contain an oath of allegiance which, however, appears in a very different context immediately after the first section of curses.[49] Here the oath is taken in a context of fear rather than trust and the relationship established between the treaty partners is consequently quite different from that of the Hittite treaties.

3) *Absence of blessings.*—In keeping with the harsh tone in the Assyrian treaties another structural difference arises. In the Esarhaddon treaties no blessings are enumerated for keeping the treaty stipulations. This is one of the permanent features of the Hittite treaties. Its absence is another rather important difference when one is comparing the two groups of treaties not only from the structural viewpoint, but also with respect to the nature of the relationship which is established.

4) *Conclusion.*—On the basis of these observations it appears that M. Kline has adequate foundation for his assertion that the Assyrian treaties are essentially different from those of the earlier Hittites.[50] Although certain elements are similar, as is to be expected in treaties between a greater and

---

49. Wiseman, *Iraq* 20 (1958) 66-68, lines 494-512.

50. Mendenhall, Albright, Bright, Külling and others are in agreement with Kline on this point. Mendenhall (*Law and Covenant,* 30) says, "This covenant type is even more important as a starting point for the study of Israelite traditions because of the fact that it cannot be proven to have survived the downfall of the great Empires of the late second millennium B.C. When empires again arose, notably Assyria, the structure of the covenant by which they bound their vassals is entirely different." He notes further (ibid., n. 19) "In all the materials we have the 'historical prologue' is missing, and only the Assyrian deities are listed as witnesses. The entire pattern is also radically different. It is, of course, possible that the form survived elsewhere, but the writer has been able to find no evidence for it. We should also expect that even if it did survive, more or less far-reaching changes in the form would also have taken place." Albright (*From the Stone Age to Christianity* [New York: 1957²] 16) agreeing with Mendenhall's analysis comments: "The structure of half a dozen Assyrian, Aramaean, and Phoenician treaties which we know from the eighth century B.C. and later, is quite differ-

lesser power, these similarities are not sufficient to warrant the statement of Wiseman that, "the form of treaties was already 'standardised' by the Hittite Empire and this text [i.e., the Vassal treaty of Esarhaddon] shows that it remained basically unchanged through Neo-Assyrian times."[51]

b. The Aramaic treaties from Sefire compared with the vassal treaties of Esarhaddon and with the Hittite suzerainty treaties.

1) *Similarities of the Sefire treaties to the Assyrian treaties.*—With the presently available Aramaic treaties from Sefire[52] one finds no historical prologue[53] or *Grundsatzerklärung* as is found in the Hittite treaties. In this respect it can be said that the Aramaic treaties are closer to the Esarhaddon treaties than they are to the Hittite treaties. In addition, the stipulations which remain preserved are decidedly one-sided. They regulate the conduct of the vassal towards the more powerful partner, but are not reciprocal except in the matter

ent." See also, Bright, *A History of Israel,* 148-149; Külling, *Zur Datierung der "Genesis P-Stücke,"* 288-289.

51. Wiseman, *Iraq* 20 (1958) 28. McCarthy (*Treaty and Covenant,* 80 ff.) supports Wiseman on this matter commenting: "It is said that the Assyrian and other treaties of the first millennium B.C. are entirely different in structure from the Hittite form in the second millennium. It seems to me that the analysis just completed fails to bear this out." More recent and even more dogmatic on this point is Weinfeld (*Deuteronomy and the Deuteronomic School* [Oxford: 1972] 60) who comments: "There is no justification, then, for regarding the formulation of the Hittite treaties as being unique, nor is there any basis for Mendenhall's supposition that only Hittite treaties served as the model and archetype of the Biblical covenant." Cf. also idem, *TDOT,* II, 267.

52. Cf. n. 44 above.

53. Fitzmyer (*The Aramaic Inscriptions of Sefire,* 122) comments: "One element in particular is significantly absent, the historical prologue. Whatever reason may be assigned for the omission of this element in the Aramaic treaties, the absence of it constitutes a major difference between the Aramaic and Hittite treaties. This element is basic to the Hittite conception of the covenant; it constitutes the 'legal framework' of the Hittite suzerainty treaty. Hittite suzerains recalled their favors toward the vassals as well as those of their predecessors in order to establish the obligation of the vassal's loyalty and service.

Indeed, it is precisely this element which is absent from covenants of the first millennium B.C., whether they be Aramaic or Assyrian. This qualification seems to be necessary in view of the claim made by Wiseman that the covenant form 'remained basically unchanged through Neo-Assyrian times.' "

of fugitives.[54] In the Hittite treaties, however, there is a solidarity of the two treaty partners so that the head partner promises protection for his vassal. He also promises that the enemies of the vassal will be defeated when the vassal remains loyal to his suzerain.[55] Both the treaties of Sefîre and the Assyrian treaties lack any such protection clause for the vassal.[56] In the Aramaic treaties the section which calls upon the gods as witnesses follows immediately after the introductory paragraph. This also deviates from the Hittite form which refers to the gods after the stipulations rather than before. In this respect the Aramaic treaties are in agreement with those of Esarhaddon.

2) *Similarities of the Sefîre treaties to the Hittite treaties.* —There are certain features of the Aramaic treaties, however, which seem closer to the Hittite treaties than to the later Assyrian treaties of Esarhaddon. In the selection of gods called upon as witnesses to the treaty the Aramaic treaties cite the gods of KTK and Arpad, that is, the gods of both the great king and the vassal. The Hittite treaties also name the gods of both partners as witnesses, while the Assyrian treaties name only the Assyrian gods. The Sefîre treaties also more

---

54. In the case of fugitives the treaty says: "and/if a fugitive of mine flees to one of them, and their fugitive flees and comes to me if he has restored mine, I shall return/ his and you shall no/t cause me trouble yourself. And if you do not do so, you will have betrayed this treaty." This is the only place which records any obligation placed on the more powerful partner. Cf. Rosenthal, *BASOR* 158 (1960) 28-31.

55. Fensham (*VT* 13 [1963] 140) comments: "One of the most humane stipulations in the Hittite treaties is the promise of protection of the vassal against enemies. This protection might have been promised to safeguard the head partner's kingdom, but was still a most encouraging experience for the vassal. There was no enemy to fear. Under such conditions small kingdoms could prosper and times of peaceful co-existence could develop." See, e.g., the protection clause in the treaty between Muwattalis̆ and Alaks̆andus̆ of Wilus̆a (Friedrich, MVÄG, 1930, 56-57).

56. Fensham (ibid., 141) comments: "It is immediately clear from the treaties of Esarhaddon and those of Sefîre that no clauses of protection of the vassal are inserted. Both the Assyrian and Aramaean treaties are one-sided and have no humane attitude to the vassal. . . . Especially the Assyrian treaties show on the one hand, a lack of consideration for the minor partner and on the other hand, strict commandments and rigorous maledictions."

closely resemble the Hittite treaties than the Assyrian treaties in the clauses which protect the rights of the head partner. The subject matter of these clauses is much broader in the Sefîre treaties than in the Assyrian treaties (this is perhaps to be expected since the Assyrian treaties are concerned exclusively with the succession problem). In addition, the style of the formulation is closer to that of the Hittite treaties than to that of the Assyrian treaties.[57]

3) *Conclusion.*—It may be concluded, then, that the treaties of Sefîre exhibit certain close affinities with the earlier Hittite treaties, but at the same time they also contain important differences, particularly the absence of a historical prologue and *Grundsatzerklärung,* and the one-sided nature of the stipulations.[58]

> *c. Implications of the treaty-covenant analogy for the date of Deuteronomy.*

From the present evidence it appears that the Hittite suzerainty treaties can be said to represent a unique early form which is not duplicated in the later treaties of either Esarhaddon or Sefîre. Connected with the difference in form is the distinctive spirit reflected in the Hittite treaties which

---

57. Cf. Fensham, ibid., 138. Fitzmyer (*The Aramaic Inscriptions of Sefîre,* 124) also points out certain similarities between the Sefîre treaties and those of the Hittites. He notes: "Several of the stipulations in the Hittite treaty between Mursilis and Duppi-Tessub of Amurru end with a formula which is quite similar to the concluding clauses in these steles: 'If you do (or do not do) such things, you act in disregard of your oath.' This is the Hittite counterpart of the Aramaic *whn lhn* clause. Still more significant is the alternate formula: 'you act in disregard of the gods of the oath.' Cf. Sf I B 27, 33; II B 9; III 4, 14, 17, 23. Dupont-Sommer has also called attention to the striking parallel in Sf III 4-7 to the Hittite treaty of Mursilis with Duppi-Tessub, (§13): 'If anyone of the deportees from the Nuhassi land or of the deportees from the country of Kinzu whom my father removed and I myself removed escapes and comes to you, (if) you do not seize him and turn him back to the king of the Hatti land, and even tell him as follows: 'Go! Where you are going to, I do not want to know,' you act in disregard of your oath" (see *ANET,* pp. 203-5)."

58. This conclusion seems warranted on the basis of presently available evidence. It should be noted, however, that we have only three Aramaic treaties from Sefîre and none of these is complete.

is rooted in the fact that gratitude and respect of the vassal for the suzerain is an essential characteristic of the treaty relationship. As we have noted the Assyrian treaties are of a different structure and also an entirely different mood or spirit. The treaties of Sefire exhibit more similarities to the Hittite treaties than do the Assyrian treaties, but they still lack the important historical prologue and *Grundsatzerklärung* which are vital to both the form and spirit of the Hittite treaties.

M. Kline, therefore, speaks with good reason of the "evolution of the documentary form of suzerainty treaties."[59] He admits that the differences should not be exaggerated and that it is "indeed one species that we meet throughout Old Testament times."[60] Yet he does find a definitely discernible evolution, and as we have noted, Deuteronomy corresponds more closely in its structure and spirit to the earlier Hittite treaties than it does to either the 8th century Sefire treaties or the 7th century Assyrian treaties. Kline's conclusion, which in our view has a great deal of merit, and which deserves more attention than it has thus far received, is that "while it is necessary to recognize a substantial continuity in pattern between the earlier and the later treaties, it is proper to distinguish the Hittite treaties of the second millennium B.C. as the 'classic' form. And without any doubt the book of Deuteronomy belongs to the classic stage in this documentary evolution. Here then is significant confirmation of the prima facie case for the Mosaic origin of the Deuteronomic treaty of the great king."[61]

---

59. Kline, *Treaty of the Great King,* 42.
60. Ibid.
61. Ibid., 43. J. A. Thompson (*Deuteronomy: An Introduction and Commentary* [TOCT: London: 1974] 51, 52) expresses reservations about the strength of Kline's argument. He comments: "The possibility must be allowed that Deuteronomy was cast in the shape of an ancient treaty by someone who wrote long after Moses' day." In addition, he questions the view that the historical prologue was uniquely characteristic of treaties of the 2nd millennium B.C., citing an article by A. F. Campbell ("An historical prologue in a seventh century treaty," *Bib* 50 [1969] 534-535). Thompson concludes: "Hence the fact

Such a conclusion is admittedly in sharp contrast to the entrenched position of critical Old Testament scholarship on the origin of Deuteronomy. W. M. D. deWette in 1805 first advanced the view that Deuteronomy (which, as others before him, he regarded as Josiah's law-book) originated in the 7th century B.C. Although deWette's thesis has been attacked from various angles in the century and a half since its promulgation, it has remained the dominant critical viewpoint.[62] Only recently have serious reservations about his theory

that Deuteronomy has a historical introduction is not necessarily an argument for a date in the second millennium, although it may be." In response to these objections it should be noted that the "historical prologue" found by Campbell in a seventh century document is not a clear cut example. Cf. the comment by E. F. Campbell, Jr. (no relation to A. F. Campbell!) that "the reading is far from clear" (*Int* 29 [1975] 149, n. 13). See further the original publication by K. Deller and S. Papola, "Ein Vertrag Assurbanipals mit dem arabischen Stamm Qedar," *Or* 37 (1968) 464-466. In addition, while the possibility that someone cast Deuteronomy in the shape of the treaty form long after Moses' day cannot be totally ruled out, Kline's position is scarcely invalidated in this way and his model still has a great deal of evidence in its favor. Kline comments (*The Structure of Biblical Authority*, 10): "If it is once recognized that the Deuteronomic treaty must have been produced whole for a particular occasion, the pervasive orientation of the book to the situation of Israel in the Mosaic age and especially the central concern of this treaty with—of all things—the dynastic succession of Joshua, always awkward for advocates of a seventh-century origin of the book, become quite inexplicable for them."

62. It is not possible for us here to discuss the history of the debate surrounding the origin of the book of Deuteronomy. For a representative statement of deWette's theory see: Driver, *Deuteronomy*, ICC; idem, *Introduction*, 69-103. For a more recent survey of Deuteronomy studies see the discussion and literature citations in E. W. Nicholson, *Deuteronomy and Tradition* (Oxford: 1967). Nicholson (ibid., 37) notes: "The problems surrounding the date, authorship and provenance of Deuteronomy are amongst the most controversial in the study of the Old Testament. At one time or another almost every period in Israel's history from Moses to the exile has been advocated as the date for its composition, whilst its authorship has at various times been attributed to Moses, Samuel, levitical priests, the Jerusalem priesthood, or prophetic circles. Similarly, the origin of the book has been traced to Jerusalem, Shechem, Bethel, and elsewhere." See further the extensive survey of R. J. Thompson, *Moses and the Law in a Century of Criticism Since Graf* (SVT XIX; Leiden: 1970). Thompson (p. 163) concludes: "In 1965 then, a century after its publication, the Grafian hypothesis is still favoured by the majority of scholars. Prophecies of its demise by Orr in 1905, Sayce in 1910, Neubauer in 1918, Du Bose in 1923, Urbach and Coppens in 1938, Levy in 1947 and Ginsberg in 1950 have not been fulfilled. Instead, it has turned the tables on its critics and eroded the Conservative bastions in Jerusalem and Rome and made inroads into evangelical Protestantism."

begun to gain wider acceptance, and this has been due in great measure to the reevaluations of the origin of the book arising from the recognition of the "covenant form" in its structure.[63] Although no consensus has developed concerning the historical conclusions to which the covenant form may point (see Appendix), there is a recognition by many that at least a *Grundschrift* of the book emanates from a time much earlier than Josiah and has its roots in the covenant traditions associated with the amphictyonic center of Shechem.[64] As was noted above, however, in connection with the "covenant form" in Exodus 19-24, there are good reasons to look back even beyond the Shechem ceremony to the Sinai event itself for the origin of Israelite unity and adoption of the covenant form. While one can never speak in terms of "proof" in matters of this sort, it appears to this writer that M. Kline and K. Kitchen have constructed a model which is consistent with available evidence and which provides a basis for the pursuit of Deuteronomic studies which is superior to either the Wellhausian or other more recent models which reject Deuteronomy's Mosaic origin.[65]

---

63. See: G. von Rad, *Studies in Deuteronomy* (SBT 9; London: 1953); idem, *Deuteronomy*; G. E. Wright, "Deuteronomy," *IB*, II (New York: 1953); Muilenburg, *VT* 9 (1959) 347-365; Kline, *Treaty of the Great King*; Nicholson, *Deuteronomy and Tradition*; Kitchen, *Ancient Orient and Old Testament*, 90-102, 128; idem, "Ancient Orient, 'Deuteronism,' and the Old Testament," in *New Perspectives on the Old Testament*, ed. J. B. Payne (Waco: 1970) 1-24.

64. See the discussion in the Appendix. Muilenburg (*VT* 9 [1959] 347, 348, 350) comments: "It has become increasingly clear that behind the promulgation of the Deuteronomic Code of 621 B.C. lies a long history of literary and cultic activity. . . . The present book of Deuteronomy is composed of various strata of tradition, but at its base there is a *Grundschrift* emanating from a much earlier period than the time of Josiah. . . . It is now generally held that the Reformation of 621 was a movement of restoration, and that its ultimate origin is to be discovered in the amphictyony of Shechem. . . . The problem of the dates of the Elohist and of *Urdeuteronomium* needs review. The arguments which led to the eighth century date of E have little force today in view of modern reconstructions of the early history of Israel and Israel's early literary history. If the origins of Deuteronomic language, style, and literary structure are to be traced to the latter part of the eighth century and before that period to the Shechemite amphictyony in the period of the settlement, then it is clear that the history of Israel's religious faith requires restatement."

65. K. A. Kitchen ("Ancient Orient, 'Deuteronism,' and the Old Testa-

Section 2
The Covenant Form in I Samuel 11:14–12:25.

A. Characteristic Features of the Covenant
Form in I Samuel 11:14–12:25.

The presence of certain characteristic features of the Old
Testament covenant form in I Samuel 12 has been noted
previously by a number of scholars.[66] Although here no more
than in other covenantal pericopes does one find a stereo-
typed adherence to a tightly constructed literary pattern
modeled on the extra-biblical treaty form, nevertheless elements of the terminology and structural features generally
characteristic of covenantal pericopes elsewhere in the Old
Testament are present. Bearing in mind that in this instance
they are utilized in the unique setting of a ceremony associ-

ment," in *New Perspectives on the Old Testament*, 4) has aptly summarized this
position as follows: "The present writer [Kitchen] cannot see any legitimate way
of escape from the crystal-clear evidence of the correspondence of Deuteronomy
with the remarkably stable treaty or covenant form of the fourteenth-thirteenth
centuries B.C. Two points follow here. First, the basic structure of Deuteronomy
and much of the content that gives specific character to that structure *must*
constitute a recognizable literary entity; second, this is a literary entity *not* of the
eighth or seventh century B.C. but rather from ca. 1200 B.C. *at latest.* Those who
so choose may wish to claim that this or that individual 'law' or concept appears
to be of later date than the late thirteenth century B.C.; but it is no longer
methodologically permissible gaily to remove essential features of the covenant-
form on a mere preconception (especially if of nineteenth-century [A.D.] vin-
tage) of what is merely thought—not proven—to be 'late.' "

66. Muilenburg (*VT* 9 [1959] 361) says of I Samuel 12 that "it is often said
that the report has been fashioned after the model of Joshua xxiv, but it is more
likely that both accounts go back to the literary genre which receives its classical
form in the Sinaitic pericope and was perpetuated in the active cult at the
amphictyonic centers. Here we have the same terminology, the same style, the
same major motifs, key words, historical memories, and other characteristic
features of the covenant *Gattung*." Baltzer (*The Covenant Formulary*, 67) says,
"In short, the schema of the covenant renewal is preserved almost intact. All that
is missing is explicit mention of a new ratification on the part of the people."
McCarthy (*Treaty and Covenant*, 143) comments, "What we have in all this is the
application of the covenant structure to a special end, a warning about the
dangers of monarchy in Israel." See further the discussions of A. D. Ritterspach,
*The Samuel Traditions: An Analysis of the Anti-Monarchical Source in I Samuel
1-15* (unpublished Ph.D. dissertation, Graduate Theological Union, 1967) 260-
263, and Birch, *The Rise of the Israelite Monarchy*, 113-121.

ated with the establishment of kingship in Israel, and that this chapter is not the text of the concluding of a covenant, but rather the description of an assembly led by Samuel in which covenantal issues were of central importance, it is not surprising that the arrangement of the features of the covenant form exhibits a certain freedom. Nevertheless, it is clear that Samuel's words and actions at the Gilgal assembly are not simply *ad hoc* remarks or an arbitrarily constructed agenda of his own invention, but rather follow well established legal-ceremonial forms of the covenant tradition. Elements of the covenant form which are particularly noticeable are: 1) the appeal to antecedent history (I Sam. 12:6-12); 2) the challenge to the basic covenantal obligation of undivided allegiance to Yahweh introduced by the transitional *and now* (I Sam. 12:13a, 14a, 15a, 20-21, 24); 3) blessing and curse sanctions (I Sam. 12:14b, 15b, 25); 4) a theophanic sign (I Sam. 12:16-22).

It is our purpose to examine each of these elements in order to ascertain its function in the chapter and, in addition, to determine what implications this combination of features has for denoting the character of the Gilgal assembly as well as the unity of the description of the assembly contained in I Samuel 11:14–12:25.

1. Appeal to antecedent history (I Sam. 12:6-12).

As was noted above the use of a historical summary is a characteristic feature of the Old Testament covenant form.[67] Such summaries are utilized in different ways in different covenantal contexts, but the central idea that Yahweh's gracious acts in history provided the basis for Israel's obligation of loyalty and service to Yahweh, which was to be expressed in obedience to the covenantal law, remains constant.[68] Here

---

67. See above, 139. Although the presence of a brief historical summary is an important characteristic feature of the covenant form, it does not follow that its use is confined only to passages displaying all aspects of the covenantal form.

68. The presence in Old Testament literature of brief historical summaries

(I Sam. 12:6-12) Samuel utilizes a historical recapitulation of
the "righteous acts of Yahweh" in order to judicially estab-

of Yahweh's previous relationship to his people has long been recognized and
various theories have been advanced to explain the origin and function of these
summaries. G. von Rad (*The Problem of the Hexateuch*, 1-78) considered Deut.
26:5b-9 to be presumably the earliest example known to us of a distinct literary
type (*Gattung*) which he termed the "historical credo"; this literary type constituted the nucleus around which the entire Hexateuch was constructed. (It would
lead us too far astray to discuss here von Rad's separation of the Exodus and
Conquest traditions from the Sinai tradition and the relationship of this to his
credo thesis [see above, Section 1,D,1].) For a critique of von Rad's position on
this issue see: Weiser, *The Old Testament: Its Formation and Development*,
83-88; and, Huffmon, *CBQ* 27 [1965] 101-113.) Von Rad (ibid., 8) found other
examples of this same literary type in Deut. 6:20-24 and Josh. 24:2b-13, and
concluded that, "the solemn recital of the main parts of the redemption narrative
must have been an invariable feature of the ancient Israelite cultus. . . ." He
mentions (ibid., 9) I Sam. 12:8 as a free adaptation of the Credo in the cultic
setting of the Mizpah (rather than Gilgal, see above, 9, 127-128) assembly. Although
von Rad's thesis has been widely accepted, C. H. W. Brekelmans ("Het 'historische
Credo' van Israel," *TvT* 3 [1963] 1-11) has challenged von Rad's contention that
the short historical Credo is an independent *Gattung*. He points out that the
historical summaries in Deut. 6:20-25; Ex. 12:26-27; 13:14-15; Josh. 4:6-7, 21-24
are not properly treated when they are separated from their context and that they
are more properly assigned to the *Gattung* of "catechetical instruction" than to
that of "historical credo." Brekelmans then notes that the historical summary in
Josh. 24:2b-13 must be viewed in connection with its appearance in a chapter
which is a description of a covenant renewal ceremony at Shechem. He points out
that verses 2b-13 are an integral part of the *Gattung* to which the chapter belongs
which is that of the "covenant formulary." Von Rad (*Old Testament Theology* I,
122, 123) considers Josh. 24:2b-13 to be representative of the transformation of
the Credo into words spoken by God (Gottesrede). Brekelmans comments, (ibid.,
8) "De stilering als 'Gottesrede' van Jos. 24 kan men dan ook niet voorstellen als
een omvorming of een afwijking van de oorspronkelijke belijdenisformule. Van
een 'formgeschichtliche' ontwikkeling van een naar het ander kan geen sprake
zijn. Beide, de katechese en het Verbondsformulier zijn eigenstandige litteraire
grootheden, die in het geheel niet uit elkaar zijn ontstaan. Dat de feitelijke
heilsdaden die in beide ter sprake komen vrijwel hetzelfde zijn, komt hieruit
voort, dat de vermelde heilsdaden het wezen van Israëls godsdienst raken. Daar-
door werden deze feiten op alle terreinen van het godsdienstig leven benut: bij de
verbondshernieuwing, in de katechese en ook in de eredienst." Brekelmans then
protests against von Rad's separation of Deut. 26:5-9 from verse 10 (noting
particularly the *we'attâ* with which verse 10 begins) because the historical summary provides the basis for the motivation to bringing the first fruits. He
comments, "Het zg. Credo is dus inleiding, historische proloog en motivering van
het opdragen der eerstelingen uit dankbaarheid voor de weldaden door God aan
Israël bewezen. Men doet ook hier de tekst geweld aan, wanneer men de vv. 5-9
van v. 10 scheidt alsof zij niet met elkaar te maken hebben. Het lijkt mij niet
onmogelijk, dat de litteraire vorm van deze verzen zeer sterk beïnvloed is door het
zg. Verbondsformulier: men zou er de historische proloog en de loyaliteitsverklar-

lish Israel's apostasy in requesting a king.[69] For this purpose
it is important for Samuel to bring the historical summary up

---

ing, verbonden door *w^e'attâ*, in kunnen herkennen. Dan zouden we hier een
liturgische toepassing van het Verbondsformulier voor ons hebben. Dit lijkt
minstens waarschijnlijker dan de verklaring, die von Rad heeft voorgesteld."
    In our opinion J. P. Hyatt ("Were There an Ancient Historical Credo and an
Independent Sinai Tradition?" in *Translating and Understanding the Old Testament* [H. G. May Festschrift; New York: 1970] 152-170) is correct when he says:
"We must agree with Brekelmans that von Rad has not successfully isolated a
Gattung that can correctly be called 'historical Credo.' What he calls by this name
are in fact historical summaries, short or long, embedded within *Gattungen* that
should be designated as catechesis, covenant formulary (or more fully: the form
for ceremony of covenant making or renewal), or prayer to be made with the
offering of first fruits" (p. 164). It then follows that the fact that historical
summaries are utilized in various ways in Old Testament literature is simply a
reflection of the fundamental importance of the "righteous acts of Yahweh" for
the conceptual structure of the Sinaitic covenant and the essence of Israel's faith.
Th. C. Vriezen ("The Credo in the Old Testament," in, *Studies on the Psalms* [6th
Meeting, OTWSA; Potchefstroom: 1963] 5-17) who considers von Rad's credo
theory as "far from a success" and "not very probable" makes the following
comment in his discussion of the nature of the historical summary contained in
Deut. 26:5 ff.: "It is a pity that, at least according to my knowledge, we have no
formula for the presentation of tribute by vassals to great kings; specially those of
the Hittite palace would have been very interesting. A formula like the one
prescribed here seems to me to hail from the sphere of the covenant; a conception
which (as is known generally), just as that of election, dominates Dt." (15-16).
    For further discussion of brief historical summaries in the Old Testament
see: L. Rost, "Das Kleine Geschichtliche Credo" in *Das Kleine Credo und andere
Studien zum Alten Testament* (Heidelberg: 1965) 13-25; Thompson, *RThR* 27
(1968) 53-64; C. Carmichael, "A New View of the Origin of the Deuteronomic
Credo," *VT* 19 (1969) 273-289; D. J. McCarthy, "What Was Israel's Historical
Creed?" *LTQ* 4 (1969) 46-53.
    69. See above, Chapter I, 24-31 Baltzer (*The Covenant Formulary*, 66)
comments, "The antecedent history in vv. 8-13, together with the introduction in
v. 7, is clearly defined. . . . The antecedent history extends from Jacob to the
suppose [sic] present. It recounts Yahweh's saving acts in contrast to the sins of
Israel. The period down to the occupation is treated very concisely, the period of
the Judges in more detail. Despite the apostasy of Israel, Yahweh has kept the
promise made in the covenant—this is the tenor of the discourse. In the express
listing of sins, this antecedent history is closely related to those discussed in the
previous section, in the circumstances of a covenant renewal occasioned by
Israel's sin." In contrast to Baltzer, McCarthy (*Treaty and Covenant*, 142) seems
to miss the import of the use of the appeal to antecedent history by Samuel when
he says, "The history which is cited, rather than giving a ground for accepting
what follows, leads up to a *reprobation of kingship* (emphasis mine). After
pointing up the infidelity of Israel and its results in the era of the judges, it
concludes with what must be taken as a negative view of the monarchy. Kingship
is an imitation of the ways of the nations; Yahwe is Israel's king. This is hardly a
proper historical prologue to the presentation of the king, for the implication is

to date[70] which he does not only by mentioning his own role as a deliverer sent by Yahweh (I Sam. 12:11), but also by pointing out the implicit rejection of the kingship of Yahweh which was involved in Israel's request for a king to lead them in battle when Nahash the Ammonite threatened her borders.

2. The challenge to the basic covenantal obligation of undivided allegiance to Yahweh introduced by the transitional "and now" (I Sam. 12:13a, 14a, 15a, 20-21, 24).

The וְעַתָּה with which verse 13 begins is characteristic of the transition from the historical recapitulation to the "statement of substance"[71] in a number of covenantal con-

---

that the kingship involves some infidelity. This is scarcely motivation for accepting the king; it would point rather to rejection." It may be questioned, however, if we really have a "reprobation of kingship" implied in these verses if the implication is given that "kingship involves some infidelity." It is not kingship itself which is reprobated or which involves infidelity. It is Israel's disloyalty to Yahweh as expressed in her wrongly motivated desire for a king which is the issue, not kingship in and of itself. On the other hand, the intent of v. 12 is not to give "motivation for accepting the king." As is repeatedly (vv. 9a, 10a) the case in the historical summary (vv. 6-12) Israel's disloyalty is here set in contrast with the righteous acts of Yahweh.

70. When one compares the historical summaries in Ex. 19:4; 20:2b; Deut. 1:5–4:49; Josh. 24:2-13 and I Sam. 12:6-12 it is clear that on the occasions when the covenant was renewed the antecedent history was brought up to date. Kline (*Treaty of the Great King,* 52) comments, "The historical prologue of the Sinaitic Covenant had referred to the deliverance from Egypt (Ex. 20:2b). Deuteronomy begins at the scene of the Sinaitic Covenant and continues the history up to the covenant renewal assembly in Moab, emphasizing the recent Transjordanian victories. When, still later, Joshua again renewed the covenant to Israel, he continued the narrative in his historical prologue through the events of his own leadership of Israel, the conquest and settlement in Canaan (cf. Josh. 24:2-13)." I Sam. 12:6-12 extends this progressive enlargement to the end of the period of the judges.

71. See n. 5 above. Baltzer (*The Covenant Formulary,* 12, 13) considers the "statement of substance concerning the future relationship of the partners to the treaty" to be a characteristic feature of the treaty form. He notes that in the Hittite treaties the "statement of substance itself comprises primarily general imperatives. Their basic requirement is loyalty on the part of the treaty signatory." Baltzer also finds the statement of substance to be a characteristic feature of Old Testament covenantal pericopes as is seen, e.g., in Josh. 24:14; Ex. 19:5, 6; Deut. 29:8(9); Neh. 10:30(29); I Chron. 28:8. This list of Baltzer's can be enlarged and formulations of the "statement of substance" in conditional phraseology stating the general conditions of the covenant obligation are certainly to be included (see, e.g.: Ex. 23:22; Deut. 8:19; 11:13-15, 22-25, 26-28; 28:1 ff.,

texts.[72] In these places it points to the conclusion which is to be drawn from the antecedent history. In our context, the description of Samuel's presentation of the king to the people, coupled with the statement that Yahweh has chosen to give his people a human king in spite of the sinfulness of their request (I Sam. 12:13) is set between the historical recapitulation and the "statement of substance."[73] This intervening material is of particular importance here because it provides the backdrop against which the exhortation to covenant faithfulness which follows is brought to focus ("behold the king whom you have given preference to, whom you have requested"), while at the same time it conveys a very positive attitude toward the incorporation of human kingship into the theocratic structure of the nation ("and behold, Yahweh has set a king over you"). It is in this very carefully construed setting that Samuel enunciates the basic covenantal require-

15 ff.; 30:17, 18; Josh. 20:24; I Sam. 7:3). In his discussion of I Sam. 12, however, Baltzer cites only vv. 20-21 as reflective of this particular feature of the treaty-covenant form.

72. For the use of וְעַתָּה in covenantal contexts see: Muilenburg, *VT* 9 (1959) 353-355, 359, 361-363; Baltzer, *The Covenant Formulary*, 21, 28, 32, 75, 148, 149; and J. L'Hour, "L'Alliance à Sichem," *RB* 69 (1962) 5-36. L'Hour comments (ibid., 25), "Cette conjonction n'a que très exceptionnellement dans la Bible un sens temporel. Elle exprime communément la consécution logique, décision ou action, découlant d'un fait ou d'une déclaration. Très souvent elle est employée comme ici, après une narration historique et on la rencontre en particulier dans les contextes d'Alliance. Son usage cultuel en Ex 19,5 et Jos 24 paraît être technique et antérieur à son utilisation par les prophètes." See further, Laurentin [*Bib* 45 (1964) 169, n. 1 and 177, 178] who comments, "*Kai nun* n'appartient pas seulement aux formules de demande d'Alliance, mais aux formules qui scellent ou proclament cette Alliance. Ces dernières ont déjà été étudiées par Muilenburg, Baltzer et L'Hour, qui ont mis en valeur le rôle de *weʿattah* et le caractère de serment que cette locution leur confère." Even though the studies of Laurentin and Brongers [*VT* 15 (1965) 289-299] make it clear that וְעַתָּה is used in a great variety of ways and, in addition, even though וְעַתָּה is utilized in I Samuel 12 in three other places (vv. 2, 7, 10; גַּם־עַתָּה, 16) its specialized use in v. 13 as an introduction to the statement of substance following the historical recapitulation is supported by comparison with its occurrence in other covenantal pericopes (cf. Ex. 19:5; Josh. 24:14).

73. When the וְעַתָּה of v. 13 is taken as leading up to the אִם־ clause of v. 14, with the two הִנֵּה clauses of v. 13 interjected, then the wording of the covenant conditional here closely parallels that of Ex. 19:5.

I Sam. 12:13, 14: וְעַתָּה...אִם...וּשְׁמַעְתֶּם בְּקֹלוֹ
Ex. 19:5: וְעַתָּה אִם־שָׁמוֹעַ תִּשְׁמְעוּ בְּקֹלִי

ment of loyalty to Yahweh in the characteristic terminology
of "statements of substance" in other covenantal contexts.[74]
He does this at first in conditional phraseology (I Sam. 12:
14a, 15a) confronting the people with the alternatives which
were open to them as they entered the new era of the
monarchy.[75] Samuel's evident purpose is to emphasize that
allegiance to Yahweh is not to be impinged upon or chal-

74. For אֹם־תִּירְאוּ אֶת־יהוה (יָרֵא) see: Deut. 4:10; 5:29; 6:2, 13, 24; 8:6;
10:12, 20; 13:5(4); 28:58; 31:13; Josh. 24:14; II Kings 17:35, 39. For עָבַד
(וַעֲבַדְתֶּם אֹתוֹ) see: Deut. 6:13; 10:12, 20; 11:13; 13:5(4); Josh. 22:5; 24:14;
II Kings 17:35. For שָׁמַע (וּשְׁמַעְתֶּם בְּקֹלוֹ) see: Ex. 19:5; Deut. 4:30; 11:13; 27:10;
30:2, 8; 31:13; Judg. 2:2; 6:10; Ezek. 20:8. For מָרָה (וְלֹא תַמְרוּ אֶת־פִּי יהוה) see:
Ezek. 20:8; Neh. 9:26.

75. Muilenburg (*VT* 9 [1959] 363) comments that the "covenant conditional" occurs here in a form "closer to Exod. xix than to Josh. xxiv but more
expanded, yet preserving the very heart of the Mosaic formulation: וּשְׁמַעְתֶּם
בְּקֹלוֹ . . . וְאִם לֹא תִשְׁמְעוּ בְּקוֹל יהוה (14-15). . . ." Baltzer (*The Covenant Formulary*,
66, 67) does not view vv. 14 and 15 as a "statement of substance" (see above,
n. 71) and thus considers these two verses as a "departure from the structure
observed elsewhere." Part of the reason for this is Baltzer's interpretation of v. 14
in which he finds "no blessing formula such as we might expect . . ." (see above,
p. 41 ff., however, for a discussion of the interpretation of the apodosis of v. 14).
Baltzer feels that the negative character of these verses is probably due to the
redactor who omitted the blessing formula. He labels vv. 14 and 15 as "the
announcement of the curse." In taking this position Baltzer misses the import of
vv. 14, 15 as well as the correspondence of their form and function in this
pericope to the statement of substance in other covenantal contexts. McCarthy
(*Treaty and Covenant*, 142) in agreement with Baltzer, comments that vv. 14 and
15 "are a remnant of a blessing-curse formula, but the negative, threatening tone
is emphasized" because the "wish for good, the apodosis of v. 14 is missing." He
adds, "the blessing is not merely omitted, a procedure which would not call
attention to itself, but it is begun and never finished so that the reader cannot fail
to remark the absence of the blessing." In addition, McCarthy feels that vv. 14
and 15 are "peculiar in another respect." He is of the opinion that they should
assure the proper functioning of the office of the king and the proper relation
between the king and the people. In other words, he interprets this "remnant of a
blessing-curse formula" as applicable to a covenant between the king and the
people, yet he recognizes that it is difficult to fit vv. 14 and 15 with this concept.
He comments, "But this is not the case; vv. 14-15 look to the relation of the
whole nation to Yahweh. This may well reflect Israel's overriding concern with its
fundamental covenant relationship, but it is not quite to the point here." Leaving
aside the question whether or not two covenants existed in connection with
kingship in Israel (one between the people, including the king, and Yahweh; and
the other between the king and the people, cf. II Kings 11:17) it seems clear to
this writer that the focus of vv. 14 and 15 on Israel's fundamental covenant
relationship to Yahweh precisely at the moment of the inauguration of the
monarchy is very much to the point (see above, Chapter I, pp. 41-46) and, in fact,
the central concern of the Gilgal assembly.

lenged in any way by the accession of the human king whom he had just presented to them, yet at the same time he clearly indicates that kingship in itself need not be in conflict with covenant fidelity to Yahweh.

After the unusual thunder storm (I Sam. 12:16-18) and the people's response to it by repentance and confession of their sin in requesting a king (I Sam. 12:19), Samuel reassures them, but he then again emphasizes their fundamental covenantal obligation of undivided allegiance to Yahweh with two additional exhortations:

I Samuel 12:20b, 21[76]

. . . only do not any longer turn away from following Yahweh, but serve Yahweh with all your heart.

And turn not away after vain things which do not profit or deliver because they are vain things.
I Samuel 12:24[77]

Only fear Yahweh, and serve him faithfully with all your heart, for consider what great things he has done for you.

The threefold repetition of the challenge to covenant faithfulness in the brief compass of this description of the Gilgal gathering suggests in itself the prominent place which covenant renewal occupies in the proceedings of the assembly.

3. Blessing and curse sanctions (I Sam. 12:14b, 15b, 25).

Samuel's formulation of the basic covenantal obligation in a conditional expression connects directly with the blessing and curse sanctions of verses 14b and 15b. If Israel remains loyal to Yahweh with the introduction of human kingship into her national life she will then be continuing to recognize Yahweh as her sovereign (והיתם ... אהר יהוה),[78] and therefore can expect to enjoy the benefits contingent

76. See above, Chapter I, 53-55.
77. See above, Chapter I, 59-60.
78. See above, Chapter I, 41-46.

upon that loyalty. If she turns away from following Yahweh, his hand will be against her as it was against her fathers.[79] The warning inherent in the curse sanction of 14b is emphasized again in the concluding statement of the chapter (v. 25) where it is said that persistence in wickedness (i.e., rejection of the kingship of Yahweh in whatever form this may take cf. vv. 17, 19, 20, 21) will lead to the destruction of the nation and its human king.[80]

4. Theophanic sign (I Sam. 12:16-18a).

Although theophany cannot be said to be a regular feature of the covenant form,[81] and in addition one might question whether or not this section of I Samuel 12 is rightly interpreted as theophanic,[82] it is nevertheless noteworthy that the covenant form is associated with theophany in a

---

79. The attachment of blessing and curse sanctions to the covenant conditional is attested elsewhere in covenantal contexts (cf. Ex. 19:5, 6; 23:22; Deut. 8:19; 11:13-15, 22-25, 26-28; 28:1 ff., 15 ff.; 30:17, 18; Josh. 24:20; I Sam. 7:3).

80. Note the similar formulation at the conclusion of certain Hittite treaties (Goetze, *ANET*[2], 205-206). In the treaty between Mursilis and Duppi-Tessub of Amurru: ". . . should Duppi-Tessub not honor these words of the treaty and the oath, may these gods of the oath destroy Duppi-Tessub together with his person, his wife, his son, his grandson, his house, his land and together with everything that he owns.

"But if Duppi-Tessub honors these words of the treaty and the oath that are inscribed on this tablet, may these gods of the oath protect him together with his person, his wife, his son, his grandson, his house (and) his country."

In the treaty between Suppiluliumas and Kurtiwaza: "If you, Kurtiwaza, the prince, and (you) the sons of the Hurri country do not fulfill the words of this treaty, may the gods, the lords of the oath, blot you out, (you) Kurtiwaza, and (you) the Hurri men together with your country, your wives and all that you have. . . . If (on the other hand) you, Kurtiwaza, the prince, and (you), the Hurrians, fulfill this treaty and (this) oath, may these gods protect you, Kurtiwaza, together with your wife, . . . May the throne of your father persist, may the Mitanni country persist."

81. The reason for this may be found largely in the fact that Yahweh addresses his covenant people through a mediator or spokesman (cf. the first person address of the covenant-treaty form in many instances), and this may or may not be accompanied by some sort of theophany as it was at Sinai.

82. See above, Chapter I, 50-51. The thunderings and rain are more an authenticating sign than a theophany in the technical sense of the word, yet the nature of the sign with its overtones of the Sinai theophany causes it to assume theophanic significance.

number of instances (cf. Deut. 31; I Kings 8; Ps. 50).[83] And
as we noted above, the manifestation of the power of Yahweh in the thunderings and rain serves a theophanic purpose
in its functional role in the proceedings of the Gilgal assembly. The people are reminded that the God who appeared at
Sinai amidst thunderings and lightnings (Ex. 19:16; 20:18) is
still concerned with his people and capable of actualizing the
covenant curses on them for their disobedience and rejection
of himself. The response of the people here (vv. 18-19) is
indicative of the deep impression which it made on them and
reminiscent of the response of their ancestors previously to
the manifestation of Yahweh's presence at Sinai (Ex. 20:18-
20). It is this remarkable act of Yahweh in sending thunderings and rain at Samuel's behest which evokes fear, repentance, and the request for intercession. At the same time this
event is described as a great thing (הדבר הגדול) which the
people are to witness (ראו), thus assuming the form of a sign
or wonder. This call to witness an extraordinary act of
Yahweh as a basis for expression of covenant allegiance to
Yahweh is also found in other covenantal pericopes (cf. Ex.
19:4a; 20:22; Deut. 29:1[2]; Josh. 23:3; 24:7a).

B. Implications of the Covenant Form in
I Samuel 11:14-12:25 for its Interpretation and Unity.

1. Implications for its interpretation.

Recognition of the covenantal character of I Samuel 11:
14-12:25 is important because it provides a perspective for
understanding the overall purpose of the Gilgal gathering
which in turn clarifies the integral relationship between the
various transactions of the assembly. Clarity on the overall
purpose of the assembly also contributes to a more complete
understanding of a number of terms and expressions appear-
ing in the report of the assembly.

---

83. See N. H. Ridderbos, *OTS*, XV, 213-226 and the literature there cited.

a. *Elucidation of the covenantal character and purposes of the Gilgal assembly.*

It has long been customary to designate I Samuel 12 as the "farewell address" of Samuel.[84] This or some similar designation of the chapter is so uniformly adopted even by proponents of the most widely divergent positions on other aspects of the analysis of the chapter that it might well be termed the traditional view. Although new attention has been drawn to I Samuel 12 in recent years because of the investigations into the covenant form initiated by Mendenhall and related to I Samuel 12 by Muilenburg,[85] Baltzer,[86] Weiser,[87] and McCarthy,[88] this has not produced a satisfactory identification of the nature of the Gilgal assembly which does justice to all the factors occasioning the gathering.

In Muilenburg's treatment of I Samuel 12 he does not break with the traditional idea of a "farewell address" when he comments that "Samuel pronounces his great *valedictory* to the people" (italics mine), yet he does point out that this was done "in language which belongs to a long history of covenant tradition."[89] His explanation for this is that I Samuel 12 as well as Joshua 24 go back "to the literary genre which receives its classical form in the Sinaitic pericope and was perpetuated in the active cult at the amphictyonic centers."[90] It is Muilenburg's purpose to point out the common features of the passages he investigates (Ex. 19:3-6; Josh. 24; I Sam. 12), but not to specify further the precise differentia-

84. Smith, *Samuel,* ICC, 81-82; Budde, *Die Bücher Samuel,* KHC, 82; Schulz, *Samuel,* EH, 164; De Groot, *I Samuël,* TeU, 123; Schelhaas, *GTT* 44 (1944) 270; Goldman, *Samuel,* SBB, 63; Caird, "Samuel," *IB,* II, 941; Gottwald, *Encyclopedia Judaica,* XXIV, 792. Note also the discussions in: Eissfeldt, *Introduction,* 13; Sellin-Fohrer, *Introduction,* 224.
85. Muilenburg, *VT* 9 (1959) 360-364.
86. Baltzer, *The Covenant Formulary,* 66-68.
87. Weiser, *Samuel,* FRLANT, 79-94.
88. McCarthy, *Treaty and Covenant,* 141-145.
89. Muilenburg, *VT* 9 (1959) 360-361.
90. Ibid., 361.

tions between the nature of the occasions with which the covenant form is connected. He thus comments with regard to I Samuel 12: "It has not been our concern here to identify the precise occasion; it is likely, however, that the events at Shechem and Gilgal(?) are thought of in some sense as covenant renewals."[91] In exactly what sense he does not say, although later he indicates that in I Samuel 12 one finds the "meeting of kingdom and covenant at the end of the old amphictyony at Gilgal(?)."[92]

From Muilenburg's study it would appear that he considers I Samuel 12 as a record of Samuel's "valedictory address" given in the context of a covenant renewal ceremony at the time of the transition between the amphictyonic and kingdom periods in ancient Israel.

As we noted above, K. Baltzer's study of the covenant formulary includes a great many more Old Testament passages than does Muilenburg's. Among these are those which he classifies as "covenant renewal" texts (Ex. 34; Neh. 9-10; Ezra 9-10; Dan. 9:4b-19; 1 QS 1.18-2.18). The "new element" which Baltzer finds in these texts which he does not find in those he initially examined (Josh. 24; Ex. 19:3-8; Ex. 24:3-4a, 7; Deut. 1-4; 28:69-30:20) is "the interpolation of a confession of sins."[93] This confession of sin then turns into a prayer for forgiveness in order that the state of *shalom* might be restored.

Baltzer next examines a number of passages (II Chron. 29:5-11; II Chron. 14:8-15:15; II Kings 22-23; Jer. 34:8-22; II Kings 18-19; Jer. 21:1-7; Josh. 7-8; I Kings 8) from which he attempts to define more precisely the specific occasions which necessitated covenant renewal. He concludes that there was no fixed date for covenant renewal, but that "the covenant had to be renewed whenever it was broken. Israel learned that the covenant had been broken when the שלום

---

91. Ibid., 364.
92. Ibid.
93. Baltzer, *The Covenant Formulary*, 50.

associated with the covenant ceased, but also definitively through Yahweh's statement."[94]

The next category of passages which Baltzer finds utilizing the covenant formulary are those associated with the confirmation or reaffirmation of the covenant in connection with transfer of authority. It is in this category that he places I Samuel 12 (otherwise including: Josh. 23; Deut. 31–Josh. 1; I Chron. 22–29; II Kings 11). Baltzer feels the necessity for this additional category of covenant texts because "the explanation that in Israel a renewal of the covenant was undertaken when the covenant had been abrogated through the sin of Israel does not . . . account for a rather sizable group of texts . . . which record a covenant renewal in greater or lesser detail."[95]

In his analysis of I Samuel 12, Baltzer, as Muilenburg, does not break with the traditional idea that the chapter contains a "farewell address" by Samuel. He comments: "the occasion of the covenant renewal is 'Samuel's abdication' " in which he introduces the king "who will succeed him in leading the nation" because Samuel has become too old for the exercise of his office (Baltzer's interpretation of Samuel's statement: "I am old and grey-headed").[96] Baltzer then concludes that "in I Samuel 12 a covenant renewal is linked with a transfer of office. Concretely, we have the transfer of the leadership of Israel from Samuel, here the type of a 'Judge of Israel,' to Saul, the 'king.' "[97]

Baltzer thus classifies I Samuel 12 as a record of a covenant renewal linked with the transfer of office. He sees the chapter as a representative of this particular sub-category of the covenant formulary which is elsewhere to be found in Joshua 23; Deuteronomy 31–Joshua 1; I Chronicles 22–29; II Kings 11. His association of I Samuel 12 with these texts

94. Ibid., 59.
95. Ibid., 63.
96. Ibid., 67.
97. Ibid., 68.

which also are concerned with covenant renewal upon transfer of office certainly has merit, yet in classifying the chapter
this way he fails to do justice to certain other important
features of I Samuel 12 which should not be overlooked in an
attempt to delineate the character of the Gilgal assembly.
Two things in particular to which Baltzer does not give
adequate attention are the serious sin of Israel in asking for a
king, and Samuel's continuing function as described in I Samuel 12:23 which Baltzer fails to even mention.

Baltzer does make the brief comment in discussing the
use of the antecedent history in I Samuel 12 that its use here
is "closely related to those discussed in the previous section,
in the circumstances of a *covenant renewal occasioned by
Israel's sin*" (italics mine).[98] This is indeed the case and
certainly needs to be included in any attempt to specify the
nature of the Gilgal assembly. In Baltzer's treatment of
Nehemiah 9-10, which he classifies as a use of the covenant
formulary at the renewal of the covenant after abrogation
because of sin, he says that the "antecedent history . . .
becomes a list of Yahweh's saving acts, in which he has
shown himself to be צדיק (9:8; cf. 9:33), i.e., in this case,
faithful to the covenant. The antecedent history is at the
same time a confession of Israel's sins. This confession also
acknowledges the justice of the curse. The prayer therefore
concludes as a plea for help."[99] I Samuel 12 shows certain
resemblances to this Nehemiah covenant renewal text which
contains a confession of sin and a plea for forgiveness in
order that the state of *shalom* might be restored (cf. I Sam.
12:19-22). Baltzer's treatment of I Samuel 12 and his designation of the character of the Gilgal assembly as covenant
renewal upon transfer of office does not give adequate attention to this factor which is prominent in its structure and
important in relation to the historical situation with which it
is connected. It is clear that the Gilgal assembly is not only

---

98. Ibid., 66.
99. Ibid., 46, 47.

concerned with transition in leadership, but also with covenant renewal after abrogation.

In addition, it must also be questioned whether it is
sufficiently accurate to maintain that I Samuel 12 really
contains a record of covenant renewal on the occasion of
"Samuel's abdication." Samuel certainly does not abdicate in
the sense of a blanket resignation and total retirement. It
might also be questioned if it is proper to speak of a "transfer
of office" from Samuel to Saul. Although Samuel does invest
Saul with certain functions which he previously had assumed
himself, there is no exact equivalence between the office of
judge and that of king. In addition, I Samuel 12:23 clearly
indicates that Samuel is not abdicating his own position of
continued leadership. This is confirmed by his important role
in the events connected with the rejection of Saul by Yahweh
and his replacement by David. The question is thus raised if it
is not misleading to designate Samuel's speech in I Samuel 12
as a valedictory, abdication, or farewell address.

It is in this context that the suggestions of A. Weiser have
served to place the chapter in a new perspective. Weiser[100]
maintains that the determination of the *Gattung* of I Samuel
12 is not helped much by the normal designations such as
"farewell address" or "sermon" as long as there is not clarity
on the form of the chapter as a whole and the relationship of
the individual structural elements within the chapter to each
other. Weiser maintains that the traditional farewell address
assessment of the chapter creates an "unüberbrückbare und
unerklärliche Kluft" between verses 1-5 and the remainder of
the chapter.[101] He, therefore, concludes that these verses do
not represent a procedure for an elderly man at the point of
retirement to step down from his office, but rather represent
a clever strategy by Samuel to secure a basis for confidence in
his own continued leadership. Weiser thus departs drastically

---

100. Weiser, *Samuel,* FRLANT, 83; cf. above, Chapter I, 18-20.
101. Ibid., 84.

from the traditional categorization of the chapter as Samuel's farewell address.

From these differences in viewpoint it becomes apparent that a significant issue which needs resolution when one attempts to specify the nature of the Gilgal assembly is that of exactly what Samuel was seeking to accomplish and how the covenant form might relate to this. Muilenburg and Baltzer view the chapter as a record of a covenant renewal ceremony in connection with Samuel's farewell and transfer of office to the king. Weiser views the chapter as a record of the way in which Samuel secured a basis for his continued function as "Repräsentant des Jahwebundes" in the restructuring of Israel's institutions as transition is made from the epoch of the judges to that of the kingdom.[102]

Weiser's position, however, has not gone without challenge. C. J. Goslinga, in our view, rightly contests Weiser's assertion that "von einer Amtsniederlegung . . . mit keinem Wort die Rede ist." Goslinga says, "Wel ontbreekt een uitdrukkelijk 'ik leg mijn ambt als richter neer,' maar Samuël doet niet, en kàn niet doen, alsof er na de instelling van het koningschap niets veranderd is. De achtergrond van heel het stuk (zie vooral vss. 2, 13) is juist dat zijn taak *in zeker opzicht* beëindigd is en hij zijn gezag aan de koning moet overdragen. Daarom vraagt hij eervolle decharge (vss. 1-5) en belooft hij spontaan wat hij voor het volk wil blijven doen, vs. 23, welk woord immers veronderstelt dat hij *op een of andere wijze* zich terugtrekt, en wel àls richter, als magistraat, als de hoogste gezagsdrager in Israël onder Jahwe" (italics mine).[103]

It is here that the recognition of the covenantal character of the Gilgal assembly is helpful by providing a perspective within which the significance of these various aspects of the Gilgal assembly can be understood and integrated.

It appears from the biblical text that covenant renewal at

---

102. Ibid., 83.
103. Goslinga, *Het Eerste Boek Samuël,* COT, 243.

times of important transition in leadership was customary in ancient Israel, being attested on at least four important occasions, namely the transition in leadership from Moses (Deut. 27; 31-34; Josh. 1); Joshua (Josh. 23, 24); Samuel (I Sam. 11:14-12:25); and David (I Chron. 22-29). Each of these occasions have their own distinctive settings differentiating them from each other, but in each case an important leader has come to the point in life where it is clear that his time of service in the leadership of the nation is drawing to a close. Each of these occasions is introduced in the biblical narrative with a similar statement by which this idea is conveyed. In Deuteronomy 31:2 Moses says, "I am an hundred and twenty years old this day; I can no more go out and come in" (cf. also Deut. 31:14, 16). In Joshua 23:2 Joshua says, "I am old and striken in age." In I Samuel 12:2 Samuel says, "I am old and grey-headed." In I Chronicles 23:1 it is said, "When David was old and full of days." In the cases of Moses and David the transition in leadership which was about to take place involved a direct *transfer of office* to another designated individual (Joshua and Solomon respectively) to whom specific tasks were assigned (Joshua was to lead the people into the promised land, Deut. 31:7, 8, 23; Solomon was to build the house of Yahweh, I Chron. 28:6, 20), and to whom the people gave their allegiance (Deut. 34:9; I Chron. 29:23-25). In the cases of Samuel and especially Joshua the transition in leadership does not involve an explicit transfer of office to another single individual who is to carry on *quid pro quo* as the departed one's successor. In Samuel's case one might at best speak of a partial transfer of office since the entire task of Samuel was not being given to the newly chosen king.

What becomes clear then, particularly in the cases of Samuel and Joshua, is that covenant renewal at the time of transition in leadership is concerned more with insuring covenant continuity than it is specifically and only with the transfer of office to another designated individual. Even in the cases of Moses and David where concern for covenant continuity focuses on a commitment to follow a designated successor by transfer of office, the most important thing is continued adherence to covenantal obligations (Deut. 31:3-30; 32:44-47; I Chron. 28:8, 9, 20). The change in leadership is important, but it is subordinated to the more weighty issue of covenant continuity and leaves the fundamental covenantal obligations for the nation undiminished.

The purpose then, of the covenant renewal ceremony described in I Samuel 11:14-12:25 is primarily to insure covenant continuity in and beyond an important transition in leadership. Here, as on other occasions, a prominent leader has become old and the nation must be prepared for the time when he no longer would serve them. But in addition this assembly was called at a time when the people had abrogated the covenant by desiring a king like the nations round about, and by requesting his appointment by Samuel. Furthermore, in spite of the wickedness of the people in their request for a king, Yahweh had told Samuel to "make them a king," and now the time had come for Saul to be inaugurated and to assume his role of leadership over the nation. Israel has thus come to the moment of a major restructuring of the administration of the theocracy. It is the combination of all these factors which created the unique situation for the calling of a covenant renewal assembly at Gilgal.

In all of this the over-riding issue is Samuel's attempt to provide for covenant continuity in the future life of the nation. This necessitated first of all repentance and confession of sin by the people for their wickedness in asking for a king, and then recognition of the continuing suzerainty of Yahweh, Israel's Great King, as she enters into the period of the monarchy.

With the establishment of the monarchy Samuel would relinquish some of his previous functions to the king, particularly that of leading the nation in war against her enemies. But this does not mean that he is simply turning his own previous responsibilities over to Saul and going into retirement. Samuel was clearly not relinquishing his prophetic function.[104] He says specifically that he will continue to instruct and guide the people in the way which they should go, and he will remain an intercessor on their behalf.[105] Here, then, is no simple transfer of office *en toto* from Samuel to Saul, but rather the initiating of a new order of administration of the theocracy in which there is a new division of responsibility among Israel's leaders. In this new order the relationship between prophet and king is to be of great significance in both the immediate and more distant future.

I Samuel 11:14-12:25 should, therefore, be understood as the record of a covenant renewal ceremony held for the dual purpose of providing for covenant continuity at a time of transition in leadership and covenant restoration after abrogation. It is misleading to characterize the chapter as either Samuel's "farewell address" or as a ceremony designed solely to enable Samuel to continue to function as "Repräsentant des Jahwebundes." Neither of these characterizations does justice to the total picture. Samuel was approaching the end of his life, and was preparing the nation to carry on without him as she entered a new epoch in her history. Yet Samuel is not retiring nor is he simply transferring his former functions *en toto* to the king. His purpose is to provide for covenant continuity by establishing the new order of the theocracy with the inauguration of Saul; by setting the pattern for the future relationship between the kings and prophets in Israel; and by calling the people to repentance and renewed allegiance to Yahweh with a view to the future well-being of the nation.

---

104. Cf. above, p. 59 (and n. 141).

105. That intercession is often associated with the prophetic function is indicated in a number of O.T. passages (cf., e.g.: Gen. 20:7; Jer. 37:3). Rowley (*Worship in Ancient Israel,* 163) comments: ". . . the prophet was not only the man who brought the word of God to man. He was also the spokesman of man to God, and as intercessor he figures frequently in the Old Testament." Cf. further: De Boer, *OTS,* III, 157 ff.; von Rad, *Old Testament Theology,* II, 51 ff.

b. Elucidation of the covenantal background for various statements and terms occurring in I Samuel 11:14–12:25.

Recognition of the "covenant form" in I Samuel 11: 14–12:25 not only aids in clarifying the significance and purpose of the Gilgal assembly, but also provides a perspective within which certain expressions and concerns in the pericope are made more perspicuous.

1) *"Renew the kingdom"* (I Sam. 11:14).—First of all, Samuel's statement, "Come, let us go to Gilgal and renew the kingdom there" (I Sam. 11:14) is placed in a new light. As we have noted, the people are invited to Gilgal in order to renew the abrogated covenant with Yahweh at a time of transition in national leadership. Samuel's primary concern at the Gilgal assembly is provision for covenantal continuity in this historical context. The presence of the covenant form and the emphasis on covenant renewal in I Samuel 12 is an added indication that the "kingdom" referred to in I Samuel 11:14 is best understood as the kingdom of Yahweh.[106] Understanding the phrase in this way clarifies the relationship between I Samuel 11:14 and 15 and provides a concise statement of the purpose of the Gilgal assembly. It is not Saul's kingdom that is to be renewed, his kingdom is rather to be established (cf. I Sam. 11:14, "they made Saul king before Yahweh in Gilgal"), but this is to be done in the context of renewal of allegiance to Yahweh. It was allegiance to Yahweh, not Saul, which had dissipated and needed reaffirmation; and it is this to which Samuel challenges the people as he presents their king to them (I Sam. 12:2, 13-15) reminding them that their wickedness was great in asking for a king (I Sam. 12:17).

2) *Israel's wickedness in asking for a king (I Sam. 12:17, 20).*—Recognition of the covenantal character of I Samuel 11:14–12:25 also contributes to a better understanding of

---

106. See above, Chapter II; Chapter III, Section 2,A.

the reason why Israel's sin in requesting a king was considered to be so serious by Samuel (cf. I Sam. 12:17, 20). As is indicated in I Samuel 8:20 the Israelites desired a king who would "go out before us and fight our battles." The Israelites were apparently gravely concerned for their national security in the face of the continuing Philistine threat, and also the anticipated hostile actions of the Ammonites under the leadership of Nahash (cf. I Sam. 12:12). In these circumstances, instead of crying out to Yahweh and requesting deliverance, they sought to provide for their security by setting a king over them to lead them in battle as was customary with the nations round about. This action constituted a most serious breach of covenant, in that it represented a lack of confidence in the covenantal promises of Yahweh, their Great King, by seeking national security in the person of a human leader. In addition, it showed complete disregard for previous demonstrations of Yahweh's covenant faithfulness in providing for Israel's defense (I Sam. 12:6-11).[107]

It is noteworthy here that one of the prominent features of the Hittite treaties is the Great King's promise of protection to his vassal against enemies. In Yahweh's covenant with Israel there is an analogous "protection clause" in which Yahweh promises to be the protector of his people when they remain faithful to their covenantal obligations.[108] Yahweh says (Ex. 23:22) "I will be an enemy unto thine enemies, and an adversary unto thine adversaries." In addition, Yahweh promised to give the Amorites, Canaanites, Hittites, Perizzites, Hivites, and Jebusites into the Israelite's hand as they enter the land of Canaan (Ex. 34:11). It is in these assurances of protection that Israel was to find her sense of national security. J. Broekhuis comments, "De oorlogen, die Israël voerde, waren Jahwe's oorlogen. Ze zijn uitdrukking van het bewustzijn van de Israëliet, dat de verbondsgod bij

---

107. See above, Chapter I, 20-40. See further, G. E. Wright's discussion of "God the Warrior" (*The Old Testament and Theology*, 121-150).
108. Fensham, *VT* 13 (1963) 133-143.

alle dingen oorzakelijk is betrokken."[109] Israel was to enter the promised land to conquer its people while maintaining her security by resting in the promises of Yahweh's protection. In Deuteronomy 20:1-4 the Israelites are told that when they go out to battle against an enemy whose forces are greater and stronger than their own, they are not to be "afraid of them; for Yahweh your God, who brought you up from the land of Egypt is with you. . . . Do not be faint-hearted. Do not be afraid, or panic, or tremble before them for Yahweh your God is the one who goes with you, to fight for you against your enemies, to save you." Because of this promise Israel was not to fear her enemies but believe Yahweh (Ex. 14:13; Num. 14:9; Josh. 10:8; II Sam. 10:12; II Chron. 20:17). Because of this promise Israel was also always to remember that her victories were Yahweh's victories, and all the glory and honor was due to him and not to the human leader in battle (Ex. 15; Judg. 5; Josh. 23:10; Ps. 18; 21).

It is the protection clauses in the covenantal formulations of Exodus and Deuteronomy which provide the explanation for Samuel's statements that Israel was rejecting Yahweh as king when they requested a human king to lead them in battle. The seeking of security in anyone other than Yahweh was tantamount to rebellion against the suzerainty of Yahweh. This abrogation of the covenant needed rectification upon the inauguration of Saul to be king. It was also important to emphasize that as Saul's kingship was established, his position as king in no way impinged on the continued sovereignty of Yahweh, and that even with a human king Israel would continue to derive her security from Yahweh's promise of protection. It is then indeed significant that Saul was inaugurated only after stating very clearly that "Yahweh has accomplished deliverance in Israel" (I Sam. 11:13) subsequent to his leading Israel to victory over the Ammonites.

109. J. Broekhuis, "De Heilige Oorlog in het Oude Testament," *ThRef* 18 (1975) 120.

3) *"Peace offerings"* (I Sam. 11:15); *"righteous acts of Yahweh"* (I Sam. 12:7); *"good and right way"* (I Sam. 12: 23).—There are other individual terms in I Samuel 11:14–12:25 which acquire fuller significance when they are seen in a covenantal context. Among these are: "peace offerings" (I Sam. 11:15); "righteous acts of Yahweh" (I Sam. 12:7); and "good and right way" (I Sam. 12:23). As we noted above,[110] the sacrifices of peace offerings at the Gilgal assembly are particularly appropriate when it is seen that the assembly is primarily concerned with covenant renewal, for these sacrifices are associated closely with the establishment of the covenant at Sinai and represent a demonstration of covenant solidarity in subsequent observances.[111] The expression "the righteous acts of Yahweh" (I Sam. 12:7) also gains in clarity when it is noted that the usage of צדק and its cognate forms occurs in covenantal contexts as a designation of covenant faithfulness (cf. Ps. 106:31; Mic. 6:5; Deut. 9:4-6; Hos. 2:21; Isa. 26:2; Zech. 8:8; Ps. 103:17[18]).[112] Here Samuel utilizes examples of Yahweh's covenant loyalty in order to set the disloyalty of Israel in bold relief.

After Saul had been presented to the people and the people had confessed their sin in requesting a king, Samuel announces that he will continue to pray for them and teach them "in the good and the right way" (I Sam. 12:23). This

---

110. Chapter II, 88-90.

111. See esp. Schmid, *Das Bundesopfer.* D. J. McCarthy (*CBQ* 26 [1964] 503) in his review of Schmid's work comments that the *selamim* sacrifice is characterized by its "relation to covenant, which it establishes, reinforces or restores. The communal meal, symbol of unity and the distinguishing mark of this rite among the sacrifices of Israel, emphasizes this relation to covenant. This is substantiated by a study of the sacrifice in its historical context. The exegesis of the relevant texts shows the meaning which the rite must have had for Israel, and again and again this is covenant."

112. Cf. Tigay, *JBL* 89 (1970) 178-186. Tigay (p. 184) suggests that צדק in v. 9 of Ps. 7 "refers not to general ethical behavior, nor even to 'innocence' in this particular case, but to the loyalty or devotion to his ally which he was accused of violating." He says further (p. 184, n. 38): "This usage of צדק and cognate forms has been noted in Aramaic inscriptions ... and a biblical covenantal context, I Kings 3:6. ..." See also Weinfeld, *JAOS* 90 (1970) 186, n. 17; Zeisler, *The Meaning of Righteousness in Paul,* 17-46.

expression is also elucidated by its setting in a covenantal context. W. L. Moran has pointed out that the term *ṭbt'* in the Sefîre treaties means "friendship" or "good relations" with specific reference to the "amity established by treaty."[113] D. R. Hillers has utilized this insight to illuminate several passages in the Old Testament where טובה occurs in contexts in which this special meaning seems to be involved (cf. Deut. 23:7[6]; II Sam. 2:6).[114] It is quite possible that טובה is also best understood in this sense in I Samuel 12:23.[115] Samuel says he will instruct the people in the way of "covenant amity." It is noteworthy that elsewhere טוב and ישר are used to describe both what Israel ought to do as well as what Yahweh in fact had done, and thus characterize the mutual obligations and relationship of the covenant partners.[116] Deuteronomy 6:18 expresses this with regard to Israel: "You shall perform what is right (ישר) and good (טוב) in the sight of Yahweh, so that it may be well with you (ייטב)." The same terms are used to describe Yahweh in Psalm 25:8, 10:[117] "Yahweh is good (טוב) and upright (ישר). . . . All the

---

113. W. L. Moran, "A Note on the Treaty Terminology of the Sefîre Stelas, *JNES* 22 (1963) 174.

114. D. H. Hillers, "A Note on Some Treaty Terminology in the O.T.," *BASOR* 176 (1964) 46-47.

115. The Hebrew construction here is unusual for two reasons. First, one would expect the vocalization of the article under the preposition ב, because of the definiteness of the following adjectives. Secondly, the feminine gender of the adjectives does not agree with the often masculine gender of דרך (*BDB*, s.v., designates דרך as "n.m. and (less often) f."). The explanation which is nearly universally adopted in the commentaries follows *GK* §126x, which says: "the omission of the article after the preposition is certainly due merely to the Masora." This explanation, however, leaves open the at least possible lack of agreement in gender. Both these matters are resolved if one views טובה and ישרה not as adjectives but as nouns. More significant than the adjectival or nominal character of the words, however, is the meaning, on which particularly with טובה new light has been thrown by the study of ancient treaties. According to *BDB* (s.v.) the nominal usage of ישרה occurs in only one other place in the Old Testament (I Kings 3:6) and this is also clearly in a covenantal context (cf. n. 110 above). For a nominal usage of טובה representing an amicable relationship between two parties, see Deut. 23:7(6).

116. Millard (*TB* 17 [1966] 115-117) has suggested that certain occurrences of the adjective טוב are also to be understood in the light of the special usage of טובה which was mentioned above.

117. See, for instance: Ps. 23:6; 100:5; 135:3, 4.

paths of Yahweh are lovingkindness (חסד) and truth (אמת) to those who keep His covenant and His testimonies." It was Samuel's concern that Israel be as loyal to their covenant obligations as Yahweh was to his.

2. Implications of the covenant form of I Samuel 11:14–12:25 for its unity.

The presence of the covenant form in I Samuel 11:14–12:25 also has significant implications for the literary criticism of the passage because it introduces new factors which must be considered in its literary analysis.

a. Clarification of the relationship between I Samuel 11:14-15 and I Samuel 12:1-25.

First of all, the relationship of I Samuel 11:14-15 to I Samuel 12 is clarified as we noted above in our discussion of the phrase "renew the kingdom." This in turn lends added support to the position developed in our exegetical discussion (Chapter II) and to the provisional conclusion which we reached concerning the literary criticism of I Samuel 11:14–12:25 (Chapter III). All the factors cited in the brief statements of I Samuel 11:14-15 are compatible with the covenant renewal emphasis of Chapter 12. The making of Saul king, the sacrificing of peace offerings and the rejoicing of the men of Israel are all subsumed under the primary purpose of the assembly, that is, that of renewal of allegiance to Yahweh at a time of transition of leadership and covenant abrogation. It is then not only possible, but indeed quite appropriate to conclude that I Samuel 11:14-15 is to be understood as lead or introductory sentences summarizing the purpose of the Gilgal assembly before further details of it are presented in I Samuel 12. It is possible that the writer took the two sections from previously existing separate sources, but there is no compelling reason to consider either the entirety of I Samuel 11:12-14, or the phrase "renew the kingdom" in verse 14 as redactional.[118]

b. *The covenant form and the structural integrity of I Samuel 12.*

Secondly, the unity of I Samuel 12 is given added credence when one rightly accepts the presence of the covenant form in this chapter. Recognition of the covenant form in I Samuel 12 provides a basis for maintaining its structural integrity over against those who either suggest that I Samuel 12 underwent redactional reworking or that it is a composite of disparate material. In addition, the covenant form has implications for the theory that the chapter is the composition of a "deuteronomistic historian" writing in the 6th century B.C. and is to be regarded as a theologically colored and largely fictitious narrative injected into the stories concerning the rise of kingship in Israel. Let us look at each of these matters in more detail.

1) *Implications of the covenant form for viewing I Samuel 12 as an original unity modified by redactional reworking.*—As we noted above (Chapter III, Section 1,A,2), a rather large number of scholars have considered I Samuel 12 as an original unity modified by redactional reworking. With a number of these scholars the chapter is viewed as either a part of, or akin to, the E strand of the Pentateuch, but evidencing a "deuteronomistic" revision. Budde, in his influential work, mentions a number of phrases which he attributes to the deuteronomist's hand, but he gives no compelling reason for excising these statements from the original composition other than their deuteronomic style.[119] The separation of such phrases from the original composition is not so

---

118. See the summary of the various positions in Chapter III, Section 1,B.
119. Budde, *Die Bücher Samuel,* KHC, 77-81. Cf. above, Chapter III, Section 1,A,2,a.

easily done, however, and Eissfeldt,[120] Caird,[121] Fohrer,[122] Mauchline,[123] Gottwald,[124] and Stoebe[125] make no attempt to separate the later material from the original because of the difficulty in establishing an adequate basis for distinguishing between them. When one recognizes the "covenant form" in the basic structure of the chapter and notices the corresponding covenant emphasis in its various parts, it is indeed the case, that indications of what may be termed "deuteronomic" influence can be found. These influences, however, pertain not only to certain isolated phrases, but to the total conception and structure of the chapter as it describes the various aspects of the Gilgal assembly. The matter of deuteronomic influence is thus important, but it must be considered in the light of the more fundamental question of the date of the book of Deuteronomy or, if one chooses, the date of the deuteronomistic school. The possibility exists that deuteronomic/deuteronomistic influence is not automatically to be confined to late editorial insertions or revisions in the report of the Gilgal assembly, but may in fact have been present in the proceedings of the assembly itself. It is our position that there is good reason for attributing Deuteronomy's origin to the Mosaic era,[126] and that consequently it is altogether possible, if not probable, that deuteronomic influences would be operative in the actions and statements of the Gilgal assembly.

There are a few statements in I Samuel 12 which are regarded by some as redactional insertions for reasons other than their deuteronomic phraseology or style. Budde and others consider verse 21 as a late gloss belonging to neither E

120. Eissfeldt, *Komposition,* 6-11.
121. Caird, *IB,* II (Samuel), 855-862.
122. Sellin-Fohrer, *Introduction,* 218-225.
123. Mauchline, *I and II Samuel,* NCB, 18-20, 31, 107-110.
124. Gottwald, *Encyclopedia Judaica,* XXIV, 787-797.
125. Stoebe, *Das erste Buch Samuelis,* KAT, 234-240.
126. See above, Chapter IV, Section 1,D.

or RD.[127] Budde and Driver, among others, view the association of the Ammonite threat with the request for a king
(v. 12) as a later insertion.[128] For both of these matters, it is
sufficient here to make reference to the comments in the
exegetical section above,[129] as neither are directly related to
the covenant form, although they are not incompatible with
it. Driver also views the reference of Samuel to himself in
verse 11 as a later expansion.[130] This, however, as we noted
in our discussion of the use of the historical summary,[131] has
an important function in Samuel's argument since he is
bringing the resumé of the righteous acts of Yahweh in
providing for Israel's defense up to date. Elimination of
Samuel's own name here would greatly weaken his indictment of the people for their wickedness in asking for a king.

Buber eliminates a number of other sections from the
chapter, the most important being the historical summary
(vv. 6-12) and the "Mirakelgeschichte" (vv. 16-19).[132] Elimination of these, however, sets aside the important role which
they play in the proceedings of the Gilgal assembly, and
removes two integral features of the "covenant form."

The position of Wallis[133] is subject to the same criticism
in that, although he develops his reasoning along different
lines than Buber, he comes to a similar conclusion concerning
the sections of the chapter which are to be viewed as redactional additions. He feels the miracle account adds nothing to
the text and is actually disturbing (vv. 16-23), and that the
summary of the conquest and period of the judges fits poorly
in the mouth of Samuel (vv. 6b-11). The association of the
Ammonite war with the request for a king (v. 12) he, as
Driver *et. al.*, views as inconsistent with I Samuel 8.

127. Budde, *Die Bücher Samuel*, KHC, 81.
128. Ibid., 80 (cf. above, Chapter III, Section 1,A,2,a); Driver, *Introduction*,
178 (cf. above, Chapter III, Section 1,A,2,b.).
129. Chapter I, 54-55; Chapter I, 38-40.
130. Driver, *Introduction*, 178.
131. See above, Chapter I, 37, and Chapter IV, Section 2,A,1.
132. Buber, *VT* 6 (1969) 156-162; cf. above, Chapter III, Section 1,A,2,e.
133. Wallis, *Geschichte und Überlieferung*, 94-96; cf. above, Chapter III,
Section 1,A,2,f.

Birch divides the chapter in two sections, verses 1-5 and verses 6-26, the latter of which he assigns to the "deuteronomistic historian" as a supplemental addition to verses 1-5. Birch regards verses 1-5 as a report added to the notice of the Gilgal assembly in I Samuel 11:12-14, and presenting Saul as functioning in the sacral-legal realm and Samuel as retiring from office.[134] Division of the chapter in this way, however, assumes an unnecessary disjunction between the two sections involved, and ascribes the central thrust of the Gilgal assembly (I Sam. 12:13-15) to the deuteronomistic addition rather than to the original account. This results in obscuring the purpose of the Gilgal assembly and does not do justice to the historical factors involved in its convocation.

2) *Implications of the covenant form for viewing I Samuel 12 as a composite of disparate material.*—The analyses suggested by Hylander and Seebass conclude that I Samuel 12 is a composite of disparate material fused together by the compiler of the book. Hylander divides the material into two sections, much as did Birch,[135] while Seebass suggests a much more complex reconstruction with his major division placed between verses 1-15 and 16-25.[136] The same objection may be made to these proposals as was made to those of Buber, Wallis, and Birch. The chapter is, in its present form, an integral whole, exhibiting various features of the covenant form, all of which contribute to achieving the purpose for which the Gilgal assembly was held. To view the chapter as a composite of disparate material does not give adequate consideration to the formal and material unity which we have been suggesting for it on the basis of our exegetical, literary-critical and genre-historical analyses.

3) *Implications of the covenant form for viewing I Sam-*

---

134. Birch, *The Rise of the Israelite Monarchy,* 113-121; cf. above, Chapter III, Section 1,A,2,g.

135. Hylander, *Der Samuel-Saul Komplex,* 237, 238, 301; cf. above, Chapter III, Section 1,A,3,a.

136. Seebass, *ZAW* 77 (1965) 288-295; idem, *ZAW* 79 (1967) 170, 171; cf. above, Chapter III, Section 1,A,3,b.

uel 12 as an independent tradition unit.—As we noted above, there are also those who have recognized the unity of I Samuel 12, but have seen this chapter as one of the many independent tradition units, which are collected in I and II Samuel.[137] Gressmann considers the chapter to be one of the later legends in this section of I Samuel, and feels that its view of kingship as a violation against God was a false idea of a later time rather than the time of which the chapter speaks.[138] After all that has been said above, we need not here discuss this position further. Weiser[139] suggests that the chapter is the product of the cult tradition of the Gilgal sanctuary, promulgated by prophetic circles with which the E source of the Pentateuch is also to be associated. Weiser refuses to discuss the implications of the deuteronomistic features of the chapter until clarity is acquired on the origin and history of the "deuteronomic style." Weiser also refuses to assign the chapter to either an E strand or to the "deuteronomistic historian." In his opinion neither approach has been able to account for the literary features of the chapter. Weiser does, however, recognize the "covenant form" in the chapter and considers this form to be evidence for its basic unity. The literary question is then shifted to the matter of the most likely explanation for the association of the "covenant form" with the description of the Gilgal assembly. Does this derive from the influence of the covenant in the life of ancient Israel at the time of the rise of the monarchy, or is this form a later derivative of cultic traditions? It is our position that there is good reason for ascribing the entrance of the covenant form into the life and literature of Israel to the Mosaic era.[140]

4) *Implications of the covenant form for viewing I Sam-*

137. See above, Chapter III, Section 1,A,1,c.
138. Gressmann, *Die älteste Geschichtsschreibung,* SAT II/1, 24-27; cf. above, Chapter III, Section 1,A,1,c,1.
139. Weiser, *The Old Testament: Its Formation and Development,* 158-170; idem, *Samuel,* FRLANT, 79-94; cf. above, Chapter III, Section 1,A,1,c,2.
140. See above, Chapter IV, Section 1,D.

uel 12 as the composition of a "deuteronomistic historian."—Others have viewed I Samuel 12 as the composition of a "deuteronomistic historian," of the exilic or postexilic age. This was the view of Wellhausen and has been adopted in its essentials by, among others, Smith, Noth, Pfeiffer, and Boecker. Wellhausen considered the chapter, in his opinion a unity, to be historically unreliable.[141] Smith considered the resemblances to D or to the deuteronomic school to be too great to be treated as secondary expansions.[142] Noth viewed the chapter as one of several key passages by which the "deuteronomistic historian" tied together and structured his history work by placing speeches in the mouths of leading figures in the historical narrative.[143] Boecker follows Noth in this position, but attempts to modify Noth's contention that chapter 12 along with I Samuel 8; 10:17-27 is basically anti-monarchical.[144]

As has been noted above, there is good reason for finding deuteronomic influences in I Samuel 12.[145] In this connection, however, the question is whether or not this deuteronomic influence is to be regarded as late (6th century or after) and whether or not it destroys the value of the chapter as a reliable description of the Gilgal assembly. The alternative to such viewpoints is that the Gilgal assembly, as described in I Samuel 12, including its purposes, words spoken, and transactions, and especially its concern with the covenant which is also evident in Deuteronomy, was a historical reality.

It is in these questions that the date of the book of

141. Wellhausen, *Composition*, 240-243; idem, *Prolegomena*, 245-256; cf. above, Chapter III, Section 1,A,1,b,1.

142. Smith, *Samuel*, ICC, xvi-xxii, 81-89; cf. above, Chapter III, Section 1,A,1,b,2.

143. Noth, *Überlieferungsgeschichtliche Studien*, 5, 54-55; cf. above, Chapter III, Section 1,A,1,b,3.

144. Boecker, *Die Beurteilung der Anfänge des Königtums*. For discussion of this matter see further below, Chapter V, Section 1,B,3.

145. These influences can be seen in both the structural elements of the chapter (the covenant form) as well as in the wording of specific phrases (cf. references to this in the text and notes of pp. 33-34, 44, 45, 46, 53, 59, 60 above).

Deuteronomy becomes extremely significant, for it is obvious that a 7th century date for its origin eliminates the possibility of its having provided a formative influence on the statements and proceedings of the Gilgal assembly. Are these statements and proceedings to be considered as historical realities, or as the creation of a late deuteronomistic historian? It is our position that the presence of the covenant form in the chapter is not a hindrance for considering the chapter as the record of a historical reality, that is, a covenant renewal ceremony at the time of the establishment of kingship in Israel. Although the acceptance of the Mosaic origin of Deuteronomy on the basis of the form critical argument derived from the treaty-covenant analogy has not been widespread, there has been an increasing willingness on the part of various scholars to accept the view that at least a *Grundschrift* of the book had its roots in the covenant traditions of Shechem associated with the tribal confederacy, and thus originated in the time prior to the rise of the monarchy and prior to the Gilgal assembly.[146] It is our position that the "deuteronomic" character of the chapter is best explained as a product of a deeply rooted living covenant tradition in the life of Israel prior to the monarchy and thus as representative of the events of the assembly itself rather than a late literary construct created to serve certain theological interests.

---

146. See above, Chapter IV, Section 1,D.

APPENDIX

As has been indicated above it is impossible here to delve
deeply into the question of the date of Deuteronomy. Nevertheless, this question is of great importance for our discussion. For this reason I am including here some amplification
to what was said above consisting primarily in brief resumés
of a few contemporary positions.

As we have noted (cf. 156 ff.), Kline and Kitchen have
concluded that the covenant form points to the Mosaic era
for Deuteronomy's origin. This approach to Deuteronomy,
however, has seemingly been ignored by many, including
some who have argued for the antiquity of the material in
Ex. 19-24 and Josh. 24 on the basis of the covenant form,
and it has been directly opposed by others. J. C. Plastaras
(*CBQ* 29 [1967] 270) in his review of Kitchen's *Ancient
Orient and Old Testament* says: "He [Kitchen] argues against
D. J. McCarthy, and in favor of the earlier unnuanced position of G. E. Mendenhall, that treaty forms similar to the OT
covenant traditions were current only during the second
millennium, but not afterwards. Well and good! But then K.
goes on to conclude that the covenant narratives could not
have taken 'fixed literary forms only in the ninth to sixth
centuries' since the writers could have had no knowledge of
the long-since obsolete covenant-forms (p. 100). K. seems to
have overlooked the very essential fact that no matter at
what date the 'Hittite' covenant-form may have gone out of
current use in the ancient Near East, Israel would have always
retained this same basic covenant-form in her cult, so that
every layer of tradition, J, E, D, or the redactional combination of these earlier sources, would all reflect the same basic
covenant structures." Such an assertion, however, leaves open

the question of when the covenant form was adopted in Israel and faces the same objections which were made above against a purely cultic derivation for the form. Even granting the point to Plastaras does not exclude an early date position, but merely provides a rationale for a late date in view of the admitted antiquity of the form itself.

It is also to be noted in this context that R. Frankena ("The Vassal Treaties of Esarhaddon and the Dating of Deuteronomy," *OTS* XIV [1965] 122-154) has argued for a seventh century date for Deuteronomy on the basis of certain points of correspondence between curse formulations in the vassal treaties of Esarhaddon and Deuteronomy. (Frankena does not discuss the implications of the differences noted above between the Hittite treaties and the Assyrian treaties except to note (ibid., 136): "The omission of blessings in the Assyrian treaties, therefore, might be due to the fact that the treaty would bestow automatically blessings on the faithful vassal.") He concludes (p. 153) that the "religious reform of Josiah was dirccted against Assyria and it is therefore tempting to regard the renewed Covenant with Yahweh as a substitution of the former treaty with the king of Assyria. . . . That the text of this Covenant should betray knowledge of the Assyrian treaties which it seems to replace seems only natural to me. The dating of Deuteronomy, moreover, would in that case find corroboration in a rather unexpected way." Although the parallels which Frankena points out in Deuteronomy and the Assyrian treaties are indeed striking, they do not invalidate the position of Kline and Kitchen. As Kline notes (*The Structure of Biblical Authority*, 10): "As for the similarities of a group of Deuteronomic curses to a section of curses in the later treaties, this is not adequate evidence to date even this particular material late, for the tradition of curse formularies extends far back into the second millennium B.C. Moreover, since the critics in question suppose that Deuteronomy developed over a period of time through a process of additions and modifications, they would be in no position to appeal to the presence of demonstrably seventh-century curse formulations (if there were such) as compelling evidence of a late origin of the treaty structure of the book as a whole." Kitchen (*Ancient Orient and Old Testament*, 99, 100, n. 49) comments: "Useful comparisons between the curses of Dt. and Neo-Assyrian treaties are made by R. Frankena . . . and M. Weinfeld. . . . However, they betray some naïvety in assuming that similarity automatically spells Hebrew dependence on late Assyrian usage. The Old Babylonian data cited by Weinfeld . . . already point toward a different answer—to a long-standing tradition going well back into the second millennium at least, which could have become known in the Westlands even before Moses."

In a different vein G. von Rad has argued for the antiquity of the form of Deuteronomy on the basis of his cultic derivation theory, but a late date for the book itself which he views as the final product of a long and complex process of development. He notes (*Studies in Deuteronomy*, 14, 15) that: "Deuteronomy in its present form is undoubtedly a literary production, but it still bears the stamp of a cultic form that has exercised an extraordinary influence on its style." He says further (p. 41) that "Deuteronomy stands in the tradition of the old Jahweh amphictyony of Shechem. Or rather, it proposes to re-introduce this old cultic tradition in its own advanced period and to set it forth as the form obligatory upon Israel for its life before Jahweh." He maintains that the Levites were the deuteronomic preachers who had the sacral and legal traditional materials at their disposal and made these relevant for their time.

E. W. Nicholson (*Deuteronomy and Tradition*) also traces the origin of the traditions underlying Deuteronomy back to the cultic life of the tribal league during the period of the judges. He (p. 45) concludes that, "the form in which Deuteronomy is cast derives from the cult and follows the liturgical pattern of the festival of the renewal of the covenant." He says (p. 120) that while Deuteronomy shows evidence of its

origin within the traditions of the amphictyony, he feels that
at the same time "it has emerged that Deuteronomy contains
no direct deposit of these old sacral traditions of early Israel.
There has been considerable development in many ways."
Nicholson regards the prophetic circles in northern Israel as
the responsible agents for the preservation and transmission
of the traditions underlying the book. He suggests that these
circles fled to the south after the destruction of the northern
kingdom and eventually drew up their program for reform
during the time of Manasseh depositing their book in the
Temple in Jerusalem where it was found during the reign of
Josiah.

M. Weinfeld ("Deuteronomy—The Present State of Inquiry," *JBL* 86 [1967] 249-262; *Deuteronomy and the
Deuteronomic School*) has opposed the cultic derivation view
of the "covenant form" noting (*JBL* 86 [1967] 253) that,
"the structure of Deuteronomy follows a literary tradition of
covenant writing rather than imitating a periodical cultic
ceremony which is still unattested." Instead of ascribing the
book to Levitical or prophetical circles he attributes it to the
court scribes of the time of Hezekiah and Josiah. He comments (ibid., 253): "if a literary pattern lies behind the form
of Deuteronomy, then it would be much more reasonable to
assume that a literary circle which was familiar with treaty
writing—in other words, court scribes—composed the book of
Deuteronomy." As was noted above, Weinfeld rejects the
view of Mendenhall *et al.* that the Hittite treaty form is
unique and that the covenant form must, therefore, be derived from the second millennium. He dismisses the lack of a
historical prologue in the Assyrian treaties as not significant
(253, n. 6). He then concludes in agreement with Frankena
that Deuteronomy reflects contemporary Assyrian treaties
rather than the earlier Hittite treaties.

Kline (*The Structure of Biblical Authority*, 14) has responded to Weinfeld's view commenting: "The oration character of Deuteronomy Weinfeld explains as a literary device:

programmatic speeches were placed in the mouths of famous persons to express the ideological views of the author (pp. 255 f.). On this point von Rad comes closer to the truth. For while he, too, deems fictional the casting of Deuteronomy in the form of a farewell speech of Moses, he does at least formally integrate this feature with the covenantal elements in the book. He identifies the speech as an office-bearer's farewell (cf. Josh. 23; I Sam. 12; I Chron. 22 and 29) and explains the presence of the covenant formulary within this and other such speeches by reference to the attested practice of renewing covenants when vassal leaders transferred their office to a successor. Unfortunately, von Rad fails to recognize in the oration form the true explanation of the hortatory trend in the Deuteronomic treaty. This feature does not derive from Levitical preaching nor from a late literary circle of court scribes, but from the historical circumstance that Deuteronomy is the documentary deposit of a covenant renewal which was also Moses' farewell to Israel. The element of parenesis already present to some extent in ancient treaties was naturally exploited to the fullest by Moses on that stirring occasion."

As we have noted, it is not possible to discuss the whole range of questions related to the date of Deuteronomy such as the relationship of the legal material in Deuteronomy to that in the Book of the Covenant and Leviticus, and the matter of the centralization of worship (Deut. 12). On these questions see especially: G. Ch. Aalders, *A Short Introduction to the Pentateuch* (London: 1949); idem, *Kanoniek;* B. Holwerda, "De plaats, die de HEERE verkiezen zal," in *Begonnen hebbende van Mozes* (Terneuzen: [1953]) 7-29; G. T. Manley, *The Book of the Law* (London: 1957); Harrison, *Introduction,* 635-662; Segal, *The Pentateuch,* 75-102.

V

THE LITERARY CRITICISM OF I SAMUEL 8-12
IN THE LIGHT OF THE COVENANTAL CHARACTER OF
I SAMUEL 11:14-12:25

It is now our purpose to apply the insights gained from our exegetical, literary-critical and genre-historical analysis of I Samuel 11:14-12:25 in a modest attempt to assess the literary criticism of I Samuel 8-12. We will begin with a general survey of the history of the criticism of this section of I Samuel. The intent here is not to be exhaustive, but rather to indicate the major directions of approach and to cite important representatives of basic positions.[1]

As was indicated above, we will divide our survey into four major categories to provide a framework for analysis.[2]

---

1. Not every investigator referred to above in our discussion of the literary criticism of I Sam. 11:14-12:25 (Chapter III, Section 1) is included in the following survey. Some of those mentioned previously have directed their attention primarily to particular parts of I Sam. 8-12 rather than the section as a whole, and in addition, we have restricted our survey here to major representatives of basic categories of approach. Our purpose is also not to recount the details of the various views, but rather to indicate the broad lines which give shape to the different positions.

2. See above, Chapter III, Section 1,A for a brief discussion of the categories which we have adopted. Notice especially the comment in n. 4 concerning the difficulty of drawing these lines too rigidly. Thus, it would certainly be possible, and in some respects even better, to place Noth in the third group. Yet as Fohrer (Sellin-Fohrer, *Introduction,* 217-218) has pointed out: "Gressmann, on the other hand, sought to explain the books as a loose compilation of individual narratives of varying scope. Noth, Sellin-Rost, Weiser, and others assume in similar fashion that large and small narrative complexes have been brought together, i.e., in part interwoven, in part strung out one after another, sometimes linked very loosely. Weiser thinks in terms of a long process of utilization and elaboration of tradition on the basis of a prophetical interpretation of history. Noth (like Sellin-Rost), following his thesis of a Deuteronomistic History, holds that the Deuteronomistic redaction linked the independent pieces together for the first time (to the extent that they do not actually derive from the Deuteronomist)."

Section 1
A Survey of the History of Criticism of I Samuel 8-12.
A. The Documentary-Source Approach

1. J. Wellhausen

J. Wellhausen, following earlier suggestions of Eichhorn[3] and Thenius,[4] developed the hypothesis that I Samuel 7-15 was composed of two main strands of narrative which he viewed as an early and a late source.[5] He maintained that I Samuel 9:1-10:16 was joined with the independent traditions in I Samuel 11:1-11, 15; 13-14 at an early date to form the early source. The later source I Samuel 7:2-8:22; 10:17-27; 12:1-25; 15:1-34 was added to the earlier material editorially by means of passages such as I Samuel 11:13, 14. It was Wellhausen's opinion that the late source reflected a deuteronomistic influence which was most apparent in its negative view of kingship. For Wellhausen the favorable and unfavorable attitude toward the monarchy was the most important factor in isolating the two strands of narrative. He comments: "In the great difference which separates these two narratives we recognize the mental interval between two different ages. In the eyes of Israel before the exile the monarchy is the culminating point of the history, and the greatest blessing of Jehovah. . . . The position taken up in the version of I Sam. vii. viii. x.17 seq. xii., presents the greatest possible contrast to this way of thinking. There, the erection of the monarchy only forms a worse stage of backsliding from Jehovah. . . . That this view is unhistorical is self-evident; . . . the idea here before us can only have arisen in an age which had no knowledge of Israel as a people and a state,

---

3. J. G. Eichhorn, *Einleitung in das Alte Testament,* (Göttingen: 1823/24⁴) III, 464-533.

4. Wellhausen, *Die Bücher Samuels,* KeH.

5. Wellhausen, *Composition,* 240-243; idem, *Prolegomena,* 245-272; cf. above, Chapter III, Section 1,A,1,b,1.

and which had no experience of the real conditions of existence in these forms; in other words, it is the offspring of exilic or post-exilic Judaism. . . . At that time . . . the theocracy *existed,* and it is from that time that it is transported in an idealised form to early times."[6]

2. K. Budde

K. Budde[7] also adopted a two source division of the narratives of I Samuel 8–12 much as did Wellhausen, but in distinction from Wellhausen he identified them with the J and E sources of the Pentateuch. He assigned the sources to different locations (Mizpah: 8:1-22; 10:17-24; 12:1-25; Gilgal 9:1–10:7, 9-16; 11:1-11, 15) and attempted to establish his case by identifying elohist terminology and themes in the Mizpah source. He considered this source to be strongly antagonistic to kingship and objected to Cornill's[8] view that the passages in chapters 8 and 10 which were opposed to the monarchy were interpolations.[9] He felt, however, that this anti-monarchial tendency was adequately accounted for only by positing its derivation from a northern E source.[10] He considered the Gilgal source as more positively disposed to the monarchy, presenting it as Yahweh's gracious response to Israel's cry for help. These two sources were combined, according to Budde, by a deuteronomistic redactor whose

---

6. Wellhausen, *Prolegomena,* 253-256.

7. K. Budde, *ZAW* 8 (1888) 223-248; idem, *Die Bücher Samuel,* KHC; idem, *Die Bücher Richter und Samuel, Ihre Quellen und ihr Aufbau* (Giessen: 1890) 167-276; cf. above, Chapter III, Section 1,A,2,a.

8. C. Cornill, "Ein elohistischer Bericht über die Entstehung des israelitischen Königtums in I. Samuelis 1-15 aufgezeigt," ZWL 6 (1885) 113-141; idem, "Zur Quellenkritik der Bücher Samuelis," *Königsberger Studien,* Bd I (1887) 25-59.

9. In speaking of Cornill's proposals, Budde (*ZAW* 8 [1888] 231) comments: "Aber so sehr er sich bemüht, die gutartige, rein sachliche Natur des 'Königsrechtes' nachzuweisen (S. 127 f): die Missbilligung des Königthums durch Samuel und die Verstockung des Volkes (vgl. dafür besonders 8, 19 f.) bleibt doch in 8, 11-20 in ihrer vollen Schärfe erhalten, so dass mit der Ausscheidung gar nichts erreicht wird."

10. He comments (ibid., 235): "Nur bei der Ableitung von E findet die starke Missbilligung des Königthums ihre Erklärung."

language is often difficult to isolate because it is so similar to E but which in certain places is clearly discernable (as, e.g., in certain expressions in I Sam. 12:9, 11, 14, 15, 17).[11]

3. H. P. Smith

H. P. Smith distinguished two documentary strands in I Samuel 8-12 following the same pattern of division previously advocated by Wellhausen and Budde. He was not convinced, however, that Budde's identification of them with the J and E sources of the Pentateuch was tenable.[12] In place of this Smith posited a life of Samuel (*Sm.*) for I Samuel 8; 10:17-25; 12, and a life of Saul (*Sl.*) for I Samuel 9:1-10:16; 11. He considered *Sl.* to be the older of the two strands and expressive of "a near and clear view of the personages and the progress of events."[13] He says the *Sm.* source is later, idealizing persons and events, and dominated by a theological idea. For this reason he concludes that "*Sm.* designed to replace the older history by one of his own which would edify his generation. This design and this method are indications of a comparatively late date—perhaps in or after the Exile."[14] Smith indicates that he adopts a two source view because of the "duplication" of certain incidents (including two or three accounts of Saul's appointment as king), as well as noticeable differences in style and "point of view." The difference in point of view is seen primarily in what Smith terms a "difference of political theory."[15] He comments: "In one account Saul is chosen as king by God, is welcomed by Samuel, is assured that God is with him and encouraged to act as he finds opportunity. His election by God is an act of grace. . . . But in other sections of the narrative the desire of the people for a king is an act of rebellion against Yahweh. Their act is

---

11. See above, Chapter III, Section 1,A,2,a.

12. Smith, *Samuel*, ICC, xv-xxii; see above, Chapter III, Section 1,A,1,b,2 and Chapter III, Section 1,B,1,a,2.

13. Ibid., xx.

14. Ibid.

15. Ibid., xvi.

an act of apostasy parallel to all their rebellions of earlier times. . . . So great a discrepancy, not in details of the narrative only, but also in the whole view of the same period, is not conceivable in one author. It can be accounted for only on the hypothesis that various works have been combined in one."[16]

4. S. R. Driver

S. R. Driver also distinguished two narrative strands within I Samuel 8-12. In agreement with Budde, Driver held that these two strands were independent narratives rather than attributing the later source to the deuteronomic author-editor as Wellhausen had done. He says that the older source regards the appointment of Saul to be king favorably, and in this source there is no indication of reluctance on Samuel's part to see the monarchy established. In the later narrative the request for a king is "viewed with disfavour by Samuel, and treated as a renunciation of Jehovah."[17] He says that it is not necessary "to suppose that this narrative is destitute of historical foundation; but the emphasis laid in it upon aspects on which the other narrative is silent, and the difference of tone pervading it, show not the less clearly that it is the work of a different hand."[18] Driver's conclusion is similar to that of Budde in which he notes affinities of the later narrative with E, which he feels indicate that it is a pre-Deuteronomic work expanded by a subsequent deuteronomistic editor.

5. O. Eissfeldt

O. Eissfeldt continued in the general pattern set by Wellhausen, Budde, Smith, and Driver although he felt it necessary to divide the earlier pro-monarchial material into two separate narrative strands, resulting in a three source theory

---

16. Ibid.
17. Driver, *Introduction*, 176; see above, Chapter III, Section 1,A,2,b and Chapter III, Section 1,B,1,b,1.
18. Ibid.

for the origin of the material in I Samuel 8-15. Initially Eissfeldt labeled these sources simply as I, II, and III, but he later identified them with the L, J, and E sources which he distinguished in the Pentateuch.[19] He assigned I Samuel 8:1-22; 10:17-21b[a]; 12:1-25 to III; I Samuel 9:1–10:16; 11:6a[a] to II; and the remaining sections, I Samuel 10:21b[b]-27; 11 (except v. 6a[a]) to I. Eissfeldt's deviation from Budde, Smith, and Driver is found then chiefly in his separation of two narrative strands in I Samuel 10:17-27 and his assignment of almost all of I Samuel 11 to L. Eissfeldt accepts as a "generally recognized result" of critical study that "there are present at least two mutually exclusive presentations of the beginnings of Israelite kingship, and that one of them, to which chs. vii-viii and xii belong, has a marked affinity to the Elohistic sections of the Hexateuch and of the book of Judges, whereas the other is in many respects reminiscent of J."[20]

The documentary source analysis of I Samuel 8-12 has had many additional advocates including among others A. Schulz,[21] R. Pfeiffer,[22] and G. B. Caird,[23] each of whom have followed the same general pattern of source division noted above with the "pro" or "anti" monarchial tendency of the

19. Cf. Eissfeldt, *Komposition*, 6-11, 56-57 (where he labels the three strands as I, II, III) with *Introduction*, 271-275 (where he designates them as L, J, and E). Eissfeldt's approach to this material in his *Introduction* is in keeping with his analysis of the Pentateuch in which he maintained that after separation of the D and P material it was not adequate to assign the remaining material to only J and E. He felt that there was evidence for an additional older L (lay) source that was "particularly crude and archaic, and although a powerful religious spirit also moves strongly through it, it is nevertheless the least touched by clerical and cultic interests" (*Introduction*, 194).

20. Eissfeldt, *Introduction*, 271. Eissfeldt's own analysis posits three accounts of Saul's accession rather than two. For a similar position see: W. A. Irwin, "Samuel and the Rise of the Monarchy," *AJSL* 58 (1941) 113-134. In this way Eissfeldt arrives at a position which is close to that of Gressmann (see below, n. 24) in its end result concerning the analysis of I Samuel 8-12. Both view I Sam. 9:1-10:16 as independent in origin and also less reliable historically than I Sam. 11.

21. Schulz, *Samuel*, EH, 174-179.

22. Pfeiffer, *Introduction*, 338-368.

23. Caird, *IB*, II, 855-868.

various narrative units providing the most significant criterion for source division. In spite of this long succession of advocates, the documentary source theory has never been without challenge. Right from Wellhausen's own time the rival fragmentary theory had its proponents, and in more recent times the more complex traditions history approach has attracted a significant number of adherents.

B. The Fragmentary Approach

1. H. Gressmann

H. Gressmann offered a distinctly different analysis of the composition of I Samuel 8-12 from that of the documentary source theory which was the dominant view of his time.[24] Following the methodology of H. Gunkel, Gressmann attempted to separate the narrative units of the book and to examine them form critically. He concluded that the book was a loose compilation by a late editor utilizing many originally independent narrative units of various literary types. Although he did not discern any connected literary sources in the book and directed his attention to the individual narrative units, he does speak of I Samuel 7:2-8:22; 10:17-27; 12:1-25 as "eine einheitliche Grösse" since Samuel is represented in these places as a judge in Israel and kingship is viewed as a "Gottesfrevel."[25] He considers all of these sections to be of late origin and comments: "Historische Kunde enthalten sie nicht; um ihres geistlichen Charakters willen wird man sie nicht als Geschichts-Erzählungen, sondern als Legenden werten müssen."[26] After discussing I Samuel 9:1-10:16 in some detail Gressmann concludes: "Nach dieser Analyse kann kein Zweifel sein, dass wir es hier nicht, wie behauptet wird, mit einer Geschichtserzählung, sondern mit einer volkstümlichen Sage zu tun haben . . . Hier nähert

---

24. Gressmann, *Die älteste Geschichtsschreibung*, SAT II/1, 24-47; cf. above, Chapter III, Section 1,A,1,c,1 and Chapter III, Section 1,B,1,a,3.
25. Ibid., 26, 46.
26. Ibid., 26.

sich überdies die Sage dem Märchen."[27] After citing characteristics of the narrative which he labels as "märchenhaft" he
concludes: "So trägt unser Kapitel durchaus das Gepräge der
Sage mit märchenhaftem Einschlag."[28]

As mentioned above, Gressmann categorizes I Samuel
10:17-27 as "Legende," but this is followed by a "Geschichtserzählung" in I Samuel 11 which is in his opinion the
only passage which gives a trustworthy account of the rise of
the monarchy in Israel. Gressmann sees a certain connection
between I Samuel 9:1-10:16 and I Samuel 11 in their present
arrangement in the text of I Samuel, but he does not consider
this connection to be original, commenting that they originally had nothing to do with each other. He says: "K. 9 verlangt
zwar K. 11 als Schluss, aber umgekehrt setzt K. 11 wenigstens ursprünglich keineswegs K. 9 voraus, sondern stand
einmal für sich allein. . . . Überdies sind K. 9 und K. 11 ihrer
literarischen Art nach völlig verschieden."[29] Gressmann views
I Samuel 12 as a late legend reflecting the same viewpoint as
I Samuel 7:2-8:22; 10:17-27.

Although Gressmann does not argue for two or three
contradictory documentary strands in the narratives of
I Samuel 8-12, his characterization of the various narrative
units as either pro or anti-monarchial is little different from
that of the representatives of the documentary source theory.
He comments: "In K. 8 wird Samuel als grundsätzlicher
Gegner des israelitischen Königtums hingestellt, das er als
eine Auflehnung wider Gott betrachtet und darum völlig
verwirft. Im graden Gegensatz dazu wird 9, 1-10, 16 erzählt,
wie Samuel auf ausdrücklichen Befehl Jahves Saul salbt;
danach ist das Königtum keine sündige, sondern eine von
Gott selbst gewollte Einrichtung. Eine dieser beiden
Anschauungen muss jünger sein; welche von beiden, darüber
kann die Entscheidung nicht zweifelhaft sein. . . . ursprüng-

27. Ibid., 34.
28. Ibid.
29. Ibid., 43.

lich galt das Königtum als eine göttliche, später, wenigstens in manchen Kreisen, als eine widergöttliche Einrichtung."[30] In commenting further on I Samuel 8 he notes: "Wie noch deutlicher K. 12 lehrt, liegt hier eine jener Erzählungen vor, die jünger sind als das Deuteronomium (=V. Mose) und sämtlich aus dem exilischen oder nachexilischen Judentum stammen."[31]

2. M. Noth

As was noted above (Chapter III, Section 1,A,1,b,3), M. Noth is of the opinion that Deuteronomy–II Kings is one great Deuteronomistic History which was written in conformity with a specific theology of history by a deuteronomistic author of the sixth century B.C. who utilized ancient traditions as well as his own compositions in the production of his work.

Noth's approach to the material of I Samuel 8-12 posits the linkage of a number of independent units by the deuteronomistic historian, in connection with a significant amount of material of his own composition. Noth considers I Samuel 9:1-10:16; 10:27b-11:15 to be old traditions about the rise of Saul to kingship.[32] He says that "the main stages by which he became king have no doubt been correctly recorded in I Sam. xi. . . ."[33] Since it was customary for the actions of the charismatic leaders of the period of the judges to have been preceded by a call, such a story (I Sam. 9:1-10:16) was placed before I Samuel 11 in the older Saul tradition without being closely connected with it. Noth comments that this story is obviously "very anecdotal," and "it must at least be doubted whether there was any thought of a future monarchy when this calling of Saul took place. . . ."[34] The re-

30. Ibid., 26, 27.
31. Ibid., 29.
32. Noth, *Überlieferungsgeschichtliche Studien*, 54.
33. Noth, *The History of Israel*, 168.
34. Ibid., 169.

maining sections of I Samuel 8-12 Noth considered to be
insertions of the deuteronomistic historian (I Sam. 8:1-22;
10:17-27a; 12:1-25). These supplemental units Noth viewed
as either original compositions of the deuteronomistic historian himself (I Sam. 8, 12) or thorough revisions of older
traditions (I Sam. 10:17-27a).[35] With the incorporation of
these materials Noth maintains that the deuteronomist expresses his fundamental doubts about the monarchy, although it was not easy for him to unite this negative view
with the older more positive traditions. Noth comments:
"Dtr hat also nicht ohne sichtliche Mühe und Gezwungenheit
die der Einrichtung des Königtums freundlich gegenüber-
stehende alte Überlieferung durch längere Zutaten im Sinne
seines negativen Urteils über diese Einrichtung zu ergänzen
versucht unter Verwertung einer ihm überkommenen alten
Tradition über die Erhebung Sauls zum König, deren Vor-
handensein ihm überhaupt das Recht zu geben schien, hier
ergänzend einzugreifen; und er hat von diesem Rechte dann
einen ausgedehnten Gebrauch gemacht."[36]

With respect to I Samuel 8-12 the end result of Noth's
analysis is not unlike that of Wellhausen in that the portions
of this material which are considered anti-monarchial are
assigned to the deuteronomist, while the other sections are
viewed as the earlier more authentic traditions expressing a
much more positive disposition towards the monarchy.[37]

---

35. Noth (*Überlieferungsgeschichtliche Studien,* 57, 58) comments that
I Sam. 10:17-27a is "vor allem in seinem Anfang ganz unzweifelhaft von Dtr
formuliert worden" but he suggests that it represents a tradition of an unknown
source on the rise of Saul to king which the deuteronomist wanted to incorporate
into the larger narrative. He then accepts Eissfeldt's designation of I Sam. 10:
21b[b]-27a as another separate tradition telling of the selection of Saul on the basis
of his height (see above, p. 353). Noth, however, does not accept Eissfeldt's view
of the connection of this unit with a larger independent source (L) and says that
"wir es hier vielmehr mit einem von Dtr verarbeiteten Überlieferungsfragment zu
tun haben."

36. Ibid., 60.

37. For Noth, cf. Chapter III, Section 1,A,1,b,3; for Wellhausen, see Chapter III, Section 1,A,1,b,1 and Chapter III, Section 1,B,1,a,1.

3. H. J. Boecker

H. J. Boecker's interest in the three pericopes in I Samuel 8-12 (I Samuel 8; 10:17-27; 12) which are frequently labeled as anti-monarchial and deuteronomistic arises from his concern with the problem which these passages present for M. Noth's view of the unity of the Deuteronomistic History.[38] For Noth there was no doubt that the Deuteronomistic History contained a clear and unequivocally negative attitude toward the monarchy.[39] But as Boecker points out, one may legitimately if not necessarily ask how Noth can correlate his view of the unity of the Deuteronomistic History with the fact that it includes not only anti-monarchial versions of Saul's kingship, but also texts which are clearly favorably inclined toward the establishment of the monarchy. This is particularly a problem as Boecker points out "wenn man nicht mehr bereit ist, mit einem mehr oder weniger zufälligen Nebeneinander oder sogar Gegeneinander verschiedener Quellen oder Traditionen zu rechnen, sondern mit M. Noth hier das Produkt einer planvollen und überlegten Geschichtsschreibung erkennt. In diesem Fall wird das Nebeneinander sachlich gegensätzlicher Berichte zu einem Problem, das, wenn es nicht ausreichend erklärt wird, die These von der Einheitlichkeit und Geschlossenheit des Werkes gefährden muss."[40]

---

38. Boecker, *Die Beurteilung der Anfänge des Königtums.*

39. Noth comments (*Überlieferungsgeschichtliche Studien,* 95): "Gleichwohl hat Dtr ... durch die Art der Einführung des Königtums in die Geschichte es ganz deutlich gemacht, dass dieses eine zeitlich sekundäre und seinem Wesen nach sogar unsachgemässe und daher grundsätzlich abzulehnende Einrichtung war...." And further (ibid., 110): "die negative Beurteilung der Einrichtung des Königtums und dessen Charakterisierung als einer sekundären Erscheinung in der Geschichte des Volkes gehörte zu den wesentlichen Zügen seiner Gesamtgeschichtsauffassung."

40. Boecker, *Die Beurteilung der Anfänge des Königtums,* 3. This problem has not escaped the notice of others. Note, e.g., the comment of Fohrer (Sellin-Fohrer, *Introduction,* 218): "Noth (like Sellin-Rost), following his thesis of a Deuteronomistic History, holds that the Deuteronomistic redaction linked the independent pieces together for the first time (to the extent that they do not actually derive from the Deuteronomist). In this case, of course, it is hard to

The solution which Boecker suggests for this problem is
based on his conclusion that it is not accurate to label the
above mentioned three passages as fundamentally opposed to
the monarchy. He sees them rather as expressing opposition
to certain aspects of kingship which involved denial of the
continued sovereignty of Yahweh in matters of concern for
both the internal and external security for the nation; but
they are not to be regarded as fundamentally opposed to
kingship as such. Boecker suggests that strong opposition to
kingship existed at the time of its institution, and that this
was related to the idea that Yahweh was king, and no human
king should usurp his position. Yet Boecker says that the
deuteronomists did not simply take over this old idea intact,
but they significantly modified it. And consequently here in
these sections of I Samuel 8-12 one finds that the "Grund-
sätzlichkeit der Alternative Jahwe oder König, auf der die
Königstumsgegner ursprünglich zweifellos bestanden haben,
gibt es bei ihnen nicht mehr. Im Gegenteil! Das Königtum
wird jetzt, obwohl sein jahwefeindlicher Ursprung nicht
geleugnet, sondern stark betont wird, doch als ein Angebot
Jahwes gesehen, ein Gnadengeschenk, das man verspielen
kann und das ganz sicher dann verspielt wird, wenn der König
im Sinne der alten Alternative an die Stelle Jahwes gesetzt
wird."[41] For Boecker the idea of kingship advanced by the
deuteronomists is not simply the product of bad experience
and a certain theological reflection, but is "zugleich Aus-

understand why the contradictory views and biases were not at least in part
subordinated to a new controlling principle by means of framework passages, as in
the book of Judges and the books of Kings." Note also the question raised by R.
A. Carlson (*David, the chosen King* [Uppsala: 1964] 24): "We might ask how the
complex in which the Davidic epoch is described, could have been preserved
intact in the D-work, as Noth, North and others have maintained. For it is an
inescapable fact that the Deuteronomic interpretation of history characterizes the
introduction of the kingship into Israel as apostasy from Yahweh (I Sam. 8:7 f.,
12:12) and on the other hand lays the blame for the fall of the two kingdoms at
the feet of the kings (II Kings 17:7 ff., 21:2 ff., 24:1 ff.). Is this due, as Noth and
North have suggested, to the fact that David, as an ideal king, was in a sense
immune from critical comment, even by the Deuteronomists?"

41. Boecker, *Die Beurteilung der Anfänge des Königtums*, 98, 99.

druck der altisraelitischen Traditionen, die für die Deuteronomisten massgebend waren."[42] The consequence which
this all has for the literary problem mentioned above is then
clear. If the deuteronomistic representation of the rise of the
monarchy in Israel is not anti-monarchial in any absolute
sense, then no irresolvable difference exists between the
various narrative units of I Samuel nor is there tension between the viewpoint concerning kingship expressed in the
books of Samuel and that in the books of Kings. This in turn
means that one cannot question the unity of the Deuteronomistic History on the basis of the different and contradictory positions which it contains concerning the monarchy.

C. The Tradition-History Approach

1. W. Caspari

The fragmentary approach of Gressmann was quickly
succeeded by various attempts to achieve some sort of synthesis between the documentary and fragmentary standpoints. One of the earliest efforts in this direction was that of
W. Caspari who suggested three distinct periods (Zeitraum)
for the development of the material contained in I and
II Samuel.[43] In the first period he posited the production of
the individual story units. In the second period he posited the
arrangement of stories which provide information over the
history of O.T. religion. In this process many of the stories
deriving from the previous period received their present form
of expression. The E source is the most important connected
work of this period. The aim of the third period is directed
primarily toward the production of more connected and
instructive narrative sequences. In this period he sees the
influence of the deuteronomistic spirit which flowered in the
exile. Caspari emphasized that his intent was to give some
indication of "einer stilgeschichtlichen Zeitfolge," but not
absolute chronology. He comments: "der Stil eines Zeitraums

---

42. Ibid., 99.
43. W. Caspari, *Die Samuelbücher* (KAT VII; Leipzig: 1926).

stirbt nicht schon damit ab, dass ein neuer Stil kommt und
einen neuen Zeitraum anzusetzen nötigt."[44]

2. Th. C. Vriezen

The general character of Th. C. Vriezen's analysis of the
books of Samuel was described above in connection with his
treatment of I Samuel 11:12-14(15).[45] He speaks of four
successive editions of the original Saul-David-Solomon history in which additional independent traditions or story
cycles were gradually incorporated with traces of this gradual
enlargement particularly evident in I Samuel 8-12. Vriezen
mentions various parallels and contradictions in the beginning
of the Saul narratives, noting in particular that the origin of
Saul's kingship is told three times (I Sam. 9, 10:17 ff., 11).[46]
His explanation for this is that one of the stories (I Sam.
11:1-11, 15) is at home in the original and larger Saul-David-
Solomon narrative, while the other two were later successive
additions. The original story tells of Saul's rise to kingship as
the result of his victory over Nahash, which led the people to
acclaim him king in Gilgal. Samuel is not spoken of in this
tradition which was part of the original politico-historical
apology not only for Solomon's succession right to the
throne of David, but also for the right of David's descendants
to the throne of Israel as the legitimate succession to Saul.
This apology for the house of David, Vriezen dates in the
time of Solomon and he suggests Zabud the son of Nathan as
a possible author. The second tradition of Saul's rise to
kingship is found in I Samuel 8:6-22; 10:17-27; 11:12-14 in
which Vriezen discerns the standpoint of Judean agricultural

---

44. Ibid., 10. The application of this framework to I Sam. 8-12 becomes
exceedingly complex and need not be discussed here in detail.

45. See above, Chapter III, Section 1,B,2,a. See further: Vriezen, "Compositie," in, *Orientalia Neerlandica* 167-189; idem, *Literatuur van Oud-Israël* 207-213.

46. Vriezen (*Literatuur van Oud-Israël*, 210) says these chapters give "veel
hoofdbrekens." The solution, however, according to Vriezen (ibid., 209) is to be
found when one presupposes: "dat wij hier verhalencycli hebben die door zelf-
standige auteurs werden geschreven; maar dan toch weer zo geschreven werden,
dat zij op elkaar waren aangelegd, als een vervolgverhaal."

circles in the time after Solomon's oppressive government
(10th or beginning of the 9th century). This tradition views
kingship as in conflict with the Jahwistic ideal, but nevertheless permitted by Yahweh. The third tradition is found in
I Samuel 9:1-10:16 in which Saul is anointed by Samuel at
the command of Yahweh in order to deliver the Israelites out
of the hand of the Philistines. This tradition Vriezen associates with a later prophetic edition of the Saul-David-Solomon
history dating at about 750 B.C. in which the hand of E or
someone from the circle of E is discernable. The final revision
of the material was made by the deuteronomist when the
entire block of material was set in his larger history work,
although Vriezen sees evidence of deuteronomistic reworking
only in I Samuel 7 and 12.

3. A. Weiser

A. Weiser considers the book of Samuel to be the result
of a process of compilation of "heterogeneous literary compositions."[47] He maintains that this character of the book is
particularly clear in the accounts of the origin of the monarchy contained in I Samuel 8-12. After noting previous
attempts to explain the literary character of Samuel by
positing either a two or three source documentary theory, he
concludes that the lack of any comprehensive and continuous
ideological plan leads to serious doubts about division into
two or three continuous literary threads. He feels that careful
analysis leads to the conclusion that: "there can hardly be
any other explanation than that here quite dissimilar literary
traditions originating in different circles have been placed
side by side without adjusting the differences between
them."[48] He illustrates this particularly by material from

---

47. Weiser, *The Old Testament: Its Formation and Development,* 159. The
position of Weiser is recounted here in more detail than that of some others
because it has initiated a trend in approach to the composition of Samuel that is
gaining in acceptance.
48. Ibid., 161.

I Samuel 8-12 and says that "even in the case of those passages which have been ascribed to the E sources (especially I.7, 8, 10:17 ff., 12, 15, 28) owing to their critical attitude towards the monarchy and their theological position, it can be pointed out that the trends of these passages when examined closely differ from each other."[49]

Weiser's proposal is that the book of Samuel is the result of a six stage process of growth.[50] In the *first stage* he posits the formation of individual traditions by the people and the court. To this stage he assigns the origin of I Samuel 9:1-10:16 as a popular saga "interwoven with themes from folktales and miracles and presenting the main persons lovingly with colourful vivacity."[51] He also places the origin of I Samuel 11 in this period and considers it to be "a historical narrative strongly stamped with realism in the style of the stories of the heroes in the book of Judges. . . ."[52] He notes, however, that because chapter 11 at no point assumes the contents of chapter 9 f., it was originally independent.

In the *second stage* comprehensive accounts were formed on the basis of the existing individual traditions. He assigns to this stage the linking of the stories of the rise of Saul in I Samuel 9 f. and 11.

The *third stage* is postulated in the collection and combination of the comprehensive accounts of the second stage and their being welded into one comprehensive tradition arranged chronologically along with the accretion of parallel and later traditions.

The *fourth stage* Weiser describes as the "prophetic formation and re-shaping of the tradition into a complete his-

---

49. Ibid.

50. Similar multi-stage growth processes are advocated by, among others: Fohrer (Sellin-Fohrer, *Introduction,* 218 ff.); Knierim ("Messianic Concept," in *Jesus and the Historian,* ed. F. T. Trotter, 20-51); O. Kaiser (*Einleitung in das Alte Testament* [Gütersloh: 1969] 124 ff.); Birch (*The Rise of the Israelite Monarchy*); Mauchline (*I and II Samuel,* NCB, 16-32); Gottwald (*Encyclopedia Judaica,* XXIV, 787-797); McCarthy (*Int* 27 [1973] 401-412).

51. Weiser, *The Old Testament: Its Formation and Development,* 163.

52. Ibid.

tory interpreted theologically. . . ."[53] He suggests that there was the prophetic interpretation of the history and its traditions "which proceeds side by side with the traditions of the people and the court, though it also stands in antithesis to them."[54] He says this is most apparent in the stories of Samuel and Saul including those which are considered hostile to the king concerning the origin of the monarchy in I Samuel 8, 10:17-27 and Samuel's retirement in I Samuel 12. These and other sections of the book according to Weiser are "probably associated together in the same intellectual and religious context of a theological presentation of history; but they do not represent a literary unity, as is often maintained."[55] (He notes here, e.g., the varying conceptions of Samuel as priest, prophet, and judge.) Weiser feels that the roots of these traditions reach back to circles around Samuel which unlike the popular tradition (I Sam. 9:1-10:16) rejects the desire of the people for a king "like the nations" on the basis of principial religious considerations. He comments: "The specially high esteem in which Samuel is held as a prophet in these passages shows that this form of the tradition was developed in the circles of the prophets who regarded Samuel as their ancestor."[56] Weiser is of the opinion that the reason for the resemblances between these narratives and the E strand of the Hexateuch is that the E source of the Hexateuch was a later product of these same circles.

The *fifth stage* which Weiser suggests is that of the deuteronomistic revision of the entire book. He considers this not to be prominent because the prophetic revision provided such a substantially compatible preparatory work, that traces of the deuteronomistic reviser's activity are few and not easily discerned.

The *sixth and final stage* of the growth of the book is to

---

53. Ibid., 170.
54. Ibid., 166.
55. Ibid.
56. Ibid., 167.

be found in a few later expansions by the insertion of certain poetic pieces of cultic origin, none of which are to be found in the section of the book concerning the rise of Saul's kingship.

Weiser elaborates further on his views of the composition of I Samuel, presented originally in his *Introduction,* in a subsequent monograph devoted entirely to the traditions contained in I Samuel 7-12.[57] In this monograph he rejects both the documentary source approach with its double account of the founding of the monarchy containing an early "pro-monarchy" source and a late "anti-monarchy" source as well as Noth's more fragmentary approach which nevertheless also regarded the "anti-monarchy" sections of I Samuel 8-12 to be late and unhistorical. In contrast to both Wellhausen and Noth, Weiser posits an early origin for the so-called "anti-monarchy" sections and suggests that they were not directed against the monarchy *per se* but are directed against a concept of kingship which was "as the nations." In support of this view he argues that each of the traditions contained in I Samuel 8, 10:17-27 and 12 contains genuine historical reflections from the time of the rise of kingship in Israel, which, however, were preserved at different localities. He ascribes the origin of I Samuel 8 to circles of like-minded friends of Samuel in Ramah. He suggests that I Samuel 10: 17-26 derives from the sanctuary at Mizpah where the tradition of the selection by lot was probably perpetuated by Benjaminites whose tribal interests were of direct concern in connection with the matter of Saul's kingship. Weiser views I Samuel 12 as a sort of parallel tradition to I Samuel 10:17-26, but suggests it originated in Gilgal instead of Ramah.[58]

57. Weiser, *Samuel,* FRLANT.

58. The procedure of dividing the materials on the basis of connection with different geographical centers of transmission has been adopted by, among others H. W. Hertzberg (*I and II Samuel,* 130-134) and K.-D. Schunck (*Benjamin. Untersuchungen zur Entstehung und Geschichte eines Israelitischen Stammes* [BZAW 86; Berlin: 1963] 80-108). This approach can be questioned, however, for its failure to give sufficient recognition to the close proximity of these

His conclusion is that each of these traditions point to the important role which Samuel played in the establishment of a new order in Israel with the inception of the monarchy.[59] He considers the desire of the people for a king "as the nations" to be a genuine historical motif and he is of the opinion that the condemnation of this desire as a rejection of Yahweh is not to be designated as a late theologumenon but an old tradition element that has been retained in various forms in I Samuel 8, 10, and 12. Nevertheless, Weiser does not regard the various component parts of I Samuel 8-12 to be representative of an actual sequence of historical events associated with the establishment of Saul's kingship, although he grants that the collector has arranged them in a way that is intended to give this impression. He comments: "Dass diese Zusammenordnung der Stoffe jedoch nur sehr äusserlich und notdürftig gelungen ist, hat man längst erkannt und dahin verstanden, dass der Sammler vorgegebene Überlieferungsstücke verwendet hat, die ursprünglich selbständig ohne gegenseitigen Bezug tradiert waren."[60] It is his opinion that the differences between the narrative units are such that harmonization in a temporal sequence is not possible and that the solution to this difficulty is to be found in a traditions history approach to them. He comments: "Das scheinbare Nacheinander der Erzählungsreihe löst sich bei kritischer Betrachtung auf in ein Nebeneinander einzelner Überlieferungsstücke, die z.T., ohne zur Deckung zu kommen, einander parallel laufen, z.t. sich zeitlich und sachlich überschneiden oder ausschliessen und es somit dem Historiker verwehren, entweder die ganze Erzählungsreihe oder auch nur den einen oder anderen Traditionskomplex in ein lückenloses Bild der Ereignisfolge zu transponieren."[61]

locations to each other. For this reason making locale the basis for distinguishing between the traditions raises a problem when they are regarded as irreconcilably contradictory versions of the same events. See S. Herrmann's review of Weiser's work in *TLZ* 89 (1964) 819-824.

59. Weiser, *Samuel*, FRLANT, 92.
60. Ibid., 47.
61. Ibid., 48.

4. B. C. Birch

B. C. Birch[62] produced a detailed study of I Samuel 7-15 which seems to be intended to undergird and advance the general position advocated by Weiser,[63] Fohrer,[64] and Knierim.[65] Birch notes that for the most part recent research on the growth and development of I Samuel is largely committed to some form of an early and late two source hypothesis. He points out that Noth's work has influenced a large number of scholars to see Deuteronomistic influence in the materials usually assigned to the late sources. In spite of many efforts to trace and explain the relationship between these two sources the conclusions have remained at variance and have been unconvincing. According to Birch a new way out of this impasse has been suggested by Weiser, Fohrer, and Knierim who point to a middle stage of editorial activity between the old traditions and the work of the Deuteronomist. The nature of this pre-Deuteronomistic stage, however, has only been vaguely identified as "prophetic," and Birch sees his work as providing substantiation for recognition of this particular stage in the growth of the material to its present shape.

The results of Birch's study can be summarized as follows: 1. The events surrounding the establishment of the Israelite monarchy produced a rich variety of traditions which seem, for the most part, to have circulated independently of one another. 2. A pre-Deuteronomistic editor is responsible for bringing these diverse traditions together into a single edition including additional material which bears his own peculiar stamp. This additional material includes the

---

62. Birch, *The Rise of the Israelite Monarchy.*
63. Weiser, *The Old Testament: Its Formation and Development,* 158-170; idem, *Samuel,* FRLANT; see also above, Chapter III, Section 1,A,1,c,2 and Chapter III, Section 1,B,1,b,5.
64. Sellin-Fohrer, *Introduction,* 215-227.
65. Knierim, "Messianic Concept," in *Jesus and the Historian,* ed. F. T. Trotter, 20-51.

following sections of I Samuel 8-12: 9:15-17, 20-21, 27-
10:1, 5-8, 16b; 10:17-19, 25; *11:12-14; 12:1-5* (italics
mine).[66] Birch maintains that the nature of these sub-sections
provides the clue to the identity of the author as prophetic;
and that this edition of the book is best attributed to northern prophetic circles in the late eighth century B.C. probably
after the fall of Samaria. 3. The final stage in the growth of
the material comes when the Deuteronomistic historian incorporated this earlier prophetic edition into his history work
making only a few additions in the process (including of
I Samuel 8-12 the following segments: I Sam. 8:8, 10-22;
12:6-24; italics mine).[67] This work according to Birch is to be
dated at least as late as the time of Josiah, although he feels
that a more precise date cannot be determined. While the
Deuteronomist, according to Birch, has a less positive view of
kingship, he is generally in sympathy with the material of the
prophetic edition and let it stand for the most part without
revision.

5. H. J. Stoebe

In his recent voluminous commentary on I Samuel, H. J.
Stoebe builds on the conclusions of previous studies of the
book and places himself within the traditions history approach to its composition.[68] He sees in I Samuel 8-12 a
composite unity which gives a description of the rise of
kingship in Israel.[69] He says that these chapters serve as a
model case, and at the same time as an Archimedian point for
the theory of source division of the book, because here two

---

66. For comment on Birch's treatment of I Sam. 11:12-14, see above,
Chapter II, n. 3; for his treatment of I Sam. 12:1-5, see above, Chapter III,
Section 1,A,2,g.

67. For comment on Birch's treatment of I Sam. 12:6-24 see above, Chapter
III, Section 1,A,2,g.

68. Stoebe, *Das erste Buch Samuelis,* KAT, esp. 64-66, 176-181; cf. above,
Chapter III, Section 1,A,2,i and Section 1,B,2,d.

69. Stoebe uses the term composite unity (ibid., 176), but the nature of this
unity differs substantially from that of the approach of "conservative biblical
scholarship" discussed below (see Section 1,D).

accounts are interwoven that are built on different presuppositions. The chapters 9:1–10:16 and 11 are relatively positively disposed towards kingship, while chapters 8, 10:17-27 and 12 reflect a decidedly negative position whose tenor must have been determined by bad experience, and therefore can be assumed to be from an essentially later time. From this fixed point, two sources can be postulated and then their course can be traced both forward and backward in the book. Stoebe is of the opinion, however, that a division of I Samuel 8–12 into two sources is inadequate, particularly in connection with the placement of chapter 11. He feels that the idea of three sources also cannot be justified. He points out that chapters 8; 10:17-27 and 12 present themselves as a very complex entity, not giving the impression of conceptual uniformity. He maintains that one cannot say that these passages are basically and uncompromisingly against the monarchy. Stoebe's conclusion is that when one concentrates on discovering a source relationship, which in any event must remain a construction, then one overlooks important statements in this section of Samuel. Therefore, in place of this approach Stoebe suggests that one must first look at the individual traditions and pay attention to what they say, trace their history as much as is possible, and note whatever changes an original account may have undergone. This renunciation of source division which is becoming a general position of recent research on I Samuel 8–12 does not, in Stoebe's opinion, lead to the acceptance of a closed single story. Stoebe concludes that this section of Samuel is the result of the fusing of two tradition complexes through which a meaningful representation of the historical process is reflected. Stoebe considers it, however, entirely possible that in the course of its formation individual sections have been inserted at places differing from the historical background which in actuality they represent.

Stoebe says that it is not to be denied that there is considerable distinction in tenor between the two tradition complexes. Nor is it to be denied that the tradition which stands in greater reserve to kingship has stronger deuteronomistic traits than does the other. Yet in Stoebe's opinion these factors are not so strong that they lead to the conclusion that these chapters should be regarded as free compositions of the deuteronomists. At the same time he does not deny deuteronomistic influences.

Stoebe considers the differences in content between the tradition units to be so uniformly linked with the names of Mizpah and Gilgal that he feels it is justified to speak of a Gilgal and a Mizpah tradition, although he notes the difficulty of the association of both Mizpah (10:17 ff.) and Gilgal (11:15) with the choice of Saul to be king. This duplicity of assertion is even more strange because both places are in the tribal area of Benjamin so that it cannot be explained by the suggestion that Mizpah was particularly dear to the writer. In Stoebe's opinion this difference can only be understood from the assumption that each of these traditions had a different historical background, and that the one reflects the designation of a charismatic leader on the basis of some special deed in a particular tribal area which then assumed royal dimensions, and out of which he was then subsequently regarded as invested with this status in a wider area.

Stoebe's conclusion is that in spite of different beginnings the two tradition complexes portray the rise of kingship over all Israel, and desire to demonstrate that this kingship is ordered after God's will. With all their differences, they are at least in their original viewpoint not contradictory, but parallels. They supplement each other. On the time of the union of the two traditions Stoebe feels that only vague suggestions can be made due to the absence of clear indicators as well as the deuteronomistic revision.

6. D. J. McCarthy

In an important article[70] on the composition of I Samuel

___
70. McCarthy, *Int* 27 (1973) 401-412.

8-12, D. J. McCarthy points out that attention has been diverted from the careful narrative construction of this entire section by concentration on the problem of the supposed pro- and anti-monarchial sources which are said to be reflected in its composition. Citing M. Tsevat,[71] McCarthy points out the pattern of contrasts which is incorporated in the section as a whole. He suggests that two genres are alternated: the "report" of assemblies, and the "story" (reports: 8:4-22; 10:17-27; 11:14-12:25; stories: 9:1-10:16; 11:1-23). The "reports" have similar internal structures which include an address by Samuel, and it is in these addresses that kingship is attacked. The "stories," on the other hand, are positively disposed toward the monarchy. McCarthy comments: "The whole apparatus of alternations serves to reinforce the basic tension of the pericope, the problem of the proper attitude toward the kingship."[72] He continues: "The section is not just about kingship, it is about kingship as a problem. . . . Chapter 8 exposes the problem of kingship among Yahweh's people, but the following story creates complications. There is something good about the man Saul in spite of the problems kingship raises, problems recalled in 10:17-19a. This creates a tension which is released when in 11:1-13 Saul is shown to act as Yahweh's own man. This is the true climax of the narrative, and it opens the way to a final resolution in chapter 12 where, with sin acknowledged and repented, kingship can be accepted into ongoing salvation history."[73] It is on this basis that McCarthy can assert that the entire section is a unity which gives a coherent account and explanation of the rise of kingship in Israel. This perspective is in sharp contrast to the long prevailing assessments of this section of I Samuel which have emphasized its disjunction rather than its unity.

---

71. M. Tsevat, "The Biblical Narrative of the Foundation of Kingship in Israel," *Tarbiz* 36 (1966) 99-109 (English summary, 116).

72. McCarthy, *Int* 27 (1973) 403.

73. Ibid., 403, 404.

Having noted this basic unity in the section as a whole, McCarthy then addresses the question of how it has acquired its present shape. After a brief survey of the variety of positions normally taken on this issue he concludes: "All theories based on source documents run into grave difficulties."[74] His reason for this conclusion is that the blocks of material separated and assigned to different sources will not stay separate with the result that these theories must "fall back on intricate fragmentations of the text, the hypothetical division of the documents into tiny pieces and their restructuring, often in a sequence different from that of the original. One is forced to think of the construction of a jigsaw puzzle."[75] Rather than a jigsaw puzzle approach to this literature, McCarthy suggests that it must be viewed as "traditional literature." The problem which he then sets out to unravel is that of tracing the history of the traditions contained in the entire section. Traditional literature, he maintains, develops in stages. The simplest stage is that of a set of individual narratives. A later stage is that of cycles of narratives in which stories concerned with a certain person or theme are clustered together. Such traditional literature, unlike written literature is "always in transition because it exists only in the telling."[76] Because traditional literature bears traces of the different times and places of its tellings, however, some of its history can be worked out.

McCarthy suggests that for I Samuel 8-12 there were three primary stages involved in its process of development.

The *first stage* is the formation of individual narratives.

The *second stage* is the grouping and retelling of the stories in cycles. In this stage he isolates three steps in the process. a) A point at which a pro-Saul cycle was told in which there was probably little emphasis on royalty, but rather on Saul as the tribal hero, a deliverer like the judges.

---

74. Ibid., 406.
75. Ibid., 406.
76. Ibid., 407.

b) A time in which the Saul cycle was linked with the David cycle and both modified by concepts from the royal ideology and the prophetic movement. This is noted in I Samuel 8-12 particularly by the addition of the "anointing" to the folktales about Saul. c) There must also have been a Samuel cycle. In these units, Samuel appears in various roles and connections as a folklore hero, as judge, as prophet, as well as related to the cult of the tribal league. McCarthy sees a consistency in this, concluding that: "Samuel represents ideals and institutions of the tribal league, often as these were remembered in later times and reinterpreted to tie into later experience."[77] Yet McCarthy is of the opinion that these Samuel narratives never acquired a structure like those of Saul and David, and remained a loose cycle.

The *third stage* is that of the organization of the traditional elements into the present unified history. The basis for this was the Saul and David cycles which were restructured by material from the Samuel cycle. Who did this? McCarthy says: "This was the work of the deuteronomistic school."[78] He bases this conclusion on two things: First, he notes that the thematic references to kingship which are essential to the entire structure are precisely the passages where deuteronomistic style is clearest. Secondly, he says: "the internal structure of the pericope is too sophisticated to be the product of accidental growth and simple retouches; it shows a controlling conception, the mark of an author, and this conception is integrated into the intricate structure of the deuteronomistic history as a whole."[79] Who then were the deuteronomists? McCarthy gives no direct answer to this, noting that von Rad associated the deuteronomistic school with levitical preaching, Weinfeld with the wisdom traditions of the scribes at the Jerusalem court. He comments: "the

77. Ibid., 408.
78. Ibid., 408.
79. Ibid., 408.

discussion continues. One suspects that several factors were at work, not one overhwelming influence."[80]

D. The Approach of "Conservative Biblical Scholarship"

The history of the critical assessment of the nature of the composition of the books of Samuel has not been without a considerable number of scholars who have regarded the books as a composite unity containing reliable and non-contradictory information over the lives and times of Samuel, Saul, and David.[81] Although I Samuel 8-12 is the section within the book which has provided the most fertile ground for attempts to separate source material and reconstruct the process of its compilation, this section has been regarded by many of these scholars as a unity of the just described nature. This does not mean that conservative biblical scholarship has ignored the discussions concerning the differences in style and emphasis between the various narratives of this section of the book, nor that they have disregarded the suggestions which have been advanced to explain these differences by many different theories of composition. Yet it remains the case that none of these theories has been successful in gaining general acceptance, and the position of "conservative biblical scholarship" has in the view of these men continued to be a viable alternative throughout the history of the debate. C. J. Goslinga, whose discussion of these matters is the most recent and complete presentation of this approach which is known to me, expresses the following conclusion concerning the composition of I Samuel 8-12: "Het geheel draagt welis-waar een samengesteld karakter, het berust wrsch. op tradi-ties van verschillende herkomst, vertoont ook afwisseling in toneel en achtergrond (Rama, Gibea, Mispa, Gilgal), maar laat zich toch lezen als een aaneengesloten verhaal, waarvan de onderscheiden pericopen elkander aanvullen, zodat men après

---

80. Ibid., 410.
81. For representatives of this approach, see Chapter III, n. 9.

tout een 'einheitliche' voorstelling ontvangt. . . ."[82] He maintains that this conclusion is indirectly confirmed by noting
that in place after place it can be demonstrated that those
who a priori have taken a critical stance toward the descriptions of the text have too easily concluded that there are
inner contradictions and unacceptable representations of the
course of events.[83]

Part of the reason for the difficulty which many have
with respect to accepting I Samuel 8-12 as a composite unity
containing a reliable account of the events surrounding the
rise of the monarchy in Israel is certainly related to the type of
historiography which is here encountered. In connection with
this aspect of the matter, A. A. Koolhaas has remarked:
"Daar het Oude Testament dus stamt uit een wereld met een
andere voorstellings-en denkwijze en de profetische geschied-
schrijving de gegevens op een bepaalde wijze rangschikt en
belicht, en daar ons over de redactie van deze hoofdstukken
practisch niets bekend is, tasten wij hier, ondanks de vele
energie en denkkracht, die door de historisch-literaire exegese
aan het boek Samuël is besteed, ten aanzien van bronnen en
tradities op vele punten in het duister en kunnen wij niet
verder komen dan te constateren, dat er achter deze hoofdstukken verschillende bronnen en tradities staan, en moeten
wij deze hoofdstukken als een creatieve synthese met een
zeer bepaalde boodschap over het onstaan van het koningschap verstaan."[84] Koolhaas also points out that what we
today might express in an argument containing several points
developed in a logical formal manner, the Semite might
express by telling several stories.[85] As Koolhaas puts it, the
Semite does not take a photograph but weaves a tapestry.
The writer of I Samuel 8-12 weaves a number of these
tapestries and then hangs them next to each other in order to

---

82. Goslinga, *Het Eerste Boek Samuël*, COT, 191.
83. Ibid.
84. Koolhaas, *Theocratie en Monarchie*, 72.
85. Ibid., 70.

present in its entirety the history of the rise of the monarchy.[86]

It is thus the conclusion of Goslinga and others of this approach that there is no compelling evidence for assuming that the Samuel books are the end result of a process of gradual growth òut of conflicting sources or traditions, nor for the idea of a series of editions incorporating revisions representing different periods of time.[87] Rather the composition of the book is best explained as the work of an author from the time of Solomon or shortly thereafter, who assembled his material from sources available to him, without engaging in extensive revision, and the book as it now stands is to be dated not later than the end of the 10th century B.C.[88]

Section 2

An Assessment of the Criticism of I Samuel 8-12 in the Light of the Covenantal Character of I Samuel 11:14-12:25

It is not our purpose in this section of our study to attempt any comprehensive reconstruction of the manner or process by which the books of Samuel were composed, but merely to demonstrate that the recognition of I Samuel 11: 14-12:25 as a report of a covenant renewal ceremony on the occasion of the institution of the monarchy in Israel provides a perspective by means of which a number of the problems around which the literary criticism of I Samuel 8-12 has centered can be viewed in a new light. Although there are many differences between the vast array of proposals which have been made to account for the literary character of the materials in I Samuel 8-12, it is nevertheless true that one or

---

86. Ibid., 71.
87. Goslinga, *Het Eerste Boek Samuël,* COT, 46.
88. Ibid., 49.

more of the following generalizations is characteristic of the majority of the reconstructions summarized above.

1. In their expression of either a favorable or unfavorable disposition toward the monarchy the pericopes of I Samuel 8-12 contain irreconcilable differences, particularly if one accepts each unit as a reliable report of the actual course of events.

2. In I Samuel 8-12 two or possibly three conflicting but parallel accounts of Saul's accession to the throne of Israel have been placed (not altogether successfully) in a chronological sequence.[89]

3. The so-called anti-monarchial sections of I Samuel 8-12 show indications of deuteronomistic influence, variously regarded as indicative of either the character of the original composition or of later editorial expansions, but in either case determinative for a sixth century or later date for their final form.

Each of these positions, whether taken separately or in combination,[90] and whether worked out precisely as stated above or in some similar form, is subject to serious questions and deserves renewed examination, particularly in the light of the covenantal perspective which I Samuel 11:14-12:25 provides for the entire sequence of events described in I Samuel 8-12.

---

89. This is usually closely associated with the separation of the narratives on the basis of contrasting attitudes toward the monarchy, but not necessarily limited to this consideration.

90. Notice, e.g., that Vriezen (see above, Section 1,C,2), avoids the usual "pro-" and "anti-" monarchial approach for dividing the narratives of I Sam. 8-12 (No. 1), yet he concludes that there are three different accounts of the origin of Saul's kingship which have been arranged in an artificial sequence (No. 2). Or notice the position of Boecker (see above, Section 1,B,3), who also rejects the "pro-" and "anti-" monarchy labels (No. 1), but attributes the modification of an original anti-monarchial tradition to the deuteronomists of the sixth century B.C. (No. 3).

A. The Ambivalent Attitude Toward Kingship in the Narratives of I Samuel 8-12 in the Light of the Covenantal Character of I Samuel 11:14-12:25

As has been noted in the above survey of the criticism of I Samuel 8-12, the division of this section into either documentary sources, independent story units, or tradition complexes which are characterized as either pro- or antimonarchial has been common procedure by the majority of critical scholars.[91] It is only recently that studies such as those of Weiser,[92] Boecker,[93] and McCarthy have challenged this long entrenched position.[94] The basis for the pro- and anti-monarchy division of sources has been the view that certain sections of I Samuel 8-12 represent Samuel as strongly opposed to the monarchy (I Sam. 8; 10:17-27; 12), while other sections present Samuel as favoring the monarchy (I Sam. 9:1-10:16; 11).[95] In our view it is certainly to be admitted that a tension exists in the narratives of I Samuel 8-12 concerning the propriety of establishing kingship in Israel, and that reservations concerning its origination are expressed in I Samuel 8; 10:17-27; and 12 while a more positive attitude toward its establishment is reflected in

---

91. Representatives of this position include: Wellhausen, Budde, Smith, Driver, Eissfeldt, Gressmann, Noth, and many more. See the discussions above.

92. Weiser, *Samuel*, FRLANT.

93. Boecker, *Die Beurteilung der Anfänge des Königtums*.

94. McCarthy, *Int* 27 (1973) 401-412.

95. W. McKane (*I and II Samuel*, TBC, 21, 22) gives a concise summary of this position. "We now pass to the other pole of the Books of Samuel where the reader is most conscious of disconnectedness and even contradiction, namely, the account of the institution of the monarchy (I 8-12). In order to explain this phenomenon a two-source theory has long been in existence and a source favourable to the institution of the monarchy (I 9.1-10.16, 27b; 11.1-15) has been differentiated from another whose attitude is unfavourable (I 8; 10.17-27a; 12). The favourable narrative has generally been regarded as the earlier and as historically credible; the other late and, if not historically worthless, certainly a representation of history which has been shaped by later dogma. These two accounts are not simply divergent, but are also in ideological conflict with each other. The one views the monarchy as ordained by Yahweh to save Israel from her enemies and the other sees it as a departure from the primitive faith and a rejection of the kingship of Yahweh."

I Samuel 9:1-10:16; and 11. While this is true in a general
sense, it must also be recognized that I Samuel 8; 10:17-27;
and 12 cannot legitimately be designated simply as totally
anti-monarchial.[96] In I Samuel 8 Yahweh tells Samuel to
"listen to the voice of the people in regard to all that they
say" (v. 7); and subsequently he repeats, "listen to their
voice, and cause a king to reign for them" (v. 22). Kingship is
therefore to be established in Israel as a direct response to the
express command of Yahweh, and this can hardly be characterized as expressing an anti-monarchial attitude. This idea is
further developed in I Samuel 10:17-27 where Yahweh is
represented as designating the person to be named king by
means of the lot. When Samuel presents Saul to the people he
refers to him as the one "whom Yahweh hath chosen"
(v. 24). I Samuel 12:1 builds from I Samuel 8:22 ("I have
listened to your voice in all which you said to me, and I have
placed a king over you.") and also includes the emphatic
statement of Samuel: "and behold Yahweh has set a king
over you" (v. 13). If one is therefore inclined to speak of pro-
and anti-monarchial attitudes in I Samuel 8-12, it must be
recognized that these attitudes are not neatly divided between two sets of contrasting narrative units as is so often
intimated, but the ambivalence is present even within the
units which have normally been labeled as anti-monarchial.
The question which this presents to the student of this
section of Samuel is that of how one is to explain this
ambivalence in attitude toward kingship. It is our suggestion
that the covenantal perspective which is to be found in
I Samuel 11:14-12:25 provides the interpretive framework

---

96. This fact is gaining increasing recognition in recent studies. Besides
Weiser, Boecker, and McCarthy, notice the comment of Stoebe (*Das erste Buch
Samuelis,* KAT, 176) that one cannot say of these sections "dass sie grundsätzlich
und kompromisslos der Monarchie feindlich gegenüberstünden." See further in a
similar vein: E. I. J. Rosenthal, "Some Aspects of the Hebrew Monarchy," *JJS* 9
(1958) 1-18; Thornton, *CQR* 168 (1967) 413-423; R. E. Clements, "The Deuteronomistic Interpretation of the Founding of the Monarchy in I Sam. VIII," *VT*
24 (1974) 398-410.

for the most satisfactory resolution of this problem, and it does so in a manner which does justice to both the positive and negative assertions about the establishment of the monarchy, without resorting to either superficial harmonization attempts or simply an appeal to a change of mind by Samuel because of divine intervention.[97]

It is our thesis that when I Samuel 11:14-12:25 is recognized as the description of a covenant renewal ceremony on the occasion of the inauguration of the monarchy, then the problem concerning the propriety of kingship in the preceding chapters is placed in its proper frame of reference. The issue in these pericopes is not that of the legitimacy of kingship itself, but rather that of the *kind* of kingship which the people envisioned, and their *reasons* for requesting it. The central question is whether or not the desired kingship would be compatible with Israel's covenant with Yahweh or would be of a type which would in effect nullify that covenant. On this basis the preceding narratives can be viewed as follows.

It was Samuel's acute perception into the improper motives of the people in asking for a king that evoked his displeasure (I Sam. 8:6) with them, and these same motives explain Yahweh's statement that by their request for a king they have "rejected me that I should not reign over them" (I Sam. 8:7). The people are said to have desired a king so that they could be "like all the nations" and so that their king could go out before them and fight their battles (I Sam. 8:20). Evidently they thought that national security could be guaranteed by such a leader. In short, their desire was for a type of kingship which was incompatible with their covenant relationship with Yahweh who Himself was pledged to be their saviour and deliverer. In asking for such a king they in effect broke the covenant, rejected Yahweh (I Sam. 8:7; 10:19), forgot his constant provision for their protection

---

97. While this latter factor may have been present, it cannot be isolated from the matter of the people's covenant allegiance to Yahweh which had been violated in connection with their request for a king.

(1 Sam. 8:8; 10:18; 12:8-11), and sought their security in a military-political establishment similar to that of their neighbors. It is for this reason that Samuel warns them by describing "the manner of the king" (מִשְׁפַּט הַמֶּלֶךְ) for which they were asking (I Sam. 8:11-17).[98] This warning given in the form of the description of contemporaneous foreign monarchies fell on deaf ears (I Sam. 8:19-20). Nevertheless, in

---

98. Mendelsohn (*BASOR* 143 [1956] 17-22) has argued that I Sam. 8:11-17 depicts the Canaanite pattern of kingship familiar to the Israelites at the time of the inception of the monarchy in Israel rather than a picture of kingship derived from and directed against Israel's own monarchy after a long and bad experience with kingship. This general position is accepted by Boecker (*Die Beurteilung der Anfänge des Königtums*, 17, 18) who says, "Die Könige in Israel haben so, wie es hier geschildert ist, nicht handeln können und haben in der Tat auch so nicht gehandelt." Boecker qualifies Mendelsohn's conclusion, however, to the extent that he says: "Die Angaben des 'Königsrechtes' sind so allgemein gehalten, dass sie nicht ubedingt auf diesen Bereich (Canaanite pattern) bezogen werden müssen. Sie könnten jedem soziologisch ähnlich gelagerten Herrschaftssystem entnommen sein. Die Deuteronomisten haben, woher auch immer, das Material für ihr abschreckendes Bild von einem Königtum genommen, das nach dem Willen des Volksbegehrens ein Königtum sein sollte, wie es 'alle Völker' haben." See further: Thornton, *CQR* 168 (1967) 413-423. Thornton (p. 418, 419) says that: "The description of the behaviour of the king given in 8.10-18, as Mendelsohn has pointed out, reflects current Canaanite practice. But it is also important to note that this description does not reflect the situation that seems to have prevailed in the post-Davidic Israelite monarchies. . . . We need not suppose then, that the picture described in I Samuel 8.10-18 is necessarily intended as a portrayal of conditions that existed under the later Davidic dynasty. Certainly there is evidence that later kings raised taxes and used forced labour, but it is questionable how far Israelite kingship in practice was as powerful and arbitrary as I Samuel 8.10-18 would suggest." See also Zafrira Ben-Barak, *"The Manner of the King" and "The Manner of the Kingdom." Basic Factors in the Establishment of the Israelite Monarchy in the Light of Canaanite Kingship* (Diss.; Jerusalem: 1972) English Summary, 19 pp., esp. Part II. After comparing I Sam. 8:11-18 with materials from the Syro-Palestinian area including the El-Amarna letters; the royal archives from Alalaḫ and Ugarit, he concludes on the basis of a tightly knit correspondence both of principle and detail that "there is a close relationship between the Biblical text of the *mišpat hammelek* and the Canaanite monarchy, an exemplar of which was in the mind of Samuel." The positions advocated by Mendelsohn, Boecker (and, although not mentioned, also Zafrira Ben-Barak) have been questioned recently by R. E. Clements *VT* 24 [1974] 398-410) who suggests (p. 404) that the list of abuses contained in I Sam. 8:11-17 "was drawn up with the very bitter memory of Solomon's exactions and excesses in mind, and that he was the ruler whose portrait was here being painted so unfavourably." It should be noted, however, that even Clements admits (ibid., 403) that "it is not possible to assert complete conformity of the royal oppressions listed in I Sam. viii 11-17 with the actual details of Solomon's political measures. . . ."

spite of Israel's apostasy, Yahweh indicates to Samuel that the time has come for Israel to have the monarchy, and Samuel is commanded to arrange for its establishment.

The next section of I Samuel 8-12 (9:1-10:16) relates the story of Saul's search for the lost cattle of his father which eventuates in his coming to Samuel for assistance, and his identification by Yahweh as the one who "shall reign over my people" (I Sam. 9:17). Subsequent to this incident, Samuel calls all the people together for an assembly at Mizpah (I Sam. 10:17-27). It is here at Mizpah that Saul's private designation is made a public one by lot. It is also here that Samuel explains to the people the "manner of the kingdom" (משפט המלכה) which is placed in written form and preserved in the sanctuary (I Sam. 10:25). In this action Samuel takes the first step in resolving the tension which existed between Israel's improper desire for a king, as well as their misconceived notion of what the role and function of this king should be, on the one hand, and the stated fact that it was Yahweh's intent to give them a king on the other. It is clear that the purpose of the משפט המלכה is to provide a definition of the function of the king in Israel for the benefit of both the people and the king-designate. This constitutional-legal description of the duties and prerogatives of the king in Israel would serve to clearly distinguish the Israelite kingship from that known to the Israelites in surrounding nations. In Israel, the king's role was to be strictly compatible with the continued sovereignty of Yahweh over the nation, and also with all the prescriptions and obligations enunciated in the covenantal law received at Sinai and renewed and updated by Moses in the Plains of Moab. In short, it was Samuel's intent to see that the משפט המלכה would be normative in Israel, rather than the משפט המלך.

After this Mizpah assembly, which served both as a constitutional convention and public proclamation of Saul as the king-designate, the people returned home to await the next step in the sequence of events by which the monarchy was

established as a continuing and formal political office in
Israel. The inauguration of Saul (cf. I Sam. 11:15; 12:1) does
not take place until after he has led Israel to victory in battle,
subsequent to which he was very careful to proclaim that
"today *Yahweh* hath wrought deliverance in Israel" (I Sam.
11:13). His purpose in this statement was to indicate in an
unmistakable manner that he regarded the victory as Yahweh's, even though it was accomplished under his own leadership. In this victory one finds the final seal of approval on
Saul, a concrete demonstration of Yahweh's continued guard-
ianship of the nation, and an occasion for Samuel's call to
assemble at Gilgal to "renew the kingdom." It was then at
Gilgal that the transition into the period of the monarchy
became official during a covenant renewal ceremony designed
on the one hand to restore covenant fellowship which had
been broken by Israel's apostasy, and on the other to insure
covenant continuity in the new era of the theocracy being
initiated. Kingship was thus formally incorporated into the
ongoing theocracy at an assembly in which Israel renewed her
allegiance to Yahweh, and recognized His continued sovereignty in the new order.[99] The problem which Israel's request
for a king had evoked had found its resolution.

B. The Narrative Sequence in I Samuel 8-12 in the Light of
the Covenantal Character of I Samuel 11:14-12:25

The second issue in the debate around I Samuel 8-12 is
that of the reality or artificiality of the sequence of events as
they are presently represented in the book. As has just been
indicated, it is our conclusion that I Samuel 8-12 is best
understood as the report of a series of events in which both
the problem surrounding the inauguration of the monarchy,
and the steps taken in resolution of that problem are de-

99. McCarthy (*Int* [1973] 412) expresses this nicely when he says: "The
fundamental thing threatened by Israel's action was the covenant relationship and
this is the formal restoration of that relationship with the kingship now explicitly
included in it. . . ."

scribed. The linking of this series of events into chronological sequence is, in our opinion, neither to be viewed as the artificial device of a late editor, nor as the result of the process of tradition growth by means of which various conflicting traditions were welded into a continuous narrative. As we have already indicated, it is our position that the tensions which are present in these narratives concerning the propriety of kingship are not properly construed when they are regarded as reflections of contrasting attitudes deriving from different periods of time or different geographic locations. These tensions are best understood when they are viewed as an authentic reflection of opposing attitudes toward kingship and the propriety of its establishment contemporary with the time of the monarchy's inception.[100] The narratives of I Samuel 8-12 are thus best understood as descriptive of the process by which the matter of the proper attitude toward, and the role of a king in Israel, was both raised and then brought to solution.

As we have noted, this process involved a number of phases:

1. The demand of the people for a king (I Sam. 8:1-5).

2. The displeasure of Samuel and his warning in the משפט המלך (I Sam. 8:6-18).

3. The persistence of the people in their demand (I Sam. 8:19-22).

4. The private designation and anointing of Saul to be king (I Sam. 9:1-10:16).

5. The public designation of Saul to be king and the definition (משפט המלכה) of his task (I Sam. 10:17-27).

6. Confirmation of Saul's designation by demonstration of Yahweh's blessing through victory over the Ammonites (I Sam. 11:1-13).

---

100. Cf. J. O. Boyd, "Monarchy in Israel: The Ideal and the Actual," *PTR* 26 (1928) 41-64. Boyd comments (42): "It is true, there are mingled here favorable and unfavorable judgments of monarchy as an institution in Israel. But who can deny that this double point of view is actually inherent in the historical situation?"

7. The inauguration of Saul at a covenant renewal ceremony held at Gilgal (I Sam. 11:14-12:25).

It is the relationship between I Samuel 11:14-15 and I Samuel 10:17-27, particularly in connection with the phrase "let us go to Gilgal and *renew the kingdom* there," which has provided what is generally advanced as the most compelling evidence for concluding that two conflicting accounts of the accession of Saul have been artificially represented as sequential and incorporated into the composite account of the establishment of kingship in Israel.[101] It is our conclusion, however, that the "renewal of the kingdom" about which Samuel is speaking has reference to renewal of allegiance to Yahweh, not to Saul, and is best understood as a call for the covenant renewal ceremony which is described in greater detail in I Samuel 12.[102] This interpretation not only provides a new perspective for understanding the relationship between I Samuel 11:14-15 and I Samuel 12, but at the same time it also removes the most widely advanced argument for positing the presence of conflicting but parallel accounts of Saul's accession to the throne found in I Samuel 10:17-27 and 11:15.

It is perhaps good here once again to emphasize that we do not intend to argue that I Samuel 8-12 is written "aus einem Guss": we have spoken repeatedly in terms of a composite unit. In our opinion there are not specific statements in I Samuel 8-12 which are contradictory, but there is variegation. It is beyond the scope of this book to pursue this

---

101. This position is adopted by advocates of otherwise widely divergent views of the composition of I Sam. 8-12. Cf. above, Chapter III, Section 1,B. Note the representative statement of Birch (*The Rise of the Israelite Monarchy*, 101): "Most scholars have regarded this verse as the clearest evidence of redactional activity in this chapter and there would seem to be little reason for challenging this conclusion. ... It would seem clear that an editor has, in the process of ordering the traditions as we now have them, attempted to harmonize an apparent duplication. Saul has already become king in 10:24 so the instance in 11:15 has been transformed into a renewal."

102. See above, Chapter II; Chapter III, Section 2,A; Chapter IV, Section 2,B,2,a.

matter more completely. But in the discussion above, particularly in Chapters I and II we have noted various points of unevenness. We refer here once again particularly to I Samuel 12:12. As we have tried to demonstrate in the exegesis of this verse, the statement that the advance of Nahash was the reason for the Israelite request for a king is not in contradiction with what is related in the preceding chapters. But at the same time I Samuel 12:12 is one of the indications that the author-redactor of I Samuel 8-12 must have made use of traditions which were not conflicting, but which did originally exist independently from each other. A similar point could be made, for example, in connection with the reference to Saul as the "anointed" in I Samuel 12:3; see the exegesis of that verse.

C. "Deuteronomic Influence" in the Narratives of I Samuel 8-12 in the Light of the Covenantal Character of I Samuel 11:14-12:25

The third characteristic of the majority of the reconstructions of the literary history of I Samuel 8-12 is the view that the anti-monarchial sections (I Samuel 8; 10:17-27; 12) show indications of deuteronomic influence, variously regarded as indicative of either deuteronomistic authorship or of deuteronomistic editorial revision. The issues here are complex. The positions advocated are quite diverse and reflect the complexity of the problem. Many authors have concluded that examination of the literary style of these pericopes leads to the conclusion that these narratives have close affinities with the E source of the Pentateuch as well as with deuteronomistic literature, and are thus to be considered products of the same circles as the E document of the Pentateuch with subsequent deuteronomistic revision.[103] The extent of the deuterono-

---

103. Cf., e.g., the viewpoints of Driver and Eissfeldt as discussed above. Driver (*Introduction,* 178) after pointing out phraseology in the "antimonarchial" strand which shows affinities with either E or the book of Judges concludes: "The similarities, partly with E (esp. Josh. 24) partly with the

mistic revision is said to be difficult to determine since the two styles have a great deal of similarity. Noth, who at least as far as I Samuel 8-12 is concerned, can appeal to Wellhausen, views our chapters as either original compositions of the deuteronomist himself (I Samuel 8, 12) or thorough revisions of older traditions (I Sam. 10:17-27a).[104] At the present time many authors are more and more directing their attention to the whole process of transmission. Some come to the conclusion that even I Samuel 8; 10b; 12 derive from sources close to the time of the events portrayed. This position does not exclude subsequent deuteronomistic revision and/or deuteronomistic responsibility for the linkage of the narratives in their present sequence.[105] Determination of the deuteronomistic influence on the section of I Samuel 8-12 is thus a matter of continuing debate, even though there is general agreement that influence of some kind is evident.

There are a number of difficulties which confront the advocates of the above positions. Budde[106] noted this long ago: if one with Wellhausen posits late deuteronomistic authorship of the sections of I Samuel 8-12 which are considered to be fundamentally opposed to the monarchy, then how does one account for the more favorable disposition toward the monarchy of both Deuteronomy itself and the so-called "deuteronomic edition" of I and II Kings as reflected in the "law of the king" in Deuteronomy 17:14-20 and the picture of David, Hezekiah, and Josiah in I and II Kings. Similar difficulties arise with the conception of

---

redaction of Judges, are evident. The entire phenomena appear to be best explained by the supposition that the basis consists of a narrative allied to that of E, which was afterwards expanded, esp. in 12:9 ff., by a writer whose style and point of view were similar to those of Dt. and the compiler of the Book of Judges."

104. Cf. the viewpoint of Noth as discussed above, Chapter III, Section 1,A,1,b,3; Chapter V, Section 1,B,2.

105. Cf., e.g., the positions of Weiser, Boecker, and McCarthy as discussed above.

106. Cf. the discussion of Budde's view above (Section 1,A,2, esp. nn. 9 and 10).

Noth.[107] These difficulties are reflected in the positions of Smith and Driver who considered the anti-monarchial narratives to be pre-deuteronomic, but subsequently expanded by a deuteronomistic editor. The difficulty with this latter position is that deuteronomic characteristics are most prominent in these narratives in connection with inseparable elements of the individual narrative structures themselves, rather than with easily removed editorial insertions. The more recent trend toward accepting a much earlier origin for the narratives once considered anti-monarchial, and to find the deuteronomists' work primarily in the structuring of the narrative sequence also does not adequately explain the deuteronomic characteristics which are inseparably linked with the internal coherence of the individual narrative units.

The position which we are advocating is that deuteronomic influence is certainly to be found in the narratives, but it is not to be considered the result of late editorializing or exilic or post-exilic authorship, but rather the reflection of a vital theological dynamic operative in and contemporaneous with the events which are here described. Such a position allows for indications of deuteronomic influence in literary expression without uniform or slavish attachment to such a style,[108] and at the same time provides a basis for understanding the ambivalence in attitude toward the monarchy, as well as the sequence of events associated with its establishment.

---

107. Cf. above, Section 1,B,3 for Boecker's solution to this problem.

108. Note the evidence for the similarity of various expressions in I Sam. 12:9 ff. not exclusively to Deuteronomy, but also to other parts of the Pentateuch, and the books of Joshua and Judges as indicated above in Chapter I, pp. 33-34, 44-46, 53, 59-60. Of the nine phrases discussed on pp. 33-34 above note the following: The first *can fairly be termed deuteronomic* since it is found there four times (6:12; 8:11, 14, 19). For the second phrase, a similar, but not identical expression *is found only* in Deut. 32:30 (cf. also Deut. 28:68). The third phrase is *not found in Deuteronomy*. The fourth phrase occurs *only once in Deut.* (1:41), but occurs previously in the Pentateuch in Num. 14:40; 21:7. The fifth phrase *occurs once in a similar form* in Deuteronomy (28:20). The sixth phrase *does not occur* in Deuteronomy. The seventh phrase *does not occur* in Deuteronomy. The eighth phrase *does not occur* in Deuteronomy but cf. Ex. 3:15; 7:16; Num. 16:28, 29; Josh. 24:5. The ninth phrase *does not occur* in Deuteronomy, but cf. Ex. 18:9, 10; Josh. 24:10; Judg. 6:9; 8:34.

As we have argued above, there is good reason to assume that the covenant traditions of Exodus and Deuteronomy were a living and vital influence in Israel's national life from its very beginning, and that the covenantal character of the assembly at Gilgal (I Sam. 11:14–12:25) is attributable to this influence.[109] The deuteronomic phraseology and theological perspective which is found in this and other sections of I Samuel 8-12 is therefore to be considered both appropriate and authentic in the description of events which were of such great significance in Israel's history.[110]

This evidence would indicate familiarity with Deuteronomy, but hardly literary dependence. Notice also the discussion in Chapter I, p. 57 where it is noted that I Sam. 12:22 expresses an idea which is prominent in Deuteronomy, but the word choice is different. On this general issue see the discussion of G. T. Manley on the deuteronomic character of the "framework passages" in the book of Judges (G. T. Manley, "The Deuteronomic Redactor in the Book of Judges," *EvQ* 31 [1959] 32-37). See also E. J. Young's discussion of how deuteronomic influences to be found in the book of Joshua are best explained (E. J. Young, "The Alleged Secondary Deuteronomic Passages in the Book of Joshua," *EvQ* 25 [1953] 142-157). As Young points out (ibid., 145) in connection with Joshua, the author "wrote in a style that was replete with the thoughts and language of earlier Scripture. But he did not copy slavishly. He had no hesitation in making minor alterations when they suited his purpose. And, although he often referred to Deuteronomy, he also referred to other parts of the Pentateuch."

109. See above, Chapter IV.

110. For advocacy of a similar position with regard to the literary character of I Kings 8 which has often been termed "Deuteronomic," note the comments of K. A. Kitchen ("Ancient Orient, 'Deuteronism,' and the Old Testament," in *New Perspectives on the Old Testament*, ed. J. B. Payne, 12, 13): ". . . it is habitual procedure in Old Testament studies, whenever certain attitudes or topics crop up in speeches or narratives of events—coinciding with supposedly 'Deuteronomic' views—to consider these occurrences spurious to the characters and situations concerned and as largely embellished, or even invented, by the Deuteronomist(s), as though it were inconceivable that such things could be thought, said, or done before the environs of 622 B.C. A classic example ca. 964 B.C.—about halfway between Deuteronomy (ca. 1200) and Josiah (622)—is the dedication of the Jerusalem temple of Solomon, where (I Kgs. 8, esp. verses 15-21, 23-53, etc.) much of his speech (esp. in its present form) is widely referred to Deuteronomic efforts in the seventh to the sixth centuries B.C. But, again, this is simply begging the question. There is no material proof of any kind that such sentiments and language must be seventh century or later, no proof that it is not of the tenth century B.C., by a speaker deliberately conscious of what is religiously 'right' (in his particular cultural context), and influenced by a basic covenant—document of ca. 1200 B.C. For Solomon in his dedication so to pay heed is no more remarkable than is the corresponding concern for religious propriety in the dedications of other temples by other Near Eastern kings all over the Biblical world, at all periods of its history (cf. Section VII, below). It is all too easy to assert there is no evidence for 'Deuteronomic' attitudes between ca. 1200 and 622 B.C., if one

D. Concluding Remarks

It has not been our purpose to enter into the entire range of literary-critical problems in I Samuel 8-12,[111] but only to touch on those for which the covenantal character of I Samuel 11:14-12:25 has particular relevance. Nevertheless, in our view, the matters which we have discussed are the central issues in the literary critical assessment of this particular section of the book.[112] It is our conclusion that the covenantal perspective of I Samuel 11:14-12:25 provides a new and supportive dimension to the approach advocated by conservative biblical scholarship which has long recognized this material as a composite unity and as historically trustworthy.[113]

has first relegated all such evidence to 622 and later on *a priori* grounds; but such a proceeding is too far-reaching to be so based, instead of being rooted in controllable facts." See further: G. van Groningen, "Joshua–II Kings: Deuteronomistic? Priestly? Or Prophetic Writing?" *JETS* 12 (1969) 3-26.

111. This has been adequately handled elsewhere. See esp.: Koolhaas, *Theocratie en Monarchie;* Goslinga, *Het Eerste Boek Samuël,* COT.

112. It is our position that differences in details of various sorts between the narrative units of I Sam. 8-12 are not of a kind which creates irresolvable conflicts between these units. We have commented on certain questions of this sort in our exegetical section above (Chapters I, and II) when these details had no direct relation to the covenantal perspective. See esp. pp. 11, n. 8; 14, n. 14; 37; 38-40; 49. For extensive discussion of similar types of problems in other sections of I Sam. 8-12 see Goslinga, ibid.

113. In our view there is nothing contained in I Sam. 8-12 which is incompatible with the position that these narratives present a reliable historical account of the establishment of the monarchy in Israel. Note the statement of M. Tsevat (*Tarbiz* 36 [1969] 99-109) who comments in the English summary: "The author rejects the opinion of many critics that this narrative (I Sam. 8:4-12:25) is intrinsically unhistorical. To this extent that it is found in these chapters, the phenomenon of opposition to the institution of the monarchy in the name of the kingdom of God, is not necessarily a retrojection of late concepts, supposedly of Hoseanic or Deuteronomistic origin." Tsevat divides I Sam. 8-12 in a manner similar to that of McCarthy (see above, Section 1,C,6) designating the five components as either "popular assemblies" or "individual actions." It is his conclusion that the stories of the assemblies expressing opposition to the monarchy (along with approval) are no less historical than the stories of "individual actions" and "nothing can be said about the relative dates of the components." See further the work of Zafrira Ben-Barak (*"The Manner of the King" and "The Manner of the Kingdom"*) who argues that "I Sam. 7-12 is a repository of reliable traditions dating from the eve of the establishment of the monarchy which reflect contemporaneous socio-political pressures. The initial and decisive editing of these traditions was carried out by a contemporary writer to whose sensitivity we owe the faithfulness with which the portrait of the age was drawn and preserved" (from Part I of the English summary).

BIBLIOGRAPHICAL ABBREVIATIONS

AJSL	*American Journal of Semitic Languages and Literatures* (Chicago).
AnBib	Analecta Biblica (Rome).
ANET	*Ancient Near Eastern Texts*, ed. J. B. Pritchard (Princeton: 1955²).
ATD	Das Alte Testament Deutsch (Göttingen).
BA	*Biblical Archaeologist* (New Haven).
BASOR	*Bulletin of the American Schools of Oriental Research* (New Haven).
BDB	F. Brown, S. R. Driver, and C. A. Briggs, *Hebrew and English Lexicon of the Old Testament* (Oxford: 1907, reprinted with corrections 1962).
*BHK*³	*Biblia Hebraica*,³ ed. R. Kittel (Stuttgart: 1937).
BHTh	Beiträge zur Historischen Theologie (Tübingen).
Bib	*Biblica* (Rome).
BibOr	Biblica et Orientalia (Rome).
BJRL	*Bulletin of the John Rylands Library* (Manchester).
BOT	De Boeken van het Oude Testament (Roermond).
BR	*Biblical Research* (Chicago).
BWANT	Beiträge zur Wissenschaft vom Alten und Neuen Testament (Stuttgart).
BZ	*Biblische Zeitschrift.*
BZAW	Beihefte zur Zeitschrift für die alttestamentliche Wissenschaft (Berlin).
BZHT	Beiträge zur historischen Theologie (Tübingen).
CambB	The Cambridge Bible for Schools and Colleges (Cambridge).
CBQ	*Catholic Biblical Quarterly* (Washington).
CentB	The Century Bible (Edinburgh).
CNEB	The Cambridge Biblical Commentary on the New English Bible (Cambridge).
COT	Commentaar op het Oude Testament (Kampen).
CQR	*Church Quarterly Review* (London).
CTM	*Concordia Theological Monthly* (St. Louis).
EH	Exegetisches Handbuch zum Alten Testament (Münster).
ET	English translation.
EvQ	*Evangelical Quarterly* (Devon).
FRLANT	Forschungen zur Religion und Literatur des Alten und Neuen Testaments (Göttingen).
GK	*Gesenius' Hebrew Grammar*, ed. E. Kautzsch, tr. A. E. Cowley (Oxford: corrected reprint 1960).

GTT	*Gereformeerd Theologisch Tijdschrift* (Kampen).
HAT	Handbuch zum Alten Testament (Tübingen).
HK	Handkommentar zum Alten Testament (Göttingen).
HSchAT	Die Heilige Schrift des Alten Testaments (Bonn).
HTR	*Harvard Theological Review* (Cambridge).
IB	*The Interpreters Bible*, ed. G. Buttrick (Nashville).
ICC	The International Critical Commentary of the Holy Scriptures of the Old and New Testament (Edinburgh).
IDB	*Interpreter's Dictionary of the Bible*, ed. G. A. Buttrick (Nashville: 1962).
Int	*Interpretation* (Richmond).
JAOS	*Journal of the American Oriental Society* (New Haven).
JBL	*Journal of Biblical Literature* (Philadelphia).
JETS	*Journal of the Evangelical Theological Society* (Wheaton).
JJS	*The Journal of Jewish Studies* (London).
JNES	*Journal of Near Eastern Studies* (Chicago).
JRH	*Journal of Religious History* (Sydney).
KAT	Kommentar zum Alten Testament (Leipzig, Gütersloh).
KBL	Ludwig Köhler–Walter Baumgartner, *Lexicon in Veteris Testamenti Libros* (Leiden: 1953). *KBL*[3]: 3rd ed., 1967 ff.
KeH	Kurzgefasstes exegetisches Handbuch zum Alten Testament (Leipzig).
KHC	Kurzer Hand-Commentar zum Alten Testament (Tübingen).
KV	Korte Verklaring der Heilige Schrift (Kampen).
LTQ	*Lexington Theological Quarterly.*
LXX	Septuagint, ed. A. Rahlfs (Stuttgart: 1971).
MT	Massoretic Text (as published in *BHK*[3]).
MVÄG	*Mitteilungen der vorderasiatisch-ägyptischen Gesellschaft* (Leipzig).
NASB	*New American Standard Bible* (New York: 1963).
NCB	New Century Bible (London).
NEB	*New English Bible* (Oxford: 1970).
Or	*Orientalia* (Rome).
OrAn	*Oriens Antiquus* (Leiden).
OTMS	*The Old Testament and Modern Study*, ed. H. H. Rowley (Oxford: 1951).
OTS	*Oudtestamentische Studiën* (Leiden).
OTWSA	Die Ou Testamentiese Werkgemeenskap in Suid-Africa (Potchefstroom).
POT	De Prediking van Het Oude Testament (Nijkerk).
PTR	*Princeton Theological Review* (Princeton).
RB	*Revue Biblique* (Paris).
RSV	*The Holy Bible, Revised Standard Version* (New York).
RThR	*Reformed Theological Review* (Melbourne).
SAT	Die Schriften des Alten Testaments (Göttingen).
SBB	The Soncino Books of the Bible (London).
SBT	Studies in Biblical Theology (London).

StANT	Studien zum Alten und Neuen Testament (München).
StSe	Studi Semitici (Rome).
SVT	Supplements to Vetus Testamentum (Leiden).
TB	*Tyndale Bulletin* (London).
TBC	Torch Bible Commentaries (London).
TDNT	*Theological Dictionary of the New Testament* (Grand Rapids: 1964 ff.); ET of *Theologisches Wörterbuch zum Neuen Testament,* eds. G. Kittel and G. Friedrich (Stuttgart: 1933 ff.).
TDOT	*Theological Dictionary of the Old Testament,* eds. G. J. Botterweck, H. Ringgren (Grand Rapids: 1974 ff.); ET of *TWAT.*
TeU	Tekst en Uitleg (Den Haag).
THAT	*Theologisches Handwörterbuch zum Alten Testament,* I, II, eds. E. Jenni, C. Westermann (München: 1971, 1975).
ThR	*Theologische Rundschau,* (Tübingen).
ThRef	*Theologia Reformata* (Woerden).
ThZ	*Theologische Zeitschrift* (Basel).
TLZ	*Theologische Literaturzeitung* (Berlin).
TOTC	Tyndale Old Testament Commentaries (London).
TvT	*Tijdschrift voor Theologie* (Nijmegen).
TWAT	*Theologisches Wörterbuch zum Alten Testament,* eds. G. J. Botterweck, H. Ringgren (Stuttgart: 1970 ff.).
VD	*Verbum Domini* (Rome).
VT	*Vetus Testamentum* (Leiden).
WZ	*Wissenschaftliche Zeitschrift* (Halle).
WMANT	Wissenschaftliche Monographien zum Alten und Neuen Testament (Neukirchen-Vluyn).
ZAW	*Zeitschrift für die alttestamentliche Wissenschaft* (Berlin).
ZThK	*Zeitschrift für Theologie und Kirche* (Tübingen).
ZWL	*Zeitschrift für kirchliche Wissenschaft und kirchliches Leben* (Tübingen).

BIBLIOGRAPHY

Commentaries cited:

Aalders, G. Ch., *Daniël*, COT, Kampen, 1962.
Ackroyd, P. R., *The First Book of Samuel*, CNEB, Cambridge, 1971.
van den Born, A., *Samuël: uit de grondtekst vertaald en uitgelegd*, BOT, Roermond, 1956.
——————, *Kronieken*, BOT, Roermond, 1960.
Budde, K., *Die Bücher Samuel*, KHC, Tübingen, 1902.
Caird, G. B., "The First and Second Books of Samuel," *IB*, II, Nashville, 1953.
Calvin, J., *Commentaries on the Book of the Prophet Daniel*, 2 vols., Grand Rapids, 1948.
Caspari, W., *Die Samuelbücher*, KAT, Leipzig, 1926.
Childs, B. S., *The Book of Exodus. A Critical, Theological Commentary*, Philadelphia, 1974.
Driver, S. R., *A Critical and Exegetical Commentary on Deuteronomy*, ICC, Edinburgh, 1901³.
Fensham, F. C., *Exodus*, POT, Nijkerk, 1970.
Gispen, W. H., *Het Boek Leviticus*, COT, Kampen, 1950.
——————, *Het Boek Exodus*, KV, Kampen, 1964³.
——————, *Het Boek Numeri*, II, COT, Kampen, 1964.
Goettsberger, J., *Die Bücher der Chronik oder Paralipomenon*, HSchAT, Bonn, 1939.
Goldman, S., *Samuel*, SBB, London, 1962.
Goslinga, C. J., *Het Boek Jozua*, KV, Kampen, 1927.
——————, *I Samuël*, KV, Kampen, 1948.
——————, *Het Eerste Boek Samuël*, COT, Kampen, 1968.
de Graaf, S. G., *Het eerste en tweede boek van Samuël*, Kampen, n.d.
Gressmann, H., *Die älteste Geschichtsschreibung und Prophetie Israels*, SAT, Göttingen, 1921².
de Groot, J., *I en II Samuël*, TeU, Groningen, 1934/35.
Hertzberg, H. W., *I and II Samuel*, Philadelphia, 1964; ET of *Die Samuelbücher*, ATD, 1960².
Holwerda, B., *Seminarie-Dictaat, Richteren I*, Kampen, n.d.
Hulst, A. R., "I en II Samuel," in *Commentaar op de Heilige Schrift*, ed. J. A. von der Hake, Amsterdam, 1956.
Hyatt, J. P., *Commentary on Exodus*, NCB, London, 1971.
Keil, C. F. *The Books of Samuel*, Grand Rapids, 1956; ET of *Die Bücher Samuels*, Leipzig, 1864⁴.
Kennedy, A. R. S., *I and II Samuel*, CentB, Edinburgh, 1904.
Kennedy, G., "Daniel," *IB*, VI, Nashville, 1956.

Kirkpatrick, A. F., *The First Book of Samuel*, CambB, Cambridge, 1880.

Kittel, R., *Die Bücher der Chronik*, HK, Göttingen, 1902.

Kroeze, J. H., *Het Boek Job*, COT, Kampen, 1961.

—————, *Het Boek Jozua*, COT, Kampen, 1968.

Leimbach, K. A., *Die Bücher Samuel*, HSchAT, Bonn, 1936.

Mauchline, J., *I and II Samuel*, NCB, London, 1971.

McKane, W., *I and II Samuel*, TBC, London, 1963.

Noth, M., *Exodus, A Commentary*, Philadelphia, 1962; ET of *Das zweite Buch Mose, Exodus*, ATD, Göttingen, 1959.

—————, *Das vierte Buch Mose, Numeri*, ATD, Göttingen, 1966.

Nowack, W., *Richter, Ruth und Bücher Samuelis*, HK, Göttingen, 1902.

Oosterhoff, B. J., "De boeken 1 en 2 Samuël," *Bijbel Met Kanttekeningen*, eds. J. H. Bavink, A. H. Edelkoort, Baarn, n.d.

von Rad, G., *Deuteronomy, A Commentary*, London, 1966; ET of *Das fünfte Buch Mose, Deuteronomium*, ATD, Göttingen, 1964.

Ridderbos, J., *Het Boek Deuteronomium*, I, II, KV, Kampen, 1963[2], 1964[2].

Rudolph, W., *Chronikbücher*, HAT, Tübingen, 1955.

Schulz, A., *Die Bücher Samuel*, EH, Münster, 1919/1920.

Smith, H. P., *A Critical and Exegetical Commentary on the Books of Samuel*, ICC, Edinburgh, 1951[4].

Stoebe, H. J., *Das erste Buch Samuelis*, KAT, Gütersloh, 1973.

Thenius, O., *Die Bücher Samuels*, KeH, Leipzig, 1898[3].

Thompson, J. A., *Deuteronomy: An Introduction and Commentary*, TOTC, London, 1974.

de Vaux, R., *Les Livres de Samuel*, La Sainte Bible, Paris, 1961[2].

Verhoef, P. H., *Maleachi*, COT, Kampen, 1972.

Other works cited:

Aalders, G. Ch., *A Short Introduction to the Pentateuch*, London, 1949.

—————, *Oud-Testamentische Kanoniek*, Kampen, 1952.

Alt, A., "Gedanken über das Königtum Jahwes," in *Kleine Schriften zur Geschichte des Volkes Israel*, I, München, 1953, 345-357.

—————, *Die Staatenbildung der Israeliten in Palästina*, Leipzig, 1930; ET: "The Formation of the Israelite State in Palestine," in *Essays on Old Testament History and Religion*, New York, 1968, 223-309.

—————, *Die Ursprünge des israelitischen Rechts*, Leipzig, 1934; ET: "The Origins of Israelite Law," in *Essays on Old Testament History and Religion*, New York, 1968, 101-171.

Albright, W. F., "The Oracles of Balaam," *JBL* 63, 1944, 207-233.

—————, "The Old Testament and the Archaeology of the Ancient East," in *OTMS*, 27-47.

—————, *Yahweh and the Gods of Canaan. A Historical Analysis of Two Contrasting Faiths*, New York, 1969.

Ap-Thomas, D. R., "Notes on some terms relating to prayer," *VT* 6, 1956, 225-241.

Anderson, G. W., "Israel: Amphictyony: 'AM; KĀHĀL; 'ĒDĀH," in *Translating and Understanding the Old Testament,* Essays in honor of H. G. May, eds. H. T. Frank and W. L. Reed, Nashville, 1970, 135-151.

Baltzer, K., *The Covenant Formulary,* Philadelphia, 1971.

Ben-Barak, Z., *"The Manner of the King" and "The Manner of the Kingdom." Basic Factors in the Establishment of the Israelite Monarchy in the Light of Canaanite Kingship,* unpublished dissertation, Jerusalem, 1972.

Bentzen, A., *Introduction to the Old Testament,* 2 vols. in 1, Copenhagen, 1952².

Berkovits, E., *Man and God: Studies in Biblical Theology,* Detroit, 1969.

Bernhardt, K.-H., *Das Problem der Altorientalischen Königsideologie im Alten Testament,* SVT 8, Leiden, 1961.

Beyerlin, W., *Origins and History of the Oldest Sinaitic Traditions,* Oxford, 1965.

Birch, B. C., *The Rise of the Israelite Monarchy: The Growth and Development of I Sam 7-15,* unpublished Ph.D. dissertation, Yale University, 1970.

——————, "The Development of the Tradition on the Anointing of Saul in 1 Sam 9:1-10:16," *JBL* 90, 1971, 55-68.

Boecker, H. J., *Redeformen des Rechtslebens im Alten Testament,* WMANT 14, Neukirchen-Vluyn, 1964.

——————, *Die Beurteilung der Anfänge des Königtums in den deuteronomistischen Abschnitten des I. Samuelbuches,* WMANT 31, Neukirchen-Vluyn, 1969.

de Boer, P. A. H., *Research into the Text of 1 Samuel I-XVI,* Amsterdam, 1938.

——————, "De voorbede in het OT," *OTS,* III, Leiden, 1943, 124-132.

Boyd, J. O., "Monarchy in Israel: The Ideal and the Actual," *PTR* 26, 1928, 41-64.

Boyle, M. O., "The Covenant Lawsuit of the Prophet Amos: III 1-IV 13," *VT* 21, 1971, 338-362.

Brekelmans, C. H. W., "Het 'historische Credo' van Israel," *TvT* 3, 1963, 1-11.

Bright, J., *The Kingdom of God,* New York, 1953.

——————, *A History of Israel,* London, 1972².

Broekhuis, J., "De Heilige Oorlog in het Oude Testament," *ThRef* 18, 1975, 108-120.

Brongers, H. A., "Bemerkungen zum Gebrauch des Adverbialen WeʿATTĀH im Alten Testament," *VT* 15, 1965, 289-299.

Bruggemann, W., "Amos IV 4-13 and Israel's Covenant Worship," *VT* 15, 1965, 1-15.

Buber, M., "Die Erzählung von Sauls Königswahl," *VT* 6, 1956, 113-173.

──────, *Kingship of God*, New York, 1967; ET of *Königtum Gottes*, Heidelberg, 1956³.

Buccellati, G., *Cities and Nations of Ancient Syria*, StSe 26, Rome, 1967.

Budde, K., "Sauls Königswahl und Verwerfung," *ZAW* 8, 1888, 223-248.

──────, *Die Bücher Richter und Samuel. Ihre Quellen und ihr Aufbau*, Giessen, 1890.

Campbell, Jr., E. F., "Sovereign God," *McCormick Quarterly* 20, 1967, 173-186.

──────, "Moses and the Foundations of Israel," *Int* 29, 1975, 141-154.

Carlson, R. A., *David, the chosen King. A Traditio-Historical Approach to the Second Book of Samuel*, Uppsala, 1964.

Carmichael, C., "A New View of the Origin of the Deuteronomic Credo," *VT* 19, 1969, 273-289.

Clements, R. E., *Prophecy and Covenant*, SBT 43, London, 1965.

──────, "The Deuteronomistic Interpretation of the Founding of the Monarchy in I Sam. VIII," *VT* 24, 1974, 398-410.

Clines, D. J. A., "Psalm Research Since 1955: I. The Psalms and the Cult," *TB* 18, 1967, 103-126.

──────, "Psalm Research Since 1955: II. The Literary Genres," *TB* 20, 1969, 105-125.

Cornill, C., "Ein elohistischer Bericht über die Entstehung des israelitischen Königtums in I Samuelis 1–15 aufgezeigt," *ZWL* 6, 1885, 113-141.

──────, "Zur Quellenkritik der Bücher Samuelis," Königsberger Studien, Bd I, 1887, 25-59.

Craigie, P. C., "The Conquest and Early Hebrew Poetry," *TB* 20, 1969, 76-94.

Cross, M., Freedman, D. N., "The Blessing of Moses," *JBL* 67, 1948, 191-210.

──────, "The Song of Miriam," *JNES* 14, 1955, 237-250.

Deller, K., Papola, S., "Ein Vertrag Assurbanipals mit dem arabischen Stamm Qedar," *Or* 37, 1968, 464-466.

Dentan, R. C., *The Knowledge of God in Ancient Israel*, New York, 1968.

Driver, S. R., *Notes on the Hebrew Text and the Topography of the Books of Samuel*, Oxford, 1913², reprinted 1966.

──────, *An Introduction to the Literature of the Old Testament*, Edinburgh, 1913⁹, reprinted, New York, 1957².

Dronkert, K., "Liefde en gerechtigheid in het Oude Testament," in *Schrift en Uitleg*, jubileum-bundel W. H. Gispen, Kampen, 1970, 43-53.

Edelkoort, A. H., *De Christus-Verwachting in Het Oude Testament,* Wageningen, 1941.

—————, *De Profeet Samuël,* Baarn, 1953.

Ehrlich, A. B., *Randglossen zur Hebräischen Bibel,* 7 vols., Leipzig, 1910.

Eichhorn, J. G., *Einleitung in das Alte Testament,* Göttingen, 1823/24[4].

Eichrodt, W., "Covenant and Law," *Int* 20, 1966, 302-321.

—————, *Theology of the Old Testament,* 2 vols., Philadelphia, 1961, 1967.

Eissfeldt, O., "Jahwe als König," *ZAW* 46, 1928, 81-105.

—————, *Die Komposition der Samuelisbücher,* Leipzig, 1931.

—————, *The Old Testament. An Introduction,* New York, 1965; ET of *Einleitung in das AT,* Tübingen, 1964[3].

Fensham, F. C., "Malediction and Benediction in the Ancient Near Eastern Vassal-Treaties and the Old Testament," *ZAW* 74, 1962, 1-9.

—————, "Clauses of Protection in Hittite Vassal-Treaties and the Old Testament," *VT* 13, 1963, 133-143.

—————, "Common Trends in Curses of the Near Eastern Treaties and *Kudurru*-inscriptions Compared with the Maledictions of Amos and Isaiah," *ZAW* 75, 1963, 155-175.

—————, "The Covenant-idea in the book of Hosea," in *Studies in the Books of Hosea and Amos,* OTWSA, Potchefstroom, 1964/65, 35-49.

—————, "Covenant, Promise and Expectation in the Bible," *ThZ* 23, 1967, 305-322.

Fitzmyer, J. A., "The Aramaic Inscriptions of Sefîre I and II," *JAOS* 81, 1961, 178-222.

—————, *The Aramaic Inscriptions of Sefîre,* BibOr 19, Rome, 1967.

Fohrer, G., " 'Priesterliches Königtum,' Ex. 19,6," *ThZ* 19, 1963, 359-362.

—————, *Überlieferung und Geschichte des Exodus: eine Analyse von Ex 1-15,* BZAW 91, Berlin, 1964.

—————, *History of Israelite Religion,* New York, 1972; ET of *Geschichte der Israelitischen Religion,* Berlin, 1968.

Frankena, R., "The Vassal-Treaties of Esarhaddon and the Dating of Deuteronomy," *OTS,* XIV, Leiden, 1965, 122-154.

Freedman, D. N., "Divine Commitment and Human Obligation. The Covenant Theme," *Int* 18, 1964, 419-431.

Friedrich, J., "Staatsverträge des Hatti-Reiches in hethitischer Sprache," *MVÄG* 31/I, 1926, 34/I, 1930.

von Gall, A., "Über die Herkunft der Bezeichnung Jahwehs als König," Wellhausen Festschrift, BZAW 27, Berlin, 1914, 145-160.

Galling, K., *Die Erwählungstraditionen Israels,* BZAW 48, Giessen, 1928.

_____, "Der Beichtspiegel: eine gattungsgeschichtliche Studie," *ZAW* 47, 1929, 125-130.

Gill, D., "Thysia and sᵉlamim: Questions to R. Schmid's Das Bundesopfer in Israel," *Bib* 47, 1966, 255-261.

Glock, A. E., "Early Israel as the Kingdom of Yahweh,"*CTM* 41, 1970, 558-605.

Goetze, A. (translator), "Hittite Treaties," in *Ancient Near Eastern Texts*, ed. J. B. Pritchard, Princeton, 1955[2], 201-206.

Gordis, R., " 'Na'ᵃlam' and other observations on the Ain Feshka Scrolls," *JNES* 9, 1950, 44-47.

Gottwald, N. K., "The Book of Samuel," *Encyclopedia Judaica*, 14, Jerusalem, 1971, 787-797.

Gray, J., "The Hebrew Conception of the Kingship of God: Its Origin and Development," *VT* 6, 1956, 268-285.

van Groningen, G., "Joshua–II Kings: Deuteronomistic? Priestly? Or Prophetic Writing?" *JETS* 12, 1969, 3-26.

Gurney, O. R., *The Hittites*, Harmondsworth, 1969[7].

Harrelson, W., "Worship in Early Israel," *BR* 3, 1958, 1-14.

Harrison, R. K., *Introduction to the Old Testament*, Grand Rapids, 1969.

Harvey, J., "Le 'RÎB-Pattern', réquisitoire prophétique sur la rupture de l'alliance," *Bib* 43, 1962, 172-196.

_____, *Le Plaidoyer prophétique contre Israël après la rupture de l'alliance*, Studia 22, Paris, 1967.

Helfmeyer, F. J., "אות," *TDOT*, I, 167-188.

Hermann, J., "εὔχομαι," *TDNT*, II, 785-800.

_____, "ἱλασμός," *TDNT*, III, 301-310.

Hillers, D. R., "A Note on Some Treaty Terminology in the O.T.," *BASOR* 176, 1964, 46-47.

_____, *Treaty Curses and the Old Testament Prophets*, BibOr 16, Rome, 1964.

_____, *Covenant: The History of a Biblical Idea*, Baltimore, 1969.

Holladay, Jr., J. A., "Assyrian Statecraft and the Prophets of Israel," *HTR* 63, 1970, 29-51.

Holwerda, B., "De plaats, die de HEERE verkiezen zal," in *Begonnen hebbende van Mozes*, Terneuzen, 1953, 7-29.

Hubbard, D. A., "The Wisdom Movement and Israel's Covenant Faith," *TB* 17, 1966, 3-33.

Huffmon, H. B., "The Covenant Lawsuit in the Prophets," *JBL* 78, 1959, 285-295.

_____, "The Exodus, Sinai and the Credo," *CBQ* 27, 1965, 101-113.

Hyatt, J. P., "Were There an Ancient Historical Credo in Israel and an Independent Sinai Tradition?" in *Translating and Understanding the Old Testament*, Essays in honor of H. G. May, eds. H. T. Frank, W. L. Reed, New York, 1970, 152-170.

Hylander, I., *Der Literarische Samuel-Saul Komplex (I Sam 1-15) Traditionsgeschichtlich untersucht*, Uppsala, 1932.

Irwin, W. A., "Samuel and the Rise of the Monarchy," *AJSL* 58, 1941, 113-134.

Jepsen, A., "Bᵉrith. Ein Beitrag zur Theologie der Exilszeit," in *Verbannung und Heimkehr*, Rudolph Festschrift, ed. A. Kuschke, Tübingen, 1961, 161-179.

——————, "צדק und צדקה im Alten Testament," in *Gottes Wort und Gottes Land*, Hertzberg Festschrift, ed. H. G. Reventlow, Göttingen, 1965, 78-89.

Jeremias, J., *Theophanie, Die Geschichte Einer Alttestamentlichen Gattung*, WMANT 10, Neukirchen-Vluyn, 1965.

Jocz, J., *The Covenant: A Theology of Human Destiny*, Grand Rapids, 1968.

Kaiser, O., *Einleitung in das Alte Testament*, Gütersloh, 1969.

Keller, C. A., *Das Wort OTH als "Offenbarungszeichen Gottes." Eine philogisch-theologische Begriffsuntersuchung zum Alten Testament*, Basel, 1964.

Kitchen, K. A., *Ancient Orient and Old Testament*, London, 1966.

——————, "Ancient Orient, 'Deuteronism,' and the Old Testament," in *New Perspectives on the Old Testament*, ed. J. B. Payne, Waco, 1970, 1-24.

Kline, M. G., *Treaty of the Great King. The Covenant Structure of Deuteronomy: Studies and Commentary*, Grand Rapids, 1963.

——————, *By Oath Consigned*, Grand Rapids, 1968.

——————, *The Structure of Biblical Authority*, Grand Rapids, 1972.

Knierim, R., "The Messianic Concept in the First Book of Samuel," in *Jesus and the Historian*, ed. F. T. Trotter, Philadelphia, 1969, 20-51.

Knight, G. A. F., *A Christian Theology of the Old Testament*, Richmond, 1959.

Köhler, L., *Theologie des Alten Testaments*, Tübingen, 1953³.

Koolhaas, A. A., *Theocratie en Monarchie in Israël*, Wageningen, 1957.

Korošec, V., *Hethitische Staatsverträge. Ein Beitrag zu ihrer juristischen Wertung*, Leipziger Rechtswissenschaftliche Studien 60, Leipzig, 1931.

Kraus, H.-J., "Gilgal—ein Beitrag zur Kultus geschichte Israels," *VT* 1, 1951, 181-199.

——————, *Worship in Israel*, Richmond, 1966; ET of *Gottesdienst in Israel*, München, 1962.

Kroeze, J. H., *Koning Saul*, Potchefstroom, 1962.

Külling, S. R., *Zur Datierung der "Genesis-P-Stücke,"* Kampen, 1964.

Kutsch, E., *Salbung als Rechtsakt im Alten Testament und im Alten Orient*, BZAW 87, Berlin, 1963.

——————, "בְּרִית bᵉrit Verpflichtung," *THAT*, I, 339-352.

——————, *Verheissung und Gesetz*, BZAW 131, Berlin, 1973.

Laurentin, A., "*We 'attah Kai nun.* Formule caractéristique des textes juridiques et liturgiques," *Bib* 45, 1964, 168-195.

L'Hour, J., "L'Alliance à Sichem," *RB* 69, 1962, 5-36.

Limburg, J., "The Root רי ב and the Prophetic Lawsuit Speeches," *JBL* 88, 1969, 291-304.

Lindhagen, C., *The Servant Motif in the Old Testament*, Uppsala, 1950.

Luckenbill, D. D., "Hittite Treaties and Letters," *AJSL* 37, 1921, 161-211.

Manatti, M., de Solms, E., *Les Psaumes*, 4 vols., Bruges, 1966.

Manley, G. T., *The Book of the Law*, London, 1957.

——————, "The Deuteronomic Redactor in the Book of Judges," *EvQ* 31, 1959, 32-37.

Mauchline, J., "Gilead and Gilgal: Some Reflections on the Israelite Occupation of Palestine," *VT* 6, 1956, 29-30.

Mayes, A. D. H., *Israel in the Period of the Judges*, SBT 2/29, Naperville, 1974.

McCarthy, D. J., *Treaty and Covenant*, AnBib 21, Rome, 1963.

——————, review of R. Schmid, *Das Bundesopfer in Israel*, CBQ 26, 1965, 502-503.

——————, *Der Gottesbund im Alten Testament*, Stuttgart, 1967².

——————, "What was Israel's Historical Creed?" *LTQ* 6, 1969, 46-53.

——————, *Old Testament Covenant: A Survey of Current Opinions*, Richmond, 1967.

——————, "bᵉrît in Old Testament History and Theology," (review of L. Perlitt, *Bundestheologie im Alten Testament*, WMANT 36) *Bib* 53, 1972, 110-121.

——————, "The Inauguration of Monarchy in Israel," *Int* 27, 1973, 401-412.

McKenzie, J. L., *The World of the Judges*, Englewood Cliffs, 1966.

Mendelsohn, J., "Samuel's Denunciation of Kingship in the Light of the Akkadian Documents from Ugarit," *BASOR* 143, 1956, 17-22.

Mendenhall, G. E., *Law and Covenant in Israel and the Ancient Near East*, Pittsburgh, 1955 (reprinted from *BA* 17, 1954, 26-46, 49-76).

——————, "Covenant," *IDB* 1, 714-722.

——————, *The Tenth Generation: The Origins of the Biblical Tradition*, Baltimore, 1973.

Millard, R., "For He Is Good," *TB* 17, 1966, 115-117.

Möhlenbrink, K., "Sauls Ammoniterfeldzug und Samuels Beitrag zum Königtum des Sauls," *ZAW* 58, 1940, 57-70.

Möller, W., *Einleitung in das Alte Testament*, Zwickau, 1934.

——————, *Grundriss für alttestamentliche Einleitung*, Berlin, 1958.

de Moor, J. C., "The peace-offering in Ugarit and Israel," in *Schrift en Uitleg*, jubileum-bundel W. H. Gispen, Kampen, 1970, 112-117.

Moran, W. L., "A Kingdom of Priests," in *The Bible in Current Catholic Thought*, ed. J. L. McKenzie, New York, 1962, 7-20.

——————, "Moses und der Bundesschluss am Sinai," *VD* 40, 1962, 3-17.

——————, "The Ancient Near Eastern Background of the Love of God in Deuteronomy," *CBQ* 15, 1963, 78-87.

——————, "A Note on the Treaty Terminology of the Sefire Stelas," *JNES* 22, 1963, 173-176.

Mowinckel, S., *The Psalms in Israel's Worship*, I, II, Nashville, 1962.

Muilenburg, J., "The Form and Structure of the Covenantal Formulations," *VT* 9, 1959, 347-365.

——————, "The Office of Prophet in Ancient Israel," in *The Bible in Modern Scholarship*, ed. J. P. Hyatt, Nashville, 1965, 74-97.

——————, "A Liturgy on the Triumphs of Yahweh," in *Studia Biblica Semitica*, jubileum-bundel Th. C. Vriezen, Wageningen, 1966, 233-251.

Nicholson, E. W., *Deuteronomy and Tradition*, Oxford, 1967.

Nielsen, E., "Ass and Ox in the Old Testament," in *Studia Orientalia*, J. Pedersen Festschrift, Copenhagen, 1953, 163-174.

North, R., "Angel-Prophet or Satan-Prophet?" *ZAW* 82, 1970, 31-67.

Noth, M., *Die israelitischen Personennamen im Rahmen der gemein-semitischen Namengebung*, BWANT III/10, Stuttgart, 1928.

——————, *Das System der zwölf Stämme Israels*, BWANT IV/1, Stuttgart, 1930.

——————, *The History of Israel*, London, 1960[2].

——————, *Überlieferungsgeschichtliche Studien*, Tübingen, 1967[3].

Nötscher, F., "Bundesformular und 'Amtsschimmel'," *BZ* 9, 1965, 181-214.

Odendaal, D. H., *The Eschatological Expectation of Isaiah 40–66 With Special Reference to Israel and the Nations*, Philadelphia, 1970.

Oehler, G. F., *Theology of the Old Testament*, Grand Rapids, n.d.; ET of *Theologie des AT*, Stuttgart, 1891.

Oosterhoff, B. J., *De Vreze des Heren in het Oude Testament*, Utrecht, 1949.

——————, *Israëlietisiche Persoonsnamen*, Exegetica I/4, Delft, 1953.

——————, *Het Koningschap Gods in de Psalmen*, Alphen aan den Rijn, 1956.

——————, *Feit of Interpretatie*, Kampen, 1967.

Orlinsky, H. M., "The Tribal System of Israel and Related Groups in the Period of the Judges," *OrAn* 1, 1962, 11-20.

Payne, J. B., "The B'rith of Yahweh," in *New Perspectives on the Old Testament*, ed. J. B. Payne, Waco, 1970, 240-264.

Pedersen, J., *Israel: Its Life and Culture*, 2 vols., London, 1926, 1940.

Perlitt, L., *Bundestheologie im Alten Testament*, WMANT 36, Neukirchen-Vluyn, 1969.

Pfeiffer, R. H., *Introduction to the Old Testament*, New York, 1941.

Plastaras, J. C., review of K. A. Kitchen, *Ancient Orient and Old Testament*, *CBQ* 29, 1967, 269-270.

Plath, S., *Furcht Gottes. Der Begriff* יִרְא *im Alten Testament*, Arbeiten zur Theologie II/2, Stuttgart, 1962.

Press, R., "Der Prophet Samuel. Eine traditionsgeschichtliche Untersuchung," *ZAW* 56, 1938, 177-225.

Quell, G., "Das Phänomen des Wunders im Alten Testament," in *Verbannung und Heimkehr*, Rudolph Festschrift, ed. A. Kuschke, Tübingen, 1961, 253-300.

——————, "The OT Term בְּרִית," *TDNT*, II, 106-124.

——————, "The Concept of Law in the OT," *TDNT*, II, 174-178.

von Rad, G., *Das Formgeschichtliche Problem des Hexateuch*, BWANT IV/26, Stuttgart, 1938; ET in *The Problem of the Hexateuch and Other Essays*, Edinburgh, 1966.

——————, Studies in Deuteronomy, SBT 9, London, 1953.

——————, "מֶלֶךְ and מַלְכוּת in the OT," *TDNT*, I, 565-571.

——————, *Old Testament Theology*, 2 vols., New York, 1962, 1965; ET of *Theologie des Alten Testament*, München, 1957², 1960.

Rainey, A., "Peace Offering," *Encyclopedia Judaica* 14, Jerusalem, 1971.

Raitt, T. M., "The Prophetic Summons to Repentance," *ZAW* 83, 1971, 30-49.

Ridderbos, Nic. H., "Die Theophanie in Ps. L 1-6," *OTS*, XV, 1969, 213-226.

Ritterspach; A. D., *The Samuel Traditions: An Analysis of the Anti-Monarchical Source in I Samuel 1-15*, unpublished Ph.D. dissertation, Berkeley, 1967.

Robertson, E., "Samuel and Saul," *BJRL* 28, 1944, 175-206.

Rogers, C. L., "The Covenant with Moses and its Historical Setting," *JETS* 14, 1971, 141-155.

Rosenthal, E. I. J., "Some Aspects of the Hebrew Monarchy," *JJS* 9, 1958, 1-18.

Rosenthal, F., "Notes on the Third Aramaic Inscription from Sefire-Sujin," *BASOR* 158, 1960, 28-31.

Rost, L., "Königsherrschaft Jahwes in vorköniglicher Zeit?" *TLZ* 85, 1960, 722-723.

——————, "Das Kleine Geschichtliche Credo," in *Das Kleine Credo und andere Studien zum Alten Testament*, Heidelberg, 1965, 13-25.

Rowley, H. H., *The Biblical Doctrine of Election*, London, 1950.

——————, *Worship in Ancient Israel, Its Forms and Meaning*, London, 1967.

Sauer, G., "הָלַךְ," *THAT*, I, 486-493.

Scharbert, J., review of E. Kutsch, *Salbung als Rechtsakt im Alten Testament und im Alten Orient*, BZAW 87, *BZ* 9, 1965, 103-104.

Schelhaas, J., "De instelling van het koningschap en de troonbestijding van Israëls eerste koning," *GTT* 44, 1944, 241-272.

Schmid, H. H., *Gerechtigkeit als Weltordnung. Hintergrund und Ge-*

schichte des alttestamentlichen Gerechtigkeitsbegriffes, BHTh 40, Tübingen, 1968.

Schmid, R., *Das Bundesopfer in Israel*, StANT 9, München, 1964.

Schmidt, W. H., *Königtum Gottes in Ugarit und Israel. Zur Herkunft der Königspradikation Jahwes*, BZAW 80, Berlin, 1966².

Schmitt, G., *Der Landtag von Sichem*, Arbeiten zur Theologie I/5, Stuttgart, 1964.

Schunck, K.-D., *Benjamin. Untersuchungen zur Entstehung und Geschichte eines Israelitischen Stammes*, BZAW 86, Berlin, 1963.

Scott, R. B. Y., "Meteorological Phenomena and Terminology in the Old Testament," *ZAW* 64, 1952, 11-25.

——————, "A Kingdom of Priests (Exodus xix 6)," *OTS*, VIII, Leiden, 1950, 213-219.

Seebass, H., "Traditionsgeschichte von I Sam 8, 10:17 ff. und 12," *ZAW* 77, 1965, 286-296.

——————, "I Sam 15 als Schlüssel für das Verständnis der sogenannten königsfreundlichen Reihe I Sam 9:1–10:16; 11:1-15 und 13: 2–14:52," *ZAW* 78, 1966, 148-179.

——————, "Die Vorgeschichte der Königserhebung Sauls," *ZAW* 79, 1967, 155-171.

Segal, M. H., *The Pentateuch. Its Composition and Its Authorship and Other Biblical Studies*, Jerusalem, 1967.

Sellin, E., *Gilgal. Ein Beitrag zur Geschichte der Einwanderung Israels in Palastina*, Leipzig, 1917.

Sellin, E.—Fohrer, G., *Introduction to the Old Testament*, New York, 1968; ET of *Einleitung in das Alte Testament*, Heidelberg, 1965¹⁰.

Simons, J., *The Geographical and Topographical Texts in the Old Testament*, Leiden, 1959.

Smith, M., "The Present State of Old Testament Studies," *JBL* 88, 1969, 19-35.

Snaith, N. H., *The Distinctive Ideas of the Old Testament*, London, 1944.

Soggin, J. A., "מֶלֶךְ," *THAT*, I, 1971, 908-920.

Dupont-Sommer, A., Starcky, J., "Les inscriptions araméennes de Sfiré (Steles I et II)," *Mémoires présentés par divers savants à l'Académie des Inscriptions et Belles-Lettres* 15, 1058, 197-351, plus 29 plates.

——————, "Une inscription araméenne inédite de Sfiré," *Bulletin du Musée de Beyrouth* 13, 1956 (appeared in 1958), 23-41 (Stèle III).

Speiser, E. A., "Of Shoes and Shekels," *BASOR* 77, 1940, 15-20.

Stamm, J. J., "Dreissig Jahre Dekalogforshung," *ThR* 27, 1961, 189-239; 280-305.

Thompson, J. H., *The Ancient Near Eastern Treaties and the Old Testament*, London, 1964.

——————, "The Near Eastern Suzerain-Vassal Concept in the Religion of Israel," *JRH* 3, 1964, 1-19.

——————, "The Cultic Credo and the Sinai Tradition," *RThR* 27, 1968, 53-64.

Thompson, R. J., *Moses and the Law in a Century of Criticism Since Graf,* SVT 19, Leiden 1970.

Thornton, T. C. G., "Studies in Samuel," *CQR* 168, 1967, 413-423.

Tigay, J. H., "Psalm 7:5 and Ancient Near Eastern Treaties," *JBL* 89, 1970, 178-186.

Tsevat, M., "The Biblical Narrative of the Foundation of Kingship in Israel," *Tarbiz* 36, 1966, 99-109.

Tucker, G. M., "Covenant Forms and Contract Forms," *VT* 15, 1965, 487-503.

de Vaux, R., *Ancient Israel, Its Life and Institutions,* New York, 1961.

——————, *Studies in Old Testament Sacrifice,* Cardiff, 1964.

——————, "The King of Israel, Vassal of Yahweh," in *The Bible and the Ancient Near East,* New York, 1971.

Vos, G., *Biblical Theology, Old and New Testaments,* Grand Rapids, 1948.

Vriezen, Th. C., "De Compositie van de Samuël-Boeken," *Orientalia Neerlandica,* Leiden, 1948, 167-189.

——————, "The Credo in the Old Testament," in *Studies on the Psalms,* OTWSA, 1963, 5-17.

——————, *The Religion of Ancient Israel,* Philadelphia, 1967; ET of *De godsdienst van Israël,* Zeist, 1963.

——————, *An Outline of Old Testament Theology,* Oxford, 1970[2]; ET of *Hoofdlijnen der theologie van het Oude Testament,* Wageningen, 1966[3].

——————, *De Verkiezing van Israel,* Exegetica, Nieuwe reeks II, Amsterdam, 1974.

Vriezen, Th. C., van der Woude, A. S., *De Literatuur van Oud-Israël,* Wassenaar, 1973[4].

Wallis, G., "Die Anfänge des Königtums in Israel," *WZ* 12, 1963, 239-247.

Weidner, E. F., *Politische Dokumente aus Kleinasien. Die Staatsverträge in akkadischer Sprache aus dem Archiv von Boghazköi,* Boghazköi Studien, 8, 9, Leipzig, 1923.

Weinfeld, M., "Deuteronomy—The Present State of Inquiry," *JBL* 86, 1967, 249-262.

——————, "The Covenant of Grant in the Old Testament and in the Ancient Near East," *JAOS* 90, 1970, 184-203.

——————, "Covenant," *Encyclopedia Judaica,* 5, Jerusalem, 1971, 1012-1022.

——————, *Deuteronomy and the Deuteronomic School,* Oxford, 1972.

——————, " בְּרִית ," *TWAT,* I, 781-808.

Weiser, A., *The Old Testament: Its Formation and Development,* New York, 1961; ET of *Einleitung in das Alte Testament,* Göttingen, 1957[4].

—————————, *Samuel. Seine geschichtliche Aufgabe und religiöse Bedeutung,* FRLANT 81, Göttingen, 1962.

Wellhausen, J., *Prolegomena to the History of Ancient Israel,* New York, 1957; ET of *Prolegomena zur Geschichte Israels,* 1905[6].

—————————, *Der Text der Bücher Samuelis,* Göttingen, 1871.

Whitley, C. F., "Covenant and Commandment in Israel," *JNES* 22, 1963, 37-48.

Wijngaards, J., *Vazal van Jahweh,* Baarn, 1965.

Wildberger, H., "Samuel und die Entstehung des israelitischen Königtums," *ThZ* 13, 1957, 442-469.

Wiseman, D. J., "The Vassal-Treaties of Esarhaddon," *Iraq* 20, 1958, 1-91.

van der Woude, A. S., "Micha II 7a und der Bund Jahwes mit Israel," *VT* 18, 1968, 388-391.

Wright, G. E., *God Who Acts,* SBT 8, London, 1952.

—————————, "The Lawsuit of God: A Form Critical Study of Deuteronomy 32," in *Israel's Prophetic Heritage,* Muilenburg Festschrift, eds. B. W. Anderson, W. Harrelson, New York, 1962, 26-67.

—————————, *The Old Testament and Theology,* New York, 1969.

Würthwein, E., "Der Ursprung der prophetischen Gerichtsrede," *ZThK* 49, 1952, 1-16.

—————————, *The Text of the Old Testament,* Oxford, 1957; ET of *Der Text des Alten Testaments,* Stuttgart, 1952.

Young, E. J., "The Alleged Secondary Deuteronomic Passages in the Book of Joshua," *EvQ* 25, 1953, 142-157.

—————————, *An Introduction to the Old Testament,* Grand Rapids, 1964[2].

Zeisler, J. A., *The Meaning of Righteousness in Paul,* Cambridge, 1972.

SUMMARY

In this study I have attempted to demonstrate by exegetical, literary critical and form critical analysis that many characteristics of I Samuel 11:14-12:25 strongly suggest that the assembly which is here described is best understood as a covenant renewal ceremony, and that there is good reason to regard this ceremony as an historically appropriate if not necessary event at this particular juncture in Israel's national existence. It is my view that the renewal of the covenant as described in this passage served a dual purpose. First, it provided for the restoration of covenant fellowship between Yahweh and his people after the people had sinned in requesting a king "as the nations" and thereby had in essence broken the covenant by rejecting the kingship of Yahweh. Second, it provided for the possibility of establishing human kingship in Israel in a manner which demonstrated that the continued suzereinty of Yahweh was in no way to be diminished in the new era of the monarchy. Samuel's purpose, therefore, in calling the people to Gilgal was to provide for covenant renewal after covenant abrogation, and at the same time to provide for covenant continuity in and through an important reorganization of the theocracy.

Chapters I and II contain a translation and exegesis of I Samuel 12 and I Samuel 11:14-15 respectively. On the basis of exegetical considerations the conclusion is reached that I Samuel 11:14-15 constitute a short resume of the gathering at Gilgal which is prefaced to the more extensive description of the same gathering which is contained in I Samuel 12. Samuel's summons "Come, let us go to Gilgal to renew the kingdom there" (I Samuel 11:14) is therefore to be understood as an invitation to Israel to renew her allegiance to Yahweh on the occasion of the inauguration of the human kingship.

Chapter III gives a survey of the history of the literary-critical assessment of these same two pericopes (I Samuel 12:1-25 and I Samuel 11:14-15 respectively) describing the various categories of critical approach and mentioning representative advocates of each. The tentative conclusion is then drawn that the content of these two pericopes gives good basis for considering I Samuel 11:14-12:25 as a composite unit describing the important ceremony at Gilgal by which Israel renewed her allegiance to Yahweh at the time of Saul's inauguration as king.

Chapter IV discusses briefly the "covenant form" in the Old Testament and concludes that the recognition of various elements of this form in I Samuel 11:14-12:25 yields useful insights into the understanding of this passage both as a whole in connection with its general purpose as well as in its various parts. In addition, the "covenant form" provides a literary basis for regarding the description of this assembly in I Samuel 12:1-25 as a unity in contrast to the variety of theories described in Chapter III which deny such a unity.

Chapter V makes use of the covenantal character of I Samuel 11:14-12:25 for an assessment of the literary criticism of I Samuel 8-12. Here the suggestion is made that the recognition of the covenantal character of I Samuel 11:14-12:25 contributes in a positive way toward the resolution of the issues which have most often been utilized as justification for the bewildering variety of critical theories for this section of I Samuel. These issues include the following: a) the ambivalent attitude toward kingship in I Samuel 8-12; b) the sequence of the various narrative units in I Samuel 8-12; and c) what is often viewed as "deuteronomistic influence" in the narratives of I Samuel 8-12.

The conclusion reached is that the "pro" and "anti" monarchial tension that is so frequently pointed to in this section of I Samuel is not to be seen as deriving from contradictory attitudes of different time periods or geographical locations, but rather as a reliable reflection of the differing attitudes toward the human kingship and toward the appropriateness of its establishment that were present at the time of its inception. The issue is not the validity of human kingship in itself, but rather the kind of kingship the Israelites desired, and the reason and motivation behind their request for a king. The issue then is not simply one of "pro" and "anti" monarchial sentiments reflected in conflicting narrative strands or units. The issue is whether the desired kingship is to be compatible with Israel's covenant with Yahweh or whether it would be of such a type that it would in effect nullify that covenant.

It is also suggested that the interpretation of the expression "renew the kingdom" (I Sam. 11:14) as an invitation to Israel to renew her allegiance to *Yahweh* (not Saul) on the occasion of the inauguration of the human kingship provides a firm refutation for the most frequently cited "proof" for the redactional harmonization of two or perhaps three contradictory stories of the establishment of Saul to be king which are often said to be juxtaposed in the narrative sequence of I Samuel 8–12.

Finally, it is suggested that "deuteronomistic influence" in this section can be best explained as a reflection of the dynamics operative in the actual course of events at the gathering in Gilgal, and that this deuteronomic perspective should not be viewed as the product of the theological orientation of a writer or redactor of a much later period.

TRANSLATION

p. 14, n. 14
Scharbert: "Also the idea of an anointing of the king by Yahweh or a man of God need not be a mere theologumenon, but may have its basis in an actually practiced sacral rite. . . . When kings in Judah were anointed by the people or by their representatives, that excludes neither the involvement of men of God nor the idea that the king is anointed as if by Yahweh."

pp. 18-19
Weiser: "a manner of declaring his indemnity, which was necessary for him in order to resign in an orderly fashion from an office (perhaps, as generally assumed, as judge)."

p. 19
Weiser: "the fact that he had conducted his life in an irreproachable manner and in conformity to the covenant."

Weiser: "also under the new relationships, Samuel wishes to be entitled and authorized to function as the 'representative of the Yahweh-covenant.'"

Weiser: "a clever step forward which provides the basis of trust for the new order which was made necessary by the institution of the kingship. . . ."

p. 23, n. 39
Boecker: "Then all the text-critical alterations of the text at this place which have been considered become unnecessary. The original text reads: 'It is Yahweh who has led your fathers out of the land of Egypt.'"

Stoebe: "Verse 6, as the lack of a continuation shows, is an insertion which anticipates the thought of verse 7 ff."

p. 26
Boecker: "In I Sam. 12:7 as also in Ezek. 17:20b the object of the legal proceeding is found in the accusative. By no means does such a matter under litigation always have to be a misdemeanor or something of that sort. That depends on the nature of the legal proceeding. In the case before us—using the language of modern jurisprudence—we do not have anything like a criminal case; that would involve a legal proceeding in regard to a misdemeanor or a felony; rather here there is portrayed a proceeding which one could designate as a 'fact-finding proceeding.'"

p. 27, n. 52
Dronkert: "The central meaning of the word is 'act according to the *mišpāṭ*.' It is difficult to say precisely what is to be understood by the *mišpāṭ*, because of the character of its usage. It is a legal value in the widest sense of the word. The legal value must be brought into practice by the *ṣedāqā(h)*. When one does that, and acts according to the *mišpāṭ*, then one is *ṣaddīq* and stands in the circle of the *ṣedāqā(h)*."

p. 28, n. 53
Dronkert: "Man can approach God. God always acts according to his purpose and concretely according to His *mišpāṭ*. That is His *ṣedāqā(h)*, His righteousness, that comes to expression in all His works. He is righteous and He acts righteously. . . . It is remarkable that the righteousness of God in the O.T., for the most part, is related to the favor of God toward man and that His justice and righteousness, for the most part, have a saving character."

p. 29, n. 55
Aalders: "Daniel recognizes fully the righteousness of the judgment which God had brought on Israel, never can any unrighteousness be laid against Him, and he accents that once again by the repetition: 'we have not obeyed the voice of Yahweh' (cf. vs. 10, 11)."

p. 30
Holwerda: "the prophetic interpretation of the events in Chapter 4, and is particularly of importance because it points to the central issue: it shows that these were not purely human and military events, but that it concerns the REDEMPTION OF THE LORD."

Holwerda: "is holding oneself to the covenant agreements, thus proving one's faithfulness."

p. 39, n. 58
Aalders: "Under this term one must include all the deeds of redemption of his people, in the first place the deliverance of Israel out of Egypt mentioned in the previous verse, but further also all other salvation-acts in which God revealed himself to his people as the faithful covenant God."

p. 31, n. 61
Goslinga: "Also these painful chastisements from God's hand can be included with his צדקות (vs. 7), for they had the purpose of bringing Israel again into a right relationship with Himself."

p. 31, n. 63
Goslinga: "The old translations have here attempted to remove a diffi-

culty. Samuel gives more detail on the period of the judges, which is relatively yet recent, vss. 9-11."

p. 32, n. 64
Schulz: "the expression 'chieftain of the army of Hazor' is supported by I Kgs 2:32 ('chieftain of the army of Israel' and 'chieftain of the army of Judah'). . . ."

p. 33, n. 66
Goslinga: "the reading Barak is nevertheless the strongest . . . all the more because the army of Sisera was defeated by him (vs. 9)."

Goslinga: "it is difficult to imagine that a copyist would write Bedan, if there had been no judge with this name. But it is also difficult to accept that Samuel would mention the oppression of Sisera (vs. 9) and not the hero that defeated Sisera. Therefore the best solution seems to be that Bedan is another name for Barak, and that this was known by Samuel's audience just as well as we, for example, know that Gideon's other name was Jerubbaal."

p. 38, n. 87
Boecker: "In I Samuel 12 the reports of the rise of the kingship are summarized and the event is definitively evaluated. Verse 12 is to be viewed as the result of such a definitive summary of differing reports, whereby once more it is shown how little the deuteronomists were history writers in the modern sense of the word. They combine in this verse the report of the Nahash incident incorporated by them in their work with the story conceived by themselves of the people's desire for a king which was taken to Samuel, whereby the ensuing essential tension obviously burdens them less than the modern reader.

p. 39
Goslinga: "one of the unevenesses, among others, that are encountered in our book, without thereby constituting a specific contradiction."

p. 40, n. 91
Koolhaas: "Thus in the Old Testament as background for the request for a king is seen: distrust in the royal rule of Yahweh, fear for the enemies and a striving in ones own strength for security and unity."

p. 40, n. 94
Goslinga: "without doubt original, and precisely in Samuel's mouth very understandable, because he saw in this request and even demand for a king a sinful act, see vs. 17."

p. 43
Boecker: "In all these places it concerns itself with a mode of expression

substantially moulded and qualified in a distinct direction. The taking up of this expression in the sense of the named parallel places may have happened in I Sam. 12:14. Just as there the recognition of a human king is the theme, so here it is the acknowledgement of the royal dignity of Yahweh. Paraphrased v. 14b reads—again outside the syntactical connection—'both you and also the king who rules over you, will recognize Yahweh your God as king.'"

p. 45, n. 102
Oosterhoff: "In Deuteronomy to fear Yahweh is to be obedient to his commandments with a heart full of deep reverence for Yahweh on the one hand, but also full of thankful love for the love that he had bestowed on his people on the other hand."

p. 45, n. 102
Oosterhoff: "Since in Deuteronomy to fear Yahweh means to keep his commandments and since these commandments for a great part concern the cultic honoring of Yahweh, the expression to fear Yahweh can acquire the meaning of 'honoring Yahweh cultically' in the manner, that he had prescribed for His people in His law."

p. 46, n. 104
Goslinga: "By far the simplest solution is to accept that an original ‎ was replaced by ‎ in transmission so that the vs. concludes with a comparison: *against you even as against your fathers.*"

p. 50, n. 115
Stoebe: "and now rain certainly does not belong to a description of a theophany."

p. 51, n. 116
Ridderbos: "When God appears in order to say something to His people (through a mediator), one speaks of a theophany; but when God appears for the deliverance of his people in battle with the enemy, it is a matter of an epiphany (the definition of the distinction shows divergencies with various authors). Such a distinction can certainly bring clarification. . . ."

p. 59, n. 144
Oosterhoff: "the cultic worship of Yahweh in contrast to the worship of idols."

p. 62, n. 7
Schulz: "That, however, is not permissible, because the text is certain."

p. 63, n. 8
Hulst: "Saul had already been anointed; by his first military act he also

shows that in fact he can be king, and thereupon the army accepts him for the future as king, and commander.

p. 63, n. 8
De Groot: "If we may take the expression 'all the people' as meaning 'all soldiers'—and in our opinion this is entirely permissible—then we do not have here simply a duplicate of the story in 10:17ff. (we would not regard even the most stupid redactor as capable of this) but we must see here a continuation and specifically the military recognition of the crowning ceremony at Mizpah (chapter 10)."

p. 63, n. 8
Koolhaas: "After the defeat of the Ammonites the kingship is renewed in Gilgal. This assembly can be seen as a continuation of the ceremony at Mizpah where the people recognized and honored Saul after his selection to be king. In Gilgal the army accepted him as king and thus confirmed his choice as king."

p. 64, n. 11
Stoebe: נחדש may neither be changed (Ehrlich נקדש, . . .) nor eliminated by an alleviating translation (Dhorme, 'inaugurate'; Klostermann, 'celebrate a national festival')."

p. 64, n. 13
Buber: "to restore the strength, consistency and validity of some thing." . . . Dhorme (inaugurate) . . . Leimback (confirm).

p. 65
Goslinga: "no basis in the text and even less in the historical situation"

p. 65, n. 16
Goslinga: "That which was done at Gilgal was not simply a repetition but a confirmation (cf. Koolhaas, p. 66) of the choice of king at Mizpah. . . ." "Now that Saul had shown what he was worth, the celebration at Gilgal also had more value and a deeper sense than that at Mizpah, 10:24. . . . Kroeze . . . says (ibid., 49, 50) that the word 'renew' shows clearly that the 'Gilgal-story' presupposes the 'Mizpah-story.'" Thus Saul was chosen king at Mizpah: "Yet at Mizpah compared with Gilgal, something was lacking. This was more something of a psychological nature. There was no noticeable change in the situation. Afterwards everyone went to his house, including Saul. Was Israel now really a kingdom?" But this is changed after the events of chapter 11. The king had acted in his role "Therefore the people now go to Gilgal to make Saul king before the LORD; not again by selection or any other formal proceeding, but by *expression of honor* by recognition of his deed. The new institution, the kingship, came into being in two steps."

p. 66, n. 17
Bernhardt: "in v. 14 one should indeed read נקדש along with Kittel instead of נחדש."

p. 66, n. 18
Wallis: "One can only renew what in the substance at hand has become perhaps antiquated or decrepit. If we consider, however, the whole of chapter 11, then we see Saul, a farmer's son, seized by the Spirit of Yahweh, take action, but not one who already previously was king. . . . A call to renewal assumes, however, the familiarity of the people with the kingdom. But the narrator relates absolutely nothing to indicate such a familiarity.

p. 66, n. 19
Wildberger: "If v. 14 speaks of the renewal of the kingdom, it stands in contradiction to v. 15, where indeed the discussion is not of its renewal, but of its initial establishment."

p. 69, n. 25
Alt: "that one may hold the conception of the kingdom of Yahweh as an original given of the religion of Israel, which would have always been indispensible to her for her self-understanding."

p. 72, n. 30
Noth: "it is not to be doubted that the old sources, to the extent that their words are contained in the fourth book of Moses, go back to very early traditions that initially were transmitted orally before they were incorporated into the narrative works of J and E.

p. 75, n. 42
Fensham: "It is definitely unnecessary to regard these words as an exilic or postexilic addition, because the idea of the eternal kingship of Yahweh shall have been expressed only in the days of deutero-Isaiah. Already in the old Hebrew poems such as Deuteronomy 32 (v. 5), Psalm 68 (v. 25), and Numbers 23 (v. 21) we encounter this idea. In addition, in the Canaanite world the kingship of a specific ruler is characterized as eternal in very early times. . . ."

p. 77, n. 49
Gispen: "And He emphasizes Israel's glorious purpose and continuing obligation: she must be a kingdom of priests (the service, which she must perform for the LORD as subjects in his kingdom, is thus of priestly nature) and a holy, set-apart, pure, given to God, belonging to God's people (v. 6a)."

p. 77, n. 51
Oosterhoff: "Even as in the other personal names in the Bible that are

constructed with *ab*, so also in the name Abimelech *ab* is a designation for God. . . . The remark of Kittel, that from the name Abimelech it appears, that Gideon did accept the kingship and that the comment in the Bible, that Gideon did not accept the kingship is the result of a later revision, is then also entirely mistaken. . . ."

p. 78, n. 53

Noth: "A great number of names brings to expression a relationship to deity or an aspect of the divine nature, which is intended to awaken and strengthen the trust of man in God. For this reason it is most appropriate to call them 'names of trust.'"

p. 78, n. 53

Noth: "Often this element is associated with the Hebrew שׁעֵ = noble (cf. Gray, p. 146f.; Köning, Wörterbuch), yet it is more likely to link it with a form of the root ישׁע (thus rightly Hommel, Altisr., Überl., p. 52 and above; Zimmern KAT³ p. 481, n. 4), for the root שׁוע also occurs frequently in Arabic as *wś'*, and שׁוע = help is yet to be found in Hebrew in תשׁועה (cf. תשׁובה תרומה תבואה) and in Peil = to cry for help."

p. 78, n. 53

Oosterhoff: "Many are the names that inform us that God is a helper. Helping belongs to the essence of God (Ps. 33:10; 70:6; 115:9; 146:5). Abiezer: 'Father is a help'; Ahiezer: 'Brother is a help'; . . . About the same meaning is to be found in the names Abishua: 'Father has delivered'; Elishua: 'God has delivered'; Melchishua: 'the king has delivered'; Joshua: 'the LORD has delivered.' The shortened name is Shua.

p. 79, n. 55

Eissfeldt: "The fact, yet to be assessed in another connection, that the personal name מַלְכִּיהוּ (Jer. 38:6) utilizing the predicate מֶלֶךְ clearly with reference to Yahweh is provable only since the time of Jeremiah, justifies the suspicion that in the above mentioned names originally not Yahweh, but another god is to be understood by the term מלך.

p. 79, n. 56

Koolhaas: "But since Yahweh's kingship was so entirely different than those of the other gods and since the title *mlk* for gods and kings was filled with an entirely different content and infused with heathen mythologies, ancient Israel in certain times refrained from using this name for Yahweh and utilized other expressions to indicate Yahweh's rulership. . . . The absence of this title, however, does not mean that the idea, which later is brought to expression by this title, was not present. . . . It witnesses to the extremely sensitive understanding of this rulership of Yahweh and that since this title was so differently utilized by other peoples, that the danger existed that Israel by the use of this title would also fill the rulership of Yahweh with a content that was in conflict with the revelation of Yahweh."

p. 80, n. 60
Koolhaas: "Although the above mentioned facts, viewed historically, certainly are valid as arguments for the late rise of kingship in Israel, yet this is not the viewpoint of the Old Testament, which regards the late rise of the kingship not as an historical, but rather as a principial question. Israel was chosen by Yahweh to be his possession, over which He Himself was king and in whose midst He lived, of which the ark as his throne was the sign. The fact that Israel lived for so long a time without a human king, is attributable primarily to the kingship of Yahweh."

p. 82, n. 64
Goslinga: "Because the people did not want to enter Canaan, they placed themselves actually outside the covenant with Yahweh, who precisely for this reason had led them out of the bondage of Egypt. The LORD did not annul the covenant as such, but places the ban on the generation that came out of Egypt, and also their children, which ban will be lifted only when the older generation is entirely gone. The 'bearing of harlotries' of the fathers undoubtedly included that the children might not be circumcised. . . . As an indication that the covenant relationship is presently again completely normal the LORD now permits those that miss the sign of the covenant to be circumcised. He thereby receives them as His people in the place of their disobedient fathers (v. 7)."

p. 83, n. 65
Goslinga: "The command to circumcise then goes out from God Himself. He thus renews His covenant with Israel and assures the people afterwards by the Passover, that He is their covenant partner in the coming battle."

p. 86
Goslinga: "On the question of what precisely we are to think about the words וימליכן etc. is probably to be answered, that Saul is anointed by Samuel. The LXX says και έχρισεν Σαμουηλ έκει τον Σαουλ and the dropping out of the Hebrew equivalent is very conceivable as a homoeoteleuton (שאול). Strongly in favor of this reading (in any case for its actual content) is the fact that Saul immediately thereafter, 12:3, 5, but also later is named with great emphasis the anointed of Yahweh (24:7; 26:9; II 1:16), and that David according to II 2:4; 5:3 was also publicly anointed."

p. 86, n. 73
Budde: "The accommodation to 10:17ff. has also gone further here in the LXX since it offers καὶ ἔχρισεν Σαμουήλ . . . εἰς βασιλέα in place of וימלכן."

p. 87, n. 76
Rudolph: "insertion on account of 23:1 whose character as a heading has been misunderstood,"

p. 89
Schmid: "The Old Testament *selemim*-offering expressed very clearly the covenant idea, that established, restored and strengthened the covenant community."

p. 102, n. 21
Noth: "essential features of his entire view of history,"
Noth: "this was temporally secondary and in its essence even improper and therefore was an institution to be fundamentally rejected in principle. . . ."

p. 102, n. 23
Noth: "Also the designation of the new king as the 'anointed of Yahweh' may be an allusion to 10:1."

p. 103
Gressmann: "historical narrative"

p. 104
Weiser: "On the question of the so-called deuteronomistic style of I Samuel 12, which is usually discussed in the form of a superficial counting of words, I have no comment: as long as no clarity has been reached concerning the essence, the origin and the history of this 'style,' it cannot serve as evidence for the literary critical problem."

p. 105
Budde: "in view of the clear structure which Rje has placed in Chapters 8ff,"
Budde: "such a great blunder, that not he (Rje) but only a revisor can be made responsible for it."

p. 107
Buber: "miracle story"
Buber: "And now, here is the king whom you desired, for Yahweh as set a king over you. If you will fear Yahweh and heed his voice, then you shall live, you as well as the king, who according to Yahweh your God has become king over you. But if you will not heed Yahweh's voice, then Yahweh's hand will be against you and against your king. Only fear Yahweh! For behold, what a great thing he has shown you! If you do evil, then you will be swept away, you as well as your king."

p. 112, n. 53
Hertzberg: "The reviewer must admit that he has never before worked through a book for the purpose of reviewing it which has even approached this book in terms of demand for patience."

p. 115, n. 64
Wellhausen: "the renewal of the kingdom in v. 14 is a highly transparent artifice of the author of chapter 8:10, 17-27 and chapter 12, which enabled him to incorporate the older chapter 11 into his version."

p. 116
Gressmann: "historical narrative"

p. 116-117
Gressmann: "If there were an inner unity, then an allusion to the secret anointing could not be missing; at the very least Samuel would have had to crown Saul, as the Greek translation (v. 15) correctly perceived, but improperly read."

p. 120
Noth: "Dtr had to obscure with regard to chapter 10:17ff by the unmotivated and unhelpful remark that now only a 'renewal of the kingdom' was being undertaken."

p. 128, n. 104
Goslinga: "Israel had to be ready for the conflict with her long time enemy and oppressor and if possible deliver the first blow. It is therefore to be assumed that the events of Chapter 11f. were very quickly followed by those of Chapter 13."

p. 129, n. 105
Ridderbos: ". . . every bringing of a (peace) offering can be termed a renewing of the covenant. . . ."

p. 141, n. 24
Notscher: "There may have been a covenantal formulation in Israel, as also Baltzer assumes on the basis of the texts which he has analyzed (Josh 24; Exod 19-24; Deut 1:1-4, 40; 5-11; 28-31). But to see therein an established literary type, would surely be to attribute too great a significance to the 'form-idea' and to underestimate the free spirited flexibility."

p. 142, n. 26
Verhoef: "The covenant idea is not only the great presupposition behind Malachi's preaching, but is also stated in so many words, while we also discover various typical elements of the covenant in his preaching."

p. 145, n. 30
Stamm: "The historical channels by which one can explain the similarity of the Hittite vassal treaties to the formulations of the Old Testament covenant, are still quite unclear."

p. 152
Grundsatzerklärung = statement of substance (cf. p. 133, n. 5)

p. 152, n. 47
Korošec: "The constant recurrence of such statements reveals that in Ḫattušaš one considered them as an essential component of every vassal treaty. . . ."

p. 162, n. 68
Brekelmans: "The characterization of Joshua 24 as 'divine-address' can also not be understood as a transforming of or derivative from the original confessional formula. There can be no talk of a 'genre-historical' development from the one to the other. Both, the catechetical and the covenant-formulary are independent literary elements that in their entirety have not arisen out of each other. The fact that the salvation deeds which are mentioned in each are nearly the same, is because the salvation deeds mentioned touch the essence of Israel's religion. For this reason these facts were used in all areas of the religious life, by the covenant renewing, in the catechization and also in the worship services."

p. 162-163, n. 68
Brekelmans: "The so-called 'Credo' is thus introduction, historical prologue and motivation for the bringing of the firstfruits out of thankfulness for the beneficent acts of God toward Israel. One does violence to the text when one separates vss. 5-9 from vs. 10 as if they have nothing to do with each other. It appears to me not impossible, that the literary form of these verses is very strongly influenced by the so-called covenant formulary; one can recognize the historical prologue and the loyalty declaration, connected by *wᵉ'attâ*. Then we would have here a liturgical application of the covenant formulary. This appears at least more probable than the explanation that von Rad has proposed."

p. 165, n. 72
L'Hour: "This conjunction has a temporal sense only rarely in the Bible. It generally expresses logical sequence, decision or action, flowing from a deed or from a declaration. Very often it is used as it is here, after an historical narrative and one discovers it in particular in contexts of covenant. Its religious use in Exod 19:5 and Josh 24 appears to be technical and earlier than its utilization by the prophets."

Laurentin: "*Kai nun* does not only pertain to formulas of request for a covenant, but also to formulas which seal or proclaim that covenant. The latter have already been studied by Muilenburg, Baltzer, and L'Hour, who have emphasized the role of *we'attah* and the character of an oath which this term confers to them.

p. 174
Weiser: "an unbridgeable and unexplainable gap"

p. 175
Weiser: "representative of the covenant with Yahweh"

Weiser: "there is no thought of . . . a resignation from office"

Goslinga: "While an explicit statement 'I lay down my office of judge' is not present, Samuel nevertheless does not act and cannot act as if nothing is changed after the inauguration of the kingship. The background of the entire account (see esp. vss 2, 13) is precisely this, that his task *in a certain sense* is ended, and that he must transfer his authority to the king. He therefore asks for an honorable discharge (vss 1–5) and spontaneously promises what he will continue to do for the people, vs 23, which in itself presupposes that he is withdrawing *in some way*, namely as judge, as magistrate, as bearer of the highest authority in Israel under Yahweh" (italics mine).

p. 178
Weiser: "representative of the covenant with Yahweh"

p. 180–181
Broekhuis: "The wars that Israel fought, were Yahweh's wars. They are an expression of the consciousness of the Israelite, that the covenant god is fundamentally involved in all things."

p. 187
Buber: "miracle story"

p. 199 n. 9
Budde: "No matter how much he strives to point out the benign, purely objective nature of the 'law of the king' (p. 127f.), Samuel's disapproval of the monarchy and the impenitence of the people (cf. esp. 8:19f.) remains intact in all its severity in 8:11–20, so that absolutely nothing is accomplished by the exclusion."

p. 199, n. 10
Budde: "Only as a derivation from E can the strong disapproval of the monarchy find its explanation."

p. 203

Gressmann: "a unified whole"

Gressmann: *Gottesfrevel* = outrage against God

Gressmann: "They do not contain historical information; as concerns their spirit or character one must regard them not as historical narratives, but rather as legends."

p, 203-204

Gressmann: "According to this analysis there can be no doubt that, contrary to what is normally maintained, we do not here have a historical narrative but rather a popular saga . . . moreover here the saga approaches the legend. *märchenhaft* = legendary

p. 204

Gressmann: "Thus our chapter bears throughout the imprint of the saga with a legendary wrapper."

Gressmann: "legend"

Gressmann: "historical narrative"

Gressmann: "To be sure chapter 9 requires chapter 11 as a conclusion, but on the contrary chapter 11 by no means presupposes chapter 9, at least originally, but rather at one time stood by itself. . . . Moreover chapter 9 and chapter 11 are entirely different in their literary style."

p. 204-205

Gressmann: "In chapter 8 Samuel is represented as fundamentally opposed to the monarchy in Israel, which he regards as a rebellion against God and therefore rejects completely. In sharp contrast to this in chapters 9:1-10:16 it is told how Samuel anoints Saul upon the express command of Yahweh; thereafter the monarchy is not sinful, but rather an institution ordained by God himself. One of these two views must be later; there can be no doubt about which of the two . . . originally the monarchy was viewed as a divine institution, later, at least in many circles, as one opposed to God."

p. 205

Gressmann: "As chapter 12 teaches us even more clearly, we have under consideration one of those narratives which are later than Deuteronomy (= the fifth book of Moses) and which in its entirety originated in exilic or post-exilic Jewry."

p. 206

Noth: "Dtr has sought therefore, not without evident difficulty and constraint, to supplement the old tradition which viewed the institution of the monarchy positively by means of lengthy additions expressive of his own negative opinion of its establishment. [He did this] by making use of an old tradition about the elevation of Saul to kingship which had come down to him and whose existence seemed to give him the right, after all, to insert the additions; and then he made extensive use of this right."

p. 206, n. 35
Noth: "above all in its beginning quite undoubtedly composed by Dtr"

Noth: "rather we are here dealing with a tradition-fragment assimilated by Dtr."

p. 207
Boecker: "if one is no longer content to recken with a more or less accidental sequence or even juxtaposition of various sources or traditions, but rather recognizes here, along with M. Noth, the product of a thought-out deliberate writing of history. In such a case the sequence of materially contradictory reports becomes a problem which, if it is not satisfactorily explained, must endanger the thesis of the work's unity and completeness.

p. 207, n. 39
Noth: "Nevertheless Dtr has . . . made it quite clear, by the manner of the introduction of the monarchy in the story, that this was temporally secondary and in its essence even improper and therefore was an institution to be fundamentally rejected in principle. . . ." "the negative assessment of the establishment of the monarchy and its characterization as a secondary appearance in the history of the people is an essential feature of his entire historical viewpoint.

p. 208
Boecker: "fundamental character of the alternative Yahweh or the king, on the basis of which the opponents of the monarchy undoubtedly originally stood, is no longer found here. Quite the opposite! The monarchy, although its anti-Yahweh origin is not denied but rather clearly shown, is now seen as something offered by Yahweh, a gift of grace which can be lost and certainly will be lost if the king is set in the place of Yahweh in the sense of the old alternative."

p. 208–209
Boecker: "at the same time the old Israelite traditions, which were decisive for the Deuteronomists."

p. 209
Caspari: "a historical sequence of styles"

p. 209-210
Caspari: "the style of a given period does not die out simply because a
newer style comes along and necessitates the initiation of a new period."

p. 210, n. 46
Vriezen: "hard nuts to crack" (paraphrase)

Vriezen: "that we have here story cycles that were written by independent
authors, but then which were rewritten in such a way that they were
connected to each other as a narrative sequence."

p. 215
Weiser: That this arrangement of the material has succeeded in only a
very external and make shift way has long been recognized and thereby it
has been understood that the collector employed extant traditions which
were originally transmitted independently without mutual relationship.

p. 215
Weiser: "Upon critical examination, the apparent succession of the
narrative units disintegrates into a series of individual tradition units,
which partly, but without complete correspondence, run parallel to each
other and partly, in time frame and subject matter, either overlap or else
exclude each other, and consequently do not permit the historian to
transpose either the entire narrative or else only the one or the other
tradition complex into an uninterrupted picture of the succession of
events."

p. 223
Goslinga: The entirety does indeed have a composite character, it rests
most likely on traditions of different origins, displays alternation of
setting and background (Ramah, Gibeah, Mizpeh, Gilgal), but it lets
itself be read as a connected story, of which the various pericopes
supplement each other, so that one afterwards receives a unified idea. . . ."

p. 224
Koolhaas: "Since the Old Testament comes from a world with different
conceptual and thought patterns, since the prophetic history writing
arranges and exposes the data in a particular fashion, and since prac-
tically nothing is known to us about the redaction of these chapters, we
remain here in the dark with respect to many points of sources and
traditions, in spite of the great energy and thought which has been given
to the book of Samuel by the historical-literary exegesis, and we cannot
come further than to establish that behind these chapters stand various
sources and traditions, and we must understand these chapters as a
creative synthesis with a very definite message about the rise of the
kingship."

Translation

p. 228

Stoebe: "'that they were fundamentally and uncompromisingly hostile to the monarchy."

p. 230, n. 98

Boecker: "'It was not possible for the kings of Israel to act in the manner described here, nor did they in fact act in such a manner.'"

Boecker: "'The declaration of the 'law of the king' is given in such general terms that it does not of necessity have to be related to this area (Canaanite pattern). The description could have been taken from any system of rulership of a sociologically similar configuration. The Deuteronomists have obtained their material from who knows where for their terrifying portrayal of kingship, which according to the wish of the people should be a kingship like "all the nations.""